The Pelican Social History of Britain
General Editor: J. H. Plumb

Joyce Youings

Sixteenth-Century England

Allen Lane

ALLEN LANE

Penguin Books Ltd

536 King's Road

London SW10 0UH

First published 1984

ISBN 0 7139 1243X

Filmset in Monophoto Bembo by Northumberland Press Ltd, Gateshead
Printed in Great Britain by
Richard Clay (The Chaucer Press) Ltd, Bungay, Suffolk

to
Ann and Harry

Contents

Editorial Foreword

Historians respond to the problems of their time almost without being conscious of the process, and the focus of their study changes with the changing times. In the nineteenth century all countries of Europe and America were preoccupied with the origins of national identity, with the need to forge a living past that would give meaning not only to the present but also to the future: Ranke, Macaulay, Michelet, Bancroft and other great historians of the nineteenth century were so preoccupied. As Britain's national identity seemed to be inexorably involved with the evolution of constitutional rights, with liberty, freedom and, particularly, democracy, it is not surprising that an ever growing number of professional historians should devote all their skills and interests to constitutional, legal and political history and that these subjects should dominate university syllabuses when they were first designed in the late nineteenth century.

The First World War, the Great Depression, and the economic disasters which followed gave great impetus to the study both of diplomatic and economic history, the one generally attracting the conservative, the other the radical historians in the 1920s and 1930s. After the Second World War interest in diplomatic history faded first or, rather, transmogrified itself into International Relations and Strategic Studies. Economic history drifted into a professional morass and developed a confused identity – the quantifiers and the econometricians moved in and so did the sociologists, especially American sociologists, hoping to establish an ideology which would refute the Marxist interpretation which had flourished within the realm of economic history.

But the problems of Western industrial society have become much more complex since the Second World War. Fantastic economic growth, and it has been fantastic these last thirty years, has created its own social tensions and, even more important, the very nature of highly industrialized society, apart from its growth, has created new conflicts. Institutions which have lasted for ten thousand years, not only in the West but also in the East, have suddenly seemed to be in jeopardy. In the last two decades there has been a mushrooming of interest among historians in the problems of demography, of the nature of the family, of the position of women, children, slaves, and servants, of the uses of leisure, of the influence of printing, of the expansion of the arts, of the importance of the images society creates for itself, and of the interpretation of class not in economic but in social terms. A new panorama of social history has spread before the eyes of scholars and led them to subjects which historians of previous generations would have thought of interest only to antiquarians.

Naturally other forms of history are not dead, even though some of them are corpse-like, but there can be little doubt that the historical imagination, for better or worse, has become intoxicated with social history: for example, the volume of work on death in the last ten years is prodigious and it is matched by the quantity of studies on childhood or marriage.

The danger of social history, which in spite of its present explosion has, in some of its aspects, long roots reaching back through G. M. Trevelyan to Macaulay and Sir Walter Scott, has been the tendency to drift into descriptive history, of how people lived and spent their days with little or no attempt to analyse why their lives, their beliefs, their activities were what they were. Also, the evidence social historians, even very good ones, used in the past, was impressionistic – diaries, letters, personal memories, together with material collected from folklorists and antiquarians. Naturally, most of this evidence related to the literate class, always, until very recent times, a modest segment of the nation.

In order to give this material greater rigour, sociological

theory, either of Marxist or capitalist bent, has been used and, often, in discussion of death, birth, education of children, or the position of women, it has been infused with modern psychological analysis. Although this has given rise to some nonsense, particularly in the history of childhood, it has given the subject, on the whole, greater intellectual weight.

As with economic history, there has also been a powerful movement which has attempted to quantify the evidence of the past in order to give a statistical basis for some of the fundamental questions of social history – average size and nature of the family, whether nuclear or extended; the age of marriage for men and women; death rates and ages at death; even an attempt has been made to quantify literacy. Huge mountains of data have been assembled and computers have hummed away merrily at great expense but the results remain extremely tentative. Before the nineteenth century record-keeping was erratic and its reliability was not easy to test. There is, too, one unknown factor of great importance – how many of the population were never recorded at all, neither their births, marriages, nor deaths? Indeed, most of the results obtained are easy to criticize and must be treated with considerable scepticism. Even so, generalizations about the family and about its size, about marriage, about bastardy, about age of death, all are firmer than they were and, because they are, help us to understand the life of the country in greater depth.

Although statistics may give shadow and depth to the picture, they cannot paint it, and social history still depends upon a great range of records. Formerly, it depended most of all on letters, diaries and imaginative literature but, although these are still of the greatest value, more attention has now been given to artefacts: to the study of houses and gardens, to newspapers, bills, and trade cards, to carriages, instruments, games and toys, indeed to everything that may throw a light on the way life was lived or the way it hurried towards its future or clung to its past. By extending its range and its depth, by encompassing a multiplicity of scenes, social history has become a far more complex and intellectually exciting discipline than it was.

Over the last ten years the flow of monographs and articles on the social history of England has increased, mushroomed like an atomic explosion, and the time is more ripe for an attempt at synthesis.

J. H. Plumb

Introduction

The people of sixteenth-century England should not be too difficult to describe. Their number was increasing but there were not as many of them, even in 1600, as there had been in 1300, and in some parts of the country they were fewer than in Roman times. English kings had once ruled a large part of France, but in 1500 their dominion had for nearly half a century been confined to an area comprising about one twentieth of western Europe. Only Calais remained as a continental bridgehead and that too was surrendered in the course of the sixteenth century. But more important, for the best part of a thousand years England had experienced no large-scale influx of people. Few of the alien merchants who had so dominated her medieval overseas trade, and who continued to do so well into the sixteenth century, had taken up permanent residence, or brought settlers in their wake. Neither the trickle of foreign artisans who maintained London's alien population nor the strangers who in the later sixteenth century moved with their families into some of the towns of south-east England made any great impact on the population at large, most of whom lived in the country. Except for some of the people of Cornwall all the English subjects of the Tudor kings and queens spoke, in regional accents and dialects, a common language. All English people, even after the detachment of their Church from obedience to the papacy at Rome, were, at least nominally, practising Christians. The country was ruled by a powerful monarchy supported by an effective administration, a national parliament and a common law. The English both regarded themselves, and were regarded, as one people, and, if we may believe foreign visitors, never ceased to proclaim

their national superiority, not in any bellicose sense but in terms
of their institutions, their material well-being and their civilized
manners and conduct. While it was largely with Londoners
and other citizens that foreigners conversed, the pride – or,
as some would call it, arrogance – was universal. Moreover,
the very ease with which so many English people migrated
within their country's own confines would seem to suggest
a common, if not an altogether ideal, way of life and common
institutions.

In fact the English people and the local societies into which
they were divided in the sixteenth century were very far from
being homogeneous. Geography, soil, climate and many
centuries of colonization and settlement, as well as retreat from
the less favourable areas, had resulted in great variety in the
size of communities and in their occupational, economic and
social structure. Within the broader framework of the English
common law both rural and urban communities had preserved,
and from time to time augmented, a multitude of varying
customs and by-laws. Antipathy to newcomers was as marked
at the local as it was at the national level, but just as in London
and other large towns aliens were accepted if they caused no
trouble and contributed somewhat to the common good, so
throughout England migrants were continually being absorbed
into communities each of whose own peculiar character remained very largely unchanged. Towards the end of the sixteenth
century an intellectual awareness of regional diversity became
associated with the ancient, but in many cases quite artificial,
administrative units, the shires or counties. This set a pattern
which has dominated local studies down to the present day,
but English regionalism is far more complex, almost every
county being itself a microcosm of the country as a whole in
the variety of its terrain and of its human settlement. It is easier
to discern the features common to such widespread phenomena
as open-field villages, isolated hill farms, market towns and
cathedral cities, than to generalize about whole counties. The
burgeoning of local historical studies since the Second World
War has led, not least for the sixteenth century, to the publica-

tion of a wealth of local case-studies which no one scholar can hope to read, let alone absorb. Indeed, the research itself has been conducted with that individualism which is itself so much a part of the English character. Comparative studies have made some progress, notably in the case of towns, but there is still a need for more agreement about the questions which need to be asked and the form in which the answers can most usefully be presented. The danger – and it is one which certainly has not been avoided in this book – is that local material will be drawn upon merely to illustrate what appears to be either typical or peculiar in the light of old generalizations rather than to serve as the basis for new and more sensitive analyses.

Records of the kind most sought after by social historians, those which list large numbers of people in some meaningful way by name, have not only survived in greater bulk for the sixteenth than for earlier centuries, but were augmented after 1500 by new compilations. Pride of place must now go to the registers of baptisms, weddings and funerals which, for a great many parishes, are complete from 1538 or not long after. Who would have thought that these one-time preserves of lawyers and genealogists would quite suddenly, or so it seemed to those unaware of what French scholars had long been teaching us, be found to hold the key to our knowledge and understanding of the dynamics of early modern society? New uses have been discovered too for the tax assessments, the muster rolls and the precious handful of local population censuses which remain for before 1600. Many of these records are among the archives of central rather than of local government. Legal records also survive in far greater quantity for the central courts at Westminster than for county assizes or quarter sessions. For local communities the records of manors, that is, of lordships, are far more plentiful, even for the sixteenth century, than those of villages and parishes, but in the case of cities and larger towns the nature of their government led not only to more records being compiled than ever before but to their being more carefully preserved. For the countryside there exists, now largely deposited in county record offices, an abundance of private

estate records, title deeds far outnumbering the more useful
accounts, rentals, and surveys. Few farmers kept records of
any kind. Ecclesiastical archives are formidable, both in their
bulk and in their technical difficulties, but here again the legal
records of bishops are more complete than those of their archdeacons. Very few parishes have preserved those invaluable
mirrors of lay involvement, churchwardens' accounts, but it
is to the Church, and indeed to its archdeacons, that we owe
the preservation of those very personal records, the wills and
the new probate inventories. At all levels of society personal
and business letters are rare and so too are private diaries and
journals, although the monastic chronicles of medieval times
had their sixteenth-century counterparts in the annals, also mostly
of public affairs, compiled very largely by civic officials. Of
rather more use to social historians are the newer descriptions
of English society and institutions. The best known of these
is the Essex parson William Harrison's *Description of England*
which, though not published until 1577, is now thought to
have been originally drafted some twenty years earlier. The
very bulk of the records, especially those of central government,
has made their modern publication very difficult, except in the
form of lists and indexes as finding-aids to research, but social
historians in particular have reason to be grateful for what has
been achieved over more than a century by local record societies
in making available, in print and in easily usable editions, so
many of the documentary sources of English history.

In spite of local diversity there are many areas of sixteenth-
century social history in which broad patterns have emerged.
We now have a fair idea of the size and geographical distribution of the country's population and of national demographic trends. A great deal is known about the nature and
incidence of plague and other epidemic diseases, and a certain
amount about such vital matters as the age distribution of the
population, the proportion who never married, age at marriage,
marital fertility and family size, as well as the extent of bastardy
and premarital conception. The occupational pattern is now
fairly clear, as also are the broad outlines of farming regions,

the location of industry, and the network of trade, both internal and sea-borne. We have some idea of the distribution of wealth, especially in respect of the ownership and tenancy of land, though less is known for sure about actual occupancy. Considerable progress has been made in the study of inheritance customs and of the market in smallholdings, including tenancies. Field systems have been intensively studied, both from maps and other contemporary records, and by fieldwork on the ground. It is no longer difficult to visualize the landscape of Tudor England. Better understanding of economic trends, especially the movement of prices, rents and wages, and of the differences between poverty and idleness, and between unemployment and underemployment, is enabling historians to judge how near England came at any time in the sixteenth century to a crisis of subsistence. The gentry are no longer a real problem but there are still many people in Tudor England who defy social classification. The social aspects of the Reformation are a continuing source of interest, especially the secularization of charitable and educational provision. Evidence of the existence of schools and of the ownership of books, to which may be added the social analysis of university admissions, is still the principal means of gauging the extent to which education was available and acquired in Tudor England; but far more significant are the attempts being made, especially with the ingenious use of records never intended to be used for such a purpose, to quantify, in the widest possible social terms, the extent of illiteracy. Local studies are revealing a great deal about the geography and social configuration of religious dissent (in particular Elizabethan Puritanism) and of Catholic recusancy. A great deal has been achieved in the analysis of the nature and incidence of crime and in the identification of the criminals and their victims. But by far the most ambitious undertakings have been the intensive study of all these elements within the confines of single communities, notably the towns but also in a few of the larger villages. With the help of computers whole local societies are being studied in dimensions undreamed-of by the compilers of traditional parish histories.

It remains to be seen how far the availability of records and the provision of resources will enable such projects to be multiplied.

Social history knows no bounds and Tudor social historians, more fortunate than their medieval colleagues in the variety of their record sources but more constrained than specialists in later centuries by the very incompleteness of their material, have spread their net very widely and concerned themselves with the totality of people's activities. Even the traditional omission of politics is becoming very difficult to justify: not only did involvement in public affairs make and mar both individual careers and family fortunes, but in the sixteenth century, for the first time in English history, government policies really began to affect people's daily lives and indeed were themselves influenced, as never before, by social and economic considerations, even if these were rarely disinterested. An example of the connection is the continued interest of Tudor governments in the manpower situation. Early in the century the country's lack of people seemed to threaten its defence capability: towards the end what appeared to be a surplus seemed to endanger public order. Landowners and employers of labour were the most obvious parliamentary pressure groups, but the influence of London on Tudor politics, especially in connection with the food supply, is still far from fully explored. Social historians need, in fact, to draw on the expertise of a wide range of specialists, not least for the proper understanding of contemporary records. They must, for example, learn from historians of Parliament how the texts of statutes evolved and from historians of the land-law how to unravel deeds of title. Many specialists are now quite deliberately endeavouring to give their studies a social dimension. The contribution of legal historians to the social history of crime has set a splendid example. Medical historians too have much to offer, not so much on the practice of medicine in the sixteenth century as in the identification of disease and its victims and in the study of the preconditions of a physically healthy society. Architectural historians now concern themselves not only with building styles and materials but with costs, with labour and also with clients and their particular needs. Archaeologists, combining excavation with the study of standing buildings, and increasingly aware of the value of documentary evidence, have contributed enormously to our knowledge of vernacular buildings, especially farmhouses and cottages, and of topography, especially that of sixteenth-century towns. The systematic study of their smaller 'finds', especially pottery and other household goods, has yet to make its full contribution to the testing of the conviction of William Harrison and other contemporary writers that in the third quarter of the century the quality of material life, for all but the very poor, was improving out of all recognition. On the whole, the interchange between social historians and specialists in contemporary literature, drama, poetry and imaginative prose has been rather less fruitful. This has been partly due to the turning away of social historians themselves from the use of literary evidence which they see as the caricaturing of Tudor society. The witches and vagabonds of the lawcourts have turned out to be more like ordinary people than their more romantic literary counterparts. A great deal of information is available about the more successful literary figures, especially those in or on the fringes of the Court, but less about minor writers and the relation of their work to contemporary life and thought. There is a need too for far more collaboration between social historians and specialists in the creative arts of the sixteenth century, especially music and painting but also all the decorative and fine arts from armour to jewellery, not forgetting domestic furnishings. But of far wider social significance is the need for a firm chronological framework for the study of folklore, and only when we also possess a historical geography of English dialect will social history really be able to comprehend the whole of people's life in the society of their time.

The search for 'hard' evidence is not without its technical pitfalls. Tudor tax assessments were never intended to reflect what men were really worth but only how they were thought to stand in relation to their neighbours. Occupational and social designations, the 'additions' required in courts of law, represented, except for those who were knights and noblemen, only their bearers' status in their own estimation. Moreover, the occupational and social, as well as physical, mobility of so many Tudor people will defeat the most meticulous attempts at classification. No quantification can be universally applied. The price indices by which we measure inflation and the real value of wages have necessarily been compiled from widely scattered evidence and the much-used Phelps Brown and Hopkins index of the cost of a 'basket of consumables' assumes that everyone, from Cumberland to Cornwall, not only ate the same food but bought all of it in the markets. Harvest patterns and the price fluctuations which accompanied them could be very local indeed. Wage-rates themselves, even those of building-craftsmen, take no account of other employment or indeed of the fact that except for the really poor, and for most people in towns, few sixteenth-century households were entirely landless. Finally, it is a sobering thought that the splendid figures now available for the country's overall population each year from 1541 are based on the registers of just over four hundred out of some ten thousand parishes in England. Statistics of almost any kind must, of course, be welcomed, provided we use our historical judgement in deciding how much weight to place upon them. It is equally important to present them in readily comprehensible terms: computers, and those who use them, tend to have a language all their own. Similar difficulties of communication all too often arise when social historians, in some cases very profitably, apply to their work some of the conceptual thinking of anthropology and sociology. Even population studies have their own terminology, but in the technique of family reconstitution surely lies the re-discovery, if such be needed, that everyone who lived in sixteenth-century England not only had his or her own name but also his or her unique life span. Moreover, in parish registers people simply have a name: they are neither rich nor poor, neither master nor servant, neither saint nor sinner, though some incumbents did find it necessary to note those who died or gave birth while, in local terms, mere birds of passage. In social history there are, of course, no great turning points or sudden revolutions but, just as in the history of nations there can be far-reaching consequences of such events as the outbreak of war or a change of ruler, so in the history both of individual people and also of families, and at all levels of society, a great deal could result from the death of an only son or from the contraction of a profitable marriage.

The arrangement of the chapters which follow may be thought to be somewhat idiosyncratic. It is intended above all to convey an impression of the passage of time, even within a single century. The first five chapters deal very largely with the period up to the mid-1530s, that which preceded not only the Henrician Reformation but also the significant rise in both population and prices. Occupations are dealt with first since the way people made their living very largely determined their identity in contemporary society. Chapters on rural and urban society are followed by attempts to describe the vertical and horizontal alignments of early Tudor people. The second group of chapters deals with the developments which particularly characterized the middle of the century. An attempt to relate the movements of population and prices is followed immediately by a necessarily brief analysis of the land-market. The course of religious change is then linked both with the clergy and with schooling. A chapter dealing with the causes and incidence of rebellion also contains some consideration of crime and litigation, thus encompassing the whole spectrum of sixteenth-century disorder. A survey of new occupational horizons is intended to serve as a background for the last five chapters which are largely about Elizabethan England. The first of these, on poverty and its relief, necessarily covers a longer time span but is placed here in order to underline the intensification of the problem towards the end of the century. Employment has a chapter to itself in an attempt to rescue it from the confusion of Tudor legislation. A chapter concerned very largely with the more successful Elizabethans compares them with those whose misfortune it was to fall some way behind.

In a chapter on communities an attempt is made to discover some of the more enduring aspects of local society, both rural and urban, with a brief consideration of those associations, both religious and secular, which linked people with more scattered habitations. The last chapter, on families, has been placed here not because of its unimportance but because only for the closing decades of the century is there sufficient material to allow more than the most speculative generalizations about the family life of those below the ranks of the gentry. On this, as on many of the topics in the book, the temptation has had to be resisted of reading back into the sixteenth century what is known for certain only of the period after 1600.

Many aspects of Tudor social history have necessarily been dealt with all too briefly, and some neglected altogether, in particular the literary and artistic history of the period. This is largely due to the author's own shortcomings but it may perhaps be defended on the grounds that to devote space to what was largely the culture of an élite while ignoring the popular, and largely oral and functional, culture of the majority of sixteenth-century people, about which so little is known, would have been to introduce an imbalance which is contrary to the purpose of the book. A more serious omission, it may be thought, is any attempt to consider how far and in what manner the people of sixteenth-century England differed from their European neighbours, including, of course, the Welsh, the Irish and the Scots. This much at least may be suggested, that in the course of the sixteenth century the English, probably more than any of their neighbours, carried over from the medieval to the early modern world not only their identity as a people but a considerable part of their community life and institutions. This continuity may well have owed a great deal to the fact that at no time between 1500 and 1600 was the country invaded by enemies from across the sea or was itself the scene of serious civil war. These very chronological perimeters, incidentally, enable us to avoid the hazards of what is coming to be regarded as more meaningful periodization. They also enable us to consider a hundred years of English history in its own right without the need, or indeed the temptation, to seek for causes of the great armed conflict between English people which in 1600 was still four decades in the future.

A book based largely on other people's research incurs many debts, the extent of which can only be acknowledged very in-adequately in the list of suggestions for further reading. The great output of recent years, especially by younger scholars, is an indication of the extent to which the study of social history has developed and shows every sign of continuing to do. My debt to the University of Exeter and its librarians in providing me with all that I have ever requested by way of books and journals is immense. From conferences with fellow historians, from conversations with colleagues, from discussions with both undergraduate and postgraduate students, from talking about social history at extramural gatherings, and from living in a city and in a rural community both of which still enshrine the long centuries of their community life, from each of these have come ideas and information, and above all the continuing urge to learn about people in the past. To the secretaries in the depart-ment of History and Archaeology at Exeter I owe a great deal for their cheerful and efficient 'processing' of my scripts. To the general editor of the series, Professor Sir John Plumb, and to the many colleagues and friends who have read all or part of this book in draft, I am immensely grateful. They have saved me from many errors and obscurities, and that I have not always followed their advice enables me to say with truth that the many which remain are my own. There are two people in particular to whom I owe not only my introduction to Tudor men and women and their documents but also the opportunity and the encouragement to pursue historical research. It is to my former teachers, Professor H. A. and Dr Lilian M. Cronne, my guides, philosophers and friends for so many years, that I offer this book.

April 1983   Joyce Youings

1. *Occupations*

Those who 'bore rule' in Tudor England saw as the ideal society one in which cobblers stuck to their lasts. Men and women, they argued, served themselves and their neighbours better if they pursued those occupations in which they had been brought up and in the exercising of which they possessed certain skills. But what particularly concerned the powers-that-be was any movement, voluntary or involuntary, of people who had been brought up in farming, into other employment, especially into industry. This, it was feared, would endanger the supply of food and other necessities. In fact throughout the sixteenth century the overwhelming majority of the country's inhabitants were engaged primarily in providing from the land, for themselves and their families, the basic needs of food and shelter. But this, as we shall see, was not incompatible with a very great deal of by-employment, that is, undertaking secondary occupations. Farming itself was not one occupation but many, for besides growing their crops and rearing their stock the farmer and his family were masters of many skills. Not only did they process from their own raw materials virtually everything they ate, drank, wore, and used for fuel, but they built shelter for themselves and their animals, and fashioned most of their own tools and implements. Long before 1500 very many English countrymen and women had developed one or other of their many secondary skills to augment their livelihood. But in spite of official forebodings few of those who followed secondary industrial occupations were likely to abandon their land unless forced to do so, for most Tudor people were by instinct tillers and graziers.

In the use they made of their land the farmers of Tudor

England were very far from being homogeneous. Both physical geography and centuries of human settlement had played their part in producing great diversity, so much so that it is almost an over-simplification to speak of farming regions. There was, of course, as there still is, the broad division between the lower-lying south and east and the hillier north and west, particularly in respect of rainfall, but the physical pattern was far more complicated. Not only were there belts of higher ground break-ing up the lowland south and east, but also considerable areas of lowland in the west and even in the north, largely in river valleys and near the coast. To a great extent this determined the distribution of the land between the largely older-settled 'fielden' or sheep–corn, that is mixed arable and pasture, areas and the relatively newly settled 'forest' or wood–pasture, where pastoral and dairy farming predominated. This distinction is fundamental in that it largely determined the nature and size of the rural communities which existed throughout the country. In fielden country the population lived mostly in fairly sizeable 'nucleated' settlements, their homesteads clustered together to form villages whose fields and pastures lay outside and around the largely residential core. Villages like this were the norm in large parts of the country, especially in the midland plain between the Malvern hills, the Chiltern ridge and the Fens, but with many extensions at all points of the compass, even west and north. In most of the west and north, and indeed in parts of the south-east, most people lived in hamlets or isolated farms. Even within counties there was great diversity, as in the 'chalk', that is sheep–corn, and 'cheese', mostly dairying and cattle-raising, parts of Wiltshire. Both north and south Staffordshire comprised largely upland country with poor soils suitable only for pastoral farming, with a central plain, well watered by the river Trent and its tributaries, supporting communities engaged in mixed farming, with nucleated settle-ments very different from the dispersed homesteads of the hill-farmers.

In the Staffordshire plain, and almost everywhere where mixed arable and pasture farming was the main occupation, the arable land lay in unfenced strips each of about one acre, usually in blocks following some more or less rational accommodation to the natural landscape or some long-forgotten quirks of early settlers. The blocks or furlongs in turn formed parts of two or more great 'fields', and the strips of land which together formed the landed resources of individual farmers were scattered widely over the whole arable area, their boundaries marked either by narrow turf 'baulks' or merely by wooden posts and stones. Not only was this medieval strip system still widespread in Tudor England but so too was the communal organization of the manuring, sowing, and harvesting of the crops, and also the regulation of the meadows and more permanent pastures. In fielden Wiltshire, and similar areas elsewhere, the farmers pooled their few sheep to form a common flock and employed a common shepherd whose task it was each evening to drive the flock from the grazing ground on to the fallow field, there to deposit overnight its indispensable fertilizer. Enclosure, both of arable land by way of redistribution of strips followed by hedging, and of common pasture, had made considerable progress in some areas. But for thousands of farmers over large parts of the country their arable land still lay widely and, as it seems to us, inconveniently and uneconomically scattered at long distances from their yards and farms. For them the obligation to fall in with whatever was agreed concerning such matters as crop rotation and the 'stinting' of pasture rights was as natural as the seasons of the year. Echoes of their deliberations reach us only when some local 'by-law' needed reiterating or some new regulation placed on record, usually on the roll of the landlord's manorial court. When in 1507 the tenants of the manor of Elmley Castle in Worcestershire imposed a penalty of 6d. on any of their number who did not ring his pigs between Ascension Day and the end of August, it is unlikely that they were suggesting a new practice. What is clear is that groups of men of very varying substance and wit, without undue fuss, not only agreed on their basic farming routine but also shared out the burdens of fencing and ditching, cleaning out dykes and water-courses, and repairing the common ways. But there their communal arrangements ended: their crops and stock, their implements and farming gear, and even their farmhouses and outbuildings were, apart from their landlords' interest, their own.

In the forest areas (usually on higher or more uneven ground where the soil was shallower and mostly unsuitable for arable farming, land on the whole of less ancient settlement) the population was more scattered but, even in 1500, not necessarily less dense. Farming there was more specialized, crops were few, and the main concern was with dairying and the grazing of large flocks of sheep on the open moorland. In Ravenstone-dale, Westmorland, in 1541 there were 181 tenants, of whom forty-three were cottagers with no land to speak of, and less than half the farms had more than five acres of arable land, the largest being only thirty-six acres. No doubt they all had stock on the fells. Farmhouses were more often isolated or grouped in hamlets of a few households. Open fields were exceptional, being confined to larger villages. Arable fields were small and irregularly shaped, but close at hand. They were often bounded, especially in the south-western counties, by massive hedge banks which served as boundaries, as shelter for crops and stock from wind and rain, and to supply timber for building and fuel. In far different country, the Fens of Lincolnshire, farmers specialized in pastoral farming, especially for meat, though in a large sample of probate inventories made in the 1530s the average herd of cattle was only ten beasts. The men of the Fens also bred horses which they sold to the coalminers of Nottinghamshire and the lead-miners of Derbyshire. Farmers in such areas followed their own individual routine with little reference to communal regulation, except perhaps in the matter of summer grazing about which they might need to reach agreement with their neighbours. There was, no doubt, mutual help at sheep-shearing time. In farming no man can be entirely self-sufficient, and invariably there was a landlord as well.

Following a century or more of retreat from marginal land it can be assumed that, taking one year with another, most early Tudor farmers were making a reasonable living. A disastrous harvest would have serious consequences, but there is no reason for thinking that real crises of subsistence were more than a very occasional occurrence. Generalizations about the livelihood of early Tudor farmers are hazardous, however. They left few records, and we can be sure that they very rarely kept accounts, since cash formed only a minor part of their reckoning. They needed it for their few essential purchases but principally for their rent. But rents were low in the early decades of the sixteenth century, the legacy of a century of a falling, or at most a stable, demand for land. Even though by the 1520s this stability was beginning to disappear, the majority of ordinary husbandmen were still enjoying its benefits. Small surpluses of grain and stock could be sold, but except in the vicinity of the larger towns, especially London, transport difficulties made the marketing of large amounts of grain uneconomic. Only in livestock was there much long-distance trade in food. The main cash crop of most farmers, both large and small, was more likely to be wool or hides.

Farming households were usually small, only for short periods extending to three generations. In most parts of the country, and especially in the sheep–corn, nucleated village areas, primogeniture was the rule of inheritance, and eldest sons rarely married until their fathers died or were incapable of running the farm. Other sons and daughters remained at home only until they married or went into service in other households. Only the more substantial farmers would employ 'day-labourers', mostly cottagers and smallholders, or living-in 'servants of husbandry'. Indeed, ordinary husbandmen with fifteen to twenty acres of arable land were more likely to spend part of their time working for wages than to employ anyone other than members of their own families. Younger sons took up tenancies wherever and whenever they could find and afford them, and, if they were lucky, married heiresses. In the forest areas inheritance customs were sometimes, though not invariably, by some form of partible inheritance. This was not always as disastrous to the viability of the farm as it would appear, for, families being small, farms were regularly re-united;

but it did accentuate the tendency for farms in these areas to be small, certainly as far as their arable land was concerned.

Whether for this or other reasons, it was especially in the forest areas that Tudor country people augmented their living in ways more enterprising, if not more profitable, than by working as farm-labourers. It has been calculated that in 'cheese' Wiltshire four out of five rural families had secondary livings. The most obvious secondary occupation, and one which already had a long history in rural England, was for farmers and members of their families to improve their skill in making woollen cloth to the point where they could work on their own or other people's materials and sell either the product or their labour for cash. Cheap rural labour had been as important as the quality of native wool in enabling the late-medieval English cloth industry to compete with its European rivals. Spinning, which required little equipment and no ancillary labour, was the obvious occupation, but the many probate inventories which list a pair of looms along with implements of husbandry testify to the large number of part-time country weavers. Indeed, the existence of so many fulling mills, power-driven by expertly engineered water-courses, the whole complex usually built and run by enterprising landlords, indicates the extent to which even the finishing of cloth was a rural industry. In some parts of England, notably in Devon and in the country around Halifax in Yorkshire, the country spinners and weavers bought and sold the wool, yarn and cloth at local markets, financing themselves from week to week. But for the most part, the rural cloth industry depended on the nearest thing in early Tudor England to an industrial magnate, the clothier. It was the essence of his function that he had no factory, though some clothiers, such as the well-known Thomas Paycocke of Coggeshall in Essex, were themselves actively engaged in weaving. The clothier, especially in the west of England, in Gloucestershire and Wiltshire, acted primarily as an entrepreneur, buying the raw wool and 'putting it out' to be carded or combed, spun, woven, etc., by a succession of craftsmen working in their own homes at piece-rates. To conduct such operations called for considerable capital, or credit, and it was this which gave clothiers what those in government circles regarded as excessively dangerous power over their employees. When, for some reason, trade was depressed, they could afford to stand off their work-force or to reduce their wages, causing distress and unrest, if not open rebellion – or so it was argued. In fact, of course, to the extent that they had other resources, most rural cloth-workers could survive a short-term crisis. The real danger to public order lay in those areas, notably in parts of the west, including Somerset, and on the Essex–Suffolk border, where, precisely because of the success of the rural cloth industry, the workers were moving in considerable numbers into large villages or small country towns such as Trowbridge and Bradford-on-Avon, Sudbury, Lavenham and Long Melford, and becoming, if not entirely divorced from their agricultural occupations, craftsmen first and farmers second. The truly rural, that is, part-time, cloth industry was in fact a source of considerable social stability.

Cloth-making was certainly the most important and most widely distributed rural by-employment, but there were later added such allied crafts as the knitting of woollen stockings which occupied the spare time of farmers and their wives in such places as the Pennine dales, and the spinning of flax and hemp. It was also natural for men accustomed not only to heavy manual labour but to handling timber and stone and providing their own fuel to be attracted, seasonally rather than part-time, to quarrying and the mining or extracting of lead, tin, copper, and, on a smaller scale, iron and silver. Most of the mining areas, from Devon and Cornwall, through Somerset, parts of Worcestershire and north Derbyshire, and so up to Westmorland and Northumberland, and also the Sussex Weald, were those in which pastoral farming predominated, enabling many of the men to be away for a substantial part of the year. It is no coincidence that lead-mining operations in the Mendips and the Peak District usually ceased around Midsummer's Day when the corn in the valleys was nearly ripe. Early Tudor Devon probably had as many tinners, mostly part-time, as she had seamen. In Cornwall, however, there were some nearly full-time tinners who farmed a few acres as a secondary occupation. In both counties they laboured in appalling conditions for small gains. In 1524, according to the coinage rolls, 432 Cornish tinners and 737 in Devon each presented less than a thousand-weight of tin, and it was reported in 1586 that miners earned barely £3 a year. Most of the profit, especially in Cornwall, went to the dealers who handled the marketing. The actual tinworks, however, each comprising several acres, were often in multi-ownership, like ships. A particular sense of community had developed among all miners, but especially among the tinners who enjoyed considerable privileges under royal charter, including free access to any land not already 'bounded'. Only these, and other extraordinary rights, such as exemption from direct taxation, from mustering with the county militia and even freedom from toll in local markets, can account for their attachment to their picks and spades, and to living conditions far worse even than those in the most primitive two-roomed, smoke-filled farmhouse.

Nearer to hearth and home, every village of any size supported a handful of specialist craftsmen, making goods for sale or providing services, including wheelwrights, smiths of all kinds, millers, more rarely carpenters and masons, and sometimes brewers. In the country town of Oakham in Rutland in the 1520s there were about a hundred and forty adult men, of whom about half were labourers and servants, about a quarter farmers and the rest, some thirty-four, master-men engaged in a score of different crafts. But like rural craftsmen everywhere each of them also had some land, in this case strips in the open fields. Here and there a concentration of specialist craftsmen points to an industry of more than local importance, such for example as John Leland noted in the early 1540s near Sheffield: 'There be many smiths and cutlers in Hallamshire'; and 'In Rotherham be very good smiths for all cutting tools.' At about the same time over in the depths of Worcestershire John Waldern of Belbroughton had in stock at his death, besides his farm implements, no less than 650 scythes, valued at £52, which meant that he probably owned a water-powered tilt-hammer.

Opportunities for employment as full-time building-workers, that is as carpenters, stonemasons, tilers, etc., were limited in early Tudor England, most farmhouses and their ancillary buildings being built by their owners with the help of neighbours. Work on cathedrals and other ecclesiastical buildings, on the King's Works, that is, on fortifications and royal palaces, and on the houses of the nobility and wealthier gentlemen was neither plentiful nor particularly well paid in the early sixteenth century. Reputable master-masons, however, could command high wages, especially those giants in their craft, the mason-architects. As much building work was seasonal and short-term the craftsmen were usually itinerant, moving, often in companies, to wherever employment was available. Although all were essentially wage-earners they usually owned their own tools. As was the case with all rural craftsmen they learned by working with others rather than through any formal training such as would have been normal in more settled occupations. Only in the larger towns were there master-craftsmen sufficiently established to contract to construct complete buildings, supplying both labour and materials, and in very few towns was there a masons' guild. There were also many other men whose livelihood took them far from hearth and home, moving around the countryside singly or at the most in pairs, self-employed or, to use a later term, 'masterless men'. Anyone owning a cart-horse or a team of oxen could earn a regular part-time income as a local carrier of goods, and there was an increasing need for long-distance cattle-drovers. Others to be met with on the roads of early Tudor England were the dealers in agricultural products, especially the much-maligned 'corn-badgers', and the rather more respected 'wool-broggers' or 'drivers'. These last were humble men, supplying local markets and not to be confused with the now dwindling number of wool-dealers who supplied the export trade, nor indeed with the itinerant and highly skilled wool-packers and wool-winders. The latter were unique in that in 1522 they established by royal charter their own Company of

Woolmen, but even so they found it necessary to deal in small quantities of wool as a sideline. Finally, there was an army of pedlars of small wares. For most of these itinerants, home was a farmhouse or cottage, usually in a forest area, for these parts of the country, it has been argued, were the haunt, even the nurseries, of independence, and of nonconformity in its widest sense.

Seafaring was one of the more adventurous occupations, though the total number of early Tudor Englishmen who made a full-time career of it was not large, at any rate compared with the number of clergy. Small fishing boats abounded, of course, based not only on the major seaports but also on hundreds of creeks and havens all around the country's long coastline. These would be sailed by their owners and one or more crew, and although they often made quite long voyages in search of their catch they were largely home-based and not part of the national or indeed international seafaring community. Fishing too was a seasonal occupation and most coastal fishermen will have spent much of the year as farmers or farm-labourers. Freshwater fishing was another occupation ancillary to agriculture, and fenland farmers in particular combined the rearing of cattle and horses with fishing and fowling. Those who looked to the sea for a principal livelihood, either as fishermen or merchant seamen, were more likely to concentrate in the larger seaports but there were many smaller seafaring communities, especially on the east coast. At Walberswick in Suffolk, according to an inquiry made in 1537, there lived five masters capable of taking ships to Iceland, the Low Countries and France, and eighty ordinary seamen of whom fourteen were 'able to be masters' in local waters. From very rough contemporary assessments it seems that at any one time during the early sixteenth century there were in England only about five thousand experienced mariners. Few English merchant ships at this time were over one hundred tons burthen, that is, contained more than six thousand cubic feet of cargo space, and coastal vessels were usually around thirty tons. With a complement of about one man for every three tons they were, by continental standards, overmanned, but most masters expected to lose men in the course of a voyage, if not by disease then by desertion. For ordinary seamen, even on a long voyage, no experience was necessary and ships' carpenters and gunners were often 'landsmen', that is men who had not previously been to sea. All naval and merchant ships sailing any distance would carry a large complement of soldiers, especially bowmen. Merchant ships sailing into foreign waters often carried, in addition to their masters, captains who were not seamen. Ships' companies were microcosms of life on land: gentlemen's sons, some of whom were entrusted to ships' masters at the age of eleven, expected to be treated with deference. The pay of ordinary seamen was probably even lower than that of agricultural labourers, although some Yarmouth seamen in 1514 demanded 15s. for a trip to the Low Countries and back instead of the usual 10s. Clothing was provided and there were other perquisites such as the right of every member of the crew to engage in trade on his own account and to share in the profits of any piracy. Henry VIII's success in reducing piracy did not help him to recruit seamen. It was possible after a few years at sea for a man to save enough to become the owner or part-owner of a ship. Many ships were of course owned by city merchants but landowners too invested in them. Sir John Fulford probably built his coaster, the *Dorothy Fulford*, for less than £50 and the fact that he could hire her out in 1536 for a voyage of twelve days from Dartmouth in Devon to the Isle of Wight for 50s. suggests that an owner could clear his outlay in a year or two. Shipbuilding must have provided a fairly settled full-time occupation all around the coasts, but especially in the Thames estuary. When Henry VIII built his great *Henri Grâce à Dieu* at Woolwich in 1514 he employed no less than 260 shipwrights. By 1559 some six hundred were permanently employed in the royal dockyards, many of them highly skilled aliens. Only gradually were English shipbuilders experimenting with designs of their own instead of copying foreign models. But early Tudor seamen too had much to learn. Even experienced masters knew little about either the use of scientific instruments or the observation of celestial bodies as aids to navigation, and so they tended to specialize in routes they knew and rarely sailed out of sight of land. But because so many English harbours were death-traps to the inexperienced there were good livings to be made as lodesmen (pilots), those able to guide strangers by virtue of their local knowledge. Coastal pilots formed one of the first organized professions, being examined and licensed at Hull, Newcastle and Bristol, and at London, in 1514, setting up by royal charter, and in typically medieval religious guise, the Guild of the Holy Trinity and St Clement, the later Trinity House at Deptford. It is a measure, however, of most Englishmen's extraordinary lack of interest in the sea that an Act of Parliament of 1541 included in its prohibition of all manner of sorcery the forecasting of the weather.

For young men, and even for a few young women, with some intellectual pretensions and, in the case of younger sons in particular, no prospects at home, one of the more obvious careers was in the Church, either as a secular priest or as a member of one of the religious orders. On the simple hypothesis that virtually every village community had a priest, and some more than one, and that there were more unbeneficed priests than pluralists, the secular priesthood alone would appear to have absorbed far more adult men than any other livelihood except farming. Few English people can have been more than a day's walk from at least one of some eight hundred religious houses up and down the country. Even those actually situated in towns had extensive rural ties in the estates with which they had been endowed. All the necessary social, religious and academic education could be provided for novices, and the more scholarly could be sent to continue their studies at one of the universities. Communities varied greatly in size from several dozen, not counting indoor and outdoor servants, to small households of three or four whose continued existence was always in jeopardy. Recruitment remained fairly steady until about 1530. In the whole of England, shortly before the dissolution of the monasteries, there were nearly ten thousand religious, including some two thousand five hundred friars and about two thousand women. For both men and women with administrative talents a religious house offered a variety of opportunities, including election as governor, and contacts with the outside world were frequent. In all but the poorest or most observant houses life for members of religious communities was materially every bit as comfortable as that enjoyed by the more affluent laity.

Neither low nor high birth, but only illegitimacy, was a bar to those seeking a clerical career, though except by special licence and for some university scholars ordination was not possible under the age of twenty-four. A boy aspiring to become a secular priest would first need some elementary schooling which he could usually obtain from a chantry-priest or other priest near his home. To learn the necessary Latin he would need to go to a grammar school, and if this meant leaving home he might need cash for lodging as well as fees. An alternative was to enter a cathedral song-school or to join an episcopal or other large clerical household from where he could attend school. It was not essential for those intending to become priests to go on to one of the universities. In the diocese of Lincoln between 1503 and 1528 only just over one in six of those instituted to benefices (who in turn were probably less than half of those ordained during the same period) were graduates, even though Cambridge was close at hand. Over the country as a whole the proportion of graduates among those ordained was probably less than one tenth. Apart from expensive treatises no professional training was available, and like his brother on the farm the young cleric learned his skills by watching and doing, probably learning the liturgy by attending services rather than by reading a missal. Examination by the bishop could be a rigorous test of both education and aptitude, but in most cases was only a formality. Some beneficed clergy were barely literate, but in 1532 the bishops in Convocation reaffirmed that all ordinands should be required to show evidence that they understood the epistles and the gospels. Much more important was the ordinand's possession of a 'title', that is, a guarantee of financial support. Otherwise he was supposed to show proof of a patrimony, that is, private means. Some were fortunate enough to have private patrons, lay or ecclesiastical, but most titles had to be obtained from religious houses which between them owned a very considerable number of the country's advowsons (rights of presentation to benefices). Institution fees could be as high as £5. For the many who were not instituted to benefices shortly after ordination, every year which passed lessened their chances. However, there is some evidence that from about 1520 the number of ordinands dropped quite considerably, so much so that had it not been for pluralism some parishes might have lacked incumbents. In the diocese of Lincoln this may have been due not so much to lack of candidates as to Bishop John Longland's more rigorous examinations, but the diocese of London under Cuthbert Tunstall and John Stokesley (1522–39) showed the same trend. The appropriation of rectorial income, largely the greater tithes, by monasteries had proceeded at such a pace during the century or so before the Reformation that most incumbents were vicars, their income consisting of a fixed stipend and the smaller tithes. With incomes as low as £5 a year pluralism was almost a necessity, and indeed even the Act of 1529 prohibiting plurality applied only to incumbents whose first benefice was worth more than £8 a year. Even those with single parishes were often otherwise occupied and evidence from a large number of dioceses shows that non-residence was as high as 25–30 per cent, providing considerable scope for the employment of curates. For unbeneficed secular priests there were other opportunities of employment, though usually at miserably low stipends, in the thousands of chantry chapels, on average over one per parish in the West Riding of Yorkshire and over three in London. Like parochial incumbents, chantry-priests could expect tenure for life. Failing this there were all kinds of stipendiary posts, without tenure, and innumerable opportunities of temporary employment in the recital of the masses and other intercessory prayers so beloved of wealthy testators. The more able might obtain posts as tutors or take in pupils. For those who sooner or later became rectors or even only vicars, as bachelors with their two- or three-roomed parsonage houses, their tithe and their glebe, the latter often equivalent to a small farm, life was in most cases as comfortable as it was for the more substantial of their farming neighbours. Whether the clergy constituted a profession in the modern sense of the term is arguable. They had no real career structure but they did possess, in ordination, recognized (if not high) qualifications, they controlled their own recruitment, and disciplined their own members. Much more important, they exercised a spiritual authority, and indeed spiritual functions, which set them apart from all laymen, however rich and powerful. They were accorded the courtesy title of 'Sir'. Very few moved from their first cure and it was probably after several years in a remote and troublesome parish that a priest had most need of a sense of vocation, for by then preferment was unlikely to come his way.

Many who found employment in the Church proceeded no further than the minor orders, thus remaining essentially laymen. For example, there must have been many thousands of parish clerks, assistants to the priests in everything connected with the church's worship, including the reading of the lessons and the making of the liturgical responses. Such men needed to be able both to read Latin and to sing, or at least to intone. They were also in charge of the choirboys if there were any and this involved a certain amount of teaching. They earned very little, being largely dependent on voluntary offerings and the proceeds of occasional 'clerks' ales', and many no doubt had other employment or a small farm. Other clerks in minor orders were to be found in the cathedral churches and here, too, they were required to be literate and, among a variety of duties, many of them sang in the choirs. From here those with real musical ability might become Gentlemen of the Chapel Royal which followed the Court, a very select group of some thirty choristers in all which included some of the most outstanding composers of Tudor England. Like the clergy, those who gained all or part of their living as church musicians went through no formal apprenticeship and obtained no kind of musical education except that which they could obtain by listening and doing.

It is difficult to be very precise about those who, other than the clergy, made all or part of their living in early Tudor England as teachers. In the two universities of Oxford and Cambridge the few professors were invariably in orders, as were the college fellows who did most of the undergraduate teaching. In the endowed public grammar schools the number of laymen employed as masters was increasing. Clergy or laymen, they received regular stipends and usually had security of tenure for life. Some of them were beginning to make a real effort to make learning easier and more attractive by giving their exercises a contemporary flavour. Of the many keepers of private schools, where children learned not only the basic literary skills but also in some cases languages, book-keeping and even the elementary mathematics needed for navigating and land-surveying, some were priests, but even they were not otherwise professionally qualified to teach. In the six south-western counties of England between 1500 and 1548, out of seventy known private schoolmasters only about one third were university graduates. Some private schoolmasters probably earned more from boarding their scholars than from fees. They almost invariably worked single-handed, and they had no professional organization or affiliation. Their brief appearances in the records almost certainly reflect an insubstantial contribution to popular education.

How very different was the situation with regard to those 'learned in the law'. Before practising their skills, lawyers had to spend many years studying at one of the Inns of Court or Chancery in London. Without such training they were not allowed to work in the courts. Unlike schoolmasters, there seemed to contemporaries to be very many of them in early Tudor England. In fact in 1500 the resident membership of the four Inns was still only about one thousand, smaller than that of either of the two universities, and over half of these did not ever practise as lawyers. It was already quite common for the eldest sons of landowners to spend a period at one of the Inns, largely to complete their social education, and to pick up knowledge useful to them in defending their landed inheritance. Entry, in fact, was more restricted than at the universities, being normally open only to the sons of freeholders and probably requiring a higher standard of secondary education. A student at the Inner Temple could support himself on about £10 a year, but his family would need to be substantial farmers or landowners to be able to afford that sum for at least six years, and there were no exhibitions. By the mid-1520s there were between one and two hundred practising barristers, of whom about fifty worked only in the courts at Westminster. Even leading barristers were still known technically as 'apprentices at law'. At the very top of the profession were about a dozen Sergeants at Law from whom alone were chosen the judges who presided over the king's courts at Westminster and at county assizes. Besides barristers there were the attorneys, that is, professional lawyers who occasionally pleaded for their clients in the lesser courts but whose chief function lay in providing advice, in drafting evidence, in standing in for their clients, and in the conveyancing of land. The majority of these worked in the provinces, their number varying with the litigiousness of different counties. Solicitors were even humbler practitioners, though they too were professionally trained lawyers and were not yet preoccupied with conveyancing. The law also provided a living for a host of court officers and also for those hangers-on of the Tudor legal system, some of them indeed trained lawyers, the informers. Theirs was certainly a career open to talents: the Crown's reliance on such agents must have helped to win for smugglers, and indeed for all who broke the law, more public sympathy and more favourable verdicts from juries than they deserved. Once he was learned in the common law a man's career prospects were excellent. Professional lawyers were increasingly in demand as 'surveyors' or land agents to substantial landowners, including ecclesiastical bodies, and monasteries frequently employed them as 'receivers' (treasurers), as 'auditors' or accountants, or simply retained them for their 'counsel'. They were also increasingly being engaged as part-time Town Clerks. Such posts, and the fees which came with them, could be multiplied to the point where, however small individually, they formed collectively a substantial income.

But not all the 'fee'd men' of early Tudor England were lawyers. The system permeated society, and the essence of the fee was that it represented only a portion of its recipient's livelihood. Most numerous of all were the manorial bailiffs appointed by landlords, usually from the more substantial of their tenants, and indeed, in the case of an absentee landlord, the same man was often both lessee of the home farm and also bailiff, his chief duty being that of rent-collector and keeper of accounts. But the greatest in the land did not disdain to receive fees for what were in effect secondary, if hardly onerous, offices of profit. The earl of Shrewsbury was 'chief steward' of no less than eleven religious houses, probably adding thereby some £50 to his annual income, equivalent to that from a large manor. The same principle applied to the majority of posts in the service of the Crown, especially those at county level such as clerkships of the peace, coronerships (for which fees were only paid from the reign of Henry VII), escheatorships, and so on. Most of these were held by local gentlemen with some legal training. The 1530s saw the appointment for the first time of Vice-Admirals of the maritime counties, offering to local knights and gentlemen not only influence but also profit, not in this case so much by way of fees as from the produce of wrecks.

But of course the plums of the vast number of administrative posts were those at Court, and if the royal household is included they cover a very wide range and area of recruitment. Including those who performed routine clerical duties (the writing of documents), there were over five hundred men employed in government departments, to whom some fifty were added in the course of the expansion of the 1530s and 1540s. Appointment was entirely by patronage, some in the gift of the king himself but most of the lesser posts in that of superior officers. Tenure was for life and no one lost his post when his patron died or was disgraced, for all took their oaths of loyalty to the sovereign. Salaries were fixed and barely adequate but were considerably augmented, in the case of the older posts by the issue of an annual livery or clothing, and in all cases by fees received from those who used their services, and by a host of other perquisites, including patronage in respect of lesser offices, which were usually bestowed for a consideration. There was also a daily ration, or 'diet', of food from the royal kitchen. The habit was growing under the early Tudors of great men, the king's chief ministers, taking promising men into their own personal service, whence they moved, if they were lucky, into the royal service proper. So William Paget, the son of a London artificer, after reading civil law at Cambridge, though not a cleric, entered in turn the services of Stephen Gardiner, Thomas Cromwell, Thomas Wriothesley and finally of Edward Seymour the later Protector. As one of the Principal Secretaries of State from 1543 he became a very powerful and, as things turned out for him, successful politician. Others arrived in royal service by quite different routes. Stephen Vaughan was a cloth exporter who, following successful service for Henry VIII abroad, became Under-Treasurer of the Mint, and Robert Amadas, a London goldsmith, Treasurer to Cardinal Wolsey, served from 1526 until his death in 1532 as Master of the King's Jewels. Thomas Audley, the later Lord Chancellor, who came of Essex farming stock, was Town Clerk of Colchester and a Member of Parliament before entering government service. Cromwell's protégés did not suffer from his fall from power. One of his former clerks, Ralph Sadler, who seems to have been entirely self-educated, was promoted to one of the two chief secretary-ships just before his patron's execution and was soon receiving a salary of £1,350 a year, gratuities in the region of £600, and payments in kind worth over £700, an income considerably more than that of most of the peerage. The nobility by birth were not excluded from office but they tended to attach themselves as courtiers to the king's immediate household. That household, together with those of the queen and of the royal children, brought the total number in more or less permanent residence in the Palace of Westminster to about four thousand persons.

Among these were to be found most of those few people in early-sixteenth-century England who made any sort of a living as writers. For anyone with ideas to convey, whether in print or simply in manuscript for a limited readership, patronage was both essential and prudent. It was best sought in the service of the Crown, either directly or as a member of the household of a leading politician. Original imaginative literature, in English, was rare and the more popular it was in character the more suspect it was likely to be in high places. A statute of 1543 listed printed ballads, plays, rhymes, songs and other 'fantasies' as the work of rebels and it was no doubt on this account that reputable printers and publishers shunned original romances, poetry and drama, if any was offered to them, in favour of classical texts, translations of foreign books and works of instruction, secular or religious. Most of the romantic literature of the period was conveyed orally. Noble households offered employment to minstrels, those men of varied talent who told tales as well as sang and played simple instruments. There were few professional musicians, either composers or performers, except in the larger cathedral and monastic churches and at Court, but in the larger towns there were the 'waits', originally nightwatchmen, who were often quite competent players of instruments. Some even served a formal apprenticeship, but only in London does there seem to have been a guild of minstrels. Most of these were self-employed performers engaged by the citizens for such occasions as wedding feasts and, if they were lucky, on a more regular basis by the keepers of taverns. Most were very poor, or had other employment. Finally, acting was hardly yet a full-time living, and certainly not yet a profession.

There were, then, in the sense we understand today, no real professions in early Tudor England except that of the law. However, the early sixteenth century did see, besides that of Trinity House, the establishment of at least one professional body which had a greater long-term significance than its founders can have realized. This was the foundation by royal charter in 1518 of the Royal College of Physicians. It had long been possible to read for a university degree in medicine but the syllabus was entirely academic and of little practical use. Even to be accepted as a physician it was necessary to have pursued further study in one of the great continental medical schools, and such men did not so much practise medicine as act as consultants for artisan barber–surgeons and apothecaries. The great Thomas Linacre's chief contribution to medical science in England was as translator of classical Greek medical texts into Latin. The original twenty fellows of the College were all, like Linacre, successful medical consultants, mostly at Court, and the charter was primarily intended to protect them from 'common artificers [such] as smiths, weavers, and women', and from those who could not 'discern the cunning from the uncunning'. It followed the precedent set by the foundation of the College of Arms in 1487 which conferred a similar monopoly on the thirteen heralds. In 1523 the College of Physicians' licensing powers were extended, by Act of Parliament, from London and its environs to the whole of England, only university graduates being exempt. It thus became more than a local guild and may be said to have offered for the first time a recognized professional status for medical practitioners. It also freed them from the control of the Church. In 1540 the College gained a measure of control over surgeons and apothecaries, but these 'artisans' proved more than a match for their superiors and, being indispensable to rich and poor alike, managed to avoid being governed. In the same year members of the College were exempted by statute from doing watch and ward and serving as constables, in case this endangered their patients, who were described as being mainly the Lords of the Council and the nobility of the realm.

It is a far cry from the hothouse atmosphere of life at Court to the working farmers with whom we began, but the mention of constables serves to draw attention to the great distinction in the minds of the rulers of Tudor England between those who, although neither lords nor even gentlemen, were of a 'sufficiency', by which they meant income from a stable occupation, to assume public responsibility, and those who, having neither skilled craft nor land, whether as owners or tenants, were fit, in Sir Thomas Smith's phrase, 'only to be ruled'. This last category included all children and young people up to the time they married and became heads of families, the adult poor, whether disabled or unemployed, the large number of unskilled or semi-skilled persons who did most of the heavy manual work, especially in the towns, skilled wage-earners who were not householders, the rural day-labourers and the journeymen of the urban industries and finally, in both country and town, an army of what were called servants. Most of these last were resident, provided with board and lodging, clothing, and a small annual wage. In the early sixteenth century men might expect between 20s. and 30s. a year, women rather less, money which many masters paid only when their servants had completed a whole year's service. In the households of the more substantial townsfolk there would be a fairly clear distinction between those servants employed about the master's business or in his workshop and those engaged in domestic duties. The larger rural households likewise would have both outdoor and indoor servants. Not all were young but they were usually unmarried and they were, especially the outdoor ones, notoriously mobile. Probably rather more settled were the servants employed as housekeepers by the secular clergy and the very considerable complement of servants, both indoor and outdoor, who shared in part in the life of religious communities.

2. Landlords and Tenants

Owner-occupation of land was by no means unknown in Tudor England. Not only were there very large numbers of freeholding tenant farmers, but most medium-sized landowners and landed magnates kept some land 'in hand' to supply their household needs and, in some cases, the market. But in early Tudor England the concept of absolute ownership of land was quite foreign to the common law and to all but a few very avant-garde law writers. No one but the Crown enjoyed full proprietary rights: everyone else held, by some sort of conditional tenure, of some superior lord – ultimately, and sometimes directly, of the Crown. The actual number of levels in the tenurial hierarchy must not be exaggerated: since the passage of the statute *Quia Emptores* in 1290 further sub-infeudation had been prohibited, and one of the effects of so much land falling into Crown hands in the later Middle Ages and being regranted had been to reduce the number of mesne, or intermediate, landlords.

The manor was still in 1500 and for a long time to come the key to, and the essential unit of, landownership. This was an estate which could comprise the lord's demesne, that is, the land traditionally reserved for his own occupation, and a variety of tenancies, freeholdings, customary holdings, leaseholdings and tenements 'held at [the lord's] will'. To the manor also belonged the residual ownership of woodland, pasture, fisheries, etc., the use of which was shared with the tenants, and also the essentially seignorial rights, each a source of profit, such as the holding of manor courts and of fairs and markets, the exploitation of minerals, the construction of mills, the seizure of stray animals, etc., and also such claims as a lord might still exercise over the personal possessions of his bond, or villein, tenants. Manors could vary enormously in territorial extent and, of course, in economic value. The counting of manors is therefore a very inexact way of measuring landownership. However, the manor was still the lowest estate which conferred on its owner the status of landlord, or what contemporaries would have called 'lordship', with all that that implied in non-economic terms. Even more prestigious were those territorial lordships, called honours or baronies, which comprised not single manors but a group, some of which were held of the lord of the honour, who was usually a peer, by mesne lords. Of great antiquity, honours would often include castles with their associated townships. In the West Riding of Yorkshire alone there were in the early sixteenth century about fifty such lordships, ten of them part of the Crown's duchy of Lancaster and twelve belonging to monasteries. These lordships brought in little rent to their owners but gave to those who were laymen great social prestige and political power.

When allowance is made for the number of manors owned by the Church, for those kept in hand by the nobility, and for the multiplicity of manors owned by the more important knights and gentlemen, it will be obvious that not all manors, probably rather less than half, had a resident lord. But even if only represented in his manor court by a steward, the lord of a manor had a very special personal relationship with each of his tenants and their fortunes were mutually dependent. Even freeholders, who paid a fixed and often purely nominal rent, were usually bound to attend certain sessions of the manor court and indeed if, as in Wigston in Leicestershire, they farmed between them (about twenty households) nearly 40 per cent of the village's open fields of some 2,850 acres, then they would wish to be involved in the making of agrarian by-laws. The existence of freeholders in any farming community provided an obstacle to an aggressive landlord, for they enjoyed a legal security virtually equivalent to his own. Large sub-manorial freeholdings were on the whole more common in forest areas, especially in Kent and also in the south-west of England, but even in East Anglia most farmers held some land by 'socage' tenure. In this, as in other aspects of landholding, by 1500 tenurial and personal relationships were very confused: a man might hold his land of several lords and by a variety of tenures.

Customary tenants were the successors of early medieval villeins, most of them by 1500 being copyholders, possessed of written evidence of the registration of their tenancy in the manorial court rolls. As such they and their lords were both protected and constrained by the custom of the manor, a body of local law arrived at by consensus over the centuries and still, in minor respects, being added to in the sixteenth century. It was manorial custom which determined whether the copy-holdings in a particular manor were 'of inheritance', which for practical purposes was tantamount to freehold, or at the lord's disposal, and whether entry-fines (money due from new tenants) were fixed or not. Even tenants 'at will', usually a minority, could derive some comfort from manorial custom which, during the century or so before 1500, when landlords had been glad to fill vacant holdings, had in many cases moved in favour of the tenant in occupation. Rents for customary holdings often included additional payments called 'sale of works', that is, cash in lieu of ancient labour services which in theory lords could re-impose, though few did so.

Leasehold tenancies, on the other hand, had in theory nothing to do with custom in the sense that they were the result of freely negotiated contracts, recorded in indentures, between two parties. Leases could be for lives, one, two, or three named and living persons, or for years, the former being a form of real property, protected by the courts of common law, the latter a chattel interest only. In the west of England in particular, and on estates belonging to the Church, the lease for years (usually a very long term), terminable on the death of all of certain named lives, usually three, was already very common by 1500. Clearly it had potential advantages for both parties and it was a gamble as to who got the best bargain. In fact, as with all leases for lives, most tenants sought to renew their contract while at least one of those named was still alive, and landlords were

usually only too ready to oblige. A good many leases concerned
the manorial demesne of a non-resident lord, or of a monastic
house no longer interested in farming the land itself. The
tenant of the 'chief messuage' usually had a sizeable holding. He
paid a rent which, especially in the case of monasteries, might
be partly in kind, that is, an annual render of a fixed amount of
grain and stock. He might even, and this again was a
particular feature of monastic lands, take over with the land a
flock of sheep which he undertook to restore at the end of his
term. It was not unknown for him to be able to call on
labour services from other tenants. Most non-demesne leases,
unless of newly colonized land – a rare commodity in the
early sixteenth century when demand, though buoyant, was not
yet really pressing on supply – were conversions from copyhold,
and though terminable and recorded on indentures such leases
retained a great many customary obligations such as suit of
court and the payment of a heriot, or best beast, at death,
but very rarely labour services. Entry-fines, even more than
rents, were a matter of negotiation, though either side,
according to the state of the market, might appeal to custom.
Fines were often payable by instalments, becoming, to all intents
and purposes, additions to the rents, and they must always be
borne in mind in any assessment of rent movements. The
extension of leasehold tenure, well under way by 1500, its terms
freely entered into and dictated by each of the parties' knowledge of the market and prognostications for the future, had
immense importance for the relationship between landlords and
tenants. Farm leases spelled the end of villein tenure, for once a
lord had condescended to bargain with his tenants it was
difficult to pretend that either their persons or their goods were
his to command.

Leasing also contributed towards the polarization in the size
of farms which was already in 1500 a feature of many farming
communities, especially in the fielden areas. It was two centuries
and more since villein farms had been of a standard size, most
commonly the virgate of about thirty acres. The great late-
medieval drop in population, resulting in the vacating of

farms and their piecemeal reoccupation, had in many villages
resulted in the gradual emergence of a tenant aristocracy, no
more than a handful but each in possession of a large farm of
one hundred acres and more of arable land. It is significant that
the earliest attempts by Tudor governments to deal with
agrarian problems, the statutes of 1488–9 and 1515, were
concerned almost entirely with the 'engrossing' of farms. This
was thought to be detrimental to an adequate supply of manpower for the defence of the realm. Like most Tudor agrarian
legislation these Acts did little to remedy a situation whose
causes were deeper than mere avarice. Chippenham, in north-
east Cambridgeshire, was a fairly typical sheep–corn, open-field
village, on well-drained chalk upland where conversion from
copyholding to leaseholding had not in general progressed very
far by 1500, but where there had been a drastic fall in
population since about 1400 which had left many farms
vacant. By 1544, by which time this former monastic manor
had passed into lay hands, one Thomas Bowles was lessee not
only of the demesne and its stock (for a term of forty-
six years from 1529) but also of other land, so that, with 480
acres of arable and meadow, he farmed over one fifth of the
open fields. He also leased, presumably for his exclusive use,
300 acres of heath. He was running two thousand sheep on the
common pastures and, as farmer of the demesne, exercised a
seignorial right to fold them on the village fields. All attempts
to restrain him failed and no other villager could keep sheep.
However, most of them survived with quite viable arable
holdings: out of some sixty householders about ten had farms of
fifty and more acres, twenty of thirty plus, and only fifteen were
landless. A further fifteen, however, had no more than two
acres, and presumably no grazing. But leasehold tenure was not
a prerequisite of engrossing, for one farm in Chippenham, of
101 acres, that of Thomas Rawlings, was entirely copyhold.
There were only six freeholders at Chippenham, none with
more than four acres of arable land, so they were no obstacle
to the large farmers. With similar holdings in a forest area such
men might have had extensive pastoral rights which they could

have defended. Here at Chippenham they were probably among the poorest farmers in the village. What we can never know is how far the 'engrossers' were themselves subletting, acting as what have been called 'wholesalers' of land. It would have been of no concern to the manor court and, if it was happening, may well have been more effective in providing small-holdings than any legislation.

Landownership too had its hazards. On the death of anyone known to be a freeholder of some substance an inquiry was held on behalf of the Crown by a jury of other local land-owners into the identity of his lands, their reputed value, the tenure by which they were held, and the name and age of the heir, or, if there were only daughters, the heiresses. Thousands of inquisitions *post mortem* were returned to Westminster in the course of the century, many recording nothing but a list of non-manorial freeholdings held by socage tenure and not, as the lawyers would say, 'in chivalry', that is, to use the technical phraseology, by knight-service or for the service of so many, or even fractions of, knights' fees. Fortunate landowners held whole manors by socage tenure, and even the tenure of part or all of the deceased's estate by knight-service was of relatively little consequence if the heir was already of age, that is over twenty-one, or if an heiress was over eighteen or already married. Nor were the prospects too grim if the lords of whom the parts of the estate were held were not the Crown or a powerful landed magnate of like pretensions. But death leaving a minor or unmarried heiress and a tenure by knight-service of the king put the land in question, and indeed, by the exercise of royal prerogative, the whole estate if the tenure was 'in chief', into the hands of the Crown until such time as the heir came of age or the daughters, if heiresses, had been given in marriage. In either case the Crown enjoyed the whole pro-ceeds of the estate, saving only an allowance for the ward's maintenance. The heir, if a man, could expect to pay a sizeable 'relief' when he entered upon his inheritance, and lands in wardship could be subjected to serious 'waste' by the Crown or its assigns. Foreign visitors to England found this royal ex-

ploitation of minors and unmarried heiresses a quite insupportable intrusion into family life, but of course some of the
more substantial potential victims were also beneficiaries of the
system in that they could, if it suited them, exercise the same
rights (though not that of prerogative wardship) over their
own tenants 'in chivalry'. Between 1514 and 1526 the earl of
Northumberland enjoyed an income varying between £20
and £100 a year from his wards' lands in three counties.

Wardship and its ramifications could be avoided by its
potential victims by resort to the legal device known as the 'use'
whereby all or part of a man's lands were conveyed to a permanent body of trustees. These 'feoffees to uses', as they were
called, could be replaced as and when any of them died, but their
corporate legal personality never died or fell victim to Crown
depredations. There was a great deal more to 'uses' than the
evasion or avoidance of what amounted to royal taxation. It
was, for example, at least arguable, though rarely successfully
established, that lands conveyed to feoffees to uses were not forfeit for treason, and they were a means of breaking an entail in
order to detach 'portions' for widows, daughters, and younger
sons. At the same time, the fiscal feudalism of the Crown cannot
fail to have justified in the minds of some landed magnates
pressures of various kinds on their own tenants. The medieval
idea that land was held ultimately from God as a trust only, not
to be used selfishly or exploited ruthlessly, was coming under
heavy strain. That its possession brought social and political as
well as economic advantages was the main reason why so many,
perhaps the majority, of Tudor landowners nevertheless
cherished the goodwill of their tenants.

But before considering landowners as agents of change, and
indeed in some cases as pace-setters, some attempt must be made
to discover who they were. The large number of surviving
inquisitions *post mortem* provide the chief source of information,
although the valuations contained in them were probably only
nominal. There were something like fifty thousand manors in
the whole of England, between five hundred and fifteen
hundred per county. An analysis of their owners alone can be

useful, but the best results are those which take some account
of the larger freeholdings – those comprising more than a single
farm. As an example we may take the large county of Devon
which included many, often very ancient, freehold estates, some
of them actually called manors, although not to be found in
Domesday Book. The Crown owned very little land in the
county before the later 1530s, no more than a dozen manors,
worth in all about £560 a year. These included royal estates
set aside for Henry VII's mother, the countess of Richmond
and known, even after her death, as 'Richmond's Lands'. Far
more land was owned by the Church, fourteen manors by the
bishop of Exeter, worth some £900 a year, eighteen by the
dean and chapter of Exeter Cathedral, worth about £1,100
and, far exceeding those of the secular clergy, some ninety
manors and other large estates, worth about £7,000, were
owned by the twenty-one religious houses in the county and
twenty-seven located in other counties. Of the nobility, Henry
Courtenay, marquis of Exeter, was far and away the largest
lay landowner in the later 1520s with over forty manors bringing him an income of about £1,300, although this was very
little more than that enjoyed by each of the two wealthiest
monasteries in the county, Tavistock Abbey and Plympton
Priory. Two other peers, the earl of Bath and the marquis of
Dorset, each owned some twenty manors with net incomes
of over £400, but they both had their main estates elsewhere,
as did Lord Daubeney whose thirteen Devon manors brought
him only about £150 a year. It will be obvious from these
figures how variable was the net income from individual
manors. These valuations comprise regular income from rents
and court profits but not the irregular proceeds of marketing
produce, including timber, nor, on the other hand, do they
allow for rents in arrears. Of lay landowners below the rank
of peers there were probably in Devon in the early sixteenth
century some three hundred and fifty knights, esquires and plain
gentlemen, and these between them owned nearly half the land
in the county compared with the rather less than 15 per cent
owned by the nobility and 30 per cent by the Church. Indi-

vidually they varied from John Coplestone, esquire, the head of an ancient local family, whose lands included about twenty-five manors worth £300 a year, to minor gentlemen worth no more than £20–£30. Indeed, between 10 and 15 per cent of the land in the county, as much as that owned by the nobility, was in the hands of farmers who were owner-occupiers. It is probable that in many midland counties the nobility's share was higher, and also that of the Crown. This was certainly so in the county of Lancashire. The Devon lands owned by the nobility had, in fact, been considerably depleted in 1501 on the death, without male heirs, of John Lord Dinham, leaving his considerable estate of sixteen manors to be divided between the families of his four sisters, each of whom had married a local knight or gentleman.

This picture of the widespread ownership of land is mirrored in many, if not all, other English counties. In the West Riding of Yorkshire, as in Devon, as much as 50 per cent was owned by gentlemen, and in Norfolk the figure was over 60 per cent. In Rutland and in Buckinghamshire the proportion forming parts of medium-sized estates was rather lower, possibly under 40 per cent. On the whole, most knights owned more land individually than gentlemen and many of the latter were in fact worse off economically than many substantial lease-holding and even copyholding farmers. As there were only about three hundred and fifty knights in the whole of England in the early sixteenth century, it can safely be said that nearly half the country's land was owned by mere gentlemen, each of whose estates, unlike those of the nobility, were usually confined within areas no larger than counties. Barring the failure of male heirs their position was remarkably stable. But so too was that of the nobility. Losses of land by attainder and forfeiture were rarely permanent and until the 1530s the outstanding political disaster was that suffered in 1521 by the duke of Buckingham, but his two hundred manors, which were seized by the Crown, were spread over no less than a dozen counties and his fall did little to upset the pattern in any one area except perhaps in Gloucestershire and over the border in south Wales.

On balance, during the early sixteenth century, even the older nobility was still adding marginally to its lands. As late as 1531 the marquis of Exeter paid out nearly £1,500 for six large manors. Few of the smaller estates were being augmented as yet, but a few new ones were always being founded, usually by younger sons of established lesser gentlemen whose professional success, usually as lawyers, even enabled them to outpace the senior line. The profits of trade flowed along similar routes, but supply rather than demand ensured that the early Tudor land-market was not an active one. Moreover, more than a century of falling population and stable if not falling agricultural prices had not encouraged the idea that land was a profitable investment. At best it was seen as a source, in fact the only source, of steady income, the best possible permanent endowment for a family or a corporate body.

By 1500, and even more so by the 1520s, the economy was moving again, population was beginning to show signs of growth and the market for agricultural products, though somewhat erratic, was certainly growing decade by decade. But few contemporaries, whether owners or tenants, could see beyond the vagaries of successive harvests. Subsistence, with the occasional profitable surplus, was their aim. The landowner might contemplate reoccupying all or part of his demesnes when the current leases expired but, although hired labour was expensive, he could hardly seriously consider attempting to reverse his ancestors' commutation of the labour services of his customary tenants. The struggle to attract tenants in the fifteenth century had resulted in the granting of leases of such length that many of these in the early decades of the sixteenth century still had many years to run and, as already indicated, were usually renewable, for a small 'consideration'. Rents were more or less sacrosanct, but entry-fines, especially for leases, could reflect market demand. Evidence is hard to come by, but few early Tudor landowners could extract, by way of fines, more than two years' rent, though wherever possible they endeavoured to shorten leases to under twenty-one years, the notional equivalent of three lives, bearing in mind that each had to be alive when the contract was made. As far as customary tenancies were concerned, most landlords were locked in the law of the manor court, and this, on the whole, worked to the tenants' advantage. The duke of Buckingham's agent met great resistance in Staffordshire when he tried to increase entry-fines and only by conceding to some sixty-eight tenants a greater degree of 'surety' was he able to extract a meagre £167.

Some fifteenth-century landowners – and their number can very easily be exaggerated – had striven to make up for their declining rent rolls by converting as much of their land as possible to the grazing of sheep. The demand for wool, either for export or for the home industry, was apparently insatiable. To be really effective this meant turning over to pasture large acreages of well-drained downland traditionally used for corn-growing. The forest areas offered little scope: there was little arable, the wet valleys were only of use for dairying, and the moors were already fairly fully stocked with demesne and tenant flocks. The only practicality here was to withdraw large stretches of sheep-pasture from communal use, which some landlords did, claiming it as their own, and ruining thereby their tenants' economy. The resulting disputes were not always between landlords and their own tenants: they were just as likely to be about invasions of manorial boundaries. An interesting case occurred in 1531 when royal commissioners, probably on instructions from the king's Court of Chancery, took evidence at Combe Martin in north Devon concerning encroachments alleged to have been made by the present owner of the adjacent manor of Challacombe on waste grounds called Hangman Hill and Little Hangman which the tenants of Combe Martin (a royal manor) claimed as their preserve, not only for grazing but as a right of way for fetching sand from the seashore. It is clear from the evidence that the lords of Challacombe had been endeavouring to ditch and fence the land in dispute at intervals for over sixty years, and some eighty-year-olds from Combe Martin even contrived to link the dispute with the battles between King Edward IV and Prince Edward of Lancaster, Combe Martin naturally claiming to have been on the side of the latter.

But such wrangles in wood–pasture areas pale into in-significance compared with what had happened, and was still happening in some sheep–corn, open-field areas, especially in the Midlands. Here too there had been extensive enclosure of common pastures by landlords, or by their 'agents and assigns', that is, their lessees. Sometimes there was only – though this was serious enough – overstocking of the commons. In some places it was not enclosure that was the problem. In Norfolk, for example, in the sheep–corn areas, some landlords were accused of exploiting their traditional right to graze what were supposed to be fixed numbers of sheep on their tenants' arable strips, thereby inducing the victims to endeavour to enclose their land as a defensive measure. For example, in 1520 Sir William Fermour of East Barsham in Norfolk had well over 17,000 sheep in twenty-five separate fold-courses in the county. Even where landlords and the larger farmers put their heads together it was only too likely that the smaller fry would find themselves squeezed out of the rearrangement. Especially if the common grazing was being carved up, the landless, or virtually landless, cottage labourers would no longer have anywhere to run the odd few sheep and cattle. This in turn could mean depopulation, that is, the driving of whole households off the manor and out of the village. This certainly happened in England in the early sixteenth century but probably not on a large scale and many of those turned out will eventually have found a niche elsewhere.

It was undoubtedly true that enclosure of open fields, that is, of arable ground, for the purpose of sheep-farming could also result in depopulation, provided of course that there were still farmers there to be evicted. But many of the great late-fifteenth-century sheep runs had in fact been created from deserted or nearly deserted villages. Victims there were few and from the landlords' point of view it was a sensible alterna-tive to vacant holdings. Some of the depopulation which had preceded enclosure was due to falling population, to retreat from less fertile soil, and even to devastating local outbreaks of plague. Land in Holyoaks on the border of Leicestershire and Rutland was enclosed by Sir Robert Brudenell in 1496 but recent excavations have shown that, although there had once been some two hundred houses, there were at the time of enclosure only five or six farms still inhabited. At most some thirty people were affected. But unless the reports of Cardinal Wolsey's investigations of 1517 were entirely false there had been, in certain parts of the country – chiefly the Midlands – a good deal of forcible eviction of large numbers of tenant farmers and their families and the reduction of the inhabitants of once populous villages to a shepherd and his dog. What is clear, however, both from documentary and archaeological evidence is that most of the worst depopulating enclosure took place well before the sixteenth century opened. Freeholders and leaseholders for lives could get a hearing in the king's courts, but the common law was very loath to offer protection to copyholders. They were better advised to take their cases to Chancery or the Court of Requests. Only gradually, however, did the litigation habit grow, not really until after 1540, and long before then most of the human damage had been done. As for the timing, it is tempting to draw certain conclusions from the fact that whereas the years 1462–86 had brought unusually high wool prices and great incentives to keep sheep, in the years 1487–1503 and again in 1519–36 corn prices rose to a point where landlords could with justification be told that enough was enough. Between 1518 and 1529 nearly three hundred persons were brought before Star Chamber on charges of having enclosed land since 1485. These included nine peers, thirty-two knights and over one hundred gentlemen, besides fifty-one monasteries and five Oxford colleges. About seventy-four pleaded guilty and in about one sixth of the cases there is evidence that some of the damage was required to be put right. Many offenders were pardoned, however, either by statute or by proclamation. While such efforts may have helped to inhibit enclosure for sheep, it is unlikely that there was wholesale re-conversion, or very much human resettlement, and the market for corn was never lively enough in the early sixteenth century to encourage large-scale grain production.

This necessarily brief account of the more antisocial aspects of enclosure is perhaps proportionate to its importance, especially after 1500. The partial, and even wholesale, consolidation of arable strips continued, here and there, to be carried out by agreement among all concerned, the resulting farms being, as the tenants of Mudford and Hinton in Somerset told their royal landlord in 1554, no doubt somewhat ruefully, more 'finable'. Even if there followed no radical change of land-use, villages whose fields were henceforward occupied 'in severalty' lost a good deal of communal activity, sometimes, no doubt, to the great relief of most of those concerned. But in a very large part of the country, in particular the greater part of the forest area and the fens, enclosure was not a live issue and very many open-field villages remained now and until well after the end of the century totally unaffected.

After what has been said of the stability of land ownership in the early sixteenth century it would seem superfluous to ask whether enclosure for sheep-farming was principally the work of 'new' landlords. One at least of these, and a great sheep-farmer, can be largely absolved from the charges of depopulating brought against him in 1517. This was John (by then Sir John) Spencer. Born probably about 1480 in south-east Warwickshire of a solid if not actually a gentle farming family, he certainly inherited no land, so he may have been a younger son. He first began to build up his flocks on land he leased, land which had been enclosed before he appeared on the scene. He made his first purchase of land in 1506, and subsequent purchases, including Althorp in 1508, took him into Northamptonshire. Only at Wicken, an outlying property in the south of the county, is he himself known to have converted arable land to pasture, and there he claimed to have found many vacant farms. At Wormleighton in Warwickshire the enclosure of the open fields had actually been carried out by the previous owner, William Cope, the king's Cofferer, who had been granted the manor by the Crown. That Cope, according to Spencer, had bought up freeholds in order to enclose is not perhaps the whole of his story, but Spencer himself, as he reported to Wolsey's commissioners in 1517, had by then built a new 'mansion place' there, part of which remains, had re-established four families and, with nearly sixty people living on the manor, net depopulation was, he claimed, less than twenty. He also declared that he had repaired the church and provided it with songbooks, and pleaded not to be compelled to remove his twenty-year-old hedges, whose timber, he claimed, was 'a greater commodity than either corn or grass in those parts'. He also stated that he had established his own breed of cattle whose meat he was supplying at reasonable prices to the London market. We do not know whether he was held to his promise to restore at least some of the land to arable cultivation by the following Candlemas, but his success as owner-grazier was spectacular, especially as he built up his estate from scratch before the great expansion of the land market after 1540. Spencer's beginnings as a sheep-master on leasehold land already enclosed by previous owners was almost exactly paralleled several decades later at Burton Dassett, also in Warwickshire, by Peter Temple, ancestor of the great family of Stowe in Buckinghamshire. In his case the encloser had been Sir Edward Belknap, another of Henry VII's ministers. Many of the early Tudor enclosers were members of the older landed aristocracy; some, like the duke of Buckingham around the turn of the century, enclosed in order to use the land for hunting parks.

Landownership was so dispersed that it was very rare for a single landlord to dominate a locality. No doubt to the tenant who felt himself to have been wronged all landlords appeared equally covetous, but in fact it could matter quite a lot to an individual farmer whether his principal landlord was the Crown, the Church, a landed magnate or a minor gentleman. The Yorkist kings, followed by Henry VII, had tightened up considerably on the conservation and collection of their landed revenue, but this had not often extended to the raising of rents, and on the whole tenants of Crown manors enjoyed secure and favourable terms. Good management had long been a feature of the royal duchy of Lancaster. Its lands in the north-west uplands of Derbyshire consisted largely of rough pasture

attached to scattered farms in the dales with a minimum of
arable. Between 1485 and 1520 the duchy officers gradually
increased its rents, especially those for 'herbage', that is, pasture.
Its tenants were undoubtedly profiting by now from increased
prices for the wool, meat and dairy products in which they
specialized. Complaints made in the duchy's courts of overstocking, and the evidence of probate inventories of farmers
in the High Peak with flocks of several hundred sheep, may
well indicate where the balance of advantage lay. One of the
effects of the increase in domestic beasts was to lessen the number
of the king's red deer. Otherwise we might not have heard
of the overstocking. Further north, in the royal forest of Rossendale in the Lancashire Pennines, a royal commission in 1507
effected a division of existing dairy farms with little damage
to the tenants but an increase in total rents from £105 to £170.
As copyholders the tenants had nothing to fear from the king's
Master of Wards. In faraway Cornwall, on the seventeen duchy
manors, a previously very flexible system of auctioning
customary leases, 'assessionable' every seven years, had never
recovered from the later-fifteenth-century depression, and in
the early sixteenth century the tenants were enjoying fixed fines
as well as fixed rents and were well on the way to establishing a virtually hereditary tenure.

Generally speaking, the early Tudor nobility were no more
demanding of their tenants than the Crown. One of the best-
documented estates is that of the Percies, earls of Northumberland. Their net annual revenue by way of rents remained
remarkably steady from the 1470s until 1537 when the childless
and eccentric sixth earl, having already handed over large
portions of his estates to his adherents, turned what remained
over to the Crown. His tenants had little reason either to regret
or welcome the change of landlord. Many of those who held
their lands of the greater northern landlords did so by 'tenant-
right', which obliged them to perform 'border service', that
is, to turn out when needed with horse and armour, at their
own expense, against the Scots. In return they enjoyed security
of inheritance and fixed rents and fines, a tenure equal in

practical terms to freehold, and the men of the Borders could always rely on royal support if their landlords tried to impose higher entry-fines, or 'gressums' as they were called in the north country. Attempts by southern magnates to enlarge their rentals by way of higher entry-fines were sometimes more successful but on the whole the early Tudor nobility were more concerned to keep, and if possible extend, their estates, than to oppress their tenants.

Before the Dissolution there were many who thought that the greatest raisers of rents were the religious communities: after their passing the monks were adorned with haloes as particularly benevolent landlords. Their records, which survive in abundance, show that neither was true. For the most part they reacted to the situation in which they found themselves in much the same way as their lay neighbours, except that, together with the higher secular clergy, being perpetual and undying corporations and being on the whole served by a more efficient administration than most lay landlords, they kept better records, had better memories, therefore, and were rarely benevolent by default. A typical sequence is that followed by the abbot and convent of St Augustine's, Bristol. In 1489 they let their demesne farm at Roborough in Somerset to William Harris and John Squire, and the latter's wife Joan (probably Harris's daughter) for sixty years or until the death of whichever of the three lived longest, at a rent of 60s. a year. Nearly forty years later, in 1527, when the value of the property must have been quite a lot higher, it was let to John and Margaret Bakewell and their son John, for their lives and at the old rent. This is a fairly typical example of a monastic lease, not least in the fact that no entry-fine is recorded, though at least a modest one will almost certainly have been paid on both occasions. But such evidence as there is suggests that not until the early 1530s was this more than an extra year or two's rent. Then, quite suddenly, monastic leases were being 'sold', not only for much larger sums, but also for far longer terms (sixty to eighty years, but no lives) so that, at least in the short term, landlords and tenants were combining to their joint benefit and, as things turned out, at the expense of the Crown. In more normal times the monks kept their leases short and this often enabled them, when it suited them, to reoccupy their demesnes. Their rents in kind were a shrewd protection against inflation but they also usually provided for commutation on demand, for food prices could still go down as well as up. It was, of course, the mark of a good abbot that he ran his estates efficiently and, short of merciless treatment of his tenants, increased his revenue. The only justification for clerical ownership of land was an economic one. As a landowner the Church could not avoid being closely involved in local society but its land was not so important a prop to its social and political role as was the case with laymen. When Sir Thomas More, writing of depopulating enclosure, referred to 'certain abbots, holy men no doubt', he was expressing only gentle irony, not a sense of outrage. Incidentally, in this connection it is noticeable that in the later 1520s and indeed right up to the eve of the Dissolution, when the monasteries were completing the process of withdrawing from active farming of their demesnes, it was their sheep pastures which they held on to longest. A lease of some pasture by Osney Abbey, Oxford, in 1532, actually contained a proviso allowing the abbey to resume possession at its discretion.

Plaintiffs in court were in the habit of referring to the immense power of their oppressors, but on the whole tenants of the greater landowners of early Tudor England were probably no more at risk than were those of lesser landlords. That Henry Clifford, first earl of Cumberland was 'the worst beloved that ever I heard of and especially with his tenants' was said of him in the early 1530s by his great enemy, Lord Darcy, but the remark can surely be construed as indicating that Clifford was an exception. In fact, this particular nobleman was of a particularly grasping disposition, an encloser who really did invite riots by his tenants, at Giggleswick and elsewhere. Oppression of their tenants was not, however, the preoccupation of the early Tudor landed magnate, nor, indeed, of most knights and gentlemen. It is the exceptions, which proved the rule, that we hear

about. For the majority, fully paid rents and no vacant farms
was their aim. It was only in the mid-1540s that that shrewd
new landowner, Sir John Gostwick of Willington in Bedfordshire, perceiving the way the economic wind was blowing,
warned his son and heir not to be too free in allowing his tenants
to take his timber, nor to make leases for terms longer than
twenty years. But neither should he take more for entry-fines
than one year's rent nor 'heighten' his rents unless he discovered
any of his tenants subletting to their profit. Sir John was now
an old man of sixty years. He was nobody's fool, but he valued
his reputation as a good landlord.

3. People in Towns

Only a very small proportion of the people of early Tudor England, probably not more than one in twenty, lived in cities and truly urban towns. Was it not, perhaps, with a touch of envy that the Italian, Polydore Vergil, wrote that the English 'do not so greatly affect cities as the commodious nearness of dales and brooks'? Probably as many again, if not more, lived in country towns, many of them, however, hardly distinguishable from large villages except for the proportion of their inhabitants not entirely occupied in agriculture, and for their supporting weekly markets and annual fairs. Not even the distinction of being a 'borough' could confer on a village or country town a truly urban character, and borough courts presided over by the lord or his steward were likely to be largely concerned with straying geese and unscoured ditches. The urban community proper recognized no lord but the king, and made it a condition of those who shared its privileges that they should wear no other lord's livery.

The principal cities and towns were usually recognizable by the size of their population and by the wealth, both individually and collectively, of their inhabitants. The author of the *Italian Relation* was clearly very impressed by the city of London which in 1500, even without the addition of the suburbs of Westminster, Southwark and the newly industrialized villages of East London, contained about sixty thousand people. In this, as in so many respects, it was, in England, in a class by itself, and although there were at least a dozen continental cities with even larger populations, foreign visitors were always impressed by the visual splendours of England's capital city. By their standards there were few other towns in England worth mentioning. The Italian noted only Bristol and York, but had he travelled more extensively he would have recognized the importance of Norwich, with some twelve thousand inhabitants, and several others, notably Newcastle, Exeter, Salisbury, and Coventry, each with well over five thousand. By purely insular standards there were about fifty towns in England which were really different, as places in which to live, from other communities. They were unevenly distributed over the country, so that some counties such as Sussex had hardly a town to speak of, Lewes being still only a seignorial borough. The really urban community numbered its inhabitants in thousands, whereas mere country towns counted theirs in hundreds. But size of population was not the only, or indeed the principal, characteristic which set real towns apart. They differed also in their topography, their occupational pattern and in the sophistication of their community life. Moreover, many of the older English towns, especially those such as Lincoln which still had a function as centres of county and diocesan administration, retained very distinctly urban characteristics in spite of their failure to retain their old pre-eminence in terms of population and wealth.

One of the greatest differences between the larger towns and more rural settlements lay in the area the towns occupied. Thousands of people lived and occupied themselves within a compass of the equivalent of a small sheep run. Out of Exeter's total population of about eight thousand, well over three quarters lived and worked inside walls which enclosed only ninety-three acres. A large village or country town, even if superficially industrialized, physically occupied thousands of acres of arable and pastoral land and even if, in the case of a nucleated village, their farmsteads lay in fairly close proximity, country people did not spend practically all day within earshot of their neighbours. People in towns lived very close together, despite contriving to retain quite extensive gardens and enclosed plots of land upon which to keep chickens, pigs, and even cows. There were no purely residential areas, for most people in towns worked at home: even the larger merchants' houses contained offices and store-rooms, so that nearly everyone, merchant, retailer or craftsman, lived over the shop. In most cases the area within which the townspeople lived was bounded by whatever remained of an ancient wall, or some sort of boundary such as a river bank and a ditch, and entry was through two or more gates which were locked at night and passage through which was to some extent supervised, even in daylight. Such gates, with their massive housing, would often, as it were symbolically, contain the town's lock-up or prison. Long before 1500 people had lived outside the walls, especially along the approach roads, but their connection with the town was somewhat tenuous. Most of the extramural dwellers lived in shacks which, if built against the walls, were liable to be pulled down at the slightest threat of civil disturbance. Strenuous, though not very successful, efforts were made, however, to drive out to the suburbs people pursuing noxious occupations such as leather-dressing or those, like metal-working and potting, which presented a fire risk. But not all suburban dwellers were poor craftsmen and labourers, for there were those who settled there more permanently in order to take advantage of the towns' commercial facilities, although not technically 'free' to do so. Suburbs, therefore, were always regarded with suspicion by the town élite, and, unlike so many continental towns, those in England had no administrative jurisdiction beyond their own boundaries. Even within the walls there were usually 'liberties' controlled by rival authorities such as bishops, cathedral chapters and religious houses, areas whose residents, lay as well as clerical, were not subject to the town magistrates. At the same time, some towns contained within their boundaries, though usually outside their defences, common pastures and even open fields.

There were, of course, many residents in towns who owned land in the country, land they had inherited, land they had bought as an investment, or for retirement, and even land they occupied and whose produce, especially vegetables, they sold. Town butchers too would often own or rent nearby pastures for fattening, or even rearing, cattle. But most of those who lived in the larger towns followed occupations other than that of farming. It was not necessary to live in a town to engage in industry, but it is probably true to say that the great majority of full-time craftsmen were to be found in the towns. The main reason for this was that towns provided wider marketing possibilities, especially the opportunity to stockpile one's products rather than to produce only to meet a known and limited demand. There were, however, differences of function between saddlers, shoemakers, goldsmiths and pewterers, all of whom sold their products, and tailors who usually worked on materials supplied by their customers. Perhaps of greater significance was the fact that the towns attracted and supported a far greater variety of crafts than villages. The larger the town, the more likely it was to support craftsmen such as bakers, brewers, joiners, etc., supplying goods which in villages would usually be produced at home. Towns, unlike villages, supported many more retailers supplying, for example, ironmongery, some of it purchased from country craftsmen. In the larger towns, too, would be found men calling themselves drapers, mercers, grocers, etc., who were both wholesalers and retailers, stocking manufactured goods brought from distant parts of the country or imported from overseas. In the countryside such merchandise – and it will have been of an inferior quality – was only available from itinerant pedlars. At the very apex, of course, was the city of London, whose visitors in the early sixteenth century were greatly impressed by the variety and quality of manufactured goods available in the shops, especially those of Cheapside and the Strand, the highway between the city and Westminster. Here, too, were most of the town houses of the nobility, their frontages obscured by rows of shops and movable stalls. Similarly, in many of the larger provincial towns, it was in the main or 'High' streets that were to be found both the residences of the wealthier inhabitants and the shops, especially those selling the best-quality wares. Workshops producing more humdrum articles would be in the poorer, more industrialized, quarters of the town, often near the river bank where, of course, if the river was navigable, would be a complex of wharfs and warehouses.

Most urban craftsmen plied their skills either at the back of their premises or in workshops fronting the street in full view of their customers. Few would employ skilled labour outside their immediate family, but they might have one or two apprentices in their households. Even in London there were rarely more than four or five employees and apprentices in any one workshop, but all but the poorest craftsmen would employ resident servants. For the most part craftsmen supplied a purely local clientele, including such country people as lived within the catchment area of the town's weekly market (not more than seven or eight miles if the journey was to be done both ways in one day). Here and there the number of men engaged in a single craft suggests a wider market. For example, at Northampton in 1524, fifty shoemakers were assessed for tax compared with only thirteen glovers, and at Leicester at about the same time there were twenty-seven butchers compared with fifteen bakers. The butchers were no doubt supplying the London meat market and also meeting the extensive demand everywhere for hides. Norwich, also in the mid-1520s, had no less than 131 master worsted-weavers, to which can be added at least as many again who were their employees and apprentices. But it also contained fifty-one tailors, forty-four mercers (dealers in fine imported textiles), and twenty-seven grocers. Cloth-workers appear in varying numbers in every town and although they often formed the largest group they rarely employed, even in Norwich, more than a third of the work-force. In York the 'tapiters', who were specialist weavers of worsted bedcovers and wall-hangings, ranked third in number after the merchants and tailors, even before obtaining, in 1543, a rare statutory monopoly of the industry north of the Trent.

The richest men in most towns, especially those which were seaports or on rivers with easy access to 'havens', were the merchants, that is, men engaged in trade with countries overseas. In London the cloth-exporters and the mercers were almost certainly the wealthiest, but they were exceeded in number by the grocers (who imported and sold spice and medicines), the drapers, and even by the fishmongers, skinners, merchant-tailors and haberdashers. The last of these imported and sold all manner of ornamental trifles. However, these designations represented guild affiliations and in London membership of any of the guilds of traders qualified a man to engage in any of the city's commercial occupations, a custom which the more exclusive companies such as the Mercers tried hard to resist. There were in London in about 1501 some seven hundred merchants who were liverymen, that is, of senior rank, in their guilds and companies. With younger merchants and apprentices there would have been a total of nearly two thousand, at least ten times as great as the merchant class in any of the larger provincial ports, and far more wealthy. But there were rich men in the provinces too, successful grocers like Richard Marler of Coventry and alderman Robert Jannys of Norwich being assessed for tax at figures which equalled the total of some smaller towns. Some in the provinces who called themselves merchants were probably only wholesalers. Thomas Hele of Salisbury, merchant, had in stock in his house in 1542 a large range of grocery and haberdashery and also ran a tavern next door. The fact that he owed £500 to a London haberdasher suggests that he in his turn may have been extending credit to local retailers. Merchants proper, even those from the provincial towns, by the very nature of their business possessed far wider horizons and contacts than craftsmen. William Mucklow, the son of a yeoman farmer of Halesowen, but by 1511 a resident of Worcester, carried in that year nearly five hundred bales of woollen cloth to the spring and summer fairs of Bergen-op-Zoom and Antwerp. He spent about £360, about one fifth of the proceeds, in Flanders, bringing back linen, canvas, velvet, satin, damask, sugar (two tons), pepper, spices, treacle, ginger, pins, needles, bells, girdles, pouches, thread, brushes, swan feathers, spectacles, wine, knives, leather buckets, brown paper, and two small cannon. He was, needless to say, also a retailer at home. By comparison, the clothiers, who were the merchants' nearest counterparts in the scale of their operations, were very largely country-based, and were content to sell their cloth to

the London exporters at Blackwell Hall, as indeed did most
of William Mucklow's successors. On the other hand, many
town-based merchants also carried on a considerable internal
trade, some of their purchases being sold abroad; those of York,
for instance, regularly travelled to Derbyshire to buy lead, to
Lincolnshire for grain and up the coast beyond Durham to
obtain fish. Bristol merchants combined their far-flung overseas
trade with a trade in agricultural produce, especially up the
Severn valley.

But for all its opportunities the occupation of merchandising,
especially overseas, was a perilous one. Perhaps it always had
been, but it is significant that the early Tudor York merchants
no longer travelled to Prussia, as their predecessors had done
rather more than a century earlier, nor did they or their fellows
at Bristol any longer go to Iceland or to the Mediterranean.
Even Exeter, a late-developer in these matters, having enjoyed
an enormous expansion in her overseas trade around 1500 (an
expansion which must to some degree have benefited everyone
in the city including porters and carriers), suffered a period,
if not of actual decline, at least of commercial stagnation in
the later 1520s. For Exeter, and perhaps for other towns, the
great wealth of her merchants reflected in the tax assessments
of the years 1523 and 1524 pointed backwards rather than for-
wards. London and her merchants meanwhile continued to go
from strength to strength. Whereas in 1500 their share of the
country's total export of woollen cloth was about 66 per cent,
by 1540, by which time the total had nearly doubled, it was
about 84 per cent. The merchants of early Tudor London displayed an aggressiveness, an ability to exploit whatever trade
there was, which led them not so much to explore new markets
as largely to corner the country's very restricted overseas outlets.
Two of their victims were the great ports of Bristol and Southampton, especially the latter, which suffered from an invasion
by Londoners. Then, in the 1540s, with improvements to the
navigation of the Thames, both outports watched, apparently
helpless, as not only foreign but also native ships abandoned
their wharfs for those of the capital. It could well be argued

that the national commercial recovery which seems to have begun around 1475, and accelerated after 1485, in the long or medium run benefited only the people of London. If foreign trade had been the life-blood of most early Tudor provincial towns, then indeed the period would have been one of very real urban crisis.

It is sometimes given to the elderly to survive crises with greater success, and considerably greater dignity, than the young. This was certainly the case with one of England's oldest cities outside London, that of Winchester. It had seen its function as an important seat of government taken over by London as early as the twelfth century, and even its cloth industry had long moved into the country. In the early sixteenth century its population, less than fifteen hundred excluding those in the bishop's 'soke', was hardly that of a large country town, but it still had a great cathedral, a fortified bishop's palace, and three large abbeys, and it was still the centre of the king's government of Hampshire. Each of these, especially the bishop's court to which litigants came not only from Hampshire but also from the whole county of Surrey, brought many visitors, both regular and casual, to the city. Winchester had few rich merchants but it had a multitude of brewers and innkeepers. Even they, however, if we may believe their tax assessments, were not as well off individually as the local lawyers and the bishop's lay officials. A similar situation no doubt prevailed in many other episcopal towns such as Chichester, Rochester, Lincoln and Lichfield, none of which supported a large resident population but whose inhabitants profited from a constant stream of visitors. By contrast, there were few fortress towns in early Tudor England, only Berwick, Carlisle, Durham, Pontefract, and Dover having garrisons, and these were normally very small. But, as John Leland recognized as he perambulated the country in the early 1540s, one of the chief causes of urban decay was the movement of England's only really important industry, the manufacture of woollen cloth, into the villages and even the isolated farmsteads of the country-side. He often wrote as if it was a recent development. What he did not always appreciate was that folk-memory was long and that for many towns woollen cloth manufacture had departed long ago. For some, however, for example York, and also Coventry, it was within living memory.

One of the greatest difficulties is to discover whether the number of people living in the towns of early Tudor England had actually decreased to any substantial extent and was still decreasing. Thomas Starkey, an intelligent observer writing in about 1536 on his return from Italy, was convinced that there were fewer people in the towns than before, but he may have been taken in by the special pleading of the more vociferous urban authorities. What they were saying was far from new. For over two centuries towns, at least in their own estimation, had borne the brunt of royal taxation, having been assessed at a notional 'tenth' of the movable goods of their inhabitants as compared with the 'fifteenth' contributed by the rest of the country. Their appeals for relief had won some response from Westminster, and although the attempts of the early Tudor government to assess individual people for tax in theory placed the burden on those best able to pay, the tradition of corporate pleading died hard. A frequent plea was depopulation. Bristol claimed in 1518 that it had 'about eight hundred households ... desolate, vacant, and decayed', and by 1530 was putting the figure at nine hundred, but Tudor people were not on oath when estimating large numbers. Coventry had a rather better authenticated figure of 565 houses empty in 1523 but even with its two censuses, probably unique as much for their being taken as for their records having survived, it is not clear what proportion of the desertion had taken place between 1520 and 1523.

Historians have set about calculating the population of early Tudor towns with a confidence which belies the inadequacy of surviving records. The tax assessments of the mid-1520s are indeed remarkable and make it possible to count the number of heads of settled households possessed of sufficient income from rents or movable goods, or indeed income from wages, to attract the attention of the tax assessors. One of the drawbacks of such evidence, however, is that it provides only a more

or less static picture, the next assessments, those for 1544, covering only owners of land and goods, not wage-earners, and
indeed a comparison of the lists of taxpayers in any one urban
parish in the years 1524 and 1525 (where both survive) suggests
a mobility which often strains credulity. Comparable evidence
is hard to find. At Coventry in 1520, according to information supplied to the mayor, there was a total of 6,601 people
needing to be fed from the town's dwindling supply of grain,
but this may not have been the town's normal population. In
spite of the exodus due to declining trade and industry, in a
famine situation there may well have been more people in the
town than normally lived there. A further count in 1523 revealed
a total of 5,699 persons, a drop, assuming the 1520 figure to
be reasonably accurate, of nearly 14 per cent. It is unlikely that
any other town was losing people at this rate by migration,
though losses of this magnitude were possible when plague was
raging. Another problem is to know what proportion of any
town's population was too poor to be taxed. Cardinal Wolsey's
'military survey' of 1522 was intended to list all men aged
between sixteen and sixty, able and 'unable', indicating not only
what weapons and armour, if any, each possessed but also how
much each man was 'worth', whatever that meant. Clearly
Wolsey also had a new tax assessment in mind, and his lists,
which survive for only two of the larger towns, Coventry and
Exeter, do seem to include at least the more settled poor who
scraped a living by casual labour, but whose substance, for tax
purposes, was 'nil'. It has been calculated from these and other
taxation records, that in Coventry nearly half the population
normally escaped tax on account of poverty, but that in Exeter
the proportion was about one third, about the same as at
Leicester and other towns. But not all these were living below
the subsistence level, for, as the military surveys make clear,
those assessed at 'nil' included many resident servants and even
apprentices. There was always, too, in spite of strenuous efforts
to keep it out, a floating population of professional beggars.
In 1547 when, in accordance with Henry VIII's will, a groat
(4d.) apiece was made available to the poor of London, some

twenty-one thousand were said to have benefited, and although
the metropolis was always a honeypot for vagrants, on this
occasion, no doubt, the word had spread even wider than usual.
There clearly was in all early Tudor towns, and particularly
those of any size, a large pauper substratum composed not only
of aged and disabled people, but of the able underemployed.
Whether the proportion of such people was increasing in the
early years of the century is impossible to say. It is possible
that when Bristol spoke of hundreds of empty houses it was
bemoaning the lack of settled, occupied, heads of families and
ignoring its mobile, underemployed, poor who lived in the
overcrowded tenements into which so many town houses had
been divided.

There were no new towns in early-sixteenth-century England
except perhaps for some of the former villages which had
recently embraced cloth-manufacture on a considerable scale
and were beginning to develop the outward appearance of
towns. The older and much more fully urbanized communities
had a long history and usually possessed one or more charters
from the Crown or another, usually lay, landlord, giving their
inhabitants a corporate identity, including the right to hold
property (and thence derive a regular income), to sue and be
sued, to have a seal, a borough court presided over by a mayor
(that is, a magistrate of the town's own choosing) and some
sort of governing body. Some were so ancient that such liberties
had been presumed: others were still only half-way towards
full independence. Some were even separate counties, as Bristol
had become in 1373, and Exeter in 1537 brought the number
of county boroughs to thirteen. Charters are often thought
of as merely dry legal documents – with their verbosity and
technical Latin they are certainly not easy reading – but they
enshrined the community's sense of identity as a body of people
separate from an often amorphous rural hinterland. Only
the larger nucleated village, conterminous with an ecclesiastical
parish, and without a resident lord, can have been as conscious
of being a separate and self-reliant community. Without a
charter, urban community life, however superficially lively, was

incapable of full expression. Even absentee lordship, when applied to towns, only too often comprised the profits of markets and fairs and all manner of tolls on trade, together with the profits of justice and a certain amount of political patronage. Only incorporated boroughs could own property and no town could achieve much without a source of regular income.

It is true that the exercise of urban chartered privileges was enjoyed only by a small minority of the inhabitants, but the very authority and patronage possessed by the officers and governing body enveloped all who identified themselves by their presence within the urban precincts. The mayor held a court, usually on one day every week, which dealt largely with civil cases, debt, breach of contract, and with offences against local by-laws concerning nuisances, but it also exercised a certain amount of petty criminal jurisdiction over all residents and temporary visitors. Most of the larger towns forbade their inhabitants to sue each other elsewhere in any legal action pleadable in their own courts. Town corporations were trustees of ongoing charitable funds, to some of which all poor townsfolk had access, although, as the mayors and their officers were only too well aware, it was the greater availability of lay charity which drew into the towns such a large proportion of the country's disabled people, as well as able-bodied beggars. Both petty jurisdiction and charity were already, in the sixteenth century, far more accessible and institutionalized in the towns than in the countryside where the old 'hundred' courts had almost ceased to function. The county magistrates had not yet undertaken much civil administration, nor had they much in the way of funds. Towns, moreover, had long striven to establish for their settled inhabitants a degree of privilege within their area of jurisdiction. This related in particular to the right to trade, and most of the larger towns had achieved a situation in which only freemen, that is, those formally admitted to the privilege, might trade without paying the tolls imposed on all strangers. In some towns the body of freemen played at least a minor part in the election of mayors, though in practice the process was no more democratic than was the election of the towns' burgesses in Parliament. More important was the fact that admission to the freedom was the first step towards a man's participation in town government. The proportion of freemen to the total number of adult male inhabitants varied from town to town and it cannot be assumed that where it was larger entry was easier or cheaper. A lot depended on how strictly the town's officers enforced the rules, but a small proportion of freemen might mean that craftsmen not engaged in retailing were exempt. It was often the case that the rules against trading by strangers were more strictly enforced in times of economic recession. York was a far from flourishing city in the early sixteenth century and it may have been on this account that none but freemen were permitted to sell goods to non-freemen, that is, one party to every deal had to be a freeman. But the York authorities also insisted that even craftsmen who sold only their skills, such as barber–surgeons, must be freemen. Hence the proportion of freemen in York was high, nearly 50 per cent of adult males, compared, oddly enough, with only just over 10 per cent in another old and somewhat decayed city, Winchester. In Norwich it was about 30 per cent, in Exeter 25 per cent, and in Chester about 20 per cent. It normally cost money to gain admission, often as much as £1, though sons and apprentices of freemen often paid nothing and some governing bodies exercised a discretion to admit without fine.

From the ranks of the freemen were chosen, when vacancies occurred and by simple co-option, the members of the towns' governing bodies, the councils or chambers, or, as they some-times called themselves, in accordance with their royal charters, the 'Twenty-Four' (or some such number). Being, almost invariably, the most 'sufficient' men available, those selected were largely merchants, that is, trading rather than industrial capitalists (of whom, as already indicated, there were few in the towns), and very rarely practising craftsmen. Membership was for life but very soon after election to the council a man might find himself chosen to serve for a year as mayor, that is, chief magistrate and chairman of the council. It was quite common for men to be mayor more than once, but not in consecutive years. How much store men really set by membership of the council and by the office of mayor is difficult to say. For some, and perhaps particularly for their wives, it no doubt added greatly to their self-esteem and even to their credit with their fellow townsmen. Only after serving as mayor did a man become one of the real *seniores*, or 'ancienty', the group of city elders from whom were chosen the aldermen who were held responsible for the good order of their respective city or town wards. No village constable could strike such terror into the hearts of evil-doers as city aldermen. In fact, to be 'elected' to the council, and more particularly to the office of mayor, was to be launched upon a lifetime of often quite onerous, time-consuming and expensive duties. In times of emergency all town councillors were expected, according to their 'ability', to give or lend money to the common purse. Busy men, or those with little inclination, sometimes flinched at the prospect and were prepared to face very considerable reproach among their peers, as well as heavy fines, for refusal of office, though not usually of the mayoralty. Indeed there is clear evidence, for example in York, that some of the heavier fines were paid in order to avoid the lower offices and achieve accelerated promotion on the civic ladder. Something of the same sort was happening in Ipswich too. Young Henry Tooley, merchant, later to be the town's chief benefactor, paid a fine of £6 in 1521 to escape serving as one of the chamberlains. But two years later he was elected to the 'Twenty-Four' and on three occasions thereafter held office as one of the two bailiffs, the highest of Ipswich's civic dignities. On the other hand, there were also many *ex officio* perquisites, including patronage in respect of town offices and charities, and a great deal of eating and drinking at public expense. No important decision was ever made without a 'solemn drinking', and mayors in particular were usually given generous allowances for entertaining distinguished visitors likely to be able to further the towns' interests. Councillors also had opportunities of borrowing town funds for short terms, and when serving as one of the bailiffs, or honorary treasurers, had useful cash flows at their temporary disposal. They also had opportunities for leasing city property on favourable terms.

But perhaps most important, the relatively small body of councillors was a fraternity, a very select society which in many cases, until and even after the Reformation, assumed a religious guise. Guildhalls, whose maintenance and embellishment constituted a major charge on civic funds, contained not only council chambers and court-rooms but also chapels, and the civic religious fraternities which supported them both moulded and were moulded by the way in which most town councils conducted their business. Feathers often flew, but the mayor's authority usually prevailed. Persistent offenders, and especially those guilty of using 'opprobrious' words of their fellows, were not only fined and even imprisoned by the mayor but were also required to shake hands or to share a loving cup. The robes or 'gowns', usually red and furred for aldermen and present and past mayors, blue or black for the rest of the council, testified to both hierarchy and fellowship. Even the councillors' 'mistresses' (wives) were expected to observe the status of their respective husbands. In this way the governing bodies of towns acted both as the repositories of urban privileges and the exemplars of public order. There were scandals, of course, but on the whole this communal proprietorship worked, and never better than in the early sixteenth century when, apparently, so many English towns were facing decay and desolation. The city corporation of London, which was certainly not decaying in the early sixteenth century, exhibited all the characteristics of the provincial urban oligarchies writ large. There were even those among her citizens who paid very substantial fines for exemption from office. For example, in 1541 John Richmond, armourer, utterly refused to be one of the city's two sheriffs. He himself swore that he was of insufficient substance, not having movable goods to the value of one thousand marks, but he could not find friends to confirm this. He was put in the Counter (the city's prison) in Bread Street and a guard placed on his house to prevent his goods being spirited away.

The mayor wined and dined him and shrewdly offered to buy him out for two thousand marks and many came forward with offers of loans. In the end he paid a fine of three hundred marks and was discharged.

For those who could never hope to strut upon the larger civic stage there was the opportunity – and often the compulsion – to be a member of, and to attain office in, one of the many occupational guilds which existed in the larger towns, including London. Their existence depended on there being at any given time sufficient persons engaged in one or a group of allied crafts or trades to make the association viable. This could mean any number from about a dozen to three score in the provincial towns to several hundred in London. No doubt the presence of enthusiastic individuals, prepared to whip up the rest, also counted for a lot, as did the possession of a permanent hall for meetings. Such halls, which by no means all craft associations had, were often, at least until the Reformation, used on certain feast days as chapels. Indeed, most guilds had a religious affinity with a saint. Such an alias was no doubt useful in giving to a guild of craftsmen an air of respectability in time of trouble, for the relationship between the craft guilds in provincial towns and the powers that be in the shape of the town and city councils was at best uneasy and at worst one of mutual hostility. Even before guilds had become numerous in the later fourteenth century the Crown had whenever possible delegated its powers of industrial control to the municipalities. This meant that guild ordinances, that is, by-laws, had to be submitted for civic approval, and provision was often made that all fines levied on their members by guild officers be shared with the civic authorities. Craft guilds were always suspected of using their authority to scrutinize workmanship, granted to them by the civic authorities in the interests of the consumer, to keep up prices, and of limiting entry in order to restrict production to the same end. Argument usually centred on the entry-fines charged by guilds for admission, especially to craftsmen who had not served an apprenticeship, either at all or with one of the guild's own freemen. In 1514 the Coventry 'Court Leet', as its council was called, ordered all guilds in the city to submit their records and 'if their fines be too much, to moderate them'. In 1519 it decreed that, except for the apprentices of mercers and drapers, who were to pay fines on being indentured, none should be required to pay entry-fines until they set up in business as masters on their own account. Even 'strangers', that is, those who had not served an apprenticeship in the city, were not to pay more than ten shillings. In 1523 the Coventry Court Leet forbade all by-laws limiting the number of apprentices which any master might take. This was another key issue as far as the guilds were concerned, because apprentices were thought to be a form of cheap labour whose employment was contrary to the interests of skilled workmen. In 1519 the city council at York too repealed certain guild ordinances in order to attract more young immigrants. In general the guilds seem to have held their ground concerning the number of apprentices, but in 1504 and 1531 even Parliament at Westminster saw fit to legislate over entry-fines, laying down in the latter year a maximum of 2s. 6d. It is difficult to determine how far guilds succeeded in their avowed objective of keeping up standards of craftsmanship. Their records suggest that they were far more energetic in resisting the introduction of new methods and new tools, and by and large they probably deserved their reputation of acting as obstacles to enterprise and initiative. A good deal of their battling with the civic authorities throughout the sixteenth century stemmed from attempts by the latter, largely representing mercantile interests, to exclude craftsmen from all wholesale, and especially foreign, trade. However, like the towns themselves in the early Middle Ages, the craft guilds had succeeded, well before 1500, in becoming recognized as an essential part of the established order. Some would say their heyday was already over, but if so they were a long time dying.

The most positive contribution of the craft guilds to late medieval and early Tudor society was the support they gave to the institution of apprenticeship. This was a means of ensuring a proper, if somewhat prolonged, period of industrial and/or commercial training. Boys, and sometimes girls (or perhaps one should say young men and women, for they were usually aged about fourteen and had received at least some elementary education), were placed in the households of established masters. The latter undertook, sometimes on receipt of a premium, to accommodate them for seven years (eight in the case of merchants, especially if they were going overseas for part of the time), to teach them all they knew of their craft or occupation, and to treat them as one of their own family. In 1526 one of the parish churches of York reserved four of what must have been its relatively new pews for householders and their apprentices, 'to the intent that the said masters might [over]see the conversation [behaviour] of the said apprentices'. It must be emphasized that most apprentices came from respected, settled, and often quite well-to-do families. Most guilds insisted that their fathers must be, if not actually free-holders, of free status. This was entirely consistent with the obligation placed upon the master that his apprentice should live as one of his family, and that placed on the apprentice that he should submit himself to discipline and serve only his master's interests, in particular never divulging his master's trade secrets. Apprenticeship was the industrial and commercial equivalent to service in a gentleman's or noble's household. It had no parallel in farming households where resident 'servants of husbandry', even if they stayed for more than a year, very rarely entered into formal contracts. At the age of about twenty-four apprentices normally became full members of their guild and then it was up to them for whom they worked, and for how long, as journeymen, that is, wage-earners. To set up on their own, however, as independent 'householders', they needed some initial capital, if only to pay the entry-fine for a lease of some premises. But, unlike their country cousins, they did not, if they were eldest sons, need to wait for their fathers' death or retirement before becoming independent and free to marry. The designation 'junior' occurred frequently in towns as an 'addition' or identification, but in country communities a young man was usually referred to as 'son of' until his father died. Entry to guilds by patrimony, that is, in succession to a father, was fairly rare, indicating that few boys were apprenticed to, or followed the same occupation as, their fathers. There is abundant evidence that people in towns not only followed secondary occupations, as did so many countrymen, but also changed their occupations, sometimes several times. Thus even the monopolies over their trades which guilds claimed, and their rules about the employment of 'illegal' (untrained) workmen, do not seem to have precluded occupational mobility. The guilds could better afford to turn a blind eye when the local economy was flourishing, and it may be for this reason that the custom of London in this respect was so liberal.

Like their betters on the councils, the senior members of the guilds indulged in a great deal of communal eating and drinking. At Coventry in 1524 thirty-three members of the Carpenters' Guild and their guests sat down to a harvest dinner at which they consumed seven pigs, two and a half lambs, six joints of beef, thirteen chickens, sixteen geese and thirty-five gallons of ale. This cost them 9d. each, and no doubt helped them forget the current high price of bread. Being to a large extent on sufferance as far as the civic authorities were concerned, guilds generally kept a low profile. On the whole they fulfilled whatever public obligations were placed upon them, playing their allotted part in civic pageantry and subscribing, with as much reluctance as they dared, to civic projects, including, in times of dearth, the purchase of public stores of grain. They certainly relieved the town leaders by caring for their own impoverished members, and they turned out in strength for each other's funerals, always hopeful that money would have been left for a commemorative dinner.

In London, of course, the guilds, especially those whose members were engaged in merchandising rather than in industrial occupations, were very wealthy and powerful organizations. There were some hundred and fifty guilds in all, but the ones which really dominated city affairs were the twelve 'livery' companies, organizations so large that to count for anything in them a man had to be a liveryman, a member

of the select upper section. These formed a much more inte-
grated and structured part of city government than most of
the provincial guilds, and membership of one of the leading
guilds was essential to anyone aspiring to membership of the
city's governing bodies, the Courts of Common Council and
of Aldermen. This was a world of top people whom even
Henry VIII treated with respect, and yet any of his Lord Mayors
could have been born of far more humble parents than was the
real Dick Whittington. Without the stability which London's
government provided, the succession of young men who sought
their fortunes in the metropolis would probably have found
their assimilation into its society far more painful. One of the
main constituents of urban stability both in London and the
provincial towns was the perennial civic calendar with its
regular fixtures such as the choosing and installation – with
a good deal of public oath-swearing – of the mayor. Then there
were the processions, especially on Midsummer Eve when in
many towns all guild members shuffled somewhat reluctantly
in due order of seniority behind the mayor and his fellow
councillors, all wearing their appropriate gowns. There were,
too, the two- or three-day annual fairs when all normal local
trading was suspended. These and many more secular high days
marked out the year, at least for the more settled part of the
urban population, in the same way as did seed-time and harvest,
and lambing and sheep-shearing, for countrymen. In addition,
of course, there was in pre-Reformation England a sequence
of holy days, public religious festivals common to both town
and countryside.

But as well as stability there was also much mobility, and
if the stability was based largely on institutions such as
mayoralties, councils and craft guilds, the mobility was that
of people. Just as important as the gradations of wealth to be
found in most early Tudor towns, gradations which are often
likened to a pyramid, the poor forming the wide base and the
rich the tapering tip, is the fact that probably barely half of
the people in towns were both born and buried there, and
that a higher proportion of townspeople than country people

died prematurely. Plague may well have been an important factor in limiting the growth of town populations, but without immigration, whether for relief or betterment, many Tudor towns would have withered and died. There were indeed those who wished to promote a truly urban culture such as existed in so many European towns. This meant attracting the nobility and gentry, if possible persuading them to build town mansions large enough to need and accommodate large numbers of servants. In 1530 York promoted horse-racing as an attraction for gentlemen, following a tradition already well established at Chester and Carlisle. But the towns of early Tudor England were very far from developing into the provincial social centres, that is, resorts of the county élite, which they became much later. Their own successful merchants who wished to enjoy the company of the gentry and to find daughters-in-law or sons-in-law had to purchase land in the country and to live on it.

The real cause for concern – 'crisis' is surely too strong a term – in the larger early Tudor provincial towns, and to a lesser extent even in London, was the lack of regular industrial employment for so many of their less-privileged inhabitants. The independent master-craftsmen were relatively few in number, partly due to the guild monopolies, and they had few full-time employees. The appearance of journeymen's guilds, especially in London, was a sign of the fact that so many skilled men saw themselves as permanent employees, unable to accumulate the necessary basic capital to set up on their own. Most urban capital was in trade, and even in the provincial towns many of the wealthy resident merchants operated in London. John Greenway, who lavished such wealth on the parish church in his native Tiverton in Devon, was never, as far as we know, an industrial magnate. He exported cloth through Exeter but he was also a member of the London company of Merchant Adventurers. The real industrial capital-ists were men like John Lane of nearby Cullompton, a clothier, and a great benefactor of his parish church, but the people he employed were not primarily those in the little town but country people spread over dozens of east Devon country parishes. Many of the older early Tudor towns, having lost their cloth-making, were not so much pre-industrial as post-industrial. And if England's only large-scale industry left the towns completely, what would be left? Nothing was likely to change the essentially small-scale character of most urban industrial occupations. Early Tudor governments, deluged in the 1530s with complaints from some ninety different towns about the decay of once fine town houses upon whose derelict plots, Members of Parliament were assured, rubbish accumulated and pits, cellars and vaults lay open and dangerous to passers-by, could only seek legal remedies. A series of Acts between 1534 and 1543 called upon the owners to rebuild, or at least enclose the plots with mortared-stone walls, failing which the town authorities were authorized to take possession. To hard-bitten businessmen, struggling to keep at least their trade alive, there can have seemed little future in such civic enterprise. There is no evidence that the legislation was ever acted upon.

4. *Belonging and Not Belonging*

People in Tudor England felt a natural affinity with, if not always an affection for, the place where they had been born and for those among whom they had spent their childhood. This rarely evinced itself, among the thousands who moved their habitation, in a desire to return to what, especially later in the sixteenth century, men were to call their 'country'. The true vagrants evaded most efforts to send them back to their places of birth or last residence and those migrants who prospered and settled were more likely to remember their birth-places in their wills than to return there to live. One of the ironies of the situation is that those in authority who viewed all people on the move with such fear and suspicion as potential disturbers of the peace were only too likely themselves to have left home when young, to have made their way from country to town, or from the provinces to London, from a fairly humble to a more affluent household. But in their case the first move will usually have been pre-arranged, to attend a school, to take up an apprenticeship, or to enter the service of a great man.

Equally suspect to those in high places as potential threats to the peace and tranquillity of the realm were the various ways in which people banded themselves together in associations which transcended the natural community of village and parish. There had been a time when even towns, with their larger concentrations of people and their pursuit of trading and other 'liberties', had seemed to pose a threat to authority based on ownership of land, but towns had long since established themselves as oases of order in an often troubled country, the one-time aggressive merchant guilds having become transformed into the communities of highly respectable freemen. The city of London, which around 1400 had been a place of turbulence, even in its governors, had become by 1500 a valued and willing partner in the Crown's essential job of keeping order. Guilds and companies of craftsmen and traders had likewise overcome a great deal of the early suspicions they had aroused and in their turn had become part of the established order, but under municipal, or occasionally royal, licence. It was the widespread move into the countryside of the country's only large-scale industry, the manufacture of woollen cloth, which now posed greater problems in that it appeared to place very considerable power in the hands of capitalist clothiers who, by laying off those they employed could cause unrest and even the possibility of whole 'countries' being 'up in arms'. There was, too, an old problem, but one which presented itself in a somewhat new guise in Tudor England, of how far to permit the great landed magnates to keep retainers or, as they were now often called, 'fee'd men'. There were those, indeed, who regarded with even more disfavour the considerable numbers of household servants kept by lords and gentlemen. Disparate as all these elements may appear, they all represent physical and personal attachments which were both potentially inimical to an ordered society but also, if adequately controlled, useful and even essential. Even the migrant or 'masterless' workmen – although contemporary authority did not see it this way – provided a pool of labour essential to the development of new industries, and the migrant husbandman was working out his own solution to the problem of the regional inequalities in the demand for farms. This, of course, is not to deny that there were people on the move in early Tudor England who were the victims of unsocial enclosure and engrossing, nor that the continued existence of indiscriminate alms-giving encouraged idle vagabondage.

That there were considerable numbers of people moving from place to place in the early decades of the sixteenth century was no figment of official imagination. Anyone attempting to explore in detail the population of any single parish, using (these being the only records generally available) the tax assessments of the early 1520s, is quickly conscious of a considerable turnover of names, even within the space of one year, not all of which can have been due to faulty or incomplete registration, although there is always the possibility that some heads of households slid into or out of the assessors' nets. Completely rootless families presumably escaped altogether. In the Buckinghamshire parish of East Claydon, forty-seven persons were assessed for the subsidy in 1524, nineteen of these on wages, the rest on their goods. A year later ten of these were missing, of whom Richard Terser and Richard Mede had died and were replaced by their widows, and of the remaining eight, five were wage-earners. The second list contains nine new names, four those of wage-earners. In the village of Midhurst in Sussex nearly half of those listed in 1524 were wage-earners, nearly one third of whom were missing a year later, being replaced by rather fewer of the same category, among whom, however, three were described as servants, one being a Frenchman. Almost everywhere, those assessed on their goods (the more established farmers and craftsmen) were clearly the more stable element. If the turnover of the poorer people reached this level every year, then it would appear that as much as 10 per cent of the population moved on each year. How far people moved is difficult to establish from the tax assessments. William Boxolle, a wage-earner who had left Midhurst by 1525, may be the same who appears in the list for that year for Lodsworth, some three miles away. None of his fellow migrants appear to have settled elsewhere in the county but they may have done so without being assessed for tax. Shelter, of a sort, was fairly easily provided in hastily erected shacks, and servants, that is, resident labourers, were easily accommodated in attics and outhouses. Servants in particular, and many who were very largely dependent on wages, moved not necessarily because work was not available, but almost as a matter of course, and in the hope of bettering themselves.

It is probably true of the early sixteenth century as of the later decades when more evidence is available, that the great majority of migrants were young, single people. What happened to the families of those who lost their farms and livelihood as a result of enclosure and engrossing can only be surmised. What is fairly clear is that the direction in which people moved was compounded of three elements. The first of these was the drift away from the areas of open-field, sheep–corn husbandry where, even if there had been little or no enclosure or engrossing of farms, land was not readily available for younger sons and, as these areas tended to be under tighter manorial, that is, landlord, control, there was less scope for squatting on the waste. The drift from these areas tended to be towards 'forest' areas where, as already indicated, even a very slender arable foothold gave access to considerable opportunities for grazing stock. But by 1500 some of the forest areas were themselves becoming quite densely populated and, although partible inheritance worked here to keep even younger sons near home, the people of these parts were of a more independent and less settled disposition than the open-field farmers who lived under a more regulated and even oppressive regime. Emigration out of forest areas, especially towards and into the towns, was considerable, much of it no doubt planned and purposeful, for betterment not for subsistence. This second element, the drift into the towns, followed a fairly clear pattern, from north and west towards the south and east, and from all the Home Counties towards London; and indeed it is the attraction of London which forms the third element.

Before considering these elements in detail it is necessary to look briefly at the preconditions for travel in early Tudor England, not only the actual road network but those activities which kept it open. Travel by land was not lightly undertaken. The first printed road-table of 1541 listed only nine long-distance routes, the so-called highways linking London with the chief provincial cities and thence with the remoter parts of the kingdom. No cross-country roads were mentioned, these being mere tracks linking village with village, often obliterated by flooding (as indeed were many highways) or by encroaching farmers. Only the main streets of the larger towns were cobbled, all other roads being kept firm only by traffic, with few fixed points except bridges over rivers. A statute of 1530 empowered Justices of the Peace to inquire into the state of

bridges – their upkeep being regarded as an act of charity –
and to see that nearby parishes contributed to the maintenance
of 300 feet of highway at either end. A good living could be
made conducting strangers through deep country, but they were
probably in greater danger of being waylaid by thieves at the
approaches to London. Innkeeping, except in the larger towns,
was not a common occupation in the early sixteenth century
and strangers could never be sure of a welcome. At Elmley
Castle, Worcestershire, in 1537 a village by-law ordained 'that
no tenant ... shall harbour any stranger or vagabond under
pain of 3s. 8d.'. Hence, of course, the almost exaggerated
defence of the reputed hospitality offered in the remoter parts
of the country by monasteries.

Those who travelled safest, though not without considerable
discomfort, were those engaged on the Crown's business.
Christopher Morris, Master of the King's Ordnance, sent post-
haste to Berwick on 4 January 1539, was reporting from
Fotheringhay Castle in Northamptonshire four days later, and
by 12 January had covered a further hundred miles or so to
Pontefract in Yorkshire. By 28 January he was busy at Berwick.
More regular were the journeys made by the assize judges who,
unless deterred by the existence of plague, moved twice a year
on their circuits of the county towns. Well provided with horses
and accompanied by a considerable entourage of clerical and
domestic staff, they were also themselves the cause of the
assembling of large numbers of people, local magistrates, jury-
men, litigants and lawyers. Judges were supposed not to sit
in their native counties, but they often did, and for this and
other reasons were not trusted to be impartial. It is ironic that
the jury system, the underlying principle of which was that
bodies of local men would either know or could find out the
facts relating to an alleged crime, did so little to settle men
in their own country. Quite humble people sought legal
remedies in London. Cases being heard in the Courts of
King's Bench or Common Pleas at Westminster frequently
ground to a halt, however, because of the difficulty of getting
a full jury to travel, and the Court of Chancery, which did

not require even litigants to be present in person, often had to send men into the counties with interrogatories, that is, lists of questions, to be administered on oath to local witnesses to elicit the facts. Even the establishment, or re-establishment, in the 1530s of the regional councils, in the Marches of Wales at Ludlow, of the North at York, and for a short time in 1539–40, in the West at Exeter and Tavistock, did not do much to reduce the flow of provincial litigants to Westminster. Of course a good deal of petty crime could be dealt with by the JPs with the help of parish constables, and they were also expected, at the drop of a hat, to travel with the more hefty of their household servants, tenants and neighbours, to deal with any menacing situation. They were still, in the early sixteenth century, very few in number, hardly a dozen on the active list even in the larger counties. For purely agrarian disputes between tenant farmers there were, of course, manorial courts, and mention has already been made of the mayors' courts in the larger towns. But the fact remains that quite humble people in early Tudor England were prepared to go far afield to defend their interests, if not themselves actually travelling to London, at least knowing how to initiate legal proceedings there.

Correspondence surviving in the state papers, especially during the period of Thomas Cromwell's ascendancy in the later 1530s, suggests that while some local magistrates and other gentlemen were working energetically on the King's behalf to ensure good order, especially the nailing of dangerous rumours, there was still much hidden apathy. Cardinal Wolsey made great efforts to bring JPs to Westminster to take their oath, and in 1526 he succeeded in assembling over one hundred of them in Star Chamber where he harangued them about the necessity of inquiring into criminal offences in their counties. He even made the great mistake of replacing some of the local men on the commission of the peace for the West Riding of Yorkshire by strangers from his own household. Thomas Cromwell did not repeat this mistake, but he not only encouraged JPs to communicate with him – those who wrote

clearly expected some reward for their pains, if only the promise
that they would be 'remembered' – he also expected men to
attend upon him in London, even at their great inconvenience.
Many an abbot found himself summoned to London, but the
higher clergy, both secular and religious, were always great
travellers, bishops maintaining houses in or near Westminster
and the heads of the larger monasteries having convenient
staging posts *en route* to the capital.

There were, of course, many early Tudor bishops who saw
very little of their dioceses: Wolsey himself did not set foot
in his diocese of York until shortly before his death. But even
in the absence of the bishop there was a commissary (or
deputy) who travelled a great deal, and archdeacons or their
deputies must have been almost continually on the road if, as
required, they regularly visited each of their deaneries for
the purpose of holding their courts. The employment by
the monasteries of a small army of lay officials to collect their
rents and to hold their manor courts might seem to have
enabled the monks themselves to remain within their
precincts, but when Thomas Cromwell in 1535 instructed them
to abide by their Rules, he called forth a stream of protest. The
abbot of St Augustine's in Bristol actually claimed that he encouraged his canons to take healthy exercise, in pairs of course,
in the hills! Most of the governors of the larger houses had
one or more rural retreats to which they themselves regularly
resorted, accompanied by a substantial number of servants. Lay
landowners did not, for purposes of administration, travel
around their manors, but employed bailiffs and, if they were
wealthy enough, stewards and receivers (treasurers), to see to
the holding of courts and collection of rents. But they did move
frequently between as many residences as they possessed, both
in the country and in towns, including London. They also added
to the traffic by maintaining, that is, acting as patrons of, troupes
of minstrels and players who spent considerable parts of the year
on tour, partly supporting themselves by visiting towns, country
houses and even monasteries. Thomas first duke of Norfolk
and his duchess had separate troupes of minstrels who frequently

visited Thetford Priory in Norfolk, as did Henry VIII's own players, and during the years 1525–35 the monks occasionally invited the nuns from a neighbouring house to share the entertainment. Patronage, however nominal, was essential for all itinerant entertainers to protect them from persecution as vagabonds. Even town 'waits', whose proper function was to act as night-watchmen, resplendent in civic livery or at least silver chains, playing a range of noisy instruments besides their traditional horns and shawms or hautboys, often went on tour, though any economy achieved by a saving of their wages was probably more than offset by the 'rewards' expected from civic purses by visiting groups. In spite, then, of the hazards, people in early Tudor England did travel, not only regularly within their own particular local circuit but in quite considerable numbers to and from London.

Roads, in early Tudor England, carried people rather than goods, and beasts for slaughter rather than for carriage. The cost of transporting most goods, especially grain, was in normal years disproportionate to their value. Moreover, both producers of and dealers in foodstuffs were under considerable pressure, especially when there was a real or threatened dearth, to market them locally. The diversity of agriculture within relatively small areas was in fact such that the need for long-distance trade in normal times was not very great. To this extent the very widespread antagonism towards dealers in foodstuffs had a rational basis. After about 1520 food was very rarely plentiful, and however much farmers may have rejoiced, nothing was more likely to provoke disorder among townsmen and other non-producers than the sight of foodstuffs being laden for transport to distant markets. Most farmers, however, sold their surplus crops and dairy produce, if not their stock, at local markets, carrying them the few miles in panniers slung on yokes across their shoulders and only occasionally in carts or on packhorses. There were, in fact, probably fewer regular carriers by land in business in the early sixteenth century than there had been two centuries earlier. Most of the wholesale trade centred on the seaports like Southampton or towns on navigable rivers such as Bristol and York, but water-borne trade further up-river was not extensive, except on the Severn and the Trent. Even London had little up-river trade, at any rate not above Henley, but it did have a very extensive coastal trade, especially with the east-coast ports as far as Newcastle from where came considerable quantities of coal. London's main concern was with the cross-Channel ports, especially Antwerp. Bristol probably still had the largest network, sending and receiving goods to and from south Wales, Ireland, the ports of the south-west, and south-west France and Spain. Bristol even had a sea-borne trade with Westmorland, and merchants from Chester sailed regularly to Ireland. Ships plying the south coast of England kept very close to land for fear of pirates, but Cornishmen sailed regularly to Southampton with tin for London, and also fish. Conditions were probably less hazardous on the east coast and in Lent in the 1530s fishermen from Walberswick and Dunwich in Suffolk were renting shops in York from which to sell their herrings. The only commodity worth transporting really long distances by land was woollen cloth. Most of it went to London, the drapers of Shrewsbury, for instance, going to Oswestry to buy Welsh cloth and employing regular carriers to take it, four 'pieces' (bales) of cloth per packhorse. The journey to London, about 140 miles, took a week, at about twenty miles a day, and lay either through Coventry and St Albans or via Stratford and then Aylesbury or High Wycombe. There was one carrier, Stephen Bateman, who carried cloth from Kendal to Southampton every year between 1492 and 1546, taking back imported luxuries such as raisins and figs, and raw materials for cloth manufacture such as woad, madder, alum and also canvas for wrappers. The pedlars and chapmen who hawked trinkets, ribbons and all kinds of cheap and easily portable goods around the countryside have left little record, but in about 1535 Clement Armstrong, the London pamphleteer, complained somewhat stuffily that there were too many of them bedazzling country people with their imported 'artificial fantasies ... in horsepacks and footpacks, in baskets and in budgets [bags]', especially as they tended to appear on holy days and Sundays, in church porches and even outside abbey gates. But then city men always disliked pedlars, preferring the country people to come to town for their shopping. The York city authorities actually forbade their own traders from joining them by going out on Sundays into the countryside. But then they even prohibited shopkeepers from engaging in door-to-door trading, unless specifically invited to bring goods for inspection by 'gentlemen'.

Tudor traders were under considerable pressure to 'stay put', or rather, following a tradition going right back to Anglo-Saxon times, to trade in authorized locations, partly in order that all transactions should be subject to public scrutiny, and partly so that those offering facilities for trade might profit from their enterprise by charging tolls. Markets, usually held weekly, were very numerous but were probably now rather fewer than in the fourteenth century. Fairs, like markets, were usually of great antiquity. They occurred annually, usually being spread over several days, and they attracted dealers and the more substantial consumers from far and wide. All local traders, including shopkeepers, were required to close down for the duration, but many of them took up space on the fairground for temporary stalls. At Nottingham in 1516 it was agreed between the town authorities and Lenton Priory, which owned the fair, that freemen should have priority in the assignment of stalls and pay less rent than strangers. At the great Stourbridge Fair outside Cambridge where the stalls were set up in the fields after harvest, certain sites were privately owned by Cambridge tradesmen. The fair tolls were owned jointly by the town and the university. In 1534 after one of many disputes 'all drank together at the Pompe Tavern and the university paid for all'. The corporation of London actually tried to forbid its own citizens from sending goods to provincial fairs but in 1487 Parliament was persuaded to intervene on the small traders' behalf: the resulting statute cited in particular fairs held at Salisbury, Bristol, Oxford, Ely and Coventry, besides those at Nottingham and Cambridge, and claimed that lords, both spiritual and temporal, abbots, priors, knights, esquires, gentle-

men and commoners, all had need of fairs where they could
buy, at reasonable prices, such articles as chalices, church ornaments, books, vestments, 'victual for time of Lent' (probably
salt fish), linen, woollen cloth, brass, pewter, bedding, iron
implements, flax, and wax, for all of which, so MPs apparently
agreed, they would otherwise need to go to London, 'to their
importable costs and charges'. Clearly the representatives of
the provincial towns at Westminster had seized a golden opportunity to spike London's big guns. At Bristol, however, it was
the city's leading traders, having been a party to the establishment of a Candlemas Fair in the suburb of Redcliffe in 1529,
who appealed successfully to the Crown in 1544 to have it
suppressed, claiming that they could supply all the year round
the kind of luxury goods brought to the fair by Irishmen and
strangers. The city's consumers might not have agreed. In
general, however, English fairs were no longer what they
had been, certainly no longer the regular annual resort of the
international trading fraternity. This was partly due to the
general European late-medieval commercial recession, and
partly no doubt to the short-sighted defensive tactics of the
towns.

If sufficient information was available, it would almost
certainly emerge that migration, including that of the poor,
largely followed trade. People did not move very far, probably
in one generation no further than into provincial nodal urban
centres, in spite of a far from friendly welcome. Possibly, in
the early sixteenth century, the number even of poor migrants
was not insupportable. Shrewsbury no doubt expected to admit
each year a quota of Welsh people, and Winchester its thin
stream from the south-west. Both would have been very
surprised to find themselves burdened with people from the
east of England. For those who came with prospects, in particular to take up apprenticeships, there is rather more precise
information. Bristol kept a register of apprentices, recording
1,426 in all between 1532 and 1542, including one hundred from
Ireland and 174 from Wales. Over four hundred were Bristol-
born and there were large numbers from the neighbouring

counties of Gloucestershire (185) and Somerset (147), but boys also came from Shropshire (75), Worcestershire (72) and even Lancashire (30). For some reason Bristol had no attractions for Cornish boys and only eight each came from Devon and Dorset, but eleven came, no doubt by sea, from Westmorland. Oxford, of course, drew young students from all parts of the country, but between 1516 and 1536 it also attracted over eighty apprentices, a dozen of them to serve with master-tailors and the rest mostly with the victualling trades, Oxford being by now largely non-industrial. Between 1537 and 1557 the total rose to 342 and the proportion of strangers increased, some coming from as far away as Cumberland. Nearly as many came from Staffordshire as from Berkshire but none came from the south-west. No doubt Exeter was absorbing most local boys seeking apprenticeships, and even Exeter was a long way from Cornwall. For York we have no actual evidence concerning the origin of apprentices but there are some details concerning those admitted to the city's freedom. Out of a sample of some three hundred and fifty admitted during the middle decades of the sixteenth century, nearly one third had grown up in York itself, slightly more had come from within a radius of twenty miles, and about one fifth each between twenty and fifty miles, and over fifty miles respectively. Quite a large number came from Cumberland, which we know to have been heavily over-populated and to have had close trading connections with York. Most of the Oxford apprentices were sons of husbandmen and this was probably true of Bristol and York, but few will have come from really poor households. There are some indications – but the point must not be exaggerated – that those who went to London to be apprentices were poorer than those going to provincial towns, but if this was so, it almost certainly was not true of the more important London companies, especially those whose members were merchants. London in 1430, together with Norwich in 1495, had obtained exemption from a statute of 1405 prohibiting the apprenticing of children of freeholders worth less than 20s. a year, but by 1500 all London masters will have been in a position to pick and choose their apprentices, the merchants in particular taking considerable interest in their literacy and numeracy. Although the number of boys apprenticed in London was far greater than those in any provincial town, rather fewer in proportion were of local birth, so much so that most of the mercantile and civic aristocracy of the city were first-generation. Moreover, a large number came long distances, probably over a half from north of the Trent or west of the Severn. How the initial contacts were made can only be guessed, but it is only too likely that links between parents and masters were established through trading connections. The young men may have been put in the charge of a carrier but, rich or poor, they did not ever, as far as we know, travel in search of a master.

To become an apprentice, and then a freeman, and most of all to attain guild and/or civic office, was to allow oneself to be assimilated into a society, or hierarchy of concentric societies, very different from that of the countryside. At every promotion in the urban ladder there were oaths to be sworn, the essence of which was absolute loyalty to the urban community, symbolized by the office of the mayor. In 1518 at High Wycombe – hardly more than a village with less than one thousand inhabitants – two burgesses who spoke 'unfittingly' of the mayor were threatened that a second offence would result in the loss of their freedom, whereby they would be 'reputed and taken as strangers'. But for all this there was no urban caste, and virtually no urban dynasties, at least among the urban élite, for those who rose highest were usually those most likely to plan for their sons careers in the law, in politics or in administration. In fact partible inheritance, that is, division of wealth among sons, which was customary in most towns, resulted in entire fortunes being split up once in every generation. Rarely, however, did successful city men themselves retire very far into the country. The early Tudor countryside was not bursting with 'new' landowners of any provenance, and probably contained more sons of lawyers than of merchants. In fact, whatever happened to their sons, few wealthy first-generation merchants abandoned their town houses and if they did so they very rarely returned to their place of birth, buying land elsewhere and contenting themselves with a dutiful bequest. But there were also more fundamental causes of discontinuity. It was by no means as common in England as it was in continental towns for even craftsmen's sons to follow the same occupations as their fathers and for this reason, although there was much intermarrying of sons and daughters, widows and widowers, of fellow guild members, guild attachments were purely personal and not familial. Entry to the civic oligarchy was not hereditary, nor was election to guild office. There was, however, a greater element of continuity in those families whose members neither rose to civic prominence nor fell on hard times but continued, sometimes for several generations, to make a merely competent living. But the most visible signs of civic stability were the guildhalls, not only those of the cities and towns but also those of the traders' and craft guilds, many of the latter doubling until the Reformation as chapels. That the guilds so often referred to both their governing bodies and to the meetings of those bodies as 'halls' typifies the identification of an ever-changing body of men with the more lasting stonework and timbers. The concentration of certain occupations in certain parishes or quarters of the towns had practical rather than fraternal significance. There might be good reasons why butchers should have their 'Rows', but 'Goldsmith Streets' were likely to contain the workshops of many luxury crafts besides the fashioning of plate. Practical considerations permitting, men moved in prosperity to live alongside their economic equals. Hence some urban parishes tended to be rich and others very poor.

An offence hardly less heinous in a freeman of any of the larger towns than disloyalty to the civic hierarchy was the wearing of a lord's livery. In principle these amounted to the same thing. A by-law of the city of Gloucester declared that no inhabitant was to be 'of open retaining, livery, or otherwise by oaths or promise to any gentleman dwelling without the said town, upon pain to be discommoned and put out of the said town'. This, of course, had nothing to do with normal trading relationships, nor indeed did it preclude ordinary townspeople doffing their caps to gentlemen, or their wives curtseying. Indeed, on one occasion a Worcester man was told by the city magistrates to mind his tongue when speaking of a neighbouring landowner, Sir John Bourne, 'considering he was a gentleman and of good calling in his country'. It was aimed at preventing the sort of permanent personal commitment to a powerful outsider which was implied in the wearing of a badge or some other livery such as a distinctive item of clothing, accompanied as would normally be the case by a regular annual fee or other pecuniary advantage such as the receipt of a rent charge from some part of the lord's landed estate. The Crown constantly warned the towns against such commitments, but they needed little reminder that their predecessors had fought long battles against feudal lordship. In fact, of course, this was not feudalism proper but that 'bastard feudalism' which had permeated English society in the fourteenth and fifteenth centuries. If this seems very remote from life in Tudor towns it is as well to note that in 1547 a York tailor, a freeman of the city, was made to confess that he was a servant and retainer of Sir John Ellerker, a local landowner, from whom he received meat, drink and a fee of 40s. a year, that in 1555 four weavers of Worcester were prosecuted for allowing themselves to be retained by Sir Anthony Kingston, and that as late as in 1577–8 in York there were, in one of the city wards alone, nine presentments 'for wearing of lords' and gentlemen's livery'. The gentry's main interest in building up an 'affinity' in the towns was, of course, the securing of the nomination of burgesses for Parliament.

In early Tudor society at large retaining, with its twin implications of livery and maintenance, had wider ramifications. Reference has already been made to the widespread practice by landowners of paying fees for part-time administrative services, this being extended to the paying of retaining fees to professional men – almost exclusively lawyers – for service when required. Only really wealthy landowners could afford to employ full-time administrators, and many of them did so on a scale surpassed only by the king himself, and indeed the dukes and earls, and even some mere barons, had 'courts' which to all appearances resembled, on a smaller scale, the royal Court at Westminster. When Henry Algernon Percy, fifth earl of Northumberland, drew up a list of 'those daily abiding' in his household in Yorkshire in 1512 it included four head officers, that is, chamberlain, steward, treasurer and controller, each with his own personal servants, and a very long list of gentlemen ushers, gentlemen waiters, yeoman ushers, and the heads of the various departments in the kitchen. With grooms, gardeners, etc., the whole establishment (including separate smaller ones for the earl's brothers) totalled 166, 'which is ordained by my lord and his Council and shall not be exceeded'. Each of the higher officials had a 'child' and there were six children in the chapel. One of the six chaplains was 'Master of Grammar', and one of the nine gentlemen of the chapel, all of whom were choristers or musicians, was 'Master of the Children'. To place a small boy in such a household was to give him one of the best possible starts in life, and probably also to implant in him lifelong loyalty to his patron. But aristocratic resources were not elastic and the object of Northumberland's list was to set a limit to the numbers who could be fed, whether or not they were also paid a salary or wage. These were his regular household, but from time to time, and especially at the great annual feasts, he would entertain a greatly enlarged circle of estate officials, legal counsellors, substantial tenants, and relations. Hospitality on a really grand scale was traditionally expected of the nobility, and provided it was offered only occasionally was really quite a cheap way of winning friends. On the feast of Epiphany in 1508 the duke of Buckingham entertained at Thornbury Castle in Gloucestershire no less than 519 persons to dinner and four hundred to supper, at a total cost of £13, a sum hardly to be noticed out of a total gross income of some £6,000. If his guests were drawn from each of the twenty-four counties in which he owned land, then indeed it must have seemed as if half England was assembled under his roof.

It had never been unlawful – nor did the 1504 Act against retaining alter the situation – for anyone to be retained in any domestic or administrative capacity, to be paid a fee, part of which might take the form of a beneficial tenancy of land, to be clad in his lord's colours, or even to wear his badge. It was not even illegal to enlarge one's complement of officials by creating additional posts, as did the sixth Percy earl of Northumberland when he appointed six stewards for his Yorkshire lands in place of his father's two, or to make posts virtually hereditary by regularly making joint appointments to fathers and sons. In such ways a landowner could, in proportion to the extent and value of his lands, and also their geographical spread, build up a vast network of individuals and their families who felt themselves to be personally linked with, if not actually dependent on, him. In return for their loyalty, which might be no more than application and efficiency in running his estates and giving priority to his interests, he would feel compelled to treat them magnanimously, if only by remembering them in his will, next after the Church. Many noblemen, as they faced death, were more generous towards their staff than towards their relations. They would also expect him to be their 'good lord', that is, to support them in any suits they were pressing, where a word from him might, for example, secure another office, and also in any legal proceedings in which they were involved. Here we are moving from the permissible to the impermissible, for 'maintenance', the perversion of justice, was, of course, itself a criminal offence. It was not, and never had been, easy to do this too blatantly, but in early Tudor England justice was still too frequently neither done nor seen to be done. A large part of the content of every deposition submitted to the Lord Chancellor was aimed at persuading him to hear the case, but the recurrent theme that the enemy was a man of great power or 'greatly befriended' was at least thought to be credible. Worst of all, of course, were the cases which were decided locally by a show of armed force. Sir William Gascoigne, JP, was a notorious disturber of Yorkshire's peace, having been brought before Star Chamber

eight times between 1499 and 1530. He had been removed
from the local bench by Wolsey. In 1530 forty of his men
descended on John Saintpole's estate at Carcroft, which
Gascoigne claimed was held of his manor of Burghwallis, and
seized cattle belonging to Saintpole's tenants. When Saintpole
brought the matter before quarter sessions at Wakefield,
Gascoigne turned up with one hundred men and carried the
day. But of course there was a lot that was wrong with English
justice that had nothing to do with the survival of private
armies.

Perversion of the king's justice was bad enough, but what
no government could possibly countenance was any contract
of service which allowed the possibility of that service being
used against the ruling dynasty. Any contract, 'fee'd' or not,
which did not specify the household, administrative, or professional duties involved, could only point in one direction,
military service. In fact it had long been illegal, except by royal
licence – and the Act of 1504 only reiterated this – to retain
a private army, whether in the form of a resident garrison or,
even more politically undesirable, a body of knights, gentlemen
and even substantial farmers who undertook to be available
when called. Presumably this is what Sir Thomas Darcy was
thought to have done when in 1496 he was indicted in the
Court of King's Bench for the illegal (unlicensed) distribution
of silver badges carrying his insignia of the buck's head to
nineteen persons in the West Riding of Yorkshire. By 1500
the written indenture of service was no longer fashionable –
and certainly too dangerous unless covered by a royal licence
– but there was no doubt a great deal of secret oath-taking.

However, two things about early Tudor private armies are
clear. The first is that neither Henry VII nor Henry VIII, nor
indeed the latter's children, either eradicated illegal retaining
completely or even instituted proceedings against all known
offenders. The only peer actually presented by Henry VII for
retaining was Lord Burgavenny, and Henry VIII confined his
attentions to the duke of Buckingham. Both were also suspected
of planning treachery, but Burgavenny actually survived to

retain, under royal licence, nearly one thousand men. Buckingham probably deserved his execution, for a great many of
those he accommodated at Thornbury Castle were Welsh
soldiers far in excess of his household needs and for which he
had no royal warrant, his barracks were as extensive as his
household quarters, and he openly boasted of his descent from
Edward III. His rebuilding of Thornbury was probably intended to demonstrate his power rather than to defend it, and
except that most of his fellow early Tudor peers were more
circumspect, Buckingham's splendid pile was not as outmoded
as is sometimes suggested. Never quite finished, it was intended
to be comfortable and followed, if it did not actually set, the
trend towards providing more privacy for the duke and his
immediate family when they wished to withdraw from the
hubbub and the public gaze. There may have been jealousy as
well as fear in the King's mind. Many of his victims were lesser
men. The plea rolls of the Court of King's Bench show a steady
trickle of prosecutions for retaining against mere barons and
substantial gentlemen, but in each case there were probably
other counts. Sometimes other charges were given precedence.
Thomas Lord Dacre (of the North) was dealt with in Star
Chamber by Wolsey in 1524 on charges of maladministration
of justice as the king's Warden (since 1511) of the Scottish
Marches (or Borders). In fact from his base at Naworth Castle
in Cumberland he had built up such a military following that
it was said that the country north of the Tyne 'thought there
was no other king'. He had been allowed to retain sufficient
men to deal with Scottish incursions, but he had foolishly gone
too far. For the second fact is that until well into the second
half of the sixteenth century the Crown continued to license
those of its subjects whom it thought it could trust to retain
and adorn with their livery fixed quotas of what the letters
patent for Sir William Cecil in 1553 simply called 'persons',
but what those for Henry earl of Arundel later in the same
year (after Mary Tudor's accession) declared might be gentlemen, yeomen or others. Both royal grants stipulated very firmly
that those retained should be employed exclusively in 'our'

service. The young King's death shortly afterwards must have left Cecil in a position of some anxiety. Both patents, following standard form, avoided the general prohibition of retaining by declaring that those retained were to be regarded 'as though they were daily attendant' on the patentees in their households, and 'as though they had meat, drink, livery, wages, and lodging' in their houses. In this way Tudor sovereigns neatly suspended their own laws. They would not otherwise have known, in an emergency, where to turn for an army. They had, in a sense, to harness the warhorses in society to their own chariots. It can no more be said of the sixteenth century than of the fifteenth that bastard feudalism, properly controlled by the Crown, was not a stabilizing force. All that was necessary was to ensure that those licensed to retain others themselves really 'belonged' to the Crown and that they could in their turn vouch for their retainers.

The sixteenth century had a simple answer to the second of these requirements, and it was not entirely a new idea. Who better to be enrolled than those of their tenants who in a special sense 'belonged' to those whom the Crown best trusted? They even used an archaic word to describe those who formed an informal army reserve, the 'manrede', and it was always in a context which implied that such a force was at the disposal of the landlord. Gentlemen retainers formed the nucleus only of Tudor private armies, the rest being made up of household servants and tenants, lesser freeholders, leaseholders and the more substantial copyholders, as many as were able to bear arms. A king who could write, as Henry VIII did to Sir Henry Willoughby in 1511, ordering him to 'put in a readiness as many able men as may be had, well harnessed, within your lands, authorities, realms and offices', was not in principle against private armies. A law was actually slipped through Parliament late in 1549 which threatened leaseholders and copyholders who refused their landlords' call to arms with loss of their tenancies. But this was a panic measure and no Tudor parliament would have agreed to a universal extension of northern 'tenant-right'. It was only a few months later, in April

1550, that licences were issued to members of the Council and other carefully selected persons to retain a total of no less than 2,340 persons. A large landowner who retained an array of gentlemen, each with his own 'manrede', was at the centre of a network of connections spreading over many counties. The Northern Rising of 1569 was to show how essential it was for this medieval legacy to be on a tight rein, but for two thirds of the century it was, by and large, a useful royal instrument.

There were other, more purely personal, networks of 'affinity', the links comprising annual fees or pensions granted with some formality and not always by a greater to a lesser personage. On the whole, however, there was an air of condescension, for example in the payment by the fifth earl of Northumberland of £10 a year to Mr Heneage, gentleman usher to Cardinal Wolsey, and of £5 to Master Page, Wolsey's chamberlain. It must always have been a toss-up whether such an outlay would be worth while, but most annuities were paid to, rather than by, men of power. Many urban corporations, having already retained the services of eminent lawyers as their Recorders, and even created offices for other influential people, would also charge civic purses with pure pensions for those whose interest in their affairs they thought worth arousing. The arch-pensioner of the early sixteenth century was Thomas Cromwell. If his fall in 1540 created little stir at Court, its effects in the provinces must have been electrifying, though by then, of course, the many monastic pensions he enjoyed were being paid to him by Crown officers. It was akin to the fall of a great noble, but in both cases, while it left many men cut off and masterless, it did not involve their own ruin, for there were always alternative livelihoods, and alternative masters. One thinks, for example, of the collapse of the affinity of John, first Howard duke of Norfolk, after the battle of Bosworth, and the way in which some of his lands contributed to the building up of a similar affinity by John de Vere, earl of Oxford. Pensions were, of course, very different from the one-off 'rewards' or bribes which seem to have been an essential lubricant of all administrative action. Pensions, like retaining, invariably implied a two-way commitment, a mutual pledge of loyalty and support which, though one of the parties was frequently disappointed, served to enmesh most of the wealthier and important people in the country in a complicated web of relationships of which the Crown was little more than an observer. It is not without significance that pensions had nothing to do with feudalism, nor with landholding. Nor, on the other hand, did the jungle of relationships just described point towards the ordered, structured, society dreamed of by humanist writers educated in the classics, a society in which everyone knew his place and was content. Nor did it have the simple centrifugal pattern of contemporary France. Those in England who either gave or received pensions were neither unscrupulous nor disloyal, but they did believe in self-help. Perhaps that is what the author of the *Italian Relation* meant when he commented that in England anything could be had for money.

5. Rank and Status

However equal they might be in the sight of God, Tudor people knew that they were not so regarded by their fellow men. Knights and burgesses gathered at Westminster in 1510 would not have been particularly surprised or affronted to be called upon to agree to yet another statute defining the quality of dress permitted to each rank of society from members of the royal family down to labourers and servants. But we must not confuse this apparent obsession with the outward trappings of rank, or indeed attempts to regulate diet in the same way, with a belief in the immutability of each individual's place in the social order. The sumptuary laws of late-medieval and Tudor England were concerned with the prevention not of social mobility but of social emulation. Having attained a certain eminence, whatever their birth or former status, people were free to dress and to eat like their peers.

The legislators of 1510 had no difficulty in dividing the higher nobility into dukes, earls and barons, who were permitted, respectively, to adorn themselves or their horses in woven cloth of gold, sable (the brown fur of the arctic fox), and cloth embroidered with gold and silver. Only Knights of the Garter and their betters might wear crimson or blue velvet, ordinary knights being permitted velvets of other hues in their gowns, riding coats, and doublets. When the authors of the statute proceeded to deal with those below the degree of knight they found it necessary to introduce income bands. Gentlemen with lands or fees of £100 a year might wear velvet in their doublets but only satin or damask in their gowns and coats. 'Persons' worth £20 a year might wear satin and damask in their doublets, but only silk or camlet in their gowns or coats.

All were on oath as to their income. None but gentlemen and upwards were permitted to wear imported furs. None but knights might use more than four broad yards of cloth for a long gown or three for a riding gown, or wear 'guarded or pinched' shirts of linen. Finally, after many exceptions, largely relating to officials in church and state and to members of the royal household, came clauses relating to servants of husbandry and to rural craftsmen who, together with husbandmen possessed of goods worth under £10, were limited to the wearing of cloth costing less than 2s. a yard, and for their hose not above 10d. Gowns and other apparel indicative of rank were, of course, on that account all the more valuable as heirlooms.

The Act of 1510 followed medieval precedent by offering as justification the prevention of impoverishment and of temptation to robbery, but in an Act in 1533 there was added the need, in the interests of public order, to distinguish 'estates, pre-eminence, dignities and degrees'. Acts of Parliament were clumsy instruments for defining social grades. Moreover those in power seized the opportunity of killing two birds with one stone, there being in all such Acts an element of protectionism in that all the restricted fabrics were imported. As was customary, all women were very specifically exempted, but as they were bracketed with 'heralds of arms, minstrels, players in interludes' and 'wearers of the king's livery', it would seem that at this period their dress was regarded as of little serious social consequence. There were elaborate tariffs laying down a hierarchy of fines, except for servants and labourers whose penalty on conviction was to be set for three days in the stocks. Frequent proclamations insisting that the law be obeyed, and an almost total lack of recorded prosecutions, testify to the difficulty of implementing such regulations, even with the incentives offered to informers in the shape of possession of the offending garments. However, they did reflect contemporary principles: Lord Clifford reproved his son for clothing himself and his horse in cloth of gold, 'more like a duke than a poor baron's son as he is'.

Cardinal Wolsey attempted to moderate excessive diet, laying down by proclamation in 1517 how many separate dishes might be served at one meal, from a cardinal, who might have nine, to anyone, layman or cleric, with an annual income of at least £40 a year or goods to the value of £500 who might serve three, not counting 'potages', that is, soups. There were exemptions in respect of 'brawn and other entrails', and at wedding feasts anyone could serve three dishes above his normal limit. Anyone entertaining a guest of superior degree was *permitted*, but not obliged, to serve whatever was appropriate. This was clearly not a book of etiquette. The only sanction was the risk of a summons 'to be corrected and punished at the King's pleasure, to the example of others that enterprise any such follies and sensual appetites'.

The nobility was defined in early Tudor England more clearly than any other element in society. Two centuries earlier the term had very loosely comprehended all gentlemen and even in the sixteenth century there were those old-fashioned enough to apply it to all of gentle birth. But some time before 1500 the lords, that is, barons and all above that rank, had come to be distinguished by the king's habit of summoning most of them personally to his parliaments. Peers, as we may call the lords, were assessed for taxation by special commissioners, an arrangement not entirely to their advantage owing to the scattered location of their estates, commoners being assessed only in the county of their residence. Lords could not be arrested and imprisoned pending trial for alleged petty crimes, including debt, and they had the right whatever their offence to be tried by their equals. They enjoyed many other privileges; for example, an Act of 1540 allowed them six alien servants compared with other men who could employ only two. Edward VI's first parliament allowed peers to plead benefit of clergy in respect of criminal offences even if they could not read, and spared them, if convicted, from the dreaded penalty of branding. Most important, perhaps, a peer convicted of treason was spared the horrors of burning or hanging and, with luck, fell swiftly by the executioner's axe.

But the English nobility, for all its privileges, was not a caste like that in most parts of the Continent. Things had been moving that way around 1400 when, by resorting to various legal devices such as the 'use', the greater landlords had found ways of dividing their estates between sons at death. Technically this was still possible in 1500, but with no opposition from the Crown, to whom large numbers of privileged but impoverished subjects were of little use, the old principle of primogeniture had become re-established, at least for inherited lands. Provision of small patrimonies for younger sons and of dowries for daughters had to be made out of marriage portions, the inheritances of mothers, or from purchases, leaving ancestral estates intact. Younger sons of lords enjoyed a certain social status but rarely an adequate living without finding an heiress or some other means of augmenting their income. Their numbers, however, were not great enough at any one time for their fate to be of much significance. The nobility had few children, partly, it has been suggested, through their habit of marrying heiresses, who were more likely than other wives to come of infertile stock. The two centuries since 1300 which had seen such efforts by the higher nobility to preserve and enlarge their landed empires had also been a period for them of very great political involvement, offering the prospect of gaining all or nothing, of rapid enhancement of fortune or the penalty of being caught on the wrong side. Attainder by parliamentary statute could be devastating, not only to the actual victim but to his line, for not only were all his lands forfeit, but he suffered corruption of blood whereby not only was his son disinherited, but lands which might otherwise have passed to his descendants, through him, from a remote ancestor, were also forfeit. But attainders could be reversed and Henry VII in particular held out this prospect to many of his victims as a reward for good behaviour, even restoring titles and lands to their heirs. Death, from whatever cause, leaving only heiresses was a far more serious hazard because they, or their husbands, were preferred to brothers and nephews, and as primogeniture did not apply to women, there was the additional risk of partition. This was less serious in depleting the number of noble families if the estate was really large, as was that of Ann Mowbray, who might have been Queen, but whose vast estates went, after her death in 1481, to set up the houses of Howard and Berkeley. Lower down the landed hierarchy a divided estate could simply augment very marginally two or more already powerful families. All landowners, not only the nobility, did their best to ensure a male succession, even to the extent of contriving to pass some land to a bastard son.

More by natural causes than by war the actual number of nobles had declined since 1400 from over one hundred to about sixty, the total number remaining remarkably constant for the rest of the century. Until after 1547, most of the higher nobility, old or new, were soldiers and courtiers rather than administrators: Thomas Cromwell, earl of Essex, was the great but very short-lived exception. Henry VIII usually rewarded his ministers with baronies. He liked to have his mightier subjects close to him, however, and it was the absence from Court of Edward Stafford, duke of Buckingham, coupled with his conspicuous expenditure, not only at Thornbury Castle in Gloucestershire but at his other castles at Tonbridge and Penshurst in Kent, which outraged the King. The Crown, of course, expected the nobles to rally their affinities in its service but, to the puzzlement of foreign observers accustomed to a territorial aristocracy, gave them no regular judicial or administrative responsibilities, and often little or no land, in the counties with which they were titularly associated.

Younger sons of the nobility might without fear of ridicule call themselves gentlemen, but even for them knighthood had to be conferred, either by the king or, rarely before the wars of the mid-1540s, and thereafter only very occasionally, by a military commander on the field of battle. The London chronicler, Henry Wriothesley, tells how in February 1547, at a ceremony at the Tower of London, Protector Somerset, apparently in pursuance of the late King's wish, knighted the nine-year-old King Edward, whereupon he in turn knighted the Lord Mayor, Henry Hobulthorne, this being the customary honour conferred on London's chief citizen. But although knighthood had lost most of its military significance, its currency was not yet devalued. It was normally conferred on the heads of about a dozen of the leading gentry families in each shire, there being usually about 350 in all. The system of 'distraint' involved the drawing up of lists of those regarded as eligible for knighthood on account of their substance and the fining of all but those selected for dubbing, a relic presumably of an age when to be a knight was to incur financial liabilities, almost like civic office.

For every early Tudor knight there were at least ten other landowners calling themselves gentlemen or, if they were entitled to armorial bearings, esquires. It is one of the peculiarities of the history of rank and status in England that whereas knighthood was not a hereditary right (until the creation of knights baronet by James I), its close connection, arms, were handed on from father to son, although even here the right to bear them had to be re-established by each generation. By 1500 they had lost most of their original significance as marks of identification on the battlefield, and were now very widely used on tombs, plate, seals and domestic stonework as symbols of family pride and, often fictitiously, of ancient lineage. Their military links remained in that their adoption and continued use was supervised by the king's heralds who also supervised royal tournaments, funerals, and all state spectacles. From 1530, at intervals of about twenty years (and probably rather less regularly before this), they perambulated the whole country, visiting gentlemen in their homes (where they expected lavish hospitality) or summoning them to some convenient place, seeking out any who bore arms unlawfully and, a practice peculiar to England, recording the genealogy of those who successfully established their right. As with the sumptuary laws, the object was not to obstruct social mobility but to ensure that no one pretended a status to which he was not entitled. The criteria were sufficient substance and respectable ancestry. Henry VIII's letters patent to Clarenceux, King of Arms, on

19 April 1530, authorized him to grant arms to any who 'by the service done to us or to other be increased or augmented to possessions and riches able to maintain the same', but prohibited grants to persons 'issued of [descended from] vile [unfree] blood, rebels to our person [or] heretics contrary to the faith'. To bear arms, then, was to be recognized as a man of 'good honest reputation'. In fact by 1530 it was the heralds' custom to draw the line at freehold land and/or fees worth under £10 a year, or at goods worth under £300. It was rare for men without freehold land to seek official recognition of their gentility in this way, but one of the few exceptions was John Spencer, the Midlands grazier, who, with his brother Thomas, apparently obtained a grant of arms in 1504, by which time John had large flocks on leasehold land, though he did not make his first freehold purchase until two years later. Their father, however, was a substantial Warwickshire farmer, and indeed their uncle, John's namesake, had called himself 'Master Spencer', which was the form of address normally used by gentlemen. Although a grant implied recognition of ancient lineage, its real value to the recipient was that it ensured that his descendants would be recognized as gentlemen. Thus the sixteenth century saw the ancient language and science of the age of chivalry used to oil the wheels of social mobility.

The word 'gentleman' lacked the legal connotation of 'esquire' and the status was conferred only through recognition by friends and neighbours. It was said that gentlemen could be recognized by the number of idle servants they employed, idle in the sense that they were not essential to their masters' livelihood but only to their status, being employed only on household duties. The ownership of land was not an essential prerequisite, especially for lawyers or men in the service of the Crown or the higher nobility, but the only way of ensuring that one's descendants could maintain their gentility was to acquire land, including, if possible, one or more manors. Marriage with an heiress was by far the best way to found an estate but it was only a desperate heiress who risked disparagement by marrying a landless husband. For those without even a small patrimony widows were often fairer game. But it is easy to exaggerate the number of really 'new' gentlemen. If there had been more noble houses, and if noble families had been larger, the ranks of the gentry would have been much enlarged by younger sons of the nobility. In fact, the great majority of new gentry families were founded by the gentry's own younger sons. Many of these became professional lawyers, merchants, and successful industrial entrepreneurs and were thus able to sustain their gentility. It was not regarded as shameful for a gentleman's younger son to enter trade, though he would usually aim at wholesale rather than retail trade, and at trade in preference to manufacturing industry. A rare example of the last was William Stumpe, the well-known clothier of Malmesbury in Wiltshire, but born of established Gloucestershire gentry stock. Stumpe, however, was also a businessman and a servant of the Crown. For the early Tudor gentleman with a modest landed estate the rearing of stock, with an eye to the market in meat, wool and hides, was a quicker route to wealth than large-scale arable farming. There were, of course, many sons of substantial husbandmen and of rural or urban craftsmen whose talents enabled them to break through, but the barrier between early Tudor gentlemen and their social inferiors was very real, and the competition from those of at least gentle birth very fierce.

One family which did cross the line, though even in its case there were probably memories of a far from undistinguished ancestry, was that of the Ishams. Euseby Isham of Northamptonshire would hardly have called himself a gentleman as long as he remained a modest leaseholder and farmer. He was actually an eldest son but only when his father died at an advanced age did he inherit a freeholding, and then not a manor. Of his unusually large family of twenty children, five sons and five daughters survived childhood. But he and his wife Ann, according to the family chronicle, 'did so cut their coats according to their cloth' that all the sons went to school, the eldest becoming a lawyer, steward to the earl of Bedford and finally a Member of Parliament, the second a priest and later prebendary, and the others being apprenticed to London mercers. All three of these last prospered, especially John. After going up to London, aged sixteen, in 1542, he married in due course the widow of a fellow mercer and eventually returned to his native county as lord of the manor of Lamport. Such examples can be multiplied, but they do not represent a jump from rags to riches. John Isham, incidentally, was content with his one manor and some property in and near London. But although unusual in his talented family, Euseby Isham was himself a representative of a vast number of modest freeholders and their heirs who made up for their relative poverty by their lineage. Families such as this were particularly numerous in a county of comparatively late settlement such as Devon. Often they were so old that their surname was the same as the name of their estate, though the latter was no more than a large farm. John Leigh of Leigh in the parish of Churchstow in south Devon died in 1513, his son in 1526, and in 1563 when a James Leigh died an inquisition *post mortem* found that 6s. 8d. a year was payable to Sir William Petre, as owner of the former Buckfast Abbey manor of Churchstow, for a property worth £6 per annum. James's heir, another John, was then a minor, but was succeeded by his son James. But what is more interesting is that the abbey had had a free tenant called Thomas Leigh holding 'the Leigh' in the late thirteenth century. The house still survives, its fine interior woodwork and impressive gate-house suggesting that this was no ordinary farm. To its owner, the dissolution of the abbey hardly mattered. His quit-rent could not be increased but neither could he afford to compound. Sometimes, indeed, all links of such a freeholding with a manor had disappeared, but carefully preserved was a tiny charter, perhaps of about 1200, which was all the title the family possessed. Between such landowners and those who called themselves gentlemen there was hardly any social barrier at all. Some, indeed, established their entitlement to arms. But it was very rare for their younger sons to aspire to more than the hand of a local heiress. There was no money for more than a modest schooling and then, perhaps, an apprenticeship.

For the landed élite education was for life, whatever that was expected to be, not for social betterment. The children, girls as well as boys, of the nobility, knights and gentlemen, would be taught to read and write while quite young, although those who could afford to do so would in adult life employ clerks. If full-time private tutors were not available there were parish and chantry priests. All young gentlemen (and women) were expected to be able to read, if not to compose, Latin prose and verse. Some might be sent as fee-payers to a boarding-school, and a minority, usually accompanied by their own tutors, attended one of the two universities of Oxford and Cambridge, but rarely with a view to serious, prolonged study. Large numbers of them went on to one of the London Inns of Court where, especially if they were heirs to an estate, they learned just enough law to help them in defending their inheritance, and a great deal of the essential social graces. However, for most of them the serious business of being educated had begun at about the age of twelve when they were sent to another household, preferably one superior to their own, to serve as pages – the 'children' of the Northumberland Household Book – where they performed quite menial tasks, such as waiting at table. Foreign observers found this peculiarly English custom quite barbaric, confirming their opinion that English people were incapable of parental affection. But as members of their host's family, along with other 'sojourners' such as his wards, they learned deportment, etiquette, riding, hunting, hawking, shooting and, of course, the essential military skills. A few young gentlemen joined clerical households, including those of monasteries. The large household of Bishop Fox of Winchester in the 1520s included Thomas Sandys, esquire, eldest son of Baron Sandys of The Vyne, and Sir Henry Seymour, brother of Edward, both of them being paid ten marks a year in wages besides their board and lodging. A fortunate few joined the royal household. Here above all they were educated for public life, with the possibility of a permanent post at Court. There were indeed some in early Tudor England who urged that the natural 'virtue' of young gentlemen should be nurtured by giving them a more academic education. Sir Thomas Elyot thought that they would learn more about war from Caesar than in the unreal atmosphere of the joust. Thomas Starkey, a religious conservative but also a realist, urged Henry VIII to use the wealth of the monasteries to found secular schools where promising young gentlemen could be educated to serve the state. Although he assumes that most of those selected will be gentlemen by birth, his insistence that education should impart 'virtue' seems to open the door to education for those best able to profit, irrespective of their birth. But he was not straying far from conventional thinking when he wrote: 'I trust to see now many a noble gentleman relieved [supported] by these acts [dissolving monasteries] and, exercising themselves in all feats of arms, made apt and meet to the defence of their country.' In 1496 the Scottish parliament had decreed that all aristocrats must send their sons to school. Such an idea was unthinkable in contemporary England.

Those who went to school in early Tudor England were more likely to be the sons of poorer parents and for them even a very elementary education could be crucial in determining their place in society. It was quite possible for children from quite illiterate families to learn, again largely from local priests (though their actual expertise as teachers was limited), to read and even to write English. For many no further progress was possible, but the provision of free elementary schooling, including basic Latin, had increased considerably in England in the fifteenth century and even more in the early sixteenth, to the extent that it was available within reasonably easy reach of most country boys, and most towns of any size supported at least one school. Most were run by the Church and staffed by clergy, but there was no commitment of the scholars to the priesthood, especially in the newer schools endowed by laymen. But for the great majority of English people even the new printed books were of no use to them. It is unlikely that more than one in ten ordinary husbandmen could even sign their names, though the proportion of craftsmen was probably higher and that of the more substantial farmers may have been as high as 40 per cent.

These last were those calling themselves 'yeomen'. Among the tens of thousands of peasant, or family, farmers with their bewildering variety of agricultural specialization and tenure, there had appeared by 1500 a minority who regarded themselves, and were widely accepted, as men who enjoyed a status above most of their neighbours. To a very considerable extent their distinction was economic, for on the whole they occupied larger farms, acreages of arable and/or pasture accumulated by their forebears during the previous century or so, a period when land had been readily available. They also tended to be the farmers with the most secure tenure, copyholders or leaseholders. Some were in fact freeholders, or at least held part of their land freely, though by no means all freeholders would have called themselves yeomen, many being no better off economically than poor husbandmen. The fact remains, however, that during the later Middle Ages the description 'yeoman' had gradually superseded that of 'franklin', though even the latter had come to denote stability and security rather than literally a freeholder. The word yeoman was used in other contexts, such as in royal and noble households, where the posts of yeoman usher, yeoman cook, etc., were common in the early sixteenth century and beyond, to indicate a degree of seniority among lesser ranks, and, especially in farming communities which lacked resident gentlemen, yeoman farmers were the natural leaders in community affairs, and in most parishes it was the yeomen who filled the offices of churchwarden, constable, etc. They were the select few most likely to turn up at the musters with a proper accoutrement of weapons, harness, and even a horse. Moreover, once having assumed some dignity or authority in their community, yeomen became accepted, like past-mayors in towns, as elders, that is, members of the village 'anciety'. To Sir John Fortescue, the great fifteenth-century lawyer, yeomen were the backbone of the English jury system, men who would not perjure themselves, not only for their fear of God but for the honour of their

descendants. Be that as it may, early Tudor England certainly
had a small farming as well as a mercantile and industrial
aristocracy. Moreover, just as the sons of provincial merchants
and the richer craftsmen took advantage of the increasing
opportunities for being educated beyond mere literacy, so did
the sons of yeoman farmers. While Elyot and Starkey clearly
thought of education as a prop to the existing social order,
Edmund Dudley in his *Tree of the Commonwealth* actually
warned his readers that if gentlemen did not educate themselves,
lesser men would leave them behind. It was indeed largely
yeomen's children who made their way to the universities and
who went from there into the Church, most bishops being
younger sons of yeoman farmers. A small number each year
went to the Inns of Court, involving their families in considerable expense, certainly more than the rent of a farm.
Whereas the very stability of yeomen families depended on
the custom of primogeniture in the handing on of farms, it
was part of the yeoman's way of life that cash was gradually
put by, either for the next renewal of a lease or for giving a
start in life to younger sons. For most this meant just another
farm, but many a yeoman's son progressed both economically
and socially way beyond his father. There are plenty of
examples of their becoming gentlemen and even of being
knighted, but few yeomen farmers were really envious of
gentlemen or wished themselves to join their ranks. Indeed,
many lived considerably better than the less well-to-do gentry,
but without aping their style of life. They certainly employed
servants, both indoor and outdoor, but they neither employed
the former idly (as gentlemen were said to do) nor disdained
to work with the latter. Their dress was sober and unostenta-
tious: the authors of the sumptuary laws could ignore them.

It is difficult to exaggerate the wealth accumulated by the
country-based clothiers, wealth which, like that of John Lane
of Cullompton in Devon or John Winchcombe of Newbury
in Berkshire, was lavished on their parish churches. More
important, they bought land and established, if not themselves,
at least their descendants as gentlemen, but they were not

necessarily in a hurry to leave their business activities behind them. Thomas Spring of Lavenham, the wealthy early Tudor clothier, was the third industrial entrepreneur in his line and Thomas Bailey, a clothier of Trowbridge, was succeeded in his family business by two sons and at least one grandson. They were, however, rather better placed to find gentlewomen as daughters-in-law than were the town-based commercial and industrial magnates. In fact, industrial fortunes were not so easily made in the towns of early Tudor England as in the countryside.

When William Harrison wrote his analysis of the society of early Elizabethan England he was clearly not describing anything new. After the nobility and gentry, the leading citizens and burgesses, and the yeomen (whom he called '*legales homines*, freemen born'), he went on to describe what he called 'the last sort of people in England'. These were the 'day-labourers, poor husbandmen, and some retailers ... copyholders, and all artificers [such] as tailors, shoemakers, [etc.] ... [who] have neither voice nor authority in the commonwealth, but are to be ruled and not to rule other', unless, he added, 'for default of yeomen'. It is an interesting categorization of the great mass of the non-élite and, in the light of what we know of occupations, it is interesting that Harrison should see little to distinguish poor husbandmen and craftsmen from day-labourers, that is wage-earners. Wage-earning in early Tudor England was in theory a temporary resort when times were hard, or a marking of time between apprenticeship and full master or householder status. In fact, as we know, many were full- or part-time wage-earners throughout their lives. Moreover, it is likely that for most men and women who had no real occupation and no means of working for themselves on the land or in their own workshop, their employment was very casual indeed. Probably no contemporary observer of early Tudor society would have known where to draw the line, within this large category of those whose fate it was to be dependent on others, between those who were able to live largely by their own exertions and those who, whether unable or unwilling to work, relied entirely on the charity of their fellow men. Harrison did not mention them, presumably including them with what he called labourers, but then the poor were not in the mid-sixteenth century the embarrassment, both socially and economically, which they were later to become. For the most part they were taken for granted, and in the lawcourts a favourite way of disparaging an opponent was to refer to him as only a poor man and therefore of no credibility.

The same could almost be said of early Tudor women. It was rare for them to appear as plaintiffs in the courts, especially if married, for they had nothing to lose. It was quite common for men to bequeath to their wives not only the latter's jewels and other finery but even their very apparel; in the words of the earl of Oxford in 1509, 'as well cloth as silks'. Almost immediately after the Statute of Wills of 1540 had enabled men to devise the greater part of their land by will, another statute denied to married women, along with idiots and infants under the age of twenty-one, the right to devise any land. Nor, as we have seen, did they yet feature in the statutes of apparel, even as displayers of their husbands' rank. 'The good nature of a woman,' wrote Sir Thomas Elyot in 1531, 'is to be mild, timorous, tractable, benign, of sure remembrance, and shame-fast.' Not all early Tudor women were, of course, such mild creatures, but when in 1536, on the occasion of the pulling down of the rood loft in St Nicholas Priory at Exeter, a crowd of women caused something of a riot, the main instruction to those appointed to carry out an inquiry into the disturbance was to discover whether these were not in fact men dressed up as women. It was when widowed that women really came into their own, and due to the quite common disparity in age between man and wife there were many of them. Compared with their opportunities when first married, they had consider-able freedom as widows, though the author of the *Italian Re-lation*, writing in about 1500, was being especially unkind when he remarked of English widows who, as many did, married their husbands' apprentices, that they had probably not found them displeasing before their husbands' death. He was probably right, however, in saying that widows were free to marry where they chose, 'however unsuitable the match may be as to age, rank, and fortune'. Until they remarried, as they usually did, often more than once, widows carried on farming, and in the towns were to be found running workshops and businesses, even being admitted in their own right to guilds and companies (though never to governing bodies or to office) and being assessed for tax. But any wealthy woman, whether widow or unmarried heiress, was at grave risk of abduction in a society whose law gave her husband complete control of all her property, real and personal. The statute of 1487 'against taking away of women against their wills' was little more than a restatement of existing law, intended not so much for the protection of women as for the maintenance of law and order. The case of Margaret Kebell, a twenty-five-year-old widow, abducted from her uncle's house in Staffordshire at six o'clock in the morning by Roger, son of Sir Henry Vernon, accompanied by some one hundred and twenty armed men, serves to underline the deficiencies of the common law in such matters. Although pursued by her formidable mother and her fiancé, Ralph Egerton, Margaret was carried off into Derbyshire where the Vernons were powerful landowners and there married, under threat, to Roger Vernon. What followed is not entirely clear but Margaret succeeded in bringing her husband and his accessories before the Court of King's Bench in London. Owing to legal technicalities this got her nowhere but she later managed to gain audience with the King himself at Greenwich and the matter came before the Council in Star Chamber. Justice was now done, the Vernons were heavily fined, and Margaret was eventually freed to marry the patient Ralph. Their grandson was the famous Jacobean Lord Chancellor. The Vernons no doubt took up the chase elsewhere.

Two centuries before 1500 by far the majority of English people had been born villeins, that is, unfree, their personal status arising from the nature of their land tenure. As bondmen or women they had not only been confined to pleading in their lords' courts but could not even leave home without their lords' licence nor give their daughters in marriage without seignorial approval. Worst of all, everything they possessed except life itself and livelihood, in effect all their personal goods, were at his disposal. In early Tudor England bondage was hard to prove, usually hardly worth proving and rarely enforced. However, the threat was always there, hanging not so much over poor men as over men of substance. Having long since parted company with tenure of land it was, by 1500, an essentially personal relationship with the lord of the manor and no one else – a taint of blood, the very opposite of gentility. In 1517 an officer of the duke of Buckingham reported that he had seized, among others, as the duke's bondman, John Dyx of Padbury, had released him on a surety of £40, had valued his goods at £18, and elicited that Dyx would pay 53s. 4d. for his liberty. Also claimed as one of the duke's bondmen was a Norwich innkeeper called Cooper. He was reckoned to be worth £200 in goods, for he had no less than thirty-six good beds and over £40's worth of silver. When reported to the duke, he had gone on a pilgrimage to Santiago. Like the Crown's feudal claims, such social anachronisms still had their cash value for landowners who felt no shame in exploiting them. Villeins by birth, discovered by their lords owning freehold land, could actually be dispossessed by them. This happened to one Richard Akes of Chippenham in Cambridge-shire in 1526, and to the two married daughters and heiresses of Walter Bolitout of Forncett in Norfolk in 1524. At Forncett in 1500 there had still been eight families among the tenants of the late duke of Norfolk who were of servile status, less than half the number there in 1400. By 1525 there were five and by 1575 none at all. There were other descendants of Forncett bondmen who were still paying an annual fine or 'chevage' for permission to live elsewhere, as did John Baxter of Tivets-hall, which is some six miles from Forncett, until 1556, when for a payment in the region of £120, he bought from the duke of Norfolk freedom for himself and all his descendants. Bondage was actually introduced by Parliament for a short time in 1547 as a penalty for contumacious vagabondage. It was real enough for its extinction to be called for by the Norfolk rebels in 1549, and as late as 1575 the Queen granted three hundred of her bondmen to Sir Henry Lee so that he could compel them to compound for their freedom at the rate of one third of the value of their lands.

Finally, cutting right across most of the lines dividing society (except that between men and women, for most of them were men), was England's quite considerable complement of aliens. These were people actually born abroad and, although resident, not yet made denizens, or as we should say, nationalized. English law was rigorous, at least in content if not in execution. Aliens were not permitted to own land, were taxed at double the native rates (and unlike natives were assessed at a basic minimum rate however poor they were), and were subjected to restrictions in the exercise of their crafts and trades. A statute of 1483 had forbidden them to employ other aliens or to take them as apprentices, the principle being that a condition of their residence must be that they confer some benefit on natives. An Act of 1523 allowed them two alien journeymen but, perversely, extended the ban on alien apprentices to denizens. Alien smiths, joiners and coopers were singled out for special restrictions, and in 1534 aliens were prohibited by statute from working as pewterers, printers, or bookbinders. Clearly the native lobby was very active. Denization (by royal grant) conferred access to the king's courts of law, the right to acquire, dispose of and to bequeath (but not inherit) land, but from 1515 carried no exemption from double taxation. But by long tradition the Crown and the nobility did what they could to protect aliens, whose services they found indispensable. Henry VII established two guilds in the 'liberty' of Blackfriars, one for French artisans and another for Flemish and Spanish shoemakers. Henry VIII confirmed the existence of the French guild, allowing it an annual service in the former Black Friars' church. The Hanseatic merchants from Germany and the Italians had long occupied premises which were outside the jurisdiction of the London city authorities, and the men of the Steelyard not only had their own quay, but paid customs on cloth exports at a lower rate than Englishmen.

While alien merchants were usually only temporarily resident and were few in number, even in London, alien craftsmen usually came to stay and in large numbers. There were at least three thousand in London in 1500, that is nearly one in ten of the male population. By 1540 they comprised nearly one third. Within the precincts of St Martin-le-Grand in Aldersgate Ward, only six Englishmen lived alongside 204 strangers, mostly Flemings, and Shoe Lane was almost entirely populated by aliens. In the provinces they were to be found only in the larger towns, and in very small numbers. Most were either too poor or thought it not worth the expense of becoming naturalized, but when Henry VIII went to war with France in 1544 and ordered all able-bodied Frenchmen to return home, no less than 1,900 of them sought and obtained letters of denization. Most of them were residents of long standing, some as long as fifty years. Many had English wives, who, along with their children who had been born in England, were natives, as far as the law was concerned. Indeed, assimilation into English society, especially in the provinces, had been fairly smooth. In Southampton, for example, a Florentine, Antonio Guidotti, married the daughter of Harry Huttoft, surveyor of the customs. Widows of aliens quickly found English husbands. It was in London where there were more of them and where they tended to stick together that hostility towards aliens was aroused. But only in the May Day riot of 1517 did the situation even look like getting out of hand. Most of the notorious English antagonism against strangers took the form of peaceful political pressure, which Westminster was very experienced in resisting. All that the author of the *Italian Relation* really experienced during his short stay was a determination by his English acquaintances, largely in official circles, to demonstrate their own superiority. They had reason to be sensitive, for foreign scholars, musicians and artists were usually very welcome at Court and in the houses of the nobility.

The Italian visitor also noted what seemed to him the remarkably courteous English habit of doffing caps and he clearly did not see this as a mark of respect paid by an inferior to a superior. For all their concern with 'degree', the people of Tudor England were neither class-conscious nor always quite sure where they stood. In 1508 Thomas Spring of Lavenham appeared in a list of those to whom was granted a general pardon as 'clothmaker alias yeoman alias gentleman alias merchant'. Clearly he was taking no chances where the law was concerned. Eight years later when being exempted from public office he was just plain 'clothmaker', as indeed he called himself in his will made in 1523. However, his wife Alice saw to it that the wooden screen surrounding his tomb carried representations of his newly acquired arms, as also did the parapet of the new tower he provided for Lavenham church and the chantry chapel where he is rightly commemorated as Thomas Spring, esquire. At his death he owned no less than sixteen manors in Suffolk alone and ten in other counties, together with freehold tenements in no less than one hundred parishes. But it was his eldest son and heir who effected the real transformation into country gentleman and eventually knight. With movement at such a slow pace, English society could remain remarkably relaxed and free from class tensions. As we have seen, there was quite as much happening to create vertical as well as horizontal bonds between people of varying degrees.

6. Inflation of Population and Prices

Early Tudor England was short of people. In 1300 there had probably been six million, but the two centuries which followed had brought a quite staggering fall, perhaps down to two million by the middle of the fifteenth century, scarcely higher than soon after the Norman Conquest. The causes were many and may even have included a slight but significant fall in average annual temperature. There may have been, for reasons which are not at all clear, a rise in the average age at which men and women married. Recurrent outbreaks of epidemic disease, in particular bubonic plague, were clearly important, although it is not easy to see why a disease so closely associated with conditions of life in towns should have had such a devastating effect on a predominantly rural population. All that can be said for sure is that late-medieval English society failed year by year to reproduce itself. By about 1470, it is believed, the situation was stabilizing. There may have been a small net increase in the closing decades of the fifteenth century, followed by a further slight contraction soon after 1500. Thereafter, probably by the mid-1510s, and certainly by the mid-1520s, the trend was firmly upwards but not of sufficient magnitude to challenge the veracity of Thomas Starkey's observation in 1536 that there was in England 'a great lack and penury of people and inhabitants'.

The fall in population can be traced in terms of farming households at the level of the local community. At Chippenham in Cambridgeshire a survey made in 1544 lists besides sixty occupied farmsteads a further sixty-four sites where houses had once stood. Cambridgeshire was on the whole a county of small farmers, its population high by contemporary standards. In Chippenham only about half the existing farms were of twenty acres or more and many comprised only a house, croft and under two acres of land. The latter's occupants must have depended on part-time wage-earning and either could not or would not increase their acreage. At Wigston in Leicestershire there were barely seventy households in the village in the 1520s compared with about one hundred and twenty just over a century earlier and even more before the Black Death. Here, however, a smaller population had given rise to larger farms and there was little or no untilled land. In 1541 in the villages of Foulby and Wragby in the West Riding of Yorkshire there were twenty-one cottages unoccupied as the result of a recent plague there, and in Snaith at about the same time 380 acres of former demesne arable had reverted to waste for lack of tenants. In the West Riding as a whole, however, population, in terms of occupied farms, had held its own rather better in the uplands than in the lowlands and, excluding the uninhabitable fells, this was also the case in the Lake counties of the north-west.

Unfortunately for historians, the early Tudor government's interest in listing the country's population was usually confined to those it could tax. Cardinal Wolsey came nearest to obtaining a national census in 1522 when he ordered a military survey to be made of all adult males aged between sixteen and sixty. The lists were to include not only all able men but also those physically unfit to serve. Had they all survived – and probably not all were completed or returned – we should have a complete census of the early Tudor male population, including even non-householders such as unmarried sons, living-in servants, apprentices, and the very poor, though these last are likely to have been ignored by the commissioners if they were only temporarily resident. Two years later when Wolsey commissioned assessments for a parliamentary subsidy, these were based on landed income, goods or, for the first and only time, income of at least £1 a year in wages. By comparing the very few surviving returns of the 1522 assessment with those for the subsidy made in 1524 and 1525 it has been calculated that, at any rate in the towns, the tax assessments omitted up to one third of the population. For the countryside, however, where most of the population lived, the subsidy coverage can be shown to have been reasonably complete as far as heads of settled households were concerned. For example, in Happing Hundred (a group of parishes) in Norfolk, the subsidy assessments contain only about 10 per cent fewer names than the muster of 1522, namely 674 compared with 746. Using the remarkably comprehensive subsidy assessments, and assuming an average family size of 4.75, it is possible to make a reasonably accurate calculation of the total settled population of most counties and parishes in the mid-1520s.

It goes almost without saying that the early Tudor population of England was spread very unevenly. In very broad terms the east Midlands and East Anglia had more people to the square mile than the west Midlands and the central southern counties. Areas which included large cities, especially London, show a higher concentration but there were entirely rural areas, for example the South Hams of Devon, the parishes to the north of Exeter and parts of east Somerset, which contained what was by contemporary standards the high density of over twenty taxpayers per square mile, the equivalent of ninety to a hundred persons. Considerable changes in relative density had occurred since the levying of the poll-taxes of the later fourteenth century. Sussex and Worcestershire, for example, had higher relative densities, confirming other evidence of late-medieval migration into 'forest' regions. There remained large areas, especially parts of the far north of England, where there were barely ten persons to the square mile. Over the country as a whole there were roughly forty-five, about one third of the present-day average outside the larger towns. Allowing for about 40 per cent of the population of England being under the age of sixteen, the total in the 1520s is thought to have been about 2.3 million, that is, rather higher, but not much, than at the probable rock bottom around the year 1450. Calculations based on the technique of 'back projection' from evidence derived from a non-random sample of just over four hundred parish registers put the total in 1541 at 2.77 million. If both these figures are approximately correct – and the latter in particular cannot but amaze the layman by its temerity – then it can be said that between 1525 and 1541 the population increased by about .03 per cent per annum, hardly enough for Thomas Starkey to have been aware that it was moving at all.

Other things being equal, which of course they never are, population trends should be reflected in the demand for, and hence the price of, foodstuffs and other necessities. A great deal of price data is available but it relates only to urban market prices and most of it comes from the south of England. Except for those engaged largely in pastoral farming, and in all but extreme famine conditions, farmers were self-sufficient for essential food. Moreover, in many rural areas, in spite of conversion of arable land to pasture, there was scope for re-occupation of vacant holdings and also for colonization of hitherto waste ground; against such a background population could grow quite considerably without affecting normal market prices. Perhaps even more to the point, the price of cereals was affected far more in the short term by the quality of the harvest than by increases or decreases in the number of mouths to be fed. Meat and dairy prices could likewise be affected by animal diseases. Good and bad harvests tended to come in batches, the weather factor being compounded by the run-on effect of shortage or plenty of seed corn. There were also considerable regional variations. However, price-tables drawn from as much data as is available do show unmistakable long-term trends. There was a quite perceptible rise in all commodity prices in the 1520s, especially of grain, and though they levelled out, they showed no sign in the 1530s of returning permanently to the old levels. The price of oats approximately doubled between 1500 and 1535, and that of wheat took rather longer to do the same. Meat prices rose at about the same time and increased proportionately more than cereals. Oxen were sold in the 1490s for 16s., in the 1510s for 23s., and in the 1520s for 30s. Calculations based on the price of a composite 'basket' of consumables, including cereals, meat, fish, malt, butter, and cheese, show, after a period of remarkable stability extending into the late 1510s, a sharp rise in 1520. This was, in fact, the middle year of a run of three disastrous harvests, but although there was a subsequent return to stability there was no return to the level of 1510. In the 1520s people expected prices to fall back when the harvest improved, but by the mid-1530s they were becoming aware that these were consistently higher than they remembered had been the case in days gone by. They tended to attribute this to reduced supply owing to the conversion of arable to pasture, and as wool and meat prices were still rising they may have been partly right. No one, least of all those in government circles, attributed it to an increased demand by an expanding population and, as prices were clearly rising faster than population in the 1520s and early 1530s, they were not badly wrong. There may even have been an increased demand, even from the towns and almost certainly from London, due to a rise in the standard of living. There was, too, the effect of Henry VIII's first debasement of the coinage in 1526. But his subjects, especially those who enjoyed the good harvests and stable cereal prices of the later 1530s, had not yet experienced real inflation, even by sixteenth-century standards. The country's population had to rise a good deal more before it would materially affect the relation between demand and supply.

Another possible mirror of population trends was the level of wages paid to agricultural and industrial labourers. Although there were few families, especially in the countryside, entirely or permanently dependent on wages, any appreciable increase in the size of the adult population might be expected to depress wages, especially in the fielden areas where the land was fully occupied and the demand for labour relatively inelastic. Again there are complications. For example, to the extent that, mostly before 1500, land had been converted from arable to pastoral farming, there had already occurred a reduced need for labour and this will have depressed wages quite independently of any possible growth in manpower. Wage-rates, too, tended to be fixed by custom, as well as by statutory regulation, and although employers would resist any increase, they might not necessarily respond to any slight increase in the labour supply by offering less. In fact the limited evidence available for the early decades of the sixteenth century suggests that the average daily wage-rates for semi-skilled work such as hedging, ditching, and spreading dung remained virtually steady at 4d. a day from the 1450s until about 1550. Unless there was a growing demand for labour, which is unlikely, this must mean that the supply was not yet sufficient to deprive labourers of the quite considerable advantages they had won since the period of the Black Death. Indeed, the passage of a statute in Parliament in 1514 putting a ceiling on wages, the first since 1388, suggests a renewed fear in high places of a shortage of labour. The following year, in fact, building-workers in London were exempted from the Act and allowed to take the wages they had been receiving before its passage. Building-workers generally were receiving their traditional 6d. per day.

Where population was really exerting pressure on land re-sources one might expect to find this reflected in increased rents. But here again other factors were at work. Some increases have been noted as early as the 1470s, but mostly on Crown estates, which we know were being administered more efficiently from about that time. The rent obtainable for pasture was also rising in response to the buoyant demand for animal products, especially wool. Rents for arable land in the vicinity of London rose fairly steadily during the very early decades of the century, but this reflected a demand in the markets of the metropolis which, if due to an increase in population rather than to a rise in living-standards, was probably the result of unceasing migration rather than any real increase in the indigenous population. Entry-fines and the length of leases which, as already indicated, offer a better gauge of demand than rents alone seem to suggest, in many of the more out-lying parts of the country, an actual fall in demand between 1500 and 1520. In Northamptonshire, in 1518, the duke of

Buckingham's tenants refused to exchange yearly tenancies for more secure copyholdings, presumably preferring to gamble that rents were as likely to go down as up. 'They had lever to depart the lordship,' reported the duke's exasperated official. The evidence is overwhelming, however, that by the later 1520s and early 1530s landlords, both lay and ecclesiastical, although they met great vocal resistance, were able to be more rigorous in their demands. Average rents per acre (including entry-fines) for new tenancies on the Herbert estates in the chalk country west of Salisbury more than doubled from 6d. to 13d. Even the monasteries who by then were relinquishing nearly all their remaining demesnes – though usually holding on to pasture until the last moment – found no difficulty in spite of the risks, in finding tenants, though admittedly for long terms and for fairly traditional if not lower rents. But this is not conclusive proof of population pressure for most of the monastic lessees were gentlemen and substantial farmers, encouraged no doubt by the marginal increase in market prices to lease land with vacant possession.

There seems little reason for connecting the slight increases in prices and land-values in the 1520s with any increase in the number of landless persons, especially younger sons. Even the early Tudor enclosure Acts, up to and including that of 1533, were aimed at reversing the drift of people from the land rather than at increasing the land available for landless men crying out for holdings. When Thomas Starkey implored Henry VIII in 1536 to make the former monastic demesnes available in small parcels, he had particularly in mind as tenants 'younger brethren living in service unprofitably', that is, idling, as he regarded it, in other men's households. He was looking not for charity but for encouragement to young men to marry and produce the families which he was convinced the country needed. Even his limited support for the Dissolution sprang partly from his anxiety to reduce the country's complement of unmarried men and what he called the 'let [hindrance] of natural propagation'. Indeed, he even suggested as an alternative some relaxation in the canonical law of celibacy.

Why was the rate of increase in population so low if the country's resources were so far from being stretched? Human nature being incorrigibly idiosyncratic there may have been some preference for small families, but the most potent form of birth-control was the custom whereby the eldest sons of farmers delayed marriage until becoming heads of their households. Foreign observers commented on the commonly disproportionate ages of English marriage-partners, especially the marriage of young men to widows. In the 1530s it was suggested to Thomas Cromwell that there should be a statute not only prohibiting boys from marrying before puberty but also potent men marrying elderly widows. If the corollary was also the case, that many young women married elderly men, particularly as their first husbands, then we may here have factors affecting both the size of the birth-rate and the life-expectancy of children. Until we reach a time well after the inception of parish registers in 1538 there is no way of finding out, but even in the mid sixteenth century, when population was increasing quite fast, almost one third of all those marrying are thought to have been either widows or widowers. Another limitation on family size could have been the custom of leaving to widows life-interests, and residence, in farms and businesses, thus further delaying the marriages of eldest sons. Manor-court rolls of the period actually record the granting of new joint tenancies on the remarriage of widowed mothers. But it seems more likely that the real determining factor continued to be that which it is generally agreed caused the very heavy fall in population in the later Middle Ages, heavy mortality caused by plague and other epidemic diseases.

Early Tudor England was hardly less, if indeed not more, subject to lethal disease than had been late-medieval England. As more and more evidence comes to light, it seems as if hardly a year passed without there being an outbreak somewhere, and in London diseases of many kinds were endemic. In the absence of parish registers for the early decades of the century the evidence is either literary or casual, or at best dependent on the probate of wills which tell us little or nothing about the incidence of those diseases which affected in particular the poor, especially bubonic plague. This was a disease which resulted from a bite by an infected flea, leading to the development of a 'bubo' or painful glandular swelling in the neck, armpit or groin. The chances of death were very high, perhaps 90 per cent, and usually within a period of five days. Timber-framed houses in-filled with wattle and daub, earth floors covered with rushes, and thatched roofs provided ideal conditions for the rats from which the fleas imbibed the infection. Buildings of stone and slate, which only the comparatively rich could afford, offered better protection, more perhaps than even simple hygiene, though it has been noticed by archaeologists that country people on the whole disposed of more of their household refuse. Though not infectious like virus diseases, plague does seem to have spread principally along the main highways, often from seaports, and this suggests that it could be spread by human contact, that is, by the transfer of infected human fleas. This is confirmed by the discovery that it was often confined to certain households. But there is also the possibility that infected rat fleas could survive for several days and travel long distances in merchandise. Evidence from wills points to the years 1500–1502, 1520 and 1527–8 as bringing the greatest mortality, each of these coinciding with widespread harvest failure which, while not causing plague, probably lowered people's resistance to it. However, its very widespread incidence in 1535–9, years of comparative plenty, are a warning against attributing to food-shortage levels of mortality which were due to entirely autonomous factors. Bubonic plague seems to have killed in particular older children and adolescents and, among adults, rather more men than women. It must surely have been the effect of bubonic plague on adolescents which had the greatest medium-term consequences for marriage- and birth-rates.

Interspersed between visitations of bubonic plague in early Tudor England were outbreaks of a virus disease known abroad as the 'English sweat'. It spread more rapidly than plague, being carried by travellers and even, it has been suggested, by mice and voles, and it struck indiscriminately in both town and country, at all social levels and at all age-groups, but especially at people in the prime of life between twenty and forty years of age. It was particularly virulent in 1485, 1508, 1517 (when Cardinal Wolsey suffered from it) and in 1528. If it killed its victim it did so within twenty-four hours which made it particularly horrific, a 'scourge without dread', as the devout Yorkshireman, Robert Parkyn, described it. In fact it was rather less deadly than plague, and people did often recover. Polydore Vergil described how, as early as 1485, people learned by trial and error how to react: 'Those who fell victims a third time to the disease learned how to cure themselves and easily escaped the virulence of the fever by profiting from their previous observations.' The remedy, they found, was to keep warm, avoid food and take only liquids. However, the last outbreak of 1551 can be traced in parish burial registers throughout the country. In three villages in Staffordshire, Betley, Ellastone, and Alstonefield, burials in one month in 1551 roughly equalled the annual average for the previous decade, and the death-rate earlier in the century may have been even higher. In particular the generation-susceptibility of disease may have been vital, and the temporary disappearance between 1528 and 1551 of 'the sweat', which was more lethal to young adults, may well have been one of the most important factors in enabling the English population to make a real leap forward in the 1540s, if not earlier.

For, after 1540, or at the very latest after 1544, the scene changed. A 'penury' of people, relatively stable prices, and virtually full employment began to give way to a competence if not an abundance of people, to inflation of prices (what contemporaries called a 'dearth' of goods), and to a certain amount of under-employment, if not unemployment. Between the mid-1540s and the later 1550s, the total number of people increased quite substantially, being probably well in excess of three million by 1556: the back-projection figure is 3.16 million. This represents a net average increase of slightly over 1 per cent per annum.

But now, for the first time, it is possible to watch what was happening, in flesh as it were, in towns and villages in every county in England. In 1538, in response to instructions from Thomas Cromwell, all parish priests, with varying degrees of efficiency, began to keep a record of every baptism, marriage and funeral performed in their churches. In theory the life-cycle of everyone who was born or died in England from that year is on record, and for this every social historian, while regretting that not all registers were faithfully kept or cherished, should be grateful. Almost every reasonably complete parish register shows, for most decades from 1541–50 onwards, a sur-plus of baptisms over burials, sufficient to indicate an average replacement rate of over one for one. So, in the hill parish of North Molton in Devon with a population in the mid-1520s (calculated from the tax assessments) of about seven hun-dred, the registers show that in the years 1541 to 1550 (inclusive) there were 201 baptisms and eighty-five burials, a net increase in population of over 16 per cent in ten years. The comparable figures for the 1550s show more baptisms but also far more burials, resulting in what appears to be a slowing down in the rate of growth. There is, in fact, no clear evidence of plague, and indeed a remote community such as North Molton was more likely to suffer abnormal mortality from the effects of a succession of bad harvests elsewhere, for little corn was grown in the parish itself. These calculations take no account of movement into or out of the parish, and as it will almost certainly have supplied migrants to the larger towns of the south-west the increase in residents may have been exaggerated. However, evidence from later in the century, by which time it is possible to trace complete life-cycles, suggests that most of the young men were settling down on the land or in employment locally. By the 1560s the village probably con-tained nearly one thousand people, but an increase of baptisms in the 1570s is explicable in part by the temporary presence of a colony of German miners.

There is ample evidence in surviving parish registers of the 1540s, especially in the larger towns, of quite sudden rises in mortality. These rarely coincided with rises in the price of grain, for towns, especially those near the coast, were usually able to obtain emergency supplies. It is fairly easy to identify bubonic plague as the cause because deaths occurred almost entirely in the later summer months, from July to September, with occasional extensions if the weather was mild enough to keep the fleas active. Reading in 1543 and 1544, Bristol in 1544 and 1545 and York in 1550–52, suffered very heavy mortality, sufficient to take many years for their population to recover, especially if plague returned within a decade as it did in Norwich in 1554–5. Norwich, in fact, with about twelve thousand people in the 1520s had barely increased in size at all by the mid-1550s, nor Exeter beyond its early Tudor tally of about eight thousand persons. The far smaller north Devon town of Barnstaple lost in 1546 alone no less than two hundred people, about 10 per cent of its total population. The winter brought no relief. Of 172 buried from September 1546 to April 1547, sixty had been baptized since 1538 (that is, were under eight years of age, forty being between one and five years), and twelve were infants under a year old. These last were probably no more than would have died anyway, but the loss of so many who had managed to survive to the age of one to seven years was bound to have serious long-term effects. At Wigston in Leicestershire the total number of families had risen from the seventy of the 1520s only to about eighty in 1563. This may, however, have been due to migration out of the village because of lack of vacant land or of employment. In fact one of the main consequences of the growth of rural population was an increase in migration, especially to London which, in spite of almost endemic plague, nevertheless kept on growing at a rate considerably in excess of that of the rest of the country. Also it never ceased to attract aliens, who increased from over 4,000 in 1540 to 4,500 in 1564, and on the evidence of fairly reliable censuses were to reach over 7,000 by 1571. These were first-generation residents, not a cumulative number, and most of them settled permanently and raised families to add to the number of native subjects of the Crown.

Serious as mortality from plague continued to be in certain towns, it is just possible that, as with sweating sickness, Tudor people in general were beginning by the 1540s to fight back. Those who could avoided plague-ridden areas or removed themselves and their families, showing that at least they recognized that diseases were caught by natural causes and were not simply inflicted on certain persons by God. Many victims and their families still accepted death whenever it came as God's will: Otwell Johnson, a London merchant, accepted his son's death from plague in 1545 because 'his time was come and so shall all ours at the Lord's pleasure'. Others, less fatalistic, urged the use of medicines, even though the doctors of early Tudor England had little to offer. Something could be learned from books, for instance from *A Litil Boke the whiche traytied and reherced many gode thinges necessarie for the Pestilence*, first published in 1485. Sir Thomas Elyot's *Castel of Helth*, published in 1539, taught that poor living-conditions encouraged disease through 'much people in small room living uncleanly and slutishly'. This, indeed, was a far cry from the moralists who preached that sexual indulgence opened the pores to infection. It was fairly typical of the Reformation in England that having denied to the people special masses against plague, and also the services of St Roch and St Sebastian whose especial concern was with disease, the reformed Church did not provide any replacement in the form of special prayers until 1563. It was, however, Cardinal Wolsey who was responsible in 1518 for a proclamation ordering that infected houses in London be indicated by the hanging of bundles of straw from windows and that all emerging from such houses carry white rods. In 1543 the Privy Council actually encouraged those suffering from plague to stay indoors, and some larger towns were by then taking measures such as the removal of the sick outside the walls and the turning away of strangers suspected of coming from plague-ridden areas.

It is also very clear that the birth-rate, or what was more important, the number of children to survive the crucial early years, increased in the 1540s and 1550s. Why this is so we do

not know. It is possible that the proportion of natural, that
is, non-plague, infant and child deaths actually dropped. It could
have been due to greater fertility – to larger families – and
indeed the 'gross reproductive rate' of children per marriage
at this period may even have been slightly higher than it was
later in the century. We have no means of knowing what it
was earlier. Possibly women were now marrying earlier;
possibly more of them married men nearer their own age, but
there is no reason for thinking that in this respect the
Reformation had changed anything. Moreover, it was not the
result of the dissolution of the monasteries, for not until
1549 were priests, including former monks, allowed to marry,
and this was again denied them between 1553 and 1558. Only
those who had been very young at the time of the Dissolution
can have begotten legitimate children, but at least the considerable drain, both of men and women, into the estate of
celibacy was ended. Whatever the reason, by the later 1550s
London was full of apprentices and law students born in the
early 1540s. No one anywhere spoke any longer of a shortage
of people.

Few, if any, contemporaries connected a growing population
with what was fast becoming an even more universal affliction
than plague, inflation of prices. The average price of all grains
moved up fairly steadily in the 1540s, reaching by 1550 a level
three and a half times that of 1500, and in the famine year
1556, five and a half times. The price of cattle, too, reached
a new high level in 1550 and was considerably higher in 1556,
possibly reflecting more than grain prices a rising standard of
living. The price of the basket of consumables was still rising
steadily in 1550 to very nearly double what it had been in 1540,
and was to go higher still in the bad harvest years in the mid-
1550s. To what extent even grain prices can be directly related
to population increase is debatable, to say the least. What is
certain is that after 1540 people talked and wrote a great deal
about inflation. As always, they blamed the 'covetousness' of
the retailers, and the King, or his advisers, directed their efforts
accordingly. A royal proclamation of 1544 declared that,

whereas a few years before, imported sugar had sold at 3d. and 4d. a pound, it was now only available at 9d. and 10d. 'against all reason and equity and to the great detriment of his Highness's loving and obedient subjects'. From henceforth the very best sugar was to be sold at no more than 7d. a pound. Everyone, of course, passed the buck. A solemn report to the Council in 1551 by the Drapers' Company of London stated that, compared with the situation only four years since, the price they now had to pay for woollen cloths had nearly doubled, Cheshire 'cottons' having risen from £7 the pack to £14 and even £14 10s., Hampshire kerseys from £29 to £50 and £52, 'and the prices notwithstanding, the said cloth was never so ill and falsely made'. Indeed we know from other sources that cloth which had been available wholesale in 1487 at £2 a bale was costing £7 in 1547. Assuming that most of the increase was due to the cost of the raw material it is easy to see that even if the conversion of arable land to pasture was not proceeding at the rate it had been half a century before there was little incentive as yet to go into reverse and produce more grain.

Perhaps more to the point for the great majority of the king's subjects, the tenant farmers and their families, by the middle of the century, probably for the first time for nearly 250 years, demand for land to rent would seem to have equalled, if not to have exceeded, supply. There was still a good deal of waste capable of being put under the plough, but landlords were having no difficulty whatsoever in finding tenants for vacant farms and were able to enhance their demands, especially for new leasehold takings. Precise figures are difficult to come by, except again on the Herbert estates in Wiltshire where the value of an acre of land rose between about 1535 and 1550 from 13d. to 20d. The volume of public outcry was overwhelming, but rents were still not rising as much as prices. Many landlords had perforce to be patient. Many, indeed, waited until the cost of living forced them to 'improve' their estates, but there is evidence that some landlords were actually setting the pace, putting up rents so that these actually caused rather than resulted from increases in commodity prices. William Harrison, only a few years later, was to allege that some landlords 'value their leases at a secret estimation given of the wealth and credit of the taker ... so that if the lessee be thought to be worth an hundred pounds, he shall pay no less for his term'. The iniquities of landlords were, of course, a favourite theme in the polemical writings of the time, the 'literature of complaint', and even the more balanced Sir Thomas Smith does not entirely exculpate them in his *Discourse of the Commonweal*, though he recognized that they, like almost everyone else, were the victims of the rise in prices. Each blames the other, he wrote, but all are 'as in a great press [where] the foremost is driven by him that is next to him, and the next by him that follows him, and the third by some violent and strong thing that drives him forward'.

Smith's choice for the 'violent and strong thing', the autonomous cause of inflation, was Henry VIII's debasement of the coinage in 1544, and we can well believe that as he wrote in 1549 he could still sense the outrage which people like himself must have felt at the drain on the country's human and financial resources in support of the war in France. For to the inflationary effect of the debasement was added that of royal purveyance of food and other supplies for the army. There were other factors, too, such as the growth of a market in land and, connected with this, the legalizing, between 1545 and 1552, of the taking of interest on loans. But to return to landlords and tenants, leasehold tenancies of farms were still, to use a contemporary term, 'bargains', that is, agreements between freely contracting parties. Reflecting on their helplessness at the beginning of the century, we must surely conclude that landlords would not have been able to raise their rents in the later 1540s if the demand for tenancies had not been buoyant, and here the rise in population must have been a crucial factor. The anti-enclosure Act of 1550, which followed so soon after the widespread hedge-breaking of the previous year, was clearly aimed not, as earlier Acts had been, to stop the drift from the land, but to provide for more small family farms.

Landlords were reminded that squatters on the waste, farming no more than three acres of land, 'doth no hurt and yet is much commodity to the [occupant] thereof'. This was surely an implied recognition that wherever possible land should be made available to some, at least, of a growing number of landless men caused by a growth in population.

An increasing population, with no increase in employment prospects, either in agriculture or industry, made it inevitable that wages would not rise in line with prices. It is true that skilled craftsmen in the building industry were able to demand more and that Sir Thomas Smith's fictitious capper complained that he was giving his journeymen 2d. a day more 'and yet they say they cannot sufficiently live thereon'. As always, there is the complication of part-time employment, very few people outside the towns being dependent on wages alone, and even the need by this time to allow for the increased number of possible working days since the Reformation. However, in terms of daily rates, it is clear that by the mid-1550s wages were falling well behind prices. While the average actual wage paid to agricultural labourers in southern England had risen from 4d. to 6d. a day, its purchasing power had fallen by 40 per cent since the beginning of the century. In the heavier rural industries, in particular smelting, men earned more but their wages were far from inflation-proof. In the Sidney Ironworks in Sussex, founders and fillers working at the furnace were paid 1s. 4d. and 1s. a day respectively from 1545 at least until 1556. Hammermen at the forge were paid at piece-rates which remained at 13s. 4d. a ton from 1546 through to 1560.

But towards the end of Mary Tudor's reign relief, of a sort, was at hand for wage-earners, though not in a way which most of them would have welcomed. First of all, there were disastrous harvests in 1555 and 1556. The prices of wheat, barley, oats and other arable crops shot up, and although there is no evidence of people actually starving to death the debilitating effect is reflected in an immediate drop in the number of births (or rather baptisms) registered. The harvest years 1557 and 1558 were much better but were preceded by an almost universal and deadly scourge which puzzled contemporaries called 'the new sickness'. A 'hot burning fever', it seems to have been a virus disease akin to modern influenza, and, unlike plague, it followed no seasonal pattern. In some villages it first appeared in the summer of 1556 but the greatest mortality – up to four times the previous annual average – occurred during the winters of 1557–8 and 1558–9, some villages suffering twice over. At Tamworth in Staffordshire a normal death rate of about forty a year trebled during the period March 1557 to March 1558. In many parishes registration stopped altogether, no doubt due to the sickness or death of the priest. In 1557, it was reported, the fever

raged horribly throughout the realm and killed an exceeding great number of all sorts of men, but especially gentlemen and men of great wealth. So many husbandmen and labourers also died, and were sick, that in harvest time in divers places men would have given one acre of corn to reap and carry in another. In some places corn stood and shed on the ground for lack of workmen ... And hereby so great a scarcity of harvestmen that those which remained took twelve pence for that which was wont to be done for three pence.

As with 'the sweat', not all who contracted the fever died, but a survey of wills proved in the dioceses of Canterbury, York, Coventry and Lichfield, Norwich, Worcester and Gloucester shows almost a three-fold increase during the years 1556–60, confirming (for only the fairly well-to-do made wills) that, like sweating sickness but unlike plague, it was no respecter of persons. This, if it was common to all classes, would have been equivalent to a fall of 20 per cent in the population, but calculations based on the wider social coverage of parish registers suggest an overall drop in population over the years 1557–9 of about 6 per cent. This hardly seems sufficient by itself to cause a real shortage of labour and a rise in wages of the order indicated above, but clearly there was much more temporary sickness than actual death. In Cheshire in 1559 the commissioners for the musters reported a very low turn-out due to the 'extreme diseases wherewith this shire hath been this two years past, and yet is, sore visited'. What was special about this Marian flu was its widespread territorial incidence. It caused the only overall fall in England's total population from about 1520 to the end of the century. But although it followed a period of very bad harvests, it was quite clearly not due to one of those 'crises of subsistence' which so afflicted contemporary continental Europe.

The crisis was, moreover, of insufficient duration to release the pressure on land and bring down rents. There were more than enough landless sons and brothers to take up vacant farms. But wages did rise, sufficient to bring the average agricultural rate for the 1560s to 7d. a day, and this went some way towards restoring its purchasing power until the end of the 1570s. Employers panicked and the young Queen and her ministers over-reacted, but the country was soon enjoying the fall in agricultural prices brought about by a series of good harvests and, to a certain extent, by there being fewer mouths to feed. Another contributory factor was that as a result of a fall in the overseas demand for English cloth from 1551, the price of wool was, if not falling sharply, at least no longer continuing to rise, and all incentive to convert any more arable land to pasture was disappearing. Very slowly after 1560 improved farming techniques were raising corn yields. For over two decades between the early 1560s and the early 1580s the price of grain still fluctuated from year to year but within a narrower band than at any time since before 1520. On this new plateau, however, it was running at about three and a half times its level at the beginning of the century. The price of live-stock was even less volatile, though showing approximately the same increase since 1500 as grain. In 1585 Lord Burghley declared in Parliament that England had enjoyed peace, and plenty of corn, for twenty-seven years, the figure no doubt chosen to please the Queen, but in fact he was approximately right.

By the later 1560s overall population was probably back to its pre-influenza level, the net decrease between 1556 and 1561 being followed in the next five quinquennia by percentage increases of some 4.8, 4.6, 4.3, 5.4 (1576–81), and 5.8 (1581–6),

to give, it is suggested, a grand total by the eve of the
Armada of some 3.8 million. Even Wigston in Leicestershire
was to add 50 per cent to its population after 1560, most of
it by 1580. The expansion is very visible in the excess of births
over deaths to be found in most years in all available parish
registers. There is also clear evidence of increased fertility,
where registers are complete enough to allow the reconstitution
of families resulting from marriages dating from the 1540s onwards. This was almost certainly due largely to earlier
marriages (some perhaps even induced by flu mortality) but
a greater abundance of food may also have contributed. Such
steady, if unspectacular, growth is often missed by those intent
on scouring the registers for evidence of mortality crises. In
fact the ability of early Elizabethan England to recover and
augment her population can in very large part be attributed
to her new freedom from widespread epidemic disease. Richard
Hakluyt, writing in 1584 (arguing for more Englishmen to
adventure overseas), ascribed the increase in population to 'our
long peace and seldom sickness'. With no more sweating sickness the countryside if not the towns very rarely suffered any
abnormal mortality. During the decade 1575–84 the ratio of
births to deaths in the 400 parishes where these have been counted was well over 1.5:1, a figure not to be reached again until
the nineteenth century. Even a few of the larger towns
escaped outbreaks of plague. York, having suffered terribly
from the 'new ague' of 1558, when it claimed to have lost one
third of its inhabitants, escaped further abnormal mortality until
the very end of the century. From York, and also from
Exeter and Winchester, there is evidence from the wills made
by the more substantial citizens that the average number of
surviving children increased markedly in the second half of the
century. But bubonic plague continued to wreak selective
havoc. Bristol suffered badly in 1565 and 1575, Norwich in
1579–80 and 1584–5, and York's neighbours, Hull in
1575–6 and 1582, and Doncaster in 1563 and 1582–3. London,
as always, was the worst sufferer. In 1563, as is well attested,
some twenty thousand (nearly a quarter of her population) died

from plague. Another year of heavy plague deaths was
1592–3. But even so the city's total population probably
topped 200,000 by 1600, having very roughly quadrupled since
1500 and doubled since about 1570.

It is impossible to establish an exact chronological relationship between the two mid-Tudor inflations, that of people and
that of prices, or to link either of these very precisely with
the rise in rents and the fall in the value of real wages. Until
the mid-1550s prices were increasing rather faster than
population. Both then took a knock in the later 1550s,
especially people, but from the mid-1560s until the mid-
1580s, people took the lead, though prices continued on their
steadily upward trend, as also did the economic value of land.
On the Herbert estates in Wiltshire the average rent per acre
for new tenancies rose from 20d. in the 1550s to nearly 23d.
in the 1560s and to 28d. in the 1570s. But there was bound
to be a time-lag between the level of prices and landlords'
total rentals, a time-lag which may have been rather longer
on the larger estates whose owners were slower to adapt to
changing times. Some landowners eventually more than made
up for lost time. On some of the Seymour manors, also in
Wiltshire, new rents rose from an average of 11d. in the 1550s
to 19d. in the 1560s and to 40d. in the 1570s and 1580s. In
the 1590s they very nearly reached 60d., a tenfold increase since
the beginning of the century. Rents like these were clearly a
cause of inflation, forcing tenant farmers to demand for their
produce the maximum that the market would stand. Even so,
it is very unlikely that rents in general kept up with food
prices. Rents in kind now came into their own as the best hedge
against inflation. The wily Sir Thomas Smith, when Provost
of Eton in the 1550s, had insisted on the college's tenants paying
some of their rent in wheat and malt, and he put his
experience to good use when in 1576, as one of the Queen's
Secretaries of State, he piloted through Parliament an Act 'For
the Maintenance of the Universities'. Those best able to profit
from the new situation – and indeed they had hardly looked
back since 1540 – were the larger working farmers, the yeo-

men. Ordinary husbandmen survived reasonably well into the
1580s provided that their farms were large enough to produce
a marketable surplus. Those, however, who could barely
support themselves on their land and who were dependent on
part-time wage-earning, began, quite early in the reign of
Queen Elizabeth, to suffer from the failure of wages to keep
up with prices, the result of the pressure of population on
employment opportunities. They were also, because of the
relative insecurity of their tenure, usually the first to suffer from
increased rents, and as a last resort to swell the numbers both
of vagrants and of migrant labourers. A high proportion of
those apprehended for vagrancy between the mid-1560s and
mid-1580s were young people aged between fifteen and twenty-
five. This surely underlines the importance of the demographic factor.

As long as harvests were reasonably good, few people actually
starved to death. Plague remained the great killer and dearth
of corn when it occurred tended only to precipitate the death
of the elderly and the infirm. The young survived. However,
there is some evidence that in the later 1580s the fall in real
wages was leading to later marriages, the only real guarantee
of a fall in the birth-rate. Indeed, in a country in which
agricultural production could not yet sustain a rapidly growing
population the closing years of the century might have brought
some relief. By 1591 overall population growth had actually
slackened and was down to only about 2.5 per cent per annum,
compared, as already noted, with nearly 6 per cent in the 1580s.
There were, however, some unusually bad harvests in the later
1580s when the average price of wheat shot up from its current
normal level of about 25s. a quarter to 35s. in 1586. Worse
was to come. In 1596 it reached a quite staggering 50s., eight
times what it had been a century earlier and 2.5 times its normal price in the mid-1550s. This was the result of a run of
five disastrous harvests from 1594 to 1598, largely due to very
heavy and unseasonable rainfall. Never could men remember
such great floods and so many impassable roads, and when
Titania in *The Dream* spoke of 'contagious fogs, which falling

in the land, hath every pelting river made so proud that they have overborne their continents', the audience at the Globe will have known what recent memories Shakespeare had in mind. In fact the crisis, though one of insufficient food for existing mouths, was caused more by the weather than by the increase in population. Prices soon dropped again as harvests improved, but not to the 1590 level, even by 1600. This great dearth certainly took its toll in causing debility and a consequent further fall in the birth-rate. Now, too, some people actually starved to death, but only in some of the upland regions, such as Cumberland, can harvest failure in the 1590s be shown to have caused death over a wide age-range. There was, too, for the first time in Tudor England, quite considerable mortality as the result of war by land and sea. Between 1591 and 1602 about six thousand men were sent abroad, including Ireland, from Kent alone, that is about 4 per cent of the county's population. Many eventually returned home, but diseased and unlikely to beget healthy children. The ratio of births to deaths was back to barely 1.2:1 in the 1590s, though a higher death-rate was probably more responsible than a lower birth-rate for, to use a modern expression, 'throttling back the rate of natural increase'.

Parish registers tell a dreadful tale in the middle and later 1590s, not only of death by starvation but, easily detectable from the seasonal pattern, of heavy plague mortality. Almost every town of any size suffered, mostly in 1596 and 1597. What was new, too, was that to a very considerable extent plague and bad harvests coincided. Even so the country's total population probably topped four million by the mid-1590s, an increase of well over a million people, or nearly 50 per cent, since 1541. But this was still far short of what the farmers of England had once managed to feed. Not even in the 1590s did England experience a crisis of Malthusian dimensions. Her troubles were not of that dimension. For reasons which are not entirely clear, but the decrease in plague mortality was one, and the particular balance between good and bad harvests another, the population had increased between about 1535 and about 1585 at a rate which was far short of explosive. Because of a mixture of human and natural failings, the production of food failed to meet demand and prices rose. Even when the rate of growth fell in the years after the defeat of the Spanish Armada food supplies for the first time failed, but only just, to feed the country's population. But even now neither plague nor dearth caused the rate of growth to come to a full stop or to go into reverse. This is clearly an oversimplification, as are all attempts to establish causation in human affairs, but in this case historians can perhaps understand what was happening rather better than contemporaries, each of whom could see only the effect on his or her particular circumstances.

7. The Land Market

When freehold land changed hands in later-medieval and very early Tudor England it did so mostly by inheritance, from father to son or other male relative or, if it passed to another family it was usually through the marriage of heiresses. It changed hands too by forfeiture to the Crown and subsequent royal grant, but very rarely by sale for cash. When sales did take place they were usually between friends, neighbours, business and professional acquaintances and political associates, which meant that changes in ownership had little effect on the social distribution of land. There was no real market because there was virtually no supply. That Robert Brudenell, an up-and-coming Buckinghamshire lawyer, purchased manors and other properties in no less than seven counties between 1494 and 1508 suggests that he had little choice. Indeed, he had begun in 1491 by leasing a farm in Stoke Mandeville, after which he leased his wife's late husband's estate in Leicestershire, only securing from the heirs a reversionary freehold interest for his own son. He himself was a younger son and was later able to purchase the family manors from his impecunious nephews. Not until 1514 did he buy the lordship of Deene in Northamptonshire which was to be the family's headquarters until the present day. When he died in 1531 Sir Robert, as he had become, created a trust enabling him to leave a substantial estate to his younger son Anthony, who immediately sold it to his elder brother Thomas. Although eager purchasers, the Brudenells shared with most landowners a deeply felt prejudice against regarding inherited land as a freely marketable commodity: a common description of freehold land was 'land of inheritance'. All landowners strove to conserve, and if possible augment, what they had inherited, and indeed, by means of the entail, to prevent their descendants from selling. The result was very considerable continuity of ownership. In the West Riding of Yorkshire out of a sample of seventy-four manors owned by gentlemen in 1428, forty were still owned by their direct descendants in 1535.

The lack of supply of land was matched by a general lack of ready money. Private vendors usually insisted on payment in full before completion of the purchase and in early Tudor England few people had much cash by them. In fact so innocent was the land-law of commercial considerations, or so hidebound by tradition, that it was not necessary to the legality of a conveyance that there should be any reference to a 'consideration', least of all to its exact amount. The most common title deed was still, around 1500, the feoffment or deed of gift and this only recorded that a conveyance had taken place. In law it was necessary only for the parties, or their agents, to give and receive livery of 'seisin', that is, possession, the vendor handing over a twig or a piece of turf in the presence of witnesses. A few lines of doggerel verse widely current at the time advised purchasers to make sure that the seller was of age, that the land was not mortgaged or in the hands of trustees, and that it was not bond-land, but made no mention of employing lawyers.

At the beginning of the sixteenth century the land market was much brisker at the level of the tenant farmer where changes, in this case of occupancy, in particular of copyholdings, had only to be presented in the appropriate manor court for approval. Such consideration as changed hands was of no concern to the court. By about 1520 this activity was gradually moving up-market into the area of freehold farms, part of the process of engrossing of neighbouring holdings. Such transfers were commonly effected by collusive actions in the Court of Common Pleas at Westminster, culminating in what were known as final concords, recorded in the well-known 'feet of fines', which thereafter constituted part of the title deeds. Not all of these actually involved a change of ownership, some being obtained in order to strengthen a title, but altogether the average annual number in the 1520s was under two hundred and fifty for the whole country. Twenty years later it was to be five times as many.

Certain changes in the law relating to land ownership were made in the reign of Henry VIII. Three statutes in particular were important, the Statutes of Uses and of Enrolments of 1536, and that of Wills of 1540. These were concerned with two closely related topics, the Crown's determination to maximize its profits from its 'feudal' tenants, that is, from landowners holding of the king by knight-service, and the desire of landowners to be free to devise at least part of their estates. As already indicated conveyance of lands to trustees to the 'use' of the conveyor, was a well-established and much-used means not only of evading the Crown's right to wardship and marriage but also of providing legacies for younger sons and unmarried daughters. Events actually played into the Crown's hands in 1535 when a panel of judges decided that a settlement on trustees made by the lately deceased Thomas Fiennes, Lord Dacre (of the South), had been intended to defraud the King. One effect of the ensuing Statute of Uses was to remove the whole matter from the Court of Chancery into the common-law courts proper, but more important the 'use', though not actually prohibited, was shorn of most of its attractions. In future the ownership, and hence the liability for feudal dues, of such lands remained with the beneficiaries of the trust. Another effect, probably unintentional, was utterly to preclude any devising of land by will, a situation remedied in 1540 when the ban was removed from all but one third of any land held of the Crown by knight-service. Now for the first time landowners could provide at common law for their younger sons, and such fragmentation of estates was bound to encourage the more widespread ownership of land and also the expansion of the land market. If the Statute of Uses had not been followed by the Statute of Wills, Henry VIII, by enforcing entails, might well have dealt a great blow to English social mobility. Even so, few men will have wished to go very far in dis-

inheriting their eldest sons. Perhaps equally important, certainly
to historians in their search for records, the Statute of
Enrolments of 1536 was designed to ensure that all changes
of ownership not effected in public were put on record, either
on the rolls of one of the London courts, especially that of
Common Pleas, or on special rolls kept by the county Clerks
of the Peace. Since the early 1520s there had been increasing
use, in place of the traditional deed of gift, of the exchange
between the parties of indentures of bargain and sale. Although
requiring a reference to the payment of an unspecified sum
of money these did not require public livery of seisin. Only
by insisting on enrolment could the Crown's county escheators
keep track of owners of land and be alerted to the need for
inquisitions *post mortem*. While such a provision no doubt added
to the cost of conveyancing it was not without some benefit
to landowners in an age when title deeds were often lost by
fire or theft. Clearly the 'Reformation' Parliament and its
successors were beginning to regard the buying and selling of
land between private persons as a normal part of everyday life.
It is not without significance that many of its members were
professional lawyers, but in their defence it must be said that
private buying of land was fraught with danger, as is well illustrated by suits brought before the Court of Chancery. Although
Henry's subjects might not have agreed, the Statute of Enrolments served their interests as much as those of the Crown.

Not everyone in high places, however, believed that the land
market should be freely open to anyone with the necessary
resources. An active land market was the surest way to a mobile
and, as some thought, an unstable society. It took a fanatical
moralist like the preacher Robert Crowley to warn yeomen
that the purchase of land, being covetous, was contrary to the
Ten Commandments, and it was he too who warned landowners against those who 'sniffed' out men's lands with a view
to purchase. But there were also serious proposals for prohibitive legislation. Thomas Cromwell toyed with the idea of
limiting merchants to the purchase of land worth no more than
£40 a year – which was a sizeable estate – preferring that they

employ their capital more usefully in trade. In 1559 a proposal
before Parliament would, if accepted, have prevented husbandmen, yeomen, and artificers from purchasing land worth over
£5 a year, clothiers, tanners and common butchers over £10,
and merchants over £50. The real significance of such proposals
is that nothing ever came of them.

In fact the Crown was largely responsible for the growth
of the land market and hence for the wider ownership of land.
There can be no doubt whatever that what really unlocked
the gates was the Crown making available for purchase large
quantities of its own land, beginning towards the end of the
1530s and continuing, as a steady trickle, even after the first
flood had become exhausted, right to the end of the century.
It had much to offer. The period from 1461 to 1509 has been
described as 'the golden age' of the Crown estate, not only
on account of its extent but also for its conservation and aggressive management. By resuming former Crown lands, by
acquiring the estates of some of its over-mighty subjects, and
by the absence of royal family commitments, the Yorkist kings,
followed by Henry VII, had added to the land owned by the
Crown in every part of the country. King Henry VIII in his
early years added only marginally to his landed inheritance.
However, the later 1530s were to see the Crown's estates very
substantially augmented, not least by the induced bequest of
the remainder of the great Percy estate, extending from Northumberland to Sussex, on the death in 1537 of Henry, sixth earl
of Northumberland. This period also brought a crop of attainders, notably that of Henry Courtenay, marquis of Exeter, a
great landowner in the south-west, who was executed in 1538.
Most important of all was the Crown's acquisition, by Act of
Parliament and by deeds of surrender, of the landed property
of some eight hundred religious communities. Monastic land,
worth at current valuation nearly £200,000 a year, was spread
over every county in England and comprised every possible
kind and size of property. In the West Riding of Yorkshire
where, admittedly, there was already a considerable concentration of duchy of Lancaster land, the addition of monastic

property brought the Crown's share to nearly half the land in the area. The 1540s brought further spoils, including the very substantial estate, mostly in the south-east of England, accumulated by Thomas Cromwell, earl of Essex, before his fall in 1540. With every toppling of a great man the Crown benefited, notably from that of Edward Seymour, duke of Somerset, in 1552, John Dudley, duke of Northumberland, in 1553, and from the failure of the revolt of the northern earls in 1570. Early in the reign of Edward VI there came the chantry property, far less valuable than the monastic lands *in toto* and comprising much smaller parcels, but for that very reason potentially attractive to people unable to afford to buy whole manors. Finally, the Crown estate was augmented at intervals from the 1530s to the end of the century by the appropriation of bishops' estates, the total number of their manors being reduced from about six hundred to about four hundred, though many of these, with royal approval, passed directly into the ownership of various of the king's lay subjects. Truly, the Tudor Crown would have been as rich as the legendary King Croesus if it had not gone far to match augmentation by alienation. Even Mary Tudor acquired by various attainders new lands worth over £20,000 a year, but restorations cost her more than £17,000 and, allowing for the refounding of monasteries and augmentation of bishoprics, she probably left the Crown rather poorer. Large amounts of Crown land were still being sold at the end of the century, especially between 1589 and 1599, and in the year 1589–90 alone there were over three hundred purchasers. The Tudor Crown, on balance, however, probably ended the century with rather more than it had had at the beginning. The fact that some properties which had been alienated once by the Crown were restored to it through attainder and then regranted to others, some several times over, added yet more to what may be called the land flow. In one county, that of Somerset, the Crown's estate in about 1536 was worth somewhat under £600 a year, hardly enough to endow a minor lord. Between then and the end of Henry VIII's reign there were added former monastic lands valued at about £7,600 a year, and by 1570 attainted land and other acquisitions, including bishops' lands, worth a further £8,000. By then, however, over two thirds of the former monastic land had been disposed of, together with a substantial part of the rest, but the total Crown estate in the county was still considerably more extensive than in 1536. Somerset may have been exceptional in that the Crown began with such a small share, but in Norfolk too the Crown gained on balance, having owned just over forty manors in 1535 and emerging in 1565 with nearly seventy. But such figures give little impression of the effect on the land market as a whole of the passage of quantities of land through Crown hands.

The statutes of 1536, not only the one dissolving the smaller monasteries, but also that setting up the Court of Augmentations to administer the property, were clearly drafted on the assumption that some of the land would be released. Not only would there be Crown leases immediately available of land handed over by the monks with 'vacant possession', but also grants of 'estates of inheritance', that is, of freeholds. At first nothing was said about sales, but these very soon materialized. Here at last was the supply which the market had been waiting for, the effect of which, as will emerge, was to cause a ripple. Between 1536 and 1539 (as also from 1546 to 1549) the real scramble was for free gifts or for sales at nominal prices – and many people actually exchanged land with the Crown – but from 1540 the market was in full swing. It was in December 1539 that there was set up the first of what was to be a long series of commissions to sell Crown lands, monastic and other, on each occasion up to a fixed amount in terms of annual value. Once dispersal began all (with certain exceptions) was available for purchase, so that at any given time after 1539 the supply situation depended on how much, rather than on what particular estates, was being fed into the market and this in turn depended on the Crown's immediate need for cash. The commissioners had strict instructions regarding the price, which was based on a current valuation, so there was no question of an auction, that is, of competing bids for specific properties. Except that as time went on the smaller properties, including those in towns which were mostly fixed rent charges, were allowed to be sold more cheaply, any variation in the terms depended in the very early days on the identity of the grantee rather than on the nature of the estate. All concessions had to be negotiated at a very high level, not lower than the Chancellor, or chief officer, of the Court of Augmentations, and he will have done little without the King's personal approval. The best bargains were the monastic sites, especially those with demesne land not yet formally leased by the Crown. The majority were granted before 1540, mostly to members of the Court circle. Informal caretaker tenancies, hurriedly arranged at the time of surrender, were easily terminated, but most of the other monastic property was subject to fairly long leases. Between the two extremes Crown leases were for a standard term of twenty-one years.

At first the commissioners' instructions were to sell at twenty years' purchase, that is, for a sum equal to twenty times the net current annual value, usually the gross rental less any fixed outgoings such as bailiffs' fees. All monastic property was also sold subject to the payment of a permanent, fixed, annual rent, notionally, and usually exactly, a 'tenth' of the current annual value. Later on, especially after 1550, the number of years' purchase was increased to take account of rising land-values in the light of the length of unexpired leases. By the later 1550s the rate was in some cases as high as thirty years' purchase and, by the 1590s, forty years'. Even so the sale price probably never quite caught up with the real value of land in terms of economic rent, that is, its value to the occupier. Indeed, it was probably always somewhat short even of its current price on the open market, and this no doubt ensured that the supply of Crown land rarely exceeded demand to the point where the market was flooded. In 1599 the commissioners were instructed – in view of the Crown's need for money for the war in Ireland – to obtain sixty years' purchase, and they did succeed for a short while but soon found that they could not sell quickly enough at that price to meet the Crown's pressing need. Hence, although this was a time of dearth and rising land-values, they had to drop the price to boost sales. Except over a long period the price of land was not governed by agricultural prices, for, unless he was able to 'rack' his rents, a landowner could not quickly adapt his income to prices. Men expected to pay a fair but not excessive price and most were content with an immediate return of 5 per cent on their capital outlay. Few were likely to improve on that in their own lifetimes.

In one respect, however, the Crown found it necessary to temper the wind in a manner which hardly served its own needs, that is, in conceding to most purchasers that the sale price could be paid in instalments, ofter over a period of up to two years. Some grantees managed to defer final settlement even longer, some probably never paid up in full, though the accountancy procedures of the Exchequer (with which the Court of Augmentations was amalgamated in 1554) ensured that such debts were not forgotten. Grantees, however, complained bitterly of administrative delays, especially in the early days when the Court of Augmentations was 'but new begun'. Waiting upon the pleasure of the new civil servants was likened by one exasperated suitor to 'the bishop of Rome's feigned purgatory' and, as in all dealings with Crown officials, grantees had to add to the purchase price substantial 'rewards' all the way from the Augmentations auditors, who prepared the particulars, to the Chancery clerks who produced the letters patent. But the real rub for those purchasing former monastic lands lay in the rule laid down in 1536 that on all grants 'of inheritance' there should be laid a tenure by knight-service of the Crown, with all that that implied in terms of the Crown's exploitation of its feudal revenues. Many owners of small, and especially of new, estates thus found themselves, or rather their heirs and heiresses, objects of the attention of the Master (and from 1542 the Court) of Wards. They also found that, in the event of their disposing of all or part of their grant, it was necessary to purchase from the Crown 'licences to alienate' and these too added to the cost of conveyancing.

How much of the former monastic land was actually given away by the Crown? It is difficult to be precise but at least it can be stated that, even in the very early years, there were few absolutely free gifts. Even grantees who were relieved of any actual purchase price usually found themselves burdened with a substantial annual 'tenth'. Some of those whom Henry VIII wished to favour obtained grants for their lives only, but these were more acceptable than mere leases for years. The most common 'gift' took the form of a reduction in the net current valuation, something which some grantees were able to achieve by corrupting officials. Most reductions were entirely above board, however, and were very precisely 'rated'. For example, in 1546 Sir William Petre, one of the two Principal Secretaries of State, bought the large former Buckfast Abbey manor and rectory of South Brent in his native Devon, currently valued at £137 12s. 10¼d. From this was deducted a notional 'tenth' of £23 15s. 3½d. and also the value of some land Petre was surrendering to the Crown in part exchange, leaving a balance of £42 16s. 8¼d.,

whereof the king's highness is pleased and content to give ... by the year £34 16s. 8½d., and so yet remaineth in overplus £7 19s. 11¾d., which rated at twenty years' purchase amounteth unto £159 19s 7d., whereof in hand £100 and the rest, being £59 19s. 7d., at Christmas next.

What protracted negotiations preceded such terms we can only guess. Petre was six months late in completing payment. The most extensive and concentrated generosity was the series of grants made by the young Edward VI in fulfilment of what the beneficiaries, all leading members of his Council, claimed had been his father's dying wishes. Estimates of the proportion of gifts vary from 25 per cent of all former monastic land in Devon disposed of by the Crown between 1536 and 1558 to only 12 per cent in the West Riding of Yorkshire up to 1546. The overall figure up to the end of Mary's reign was probably between 15 and 20 per cent.

For the great majority of grantees, even including those who succeeded in securing some degree of concession in the purchase price, the problem was how to raise sufficient cash. Especially in the early 1540s, there was a good deal of what today would be called 'stagging', that is, buying more than one could afford to retain and re-selling part, sometimes at a modest profit, before final settlement was due. This was not necessarily naked speculation but one of the few ways open to those with limited capital to acquire even a small permanent stake. Most of those who resold immediately no doubt had potential purchasers in mind, and many initial grantees were in fact acting as agents, working on an agreed commission. Not only was it necessary to know the ropes, but a large initial purchase with a view to immediate splitting by resale was a convenient way of mini- mizing the overhead costs by way not only of fees but also of gratuities. Many purchases by partnerships, followed by divi- sion of the property, were no doubt means to the same end. Lawyers often acted in partnership with other gentlemen, but it is rarely possible to discover who supplied the initial cash. Certainly a good many smaller properties filtered on to the market in this way. Those tenants who purchased their farms, including even freeholders who purchased the extinction of ancient quit-rents, were most likely to buy second-hand from agents. But even those who bought at the higher end of the market, especially towards the end of the century, often bought at second-hand from friends or, by then a well-established practice in land-conveyancing, through the agency of lawyers. In 1599, for example, the earl of Essex used his solicitor, Anthony Pembridge, to buy for him the royal manor of Little Mundon in Essex.

There can have been very few landowners in the period before 1550 or even 1560 who were able to finance further purchases out of agricultural profits, least of all out of accumulated rent income. Sales of woods, that is, of standing timber, though increasingly profitable, cannot have realized really large cash sums. The market was, however, probably greatly encouraged by the legalizing of the taking of interest. Up to 10 per cent was permitted between 1545 and 1552 and permanently from 1571. Presumably this also helped to keep the going rate of interest down, and also made it cheaper to borrow by mortgaging existing property. The mortgage itself, until later in the sixteenth century, involved an actual conveyance (a sale of the land to the lender or mortgagor), with the option of repurchase at or before an agreed date. Most landowners avoided resorting to such means in case they failed to repay, but many a property changed hands permanently as the result of a foreclosure. Although the mortgagor in such cases had little choice in the location of his new estate he will not have lent as much as the estate was worth. Indeed, it was not unknown for a mortgagor to refuse, or by some means to avoid, repayment. Later in the sixteenth century it became possible for the borrower to retain possession of his land and even to obtain the protection of the common-law courts beyond the day fixed for repayment, provided he paid the agreed interest regularly. This too must have made the raising of capital for land purchase much easier though, as always, men were still more likely to mortgage their property in order to satisfy impatient creditors, or to provide marriage portions for their daughters. By the middle years of Queen Elizabeth's reign there were some landowners, especially those actually engaged in farming, who could finance further purchases from estate profits. To this extent inflation itself was contributing to the expansion of the land market, but on the whole the chain of cause and effect was the other way round, the buoyant price of land necessitating its increasing profitability. At the same time the lack of capital generated either by industry or trade prevented the Tudor land market from creating its own inflationary spiral. Demand never greatly exceeded supply, the equilibrium being partly maintained by the net disposal (sales less purchases) of some four hundred manors by the Elizabethan aristocracy. Merchants and wealthy clothiers did, of course, augment and found estates but their numbers were very small compared with those who entered the land market with money accumulated from fees and the perquisites of office, especially under the Crown. But the effect on the land market of what may be called 'new' money must not be exaggerated. What we should be noticing is that by the middle of the sixteenth

century men were throwing off old prejudices against ration-
alizing their estates by selling parts of their inherited land. This
helped greatly to feed the market. They were coming to see
their land as a freely marketable commodity, but that did not
necessarily mean that they had come to regard it primarily as
a source of income. A carefully selected, compactly located
estate was more likely than scattered holdings to contribute to
a man's social and political status.

It is by no means easy to discover the resale price, even
of former Crown lands. And even where details are available
they need to be evaluated bearing in mind the condition of
the property, that is, how ripe it was for development – what
was called 'improvement' – this being dependent upon the
length of time since the initial purchase, and the factor of
inflation. Undoubtedly the largest short-term profits were made
by those who had been able to exploit a particular situation,
especially by buying, and later selling, undervalued Crown land.
Individual cases involving what appear to have been large
profits are not hard to find. In Yorkshire in 1539 the manor
of Appletreewick was bought by Sir Christopher Hales for
£314 and sold the same year for more than twice that sum.
The manor of Ashprington in Devon was bought in 1540 by
a member of the king's household, Francis Knolles, for just
over £500 and resold in 1542 to a merchant of nearby Totnes
for £800. Whether in either or both of these cases the local
purchaser was 'robbed' or wanted the property very badly, or
whether the original grantee by virtue of his position had
obtained a bargain, is very difficult to judge. Most profits which
can be ascertained were much more modest. Fairly typical was
the case of John Fry, a lawyer of Gray's Inn who in 1545 bought
three manors in Devon, two from a local knight, Sir Gawen
Carew, and one from the Crown. His total outlay was £839.
He subsequently sold all three to a Devon clothier, John
Willoughby, but by 1558 he could show a profit of only £161
for his enterprise. All in all, even towards the end of the century, profits made from the purchase and sale of land do not
seem to have been excessive, which is further confirmation that

as in the market for Crown grants, so in the land market generally, supply just about kept up with demand.

In any broad analysis of the effect of the expanded land market on Tudor society one can safely ignore the minority of so-called speculators and short-term profiteers. They were, as far as landed society in general was concerned, mere birds of passage, who, without having more than a marginal effect on the price of land, served a useful purpose, especially in the dispersal of the smaller units. It is difficult to generalize about their social or occupational background, but some of them at least were lawyers, some were merchants, and some were minor government officials, including most of the regional officers of the Court of Augmentations. Most were quite unknown and remained so, which hardly suggests that professional trafficking in Crown or any other land was a very lucrative occupation.

Ignoring those who bought land only to re-sell within a very short time, and hence concentrating on those who bought land with the intention of passing it on to their heirs, two fairly closely related types of purchaser assume the greatest significance in the land market. The first comprised the heads of old landed families of modest means, locked for generations in inconveniently placed estates, who were enabled from the 1540s onwards to sell outlying properties and buy land nearer home. Such a one was Sir John Fulford, the head of a very old Devon family, living (as his descendants still do) in the parish of Dunsford. Much of his inherited property lay some distance away, while the greater part of the parish, including the rectorial tithes and the patronage of the vicarage, had long belonged to the nuns of Canonsleigh fifty miles away on the Somerset border. It took Sir John a little time after the priory was dissolved in 1539 to find ways and means, but between March 1543 and July 1544 he disposed of no less than eleven of his older and outlying properties for a total of £407, enabling him in June 1544 to purchase all the Canonsleigh property in Dunsford for £548. He happened to be in the market either when business was brisk enough or the Crown was sufficiently desperate for all the cash to be called for immediately. This, as well perhaps as his distance from London, no doubt explains why Fulford bought the property, with a lot more, in partnership with a Somerset lawyer, Humphrey Colles. Each kept what he wanted, and the rest they resold. The other, and more numerous, group was that of the younger sons of established landed families who, with no more than a very modest patrimony, had become lawyers, government officials, servants of great men, or merchants, and could afford to purchase, very judiciously, sufficient land to form over the years an endowment for a new branch of the family. Such men were in no great hurry to purchase for they too needed time to accumulate sufficient capital. Like their already landed elder brothers and cousins, they bought for the long term and were more interested in the social than in the economic return, certainly until inflation really began to bite in the latter half of the century. There were, indeed, many in quite high office who, even before 1540 but especially after, paid the full price asked by the Crown or other sellers. These were the buyers who, in the long term, kept demand buoyant. Master of the Wardrobe and holder of several other lucrative government offices, Sir Ralph Sadler spent over £10,000 in the last decade of Henry VIII's reign, but in doing so he probably acquired lands worth far more than this even at the time of purchase.

But there were also men of more humble stock who had worked their passage in the king's service and for whom the availability of land offered hitherto undreamed-of prospects. One of these was John Gostwick. He seems to have been an elder son, heir to a small freehold estate in Willington, in Bedfordshire. His father probably called himself a yeoman. John's career started in Wolsey's household whence he progressed into government service under Cromwell, becoming in 1535 the first Treasurer of the new Court of First Fruits and Tenths. Until 1529 he either could not find or could not afford more than a few small tenements to add to his patrimony, but he did lease a good deal of land, including some in Yorkshire where for a time he had a post in the king's service. Through keeping his ear to the ground he was able in 1529 to purchase from the duke of Norfolk for £1,300 the whole manor of Willington. Here he quickly built himself a fine timber-and-brick house with lead water-pipes, but only in 1535 did he really begin to extend his landed interests, particularly by purchasing former monastic lands in the vicinity of Willington, lands of monasteries which he, as one of the royal commissioners, had had a hand in dissolving. His official salary was only £100 a year but he will have collected many gifts from his clients and presumably he was showing a profit by subletting his many leaseholdings. By the time of his death in 1545 Sir John Gostwick had accumulated some fifteen thousand acres. His place in history has been assured by the survival of the advice he wrote down for his son which, as we have seen, shows him to have been an efficient, businesslike but, at least towards the end of his life, certainly not a rapacious landlord.

Among the next generation of royal servants was Nicholas Bacon, a younger son of a fairly typical Suffolk yeoman, a Cambridge graduate, lawyer, Solicitor to the Court of Augmentations from 1537 to 1546, then Attorney to the Court of Wards, and finally in 1558 Lord Keeper of the Privy Seal. He made his first purchase of land, the manor of Ingham in Suffolk, in 1540, the same year in which he married Jane Fernely, daughter of a London mercer and herself shortly to be sister-in-law to Thomas Gresham. His salary was then only £10, but by 1546 he had £70 a year (and unrecorded perquisites) and he would have had no difficulty, with his city connections, in borrowing money. Between then and his death in 1578 he spent over £32,000 in purchasing land, about one third of it direct from the Crown, and only once, in 1559, did he receive a royal gift. Like Gostwick, he bought slowly and steadily, occasionally reselling the odd property, but he retained over thirty manors, half of them in his native Suffolk. So slowly did he buy that some of his later purchases could have been paid for from his landed income but by then his fees and other official earnings were at least £1,500 a year. Sadler, Gostwick and Bacon were outstanding in the scale of their purchases and therefore not typical examples of the new landowners of the mid sixteenth century. Moreover, if one rigorously excludes from those who purchased land all who had themselves inherited at least the lordship of a manor or were younger sons of substantial landowning families, the number of really 'new' men is reduced to a quite minuscule proportion of those who bought sizeable estates between the mid-1530s and the mid-1560s. Even from about 1570 to the end of the century the number was not large.

But while Bacon's yeoman origins were irrelevant by the time he entered the land market, there were plenty of yeomen still farming who bought freeholdings, usually single farms rather than the manors which, unless they were socially ambitious, did not interest them even if they could afford them. Out of a sample of over 3,000 transactions involving yeomen as purchasers between 1570 and 1640, in well over half the purchase price was under £100, implying an annual value of under £5 or between fifty and one hundred acres. Less than one in ten were for purchases above £500. But in Elizabethan England yeoman farmers supplying the market were probably better able to accumulate modest capital sums than many of the lesser gentry with no other income than fixed rents. Moreover, whereas the instinct of most gentlemen was to consolidate their lands, to build up their prestige in at least one small area, for the working farmer it made sense to buy outlying farms, often in quite distant parishes, farms whose land would complement what they occupied already. On balance, too, yeomen purchasers were more likely to be heads of families rather than younger sons. Many yeomen preferred to have their capital in their stock or at least to limit themselves to the purchase, by way of entry fines, of secure tenancies. Long leases were much sought after but they cannot have raised yeomen an inch in social status. Sometimes, however, even quite short leases were the first steps to purchases. In 1583 Robert Phillips, yeoman, paid a fine of £45 for a seventeen-year lease of the whole manor of Wispington in Lincolnshire. The rent was £8 a year. Only two years later he found over £1,000 and bought the estate. By 1603, if not before, he was styling himself 'gentleman'. But he was an exception. By and large the evidence of the land market does not show much upward mobility from yeomanry to gentry. It only shows that it was possible.

Just how long it could take is well illustrated by the case of Peter Temple. He was the younger son of a Witney merchant who had the advantage of a short spell as a student at Oriel College and subsequently at Lincoln's Inn, London (by virtue of which he could call himself a gentleman). He put behind him all thought of a professional career, if that had ever been his intention, when, in 1541, he married a cousin's widow some years older than himself and settled down, principally as a grazier, on her leasehold land at Burton Dassett in Oxfordshire. A man of many parts, raiser and fattener of sheep and cattle, wool-dealer, general trader, even bailiff for an absentee landlord, Temple took his profits when times were good and diversified his activities when they were not. It was nearly twenty years before he began buying land, and most of his early purchases were resold, no doubt at a modest if not spectacular profit. By the early 1560s he had accumulated assets of over £1,000 and he then proceeded, slowly but surely, to buy up the manor of which he had for so long been a tenant. There followed other purchases and most of them he kept. In 1571 he extended his landed interest into Buckinghamshire, but the lease he obtained of some former monastic property at Stowe still had over fifty years to run. His son John bought the freehold in the 1590s. Before going to Lincoln's Inn in 1560 John himself had spent four years as an apprentice to a wool-merchant. In 1586 he was pricked as sheriff of Buckinghamshire. The establishment of the Temple family as landed proprietors had been a long and arduous task.

Some attempt can be made to indicate, in very broad terms, what was the effect of the greatly expanded land market on the social pattern of Tudor landownership. One very obvious change in all counties was the enormous reduction in the land owned by ecclesiastical dignitaries and corporations. In the West Riding of Yorkshire this was reduced between 1535 and 1546 alone from 44 per cent to 17 per cent. Of that lost, most of it former monastic land, nearly one third had been disposed of by the Crown by the end of Henry VIII's reign. Most had gone to gentlemen, that is to smaller lay landowners, some new but mostly old, raising the total owned by gentlemen in the area from 50 per cent to over 60 per cent. During the same period the share owned by the nobility rose from about 9 to over 11 per cent. In the county of Norfolk over approximately the same period the Church's share dropped from 22 per cent to 6 per cent, partly due to Henry VIII's very profitable 'exchanges' with the bishopric of Norwich. Rather less had been sold by the Crown by 1546 than in Yorkshire but the gentlemen had already owned rather more and their share went up from 63 per cent to 71 per cent. The nobility gained only marginally here, too, from just under 10 per cent to just over 12 per cent. The years 1546 to 1555 saw a great deal more land in Norfolk being sold by the Crown. The nobility now lost ground from 12 per cent to 11 per cent, no doubt largely owing to the fall of the duke of Norfolk, but gentlemen continued to gain steadily, improving from 71 per cent to 75 per cent. This trend continued so that by 1565 the figures for the nobility and gentry were 10 per cent and 77 per cent respectively. These Norfolk figures are based on the ownership of manors and if, as seems likely, the manors owned by noblemen were on average rather larger than those of gentlemen then the actual proportion owned by the nobility may have been slightly underestimated. Nor do such somewhat crude statistics indicate how many 'new' gentlemen there were. What these and similar figures for other counties do show, however, is that during the middle third of the sixteenth century more and more land was forming part of the kind of medium-sized estate which characterized the landed resources of knights, esquires and mere gentlemen. This was, quite simply, what Professor Tawney meant when in 1940, using evidence from a handful of scattered counties, he wrote of the 'rise of the gentry'. What he had discovered was that in Elizabethan England the proportion of the landed wealth of the kingdom forming part of what he called 'medium-sized estates', already large, continued to increase. All subsequent analyses have shown how right he was!

Reference has already been made to how the release of the estates of the nobility, both by attainder, that is, via the Crown, and by sale on the open market contributed to the expansion of the land market. Broadly speaking, over the whole country, it seems that the number of manors owned by peers dropped from about 3,400 in 1558 to about 2,200 in 1600, that is, by over one third. But looking at the activities of peers in the land market alone, although in each decade between 1560 and 1600 sales were substantial, until the 1590s the net loss was reduced by around one third by purchases. Only in the 1590s did the peers fail to buy land on any scale.

There were all kinds of minor, though interesting, developments in the Tudor land market as the century wore on. Landlords were to be found purchasing their own manorial freeholdings in order to add them to their demesne or to let them to farmers. There were also instances of tenants, even copyholders, purchasing the freehold of their farms. Neither of these was common, however, and by and large the operation of the land market left both manors and their tenurial pattern intact. Far more important was the development of a market in tenancies, not so notably in the long-established transactions between tenants as in what amounts to the sale of tenancies, usually leases. Landlords had long been accustomed to exacting entry-fines, often payable in instalments and forming, to all intents and purposes, modest additions to old and accustomed annual rents. Even the exaction of fines for reversionary leases to begin at some future date was not a sixteenth-century invention. But what was new was the exaction of fines very many times larger than the old rents. It is probable that even this had been done by the monks on the eve of the Dissolution, especially for leases for exceptionally long terms. It was in a sense a process of capitalization, a marketing of land by a bargain made between landlord and tenant. The larger the fine the longer the term, and the more remote in time was the prospect of repeating the exercise. A landowner could, in this way, mortgage his estates to the great detriment of his immediate heirs. The tenant bought a period of security, time in which he, or more likely his heirs, could accumulate sufficient cash for the next occasion. At this distance in time it is very difficult for the historian to take into account, as both sides to these bargains undoubtedly did, such considerations as the agricultural potential of farms held for the long term and the ages of the tenant and his family if the lease was to be for lives. There were even competing bids, that is, auctions, in this particular sector of the private land market. Contemporaries clearly regarded it as the result of a growing demand for land. Richard Carew, writing of Cornwall in the early 1590s, noted the recent competition for farms, 'and over and above the old yearly rent they will give an hundred or two hundred years' purchase, and upward at that rate, for a fine', and this in a relatively underpopulated county, and one where in the short term there was more money to be made in tin-mining than in farming. Carew, of course, lived in that part of Cornwall which supplied the flourishing Elizabethan port of Plymouth. In the far north-west, and no doubt elsewhere, landlords arranged fictitious sales in order to levy the fines which were customary on a change of ownership. The Chancellor ruled against these general fines in 1597 but Chief Justice Coke regarded them as legal provided they were occasioned by acts of God, that is by death and succession.

The fines asked for leases of Crown lands were never substantially increased and the standard term remained twenty-one years. However, Queen Elizabeth made a habit of giving away leases, usually in reversion, no fine at all being payable, to repay debts or to reward services. Nicholas Hilliard, the miniaturist, received a reversionary lease of some land in Lincolnshire as payment for engraving the Great Seal. What is interesting here is not the value put on such royal bounties – no one expected more than modest recompense from the Queen – but the fact that such grants were normally promptly re-sold to the highest bidder, for cash. In some cases, as in that of a grant to William Byrd and Thomas Tallis, the composers, the Queen actually stipulated that the sitting tenants should be given first refusal. As most Crown land by this time was considerably under-rented, such leases could be quite profitable acquisitions. Courtiers usually disposed of them through agents, no doubt at a discount. Could the market in land go further? Such a situation is a far cry from the traditional landlord–tenant relationship. Together with the conversion of copyholdings into leaseholdings this, rather than direct agricultural exploitation, was surely the real commercialization of land. Even towards the end of the century when freehold land was more readily available, gentlemen still leased a good deal of land, much of which they sublet to farmers. It is highly probable that even yeomen did not occupy all the land they leased, but subletting is the aspect of the trade in land which has left least on record. Incidentally, Queen Elizabeth even gave away some of her woods, that is, the standing timber, to her favourite courtiers. She also, like her predecessors, sold wardships, and although not all heirs were minors, the increase in the number of land-owners, especially of those who held by knight-service of the Crown, inevitably added to the business of the Court of Wards, if not to its profitability.

The considerable expansion of the market in land in the mid and later sixteenth century brought, as another effect on English society, a great increase in business for the legal profession, not only, or even so much as, in conveyancing, but also in litigation. The actual drawing up of the deeds of conveyance remained largely in the hands of a subsidiary profession, that of the scriveners or professional writers. By the end of the century they were also acting as land-agents, either purchasing on behalf of clients or effecting introductions between sellers and buyers, though the mechanism was still very crude. To their clients it seemed that the scriveners as well as the lawyers were adept at making work for themselves: as John Norden wrote in 1607, 'In these days there go more words to a bargain of ten pound [of] land a year than in former times were used in the grant of an earldom.'

But Master John Norden himself (*c.* 1548–1625), who was the son of a Somerset yeoman farmer, was an example of yet another profession, in this case one which grew almost from scratch in Elizabethan times, which profited from the expansion of the land market. 'Mathematical practitioners' were increasingly employed to survey estates, both in listing and valuing tenancies and in making 'platts' or maps to delight not only their clients' expectations but also their eyes. Cartography, both as a science and as an art, served the Elizabethan landowner as well as, if not before, it served the traveller by land and sea. Landlords, both old and new, sooner or later wished to inform themselves of their future prospects, and to this end would arrange for a court of survey to be held at which particulars of all tenancies would be scrutinized and recorded. Where medieval landlords had been content with 'extents' listing virgates, local acres and even 'day-works', Tudor landowners called for more precision. Since 1537 when an Augustinian canon from Merton in Surrey had published *The Maner of Measurynge all maner of Land* it had been possible, by using geometric squares, rectangles, and triangles, to measure irregularly shaped fields and woods and even represent them on paper, but the real science of triangulation which revolutionized the making of maps was probably brought to England early in Elizabeth's reign by the astrologer John Dee. Before Norden, who also practised as an attorney, advanced from the mapping of manors to the mapping of counties he had used not only the plane-table but also the theodolite. Even when he had attained national fame, he retained his interest in the minutiae of fields and pastures and in his *Surveyor's Dialogue* of 1607 he endeavoured to show that the accurate mapping of estates was in the interests of both landlord and tenant. Indeed, it is difficult to exaggerate the contribution of the Elizabethan mathematical practitioners to English cultural life. Had it not been for his employment by landlords, Christopher Saxton, a professional estate-surveyor like Norden, might never have published in 1579 the first national atlas – in the form of country maps – to be printed by any country in the world. He was also one of those who alerted the Elizabethans to the aesthetic value of landscape. Even Norden's farmer had come to see in 'the field itself a goodly map for the Lord to look upon'.

8. Clergy, People, and Schools

To all Christian people only the clergy can give a child a name and admit it to full church membership, join men and women in holy matrimony, and preside over the burial of the dead. Only in exceptional circumstances such as the imminent death of an unbaptized infant, no priest being available, may laymen step into the breach, and in an age which made no provision for civil registration of marriage, only those who made their vows at the church door could expect to be regarded as truly wed. In death, as throughout their lives, Christian laymen rely upon the prayers of the clergy to protect them from the powers of darkness and to ease their passage to eternity, and in Tudor England it was the clergy who supervised the disposal of men's worldly goods. As keepers of their consciences in all their earthly dealings, as judges in the ecclesiastical courts of many of their words and actions, and as suppliers of almost everything which could be called education, the clergy governed all people's lives from the cradle to the grave. The Tudor Reformation brought many changes but its effect on the social function of the clergy was very far from revolutionary. The country's lay leaders were not unmindful of the clergy's role in disciplining and unifying society, and in particular of the power of the pulpit and the confessional as the only really effective popular media. The English Crown was in fact by tradition the great protector of the Church, of its powers, and of its resources, a position never abandoned by the post-Reformation monarchy. Above all, the Church could rely on royal support when, during the later Middle Ages and the very early decades of the sixteenth century, a minority of the king's subjects, and even some clergy, nourished a degree of disenchantment with the orthodox beliefs and practices to which the vast majority of English people still subscribed.

The Reformation in England may be said to have begun in the years 1533–4 when, by a series of Acts of Parliament, Henry VIII detached his country's Church from obedience to the Pope in Rome. Thus was he able to marry Ann Boleyn and make sure of the legitimacy of their daughter, the future Queen Elizabeth. The King and his successors, except for his daughter Mary during whose reign the papal jurisdiction was restored, now had the power, though they would not exercise it alone, of defining religious doctrine, of determining the form and content of Church services, and, by implication, of controlling the Church's institutions and their resources. The most obvious of the reforms effected by Henry VIII was in fact the dissolution of the monasteries, and only very gradually over nearly two decades were laymen in their parish churches to be required to accept changes. Except in Mary's reign, the parish clergy were largely undisturbed and indeed there were many who continued in the same benefice from before 1530 to after 1560. Their means of support remained the same and one of the reforms most necessary, the provision of parish priests able both to understand the Christian Scriptures and to teach them to their people, was still far from being achieved by the end of the century. At no time, however, was their monopoly, as ordained priests, either of the administration of the sacraments or the absolution of the penitent from their sins, ever seriously called in question. But whereas we may well wonder when, had it not been for Henry VIII's marital necessities, Protestantism would have come to England, it is unlikely that even he and Thomas Cromwell, to say nothing of Protector Somerset and Queen Elizabeth, would have carried even Parliament with them had there not already been, well before the 1530s, a good deal of dissatisfaction with the Church, with its teaching as well as with its wealth. Henry VIII's achievement was to harness popular anti-clericalism and to direct it away from the English clergy and towards the papacy. Every Tudor monarch sought to obtain as far as possible unity of religious beliefs or at least, as far as Queen Elizabeth was concerned, outward conformity. There were always those who wished to continue with the old Catholic orthodoxies, a number which in the closing decades of the century was reduced to those known then as recusants. There were also the radicals, the minority for whom reform was not going far and fast enough, the later Puritans. The latter as well as the former, in differing degrees, had their roots in the pre-Reformation Church in England, but the great majority of English people, throughout the sixteenth century, continued without either undue enthusiasm or reluctance to accept whatever spiritual beliefs and practices were offered to them. Before the Reformation and indeed until the end of Henry VIII's reign the only real dissidents were the religious radicals.

Lollardy, Lutheranism, and even Anabaptism are difficult to disentangle, except chronologically. Socially, their importance was twofold: they gave rise to the formation of separate fellowships, of secret or 'underground' groups, and they were largely confined to the families of craftsmen and merchants and to the seaports and industrial communities. They were, then, potentially socially disruptive. Those whom the Church authorities called 'Lollards', successors to a tradition of native dissidence stretching back to the late fourteenth century, were hostile to the traditional Mass, in particular to the doctrine of transubstantiation, to the necessity of confession to the clergy, and, most overtly, to the practices of fasting, of going on pilgrimages and of praying before the images of saints. Above all, they sought for all laymen direct access to the Scriptures, and much of their group activity consisted of reading and, for the majority, hearing the Bible in English. The early Tudor Lollards were mostly humble craftsmen able to maintain a certain detachment from society at large, but in Coventry in 1511–12 a minority of the forty-five persons who admitted to heresy were prominent merchants with contacts in Leicester. There were few Lollard clergy. Lollardy was, in fact, fairly easily kept under control by occasional prosecutions in the Church courts and little would have been heard of it had it not been for the activities of a few early Tudor bishops more concerned than their predecessors to root out heresy and discipline their flocks.

Anabaptists, unlike the Lollards, followed imported dogmas and only began to appear in England in the 1530s. They were great believers in independence and free will, and hence in baptism for those of riper years, a scandalous idea in a country where children were normally confirmed at the age of seven. But it was their civil disobedience, their refusal to take oaths and to bear arms, that made them anathema to governments. Over a dozen Dutch people of this persuasion were convicted and burned at the stake in London in 1535 and others were to crop up from time to time during the rest of the century, including a sect called the Family of Love which appeared in Kent in 1552, but their total numbers were never very great and they were as unpopular with other religious reformers as with conservatives.

The most important continental reforming movement which affected England before 1530 was undoubtedly Lutheranism. Grafted to a certain extent on to native Lollardy, it was much more outward-looking. It naturally took hold first, in the 1520s, in London and the seaports, from which it spread inland along the few trade-routes. Itinerant labourers and craftsmen who had already encountered native heresies were the readier to seize upon Lutheran literature brought home by English seamen. At Winchester in 1528 a resident German was reported to the bishop for allegedly denying the divine institution of confession and fasting, the value of praying to saints, and the existence of purgatory. With hindsight he appears almost a minor prophet. But alien influence can easily be exaggerated: aliens were more likely to be denounced than natives. Well before the breach with Rome, Luther's teaching had gained a great hold within one of the Church's own fastnesses, the university of Cambridge, from where it was carried into the parishes by the younger clergy and was even taken home to their convents by young monks to be passed on to novices and other residents. Without the influence spread abroad by these university-trained theologians, English Protestantism would probably not have made much progress outside London and a few other large towns in the second quarter of the century, a point underlined by the relative absence in Lancashire both of Protestantism and of graduate clergy. It was to this fraternity of university scholars that English Lutherans looked for their vernacular scriptures. William Tyndale, a Gloucestershire man and perhaps the greatest of the translators, was forced to flee to the Continent for his life in 1524, but printed copies of his New Testament, rendered directly from Hebrew and Greek texts (not mere translations from the Latin Vulgate as used by the Lollards), were smuggled into England in large numbers from 1526 onwards. As an old lady of eighty-five in 1610 Mrs Rose Throckmorton still remembered how her mother, the wife of William Locke, a London mercer, obtained a copy of the Gospel in English through her husband's overseas factor, 'whereupon she used to call me with my two sisters into her chamber to read to us out of the same . . . very privately for fear of trouble'. Tyndale's last refuge in England had been in the house of a wealthy London merchant, Humphrey Monmouth. Such lay self-help was bound to be interpreted as anti-clerical, more especially since many who embraced Lutheranism were also critical – some would say 'envious' – of the wealth of the Church in general, and in particular (like the earliest Lollards) of the landed endowments of the regular and higher secular clergy. At the same time, the New Testament brought men and women face to face with the life of Christ and his disciples, underlining the importance of the pastoral and educational function of the clergy, and helping to detach them from their preoccupation with local saints.

Last, but by no means least among early Tudor dissidents, there were the intellectuals, especially those, mostly laymen, who, though not themselves teachers, had a consuming interest in education, especially that of the laity. To call them humanists, in view of the present-day use of the term, is unfortunate, for they were, for all their interest in classical Latin literature, essentially orthodox Christians. They were, however, very

critical of the clergy as educators and contributed in this way
a great deal to anti-clericalism. Even the Dean of St Paul's,
John Colet, made a symbolic, though far from unprecedented,
public gesture when he entrusted the government of the newly
founded St Paul's School to a body of laymen, the Mercers'
Company of London. His aim was to encourage the diversion
of lay provision for the Church and its clergy into schools for
the laity. Indeed, to most of those who, especially in the later
1530s, were bent upon the partial disendowment of the
Church, even to Henry VIII, there occurred the laudable
thought that some of the proceeds should be used for the
provision of more lay education. But no one, least of all the
Henrician humanists, advocated even elementary schooling for
all. Their aims were quite clearly élitist. Only in St Paul's
School was a truly humanist (classical) education offered free
to all comers – in Colet's famous words, 'my countrymen,
little Londoners especially' – and even there no child was admitted who could not already read and write. By about
1520 most of the country's major grammar schools no longer
taught the traditional curriculum. Many of their teachers,
especially those who were laymen, were well read in the classical authors, if only through the textbooks which, especially
with the availability of print, were perhaps the greatest legacy
of the humanists. These teachers, especially bearing in mind
their close links with continental scholars, above all with the
great Dutch teacher, Desiderius Erasmus, formed a part of what
was a truly international intellectual fraternity. English human-
ism had its roots, of course, in the two universities but, even
before the Reformation, it had grown in something essentially
extramural, even metropolitan.

The contribution of London to early anti-clericalism can
hardly be exaggerated. The city, as contrasted with the seat of
government out at Westminster, was a young person's world. Its
apprentices travelled to and from the Continent on their masters'
business, and the willingness of many of the London parish
churches in Edward VI's reign to be Protestant pace-setters
probably had its roots back in the 1520s, contemporaneously

with the theological ferment enjoyed by the young men of Cambridge. Indeed, remembering the clamour in London by the common lawyers at the time of the Hunne case in 1514, may it not be that what was then London's only 'university', the Inns of Court, promoted the first overt lay challenge to the ecclesiastical establishment? Richard Hunne was a wealthy merchant-tailor who challenged the Church's right to take his dead child's robe as a 'mortuary'. He was strangled to death as he lay in the bishop of London's prison. However, Thomas More, the Church's staunchest defender, was also a Londoner, by birth, by upbringing and by his membership of the Mercers' Company. He was also a common lawyer. Learned men, whether theologians, classicists or lawyers, while often very good at encouraging disrespect towards authority, are rarely leaders in the field. Intellectual curiosity can be a bar to the real conviction which leads to action. The real initiative has to come from the politicians.

Moreover, early Tudor London, or the two universities, was not England, and the politically initiated reformation when it came had to be brought home to every parish church in the country. Here, in the 1520s and early 1530s, the picture was predominantly one of orthodoxy, or at least convention. Church courts were occupied for the most part not in rooting out heresy but in punishing men and women for sexual offences, especially bastardy. The court of the archdeacon of Norwich in the year 1532–3 dealt with sixty-three sexual offences and only nineteen cases of non-observance of the Sabbath and of saints' days, and while three people were accused of absence from church, four were in trouble for being there and causing disturbance. Churchwardens' accounts perhaps offer more reliable evidence for they show how parishioners spent their money. Until the later 1530s such accounts as survive show little change from traditional expenditure such as the repainting and clothing of the images of saints, but more parishes were installing new pulpits, and as early as the 1520s some were also finding money for 'seges', that is, seats or benches, often with elaborately carved ends. This was probably due less to a resignation to more and longer sermons than to a fashionable desire among the laity for comfort, the climax to the great late-medieval and early Tudor rebuilding of English parish churches. In York, bequests by wealthy citizens for this purpose began to feature in wills soon after 1500, and in many rural parishes all over the country the installation of benches was in full swing by the 1530s. Attempts to date those which have survived purely on the evidence of the style and subject-matter of their carving ignore the fact that in such matters pagan traditions died hard, the religious changes being largely irrelevant.

Analysis of a very large number of early Tudor wills has shown a steady stream of lay bequests to the Church persisting into the decade 1501–10, although the peak for gifts towards the repair of the fabric of parish churches had by then already passed. The first decade of the century saw a great deal of money being left for the saying of prayers for the deceased and their families, including the founding of chantry chapels. No less than forty-nine were founded in Yorkshire during the first thirty years of the century. However, by the 1520s most people were only leaving money for the saying of set numbers of masses after their death. Bequests to religious corporations had fallen off quite considerably by then, except to the houses of friars, but people continued to leave small sums to individual monks and nuns, especially those who were their relations, acceptance of which was apparently not prohibited. Bequests to augment the income of the secular clergy, never very great, actually rose overall during the first thirty years of the century and this is significant in view of the fact that there is little sign among the laymen who embraced ideas of reform of any concern about the very low income of the parish clergy, especially that of curates and other stipendiary priests.

The main source of the parochial clergy's income was tithe, whose payment, both in parishes appropriated by monasteries and in non-appropriated parishes, was a frequent matter of dispute. Only the really poor could avoid liability for a levy which the Church's law laid on all material gains, crops, stock, wages and, though much more difficult to assess, trading profits. There is no evidence that even the most outspoken critics of Church wealth actually encouraged laymen to withhold their tithe, or indeed that early Tudor people were any more reluctant than their forebears to pay up. The frequent provision in wills of small sums for 'tithes forgot' was no Tudor innovation. What appears to have roused more lay resistance on the eve of the Reformation was the Church's demand for mortuaries, the traditional payment to the parish priest of the deceased parishioner's second best beast or other possession, the best, in the case of a tenant farmer, being due to his lord as a 'heriot'. However, it would be wrong to imagine that parsons and people on the eve of the Reformation were at loggerheads. Parish churches, especially in rural areas, were the centres of community life, of plays and pageants, and of many purely secular activities, of family gatherings and of most fun and games, of church-ales and musters, and, largest by far of the gathering of people under one roof, of religious festivals. Few people any longer went on long-distance pilgrimages – even Canterbury Cathedral was feeling the pinch of fewer visitors and fewer offerings long before the Reformation – but both on holy days and at other times people did visit neighbouring parishes, especially those fortunate enough to possess shrines offering immediate, and, by way of relics, actual physical, access to particular saints.

The Reformation Parliament during its first session in 1529 passed a number of Acts intended by its lawyer members to remedy some of what they considered to be the worst abuses of the clergy, in particular non-residence. Perhaps the most interesting part of the statute against plurality of benefices was its exemption of those whose first living was worth under £8 a year, for the *Valor Ecclesiasticus* of 1535 was to show that over half the incumbents of the country's parochial benefices claimed to have incomes of under £10 a year, and a third to be receiving less than £5. The same statute also prohibited the clergy from leasing land to farm and from engaging in trade. Mortuaries too were dealt with by Parliament, being made

payable in future only by those with personal estate of ten marks
(£6 13s. 4d.) and over, and even parishioners worth £40 and
over in goods were not to be required to contribute more than
10s. Clearly laymen were now on the offensive and a proposal
in 1531 that it should be made an offence for any layman 'to
say or report that there is no good priest', or for any clergy-
man to say 'that laymen love not priests', was not pursued.
But the parliamentary attack, after culminating in the Sub-
mission of the Clergy in 1531, moved over to matters quite
beyond the comprehension of ordinary parishioners, most of
whom knew nothing about appeals to Rome or the consequences of their restraint. They did know, however, in 1533
if not before, that the King was putting aside Queen Katherine,
and, if they barely understood his reasons, they certainly felt
sorry for a wronged wife. Alien she might be, but her badge,
that strange foreign fruit the pomegranate, had appeared on
sculptured capitals and carved screens in many parish churches
up and down the country. For Ann Boleyn most people had
scant regard, certain persons in Cornwall being committed to
the stocks and the pillory in December 1533 for speaking
seditious and 'opprobrious' words of the Queen's grace.

But the people of Cornwall, shortly after Ann Boleyn's be-
heading three years later, were to learn from Henry's new archbishop, Thomas Cranmer (for it was surely his doing), what
kind of work pattern was required of all good Protestants. In
1536 Convocation, the parliament of the higher clergy, decided
that the number of holy days was the cause of 'much sloth
and idleness, the very nurse of thieves, vagabonds, and divers
other unthriftyness and inconveniences [such] as [the] decay
of good misteries and [useful] arts'. Holy days, having been
instituted by men not by God, were described as the occasion
of 'excess, riot and superfluity', and excuses for wasting good
weather when all should be busy bringing in the harvest.
Sundays remained sacrosanct, but, with certain exceptions, all
church dedication feasts were henceforth to be celebrated on the
first Sunday in October and although the feasts of patron saints
could be observed, all might work on such days. From July

to September, the months of the harvest, and during the three law terms, holy days were forbidden entirely except for the feasts of the Apostles, of the Blessed Virgin Mary, St George, Ascension Day, the nativity of St John the Baptist, All Hallows and Candlemas. In 1541 the feasts of St Luke, St Mark and St Mary Magdalene were restored. Henry VIII relieved those of his subjects who could afford the luxury from some of the rigours of the Lenten fast, permitting them, in March 1538, because of the scantiness and high price of fish, to consume milk, butter, eggs, cheese and other 'white meats'. His proclamation added that he did not expect them to 'abuse or turn the same [privilege] into a fleshly or carnal liberty' but to continue to mortify their flesh in accordance with their Christian profession. Queen Elizabeth, as is well-known, restored the full rigours of weekly fish-eating in the interests of her navy.

Just as the medieval Church had in so many respects, including the Lenten fast, accommodated itself to economic and social necessity, so it is difficult during Cranmer's primacy to disentangle religious reform from social discipline. The restriction of holy days had much to do with fears in high places about the potential for disorder of large gatherings. Thomas Cromwell's Injunctions to the Clergy in 1536 laid down not only that children and servants were to be taught the Lord's Prayer, the Creed, and the Ten Commandments in their mother tongue (not a novelty but the emphasis was a sign of the times), but also that they should be put 'either to learning or to some other honest exercise, occupation, or husbandry', lest they fall into idleness and begging. Images and their worship had long been a target of Protestant barbs, and of course the devotion of the laity to the saints was an obstacle in the way of the God-centred religion of the reformers, but they also attracted offerings which might be better used if placed in parish poor-boxes. Cromwell's first Injunctions to the Clergy in 1536 merely forbade them to 'extol' reputed 'relics' of saints or the miracles attributed to them, but parishioners were also to be dissuaded from attributing particular powers to individual saints, an admonition which, if obeyed, must have cut deep into popular beliefs. However, the instruction to the clergy to tell their people that 'it shall profit more their souls' health if they bestow that on the poor and needy which they would have bestowed upon ... images or relics' indicates how far the Supreme Head or those who spoke on his behalf were in 1536 from abandoning completely the doctrine of justification by works. Two years later the clergy were ordered to remove 'feigned' (counterfeit or false) images, which attracted the worship due to God alone. No candles, tapers or wax effigies were to be set before images, these last having been very popular as reminders to the saints of people's physical ailments. How quickly parishes responded is difficult to discover. Some did so with alacrity: four men in the small parish of Rewe near Exeter removed a large collection of garments, coins, rings, girdles, and even silver ships offered in times past to certain images in their church. They claimed they were only obeying the King's injunctions and that the goods had been sold for the maintenance of the fabric, but they reckoned without the lay lessee of the rectorial income who took them to Chancery. Images were not ordered to be completely removed from English churches until 1547, which, intentional or not, was a slight concession to their undoubted importance as visual aids to unlettered congregations. In practical terms, the loss of offerings to saints was, in proportion to their resources, as great a loss to parochial finances as it was to the great monastic churches, and unlike the latter the parishes had to carry on and find alternative sources of income, church-ales and the like.

If the loss of their saints who, after all, had been a great source of comfort to ordinary parishioners, was a long-drawn-out process, so also was their relief from the fear of purgatory, the fear which had induced so many people to provide in their wills for the saying of the prayers which they believed would lessen the pains and the period of their coming agony. As early as 1534 Cranmer forbade the clergy to preach about purgatory, although he himself was still reserving judgement on its existence. The King was probably never converted and the Act of Six Articles of 1539 reaffirmed the utility of prayers for the dead, though admitting that the Scriptures were silent on the details of purgatory. The same position was taken by the bishops in Convocation in 1543 but Cranmer managed to include the important reservation that prayers should be offered not for specific souls but for all Christian people. Not until the very end of the reign of Edward VI did Cranmer's Articles of Religion, the basis of Queen Elizabeth's Thirty-nine Articles of 1563, finally condemn the doctrine of purgatory, along with the worship of saints, as 'repugnant to the word of God', but by then things had happened which must have had a far more powerful effect on popular belief in purgatory than official directives. These were the dissolution of the monasteries and the chantries, both of them, but especially the latter, essentially intercessory institutions. The legacy, respectively, of many centuries and of many generations, they disappeared from England between, very roughly, 1536 and 1550. As Bishop Hugh Latimer, one of the period's most radical religious reformers was to declare, '[as] the founding of monasteries argued purgatory to be, so the putting of them down argueth it not to be'.

In every other respect the importance of the Dissolution in the period 1536–40 as an integral part of the Henrician Reformation is arguable. Many small religious communities had been dispersed before the Reformation and their endowments diverted either to other religious uses or into Crown hands, notably by Cardinal Wolsey, and many of the larger houses continued to exist until 1539–40 within what was virtually a national Church. The effect of the confiscation and disposal by the Crown of most of their landed property was very important in relation to the land market and the social distribution of landownership, but the recipients were not all enthusiastic Protestants. In 1559 when England once again became Protestant there were Catholics in both Houses of Parliament who were in favour of the royal supremacy (though not of religious uniformity) because it was likely to facilitate their recovery of lands restored by Mary Tudor to the Church. Even the social significance of the Dissolution can be exaggerated:

the loss of monastic charity was not really serious and may even have had a positive value in reducing the amount of casual alms-giving. Perhaps the greatest single effect of the Dissolution on parish life was the passage of so many impropriated rectories and even vicarages, with the advowsons (rights of presentation) of an even greater number of these parochial benefices, via the Crown into lay hands. In the diocese of Canterbury the amount of lay patronage more than doubled between 1533 and 1553, from 16 per cent to 38 per cent, a surprisingly high proportion in an area so dominated by the primate, but the situation was not dissimilar in other dioceses. Advowsons were, and still are, a form of real, that is freehold, property, and, along with tithes, could be bought, sold and also leased. Not until the Church was riven by Puritanism in Elizabeth's reign was the true religious significance of the enormous lay intrusion resulting from the Dissolution made clear, although the situation was little different from that in the early twelfth century when most parochial benefices had been in the gift of their lay founders or their descendants. To the extent that the new lay rectors were committed by the terms of their grants to appoint stipendiary vicars, parishes formerly dependent on the uncertain ministrations of religious houses, especially those of Augustinian canons, may have found themselves pastorally better served. By and large, however, lay possession of the revenues of the parish clergy was an obstacle to the improvement of the lesser clergy's standard of living. Pluralism and non-residence continued to be widespread. The collection of tithes and other parochial income had often been leased to laymen by the monasteries, so in this respect many parishioners will have noticed little difference, at least not until inflation made the new owners dissatisfied with old monetary compositions and anxious to collect the tithe once more in kind. Clerical rectors had the same idea and tithe cases became even more numerous in the Church courts. The Reformation had given no comfort to laymen as payers of tithe: in 1536 an Act of Parliament required everyone to pay whatever was customary in his parish. Offenders were still to be cited in the ecclesiastical courts but for the first time JPs were brought in to imprison recalcitrant offenders. In 1540 a further statute allowed laymen, as lessees or owners of tithe, to sue in the ecclesiastical courts. In the court of the archdeacon of Lincoln tithe causes (actions) increased from 4.4 per cent of all causes in the year 1536–7 to 29.5 per cent in 1544–5. In 1549 yet another Act of Parliament did exempt day-labourers from the payment of tithe on their earnings, and also, for a period of seven years, the occupiers of newly cultivated land, this being part of the government's effort to encourage tillage and reduce the price of grain, but it underlined the duty of all parishioners to make their voluntary offerings to the parson or his assigns, dues later turned into the annual Easter offering. This Act had its more rigorous aspects, however, in that it did away with the ancient practice of allowing tithe-payers, on oath, to assess their own liability.

The significance for the ordinary parishioner of the dissolution of the chantries early in the reign of Edward VI was rather different. Although existing only in a minority of parishes, chantries were far more an integral part of secular religious life than the monasteries, and although, even in the most traditional parishes, there was no longer much enthusiasm for the provision of prayers for the dead, many people must have felt very deeply disturbed at the flaunting of the wishes of their ancestors. Any assault on prayers for the dead could be regarded as an attack on family piety. On a more practical level the disappearance of the chantry priests meant the loss of a good deal of non-institutional elementary education. When, in 1549, men from Devon and Cornwall were rebelling against the use of the new English Prayer Book, their objection to the new order of confirmation was on the grounds that children would never learn the words unless they had been to school, evidently in those parts now a remote possibility.

Many of the endowed grammar schools too were attached to institutions which were basically chantries or had developed out of them. These were declared to be exempt from royal confiscation of their endowments and there were many interested parties bestirring themselves towards the end of

Henry VIII's reign in the hope of saving old foundations by giving them educational functions. For example, some time before 1548, chantries in Bromsgrove, King's Norton, and Stourbridge in Worcestershire were transformed by their respective trustees into what were primarily grammar schools. Elsewhere the metamorphosis of neo-religious into purely craft guilds led to the disappearance of their priest-schoolteachers. At Worcester, the town's Trinity Guild ceased to provide a school and in 1541 a new free grammar school was provided as part of the King's package setting up the new cathedral out of the dissolved priory. This meant, however, that in Worcester secondary education remained the preserve of the Church. Endowed schools which had no explicit intercessory function, however much their founders had intended the whole ethos of the education to be Christian, were left intact. Winchester and Eton, being attached to colleges of secular priests, were undisturbed. Authentic stipends payable to schoolmasters, clerical or lay, out of the confiscated chantry property were honoured by the Crown, although the recipients were placed under no obligation to continue to teach.

While there was no official intention of reducing the facilities available for either elementary or secondary education there were no strenuous efforts made to increase the number of schools by using some of the resources taken from the Church. The new cathedrals, with their schools, were Henry VIII's only contribution to educational facilities, but in them the curriculum, as in the monasteries they replaced, was of necessity subordinate to the needs of cathedral worship. The so-called 'free grammar schools of Edward VI' were very largely refoundations, only a few such as Bath, Birmingham, Shrewsbury and Spilsby in Lincolnshire being entirely new. Some of the Church's former resources found their way via laymen into new or enlarged endowed grammar schools, and to this extent the Reformation played a marginal role in continuing the already strong tradition of the founding by laymen of schools for children with professional or administrative careers in mind. The overall effect of the Henrician and Edwardian

Reformation was, then, marginally to increase the provision of secondary education but to put a good deal of elementary education at risk. Children 'meet for learning' were slightly better provided for in 1560 than in 1530, but the general literacy rate had not been anyone's concern and had probably not improved. The real difficulty, probably as great in 1560 as thirty years earlier, was to find adequate schoolmasters. For university graduates the Church still offered a better living, or at least greater security.

It is as impossible to ignore as it is difficult to assess the effect of printing on English culture in general and on religious education in particular. Obviously printed books could be circulated more widely and more cheaply than manuscripts. But whether they were read and whether, as a direct result of printing, there were more learned or even literate men and women in England are difficult questions to answer. Wealthy people had always been able to afford to buy what they wanted to read and those most able to read had always had access to libraries. With print there is no doubt that ownership of books became more fashionable. The printed Bible and other devotional literature undoubtedly played an important part in the spread of Protestantism (and, in Mary's reign, of Catholicism) but their availability in parish churches came about very slowly. There is, too, the inescapable fact of government censorship. Even Henry VIII's Latin grammar was required to be used to the exclusion of all rivals.

So far we have been dealing with the more negative, or at best neutral, impact of the religious changes on ordinary Tudor people. Equally important, if not in the long run more so, was the legalizing and indeed active promotion of the use of vernacular scriptures and liturgy. As early as June 1530 when Henry VIII was devoting himself almost exclusively to obtaining his 'divorce' from Rome, he issued a proclamation with an interesting twofold message. First, no doubt in order to demonstrate his orthodoxy, his subjects were ordered to put away 'blasphemous and pestiferous English books', especially those printed abroad. No doubt he had in mind particularly

Tyndale's New Testament. But after denying any need for the whole Bible to be made available in English, or for the Scriptures to be expounded other than by priests in their sermons, he promised that if his subjects would abandon 'all perverse, erroneous, and seditious opinions', it was his intention to commission 'great, learned, and Catholic persons' to translate the Scriptures into the English tongue. By 1535 the former English friar, Miles Coverdale, had published on the Continent the first complete English Bible, having borrowed much of his translation of the New Testament from Tyndale. His own limitations as a scholar (he knew little Hebrew) were more than balanced by his command of the English language. For over four hundred years English people have enjoyed singing, if not always quite understanding, his version of the Psalms. The first edition of Coverdale's Bible appeared in England, with royal approval, in the same year, printed by a Dutch resident of Southwark. A rival version published shortly afterwards also had overseas connections, its translator, 'Thomas Mathew', being John Rogers, chaplain to the English merchants in Antwerp. A third version, by Coverdale, was actually set up in type in France and only with difficulty were the printed sheets brought by Thomas Cromwell to England in 1539. By then the Bible was, by contemporary standards, potentially big business, for, tentatively in 1536, and with more conviction in 1538, royal injunctions had ordered every parish church in the country to obtain a copy of the whole Bible in English so that all laymen able to do so might read. Neither the new-found enthusiasm of some of the bishops, nor the possible influence of Ann Boleyn, nor even Cromwell's efficiency and business instincts, can detract from the part played by Henry VIII, but Cromwell should be allowed the credit at least for limiting the price to what every parish should have been able to afford. The King later thought it necessary, in the interests of public order, to restrict Bible-reading to noblemen, gentlemen, and substantial merchants. Only a society which took sumptuary legislation in its stride could have accepted, without public protest, the statutory denial of the vernacular Bible in 1543 to women (except gentlewomen), artificers, apprentices, journeymen, serving-men under the degree of yeoman (in noble households), husbandmen and labourers. Luther's encouragement to women to think for themselves had not gone entirely unheeded in England but it is very unlikely that any but gentlewomen and a few wives of merchants and urban craftsmen could read the Bible or any other literature. Henry VIII's no doubt quite sincere revulsion, communicated to Parliament in 1545, to the word of God being 'disputed, rhymed, sung, and jangled in every alehouse and tavern', has its modern echoes in the objections once raised to the broadcasting of religious services, that men might be listening in public houses with their caps on.

The repeal of the later Henrician statutory restraints on reform by his son's first parliament opened the door to great changes in parochial religious life. As recently as 1539 Henry VIII had urged the clergy to explain to their congregations the significance of holy water, Candlemas, the giving of ashes and the bearing of palms. Quite suddenly, in 1547–9, it was all changed. To the real conservatives the loss of the Act of Six Articles in particular infringed their liberty to worship in the old way. To a 'reactionary' priest like Robert Parkyn, vicar of Adwick-le-Street near Doncaster, the abrogation of old ceremonies spelled loss rather than release. He regretted the disappearance of processions, of the bearing of candles in men's hands, and of the sanctifying of the ashes, that the Passion was no longer read in Latin at Mass but in English only, that no altars were washed on Easter Thursday, no Maundy given, no fire lit on Easter eve and no paschal candle, and on Rogation days no procession around the fields, 'but cruel tyrants did cast down all crosses standing in open ways despitefully'. But perhaps his parish had conformed more than others, for in 1550, when all stone altars were required to be replaced by wooden communion tables, it was still necessary to reaffirm the outlawing of the invocation of saints, of the use of bede-rolls, of images, relics, holy bread and water, ashes and palms.

How rapidly did Protestantism take hold in England? Evidence derived from the verbiage of wills, though biased in that it probably reflects the beliefs of local scribes (many of them, however, parish priests) and certainly of older people, is probably the nearest we shall ever get to gauging popular religious trends. The crucial section is the opening sentence where the traditional testator invoked the saints, but the Protestant commended his soul to God alone. Much can be learned too from any provisions regarding funeral arrangements. The London chronicler Wriothesley thought it sufficiently eccentric to be worth remarking that Alderman Humphrey Monmouth, draper and friend of Tyndale, left instructions in 1537 that he should be buried without candles, bells or chanting priests and that instead of leaving money for masses he provided for the preaching of thirty sermons, each to be followed by a *Te Deum* praising God for the King. Monmouth was a thoughtful man, however, or perhaps he did not want to cause trouble, for he instructed his executors to pay to his parish church all customary charges as though he had all the traditional rites. Very few wills proved in the 1530s were other than entirely traditional. Such trends as can be detected in the 1540s were towards neutrality, omitting the saints but with no clear commitment to new doctrines. In London, and surprisingly in the county of Yorkshire (especially in Halifax and the textile districts of the West Riding), and also in Nottinghamshire, as many as a quarter were neutral. In Kent by the later 1540s over half of those who died showed more positive signs of Protestant belief, but this was a county that was not only traditionally avant-garde but was influenced by Cranmer and by the preaching tours of university men which he organized.

With the knowledge of hindsight it is possible to project certain trends back into the years before the Reformation. For example, far more chantries had been founded in the north and west in the early sixteenth century than in the Midlands and south-east. This surely implies, in the former, not so much a resistance to change as a different time scale. It took considerably longer for Cambridge graduates to penetrate into

Lancashire, either as parish clergy or itinerant preachers, and
when they got there they had little indigenous dissent to work
on. Town and country had exhibited similar trends, far less
money having of late been subscribed for chantries in the former
than in the latter. This may have been partly due to urban
decay but we would be unwise to conclude that poverty
necessarily bred religious radicalism. It was the rich Londoners
rather than the poor who led the way. Analysis of 'professors
of the Gospel', as the reformers called themselves, between 1525
and 1558, known very largely through the pages of John Foxe's
Book of Martyrs, does in fact indicate a concentration in the
towns, over 60 per cent if London and the two university
cities are included, and over 30 per cent without them, compared with nearly 40 per cent in rural parishes. But if market
towns are included with the villages, the rural total is over
50 per cent compared with some 47 per cent in the urban areas
proper. Whichever way, bearing in mind the predominantly
rural location of the population, it is clear that a higher proportion of people in towns than in the country were Protestant
activists. However, on the evidence of wills there was less inclination towards reform in York itself (about one in twenty)
than in its rural hinterland. Exeter too remained very attached,
though with certain outstanding exceptions, to the old ways.
One of its exceptions was John Hooker, later to be City
Chamberlain, who as a young man in the later 1540s was one
of the few Englishmen at that time to travel abroad and sit
at the feet of the great continental reformer theologians such as
Peter Martyr who held court at Strasbourg. It must have
exasperated Hooker to see how slowly the parish churches of
his native city acquired their Bibles and later their copies of
Erasmus's *Paraphrases*.

The towns might have been expected to set the pace of change
because it was to them that there came, from the 1530s onwards,
the succession of licensed preachers. They attracted large crowds
but often more abuse than enthusiasm. This was the last thing
the government wanted and the more effective they were the
more they tended to arouse the passions of both the diehards

and the radicals. Londoners enjoyed the most regular entertainment of this kind, especially at Paul's Cross, just as they were the most frequent witnesses of public executions and burnings. The provincial towns were also, from time to time, arenas for such spectacles: if not always the scene of the death of traitors, they were at least the recipients of their dismembered 'parts'. Many extremists, including, while Henry VIII lived, both conservatives and reformers, having been persuaded to confess their errors, merely bore the symbolic faggot.

How could anyone be sure, even after 1547, for how long and how far reform would proceed? Wise men hedged their bets. In Edward VI's reign William Gatchet of York asked to be buried 'according to the King's affairs' but left a shilling to his parish priest to pray for him. What may be called 'neutral' or uncommitted wills were very common, for Protestant conviction did not yet run very deep. In 1549 Sir William Paget warned Protector Somerset that although 'the old religion is forbidden by a law ... the use of the new is not yet printed in the stomachs of eleven of twelve parts in the realm'. He may well have been right. To a large extent this was due to the failure of the clergy, either through ignorance or wilfulness, to instruct their flocks. The new liturgy was widely misunderstood. During the early stages of the rebellion in Devon and Cornwall in 1549, partly sparked off by the new Prayer Book, some of the leaders, whether priests or laymen is not clear, apparently believed that for men and women to enter the chancel of a church to receive communion was immoral. Until then they had done this only immediately after being joined in matrimony. How many laymen, without professional help, could understand the Bible's message? How many could read it for themselves? Indeed, the conservative bishop of Winchester, Stephen Gardiner, was probably not far out when he said that most English people were not even very good hearers.

However, by 1550, religion was very visibly changed. Hundreds of the former monastic churches were in ruins or had been converted to residential or parochial use, their precinct walls no longer even a symbolic barrier between the religious and secular world. Only the cathedral churches, new and old, showed little change, their most notable ornaments, the great tombs of medieval kings and bishops, remaining intact. By comparison parish churches must have looked bare and colour-less, bereft not only of their smaller images but also of their great roods, and some even of their late-medieval and early Tudor screens. The long-expected raid on their goods, that is, their plate and vestments, was soon to be in full swing and had indeed been anticipated by many parishes. When the royal com-missioners came to St Olave's in Exeter they were told, by no doubt poker-faced wardens, that 'by the consent of the parish' they had sold a good deal of their plate to pay for a new font, an iron 'desk' (or lectern), a pulpit and 'the painting of God's word about the church'.

The reign of Mary Tudor, with its nearly total official rejection of Protestantism, was perhaps exactly what the parishes needed, a breathing-space. It was amazing how much discarded church furnishing miraculously reappeared. About eight hundred people, largely men and women of some substance, found Mary's regime so insupportable that they fled abroad, nearly half of them from London, the Home Counties and East Anglia. Most of the martyrs too, in this case largely men and women of small means, came from the south-east, but that may have been largely due to the zeal of Cardinal Pole and Bishop Bonner of London. Every death by burning lessened Mary's chances of success, but even John Hooker of Exeter, who liked nothing better than a good sermon, apparently decided that the preservation of order was worth a Mass. If he was a member of an underground congregation, even his later voluminous city chronicles revealed nothing about it. However, Mary's short reign ensured that the break with the past would never again be so complete, for in spite of the horrors of Smithfield there were lasting gains. Some of the colour and the pageantry came back into the churches for good, so that further iconoclasm by the Puritans was to be very hard work indeed.

But Mary's reign did little to halt the decline in parochial

church music brought about by the Reformation, and in particularly by the new Prayer Books of 1549 and 1552 which contained almost none of the provisions for liturgical music which
had been such a feature of the old diocesan 'rites'. In this
respect England had cut herself off completely from Lutheranism, Cranmer apparently being influenced by Calvinism and
even by the extreme Zwinglian views of Bishop John Hooper
of Gloucester. A further factor was the post-Reformation decay
and disappearance of organs which accompanied, if they were
not directly due to, the removal of rood lofts. To moderate
Protestants choirs were seen as a hindrance to the audibility
of the vernacular liturgy, and to extremists the singing of hymns
and anthems contravened the principle that only the words of
the Scriptures should be heard. The Psalms of David were 'lined
out', that is, recited in the vernacular by parish clerks to be
repeated by largely illiterate congregations, but even the clerks
lost a good deal of their former status when the minor orders
were abolished in 1559. The metrical versions of the Psalms,
in simple harmonic style by Sternhold and Hopkins, were first
made widely available soon after Elizabeth's accession, but they
were intended for domestic not congregational use, and they
were likened by the Queen to 'Genevan jigs'. Many of the
clergy resisted their liturgical use, especially in the cathedrals,
but the demand of laymen to be allowed to exercise their lungs
at the end of a long sermon seems to have spread into the
churches from open-air gatherings at Paul's Cross and elsewhere, and by no means all who sang the Psalms were Puritans.
Church bells, in spite of Puritan efforts, were never entirely
silenced, but in parish churches choirs became a rarity. It was
otherwise, of course, in the cathedral churches where a high
degree of musical professionalism survived, though not everywhere to the high standards attained in the Chapel Royal, in
Westminster Abbey and at Windsor. Here, at least, and in some
of the college chapels, not only did the traditional liturgical
music flourish but it reached new heights of excellence under
the influence and example of composers such as Thomas Tallis
and William Byrd, not forgetting the support of the Queen

herself. The effect of such music in setting new standards for secular music can hardly be exaggerated.

In theory the dissolution of the monasteries and chantries should have left England with a surplus of clergy. It was no part of Cromwell's or Henry's plan to make martyrs and elaborate provision was made for pensioning off the dispossessed but all the men also had the option of receiving licences to seek employment as secular clergy. The nuns probably had little alternative but to return to an uncertain welcome by their families, unless they were abbesses who, like their male counterparts, had more than adequate pensions. Underlying all the official pension arrangements was a kind of rough logic which related them to age, security, and the financial resources which, as members of their communities, the religious were losing, rather than to their individual needs. They were, after all, all members of a hierarchical society. For the rank and file of both sexes pensions which were adequate in the 1530s (and not all were) soon became quite inadequate with inflation. But they were in this respect little worse off than most unbeneficed clergy. For some, particularly the older generation, re-entry into the world was a personal tragedy, but for many of the younger men and women, especially those who had entered religion while no more than children, it no doubt offered all the excitement of a new start. The great majority needed a supplementary income and that so many of the men found clerical employment in due course can only have been due to the fact that fewer priests had been ordained in the 1530s. In the large diocese of Lincoln, whereas between 1520 and 1535 the number ordained each year never fell below fifty-five, between 1536 and 1546 it never rose about thirty. In the diocese of Durham no priests at all were ordained between 1536 and 1544 and even in London there was a sharp drop after 1537. The result was an actual shortage of priests in these dioceses and as well as many ex-monks many previously unbeneficed secular clergy were able to obtain secure employment. In Kent, however, there continued to be a surplus, probably due to the magnetism of Canterbury, and also to the continuance of a high rate of pluralism. Whether or not there was overall a reduction in clerical under-employment, it is clear that the 1540s and 1550s saw no improvement in the intellectual calibre of the parish clergy. Graduates were still a minority. Moreover, clerical marriage, one of the attractions of continental reform, was for long denied to the English clergy. The reaffirmation of clerical celibacy in 1539 obliged Archbishop Cranmer to send his wife home to Germany and in 1549 it was only with the utmost reluctance that Parliament lifted the ban on clerical marriage. The enthusiasm with which so many of the clergy then took wives was never matched by the approval of their parishioners. Those who had previously gossiped about clerical 'concubines' would very readily have echoed the diehard Robert Parkyn's reference to priests 'using [women] as their wives'. Consciously or not, Parkyn makes an interesting conjunction when he refers to married priests who 'would make no elevation at Mass after consecration [as in the new Prayer Book], but all other honest priests did according to the old laudable fashion'. It was in fact one and the same parliament which authorized both the marriage of priests and the English liturgy. Many of the priests who married before 1553 were not in fact dedicated reformers, and indeed the issue of clerical marriage was not a theological one. Moreover those parts of the country where, when the ban was reimposed in Mary's reign, the greatest number of clergy chose to be deprived of their English cures rather than of their wives, bears no particular resemblance to the geographical distribution of early Protestantism.

The task of the immediate post-Reformation generation of parish clergy was certainly not made any easier by the convolutions of a state-ordered religion. The examples of parish priests whose pastorate spanned the whole period from the 1530s to the 1560s and beyond, including Robert Parkyn, are legion and it was very much to their credit that the people's Christian faith itself survived. Uncertainty, even in the mind of Archbishop Cranmer, concerning the nature of the eucharistic elements, led to a great deal of popular irreverence and ribaldry concerning the sacrament of the altar. Moreover, as in medieval times, paganism and local folk-cultures were never very far below the surface, though perhaps not as much in England as on the Continent. In 1542 Henry VIII and Parliament made it a felony, and hence punishable by death, to practise witchcraft or indeed any other occult art, even including the supernatural discovery of stolen goods. The Devil was, of course, a reality to all faithful Christians and everyone was aware of the dangers of being 'possessed', but the rite of exorcism had rarely been used in pre-Reformation England and cases of witchcraft had not often come before the Church courts. It is tempting to connect the Act of 1542 with religious conservatism, but possibly it reflected only the King's own determination to achieve, by statute, 'unity of opinions'. There is no evidence of any judicial proceedings, and its repeal in 1547, along with so much other Henrician legislation, probably went unnoticed. By 1563, when a further Act was passed, the situation had changed somewhat. The impact of the doctrinal changes, at the popular level, had been largely negative and in the vacuum thus created certain unhappy people were encouraged to exploit their neighbours' credulity. Certainly by 1563, if not in 1542, there was felt by many influential people to be a need for the state as well as the Church to arm itself. The Church courts in England, in particular those of the archdeacons, continued in business, and indeed were very busy for the rest of the century, but had little desire or encouragement to extend their sphere of operations. Indeed it was no part of Protestant doctrine to fight black magic with any other kind of supernatural weapon and exorcism as a religious rite was abandoned, in the second Edwardian Prayer Book, even from the ceremony of baptism. Few laymen and no orthodox priests doubted the power of the Devil, but his influence had to be resisted by personal faith and prayer. Any more positive action against witchcraft had to come from the lay power as part of its business of providing justice and keeping the peace. The Act of 1563 was to survive until 1604 and there is some, though very localized, evidence of its implementation. Ironically, its effect was probably to increase popular belief in witchcraft, belief which was condemned by both Protestants and Catholics alike. Both the exercise and the fear of witchcraft in later Tudor England, neither of which must be exaggerated, were largely the result of the failure of both Church and State to inject into people's minds any real enthusiasm for the reformed faith. The real challenge which faced the clergy and people of Elizabethan England was to maintain, especially at parish level, a sufficient uniformity of belief and practice to avoid the religious conflict which was so weakening community life on the continent of Europe.

9. Armed Rebellion, Popular Commotions, Mere Lawbreaking, and Litigation

The idea of a 'Tudor despotism' dies hard. Death by the axe was a hazard faced by all in high places, and death by fire or the rope was the fate of countless people at all social levels below that of the peerage. By no means all were convicted by due process of the law. But just as the tolerance of Tudor governments was, to say the least, limited, so also were its resources. Even convicted, let alone notorious, criminals could escape punishment on a legal technicality, including benefit of clergy, and many, especially those guilty of assembling in arms against the king's or the queen's peace, were never found. Above all, when faced with widespread popular defiance, no Tudor government from that of Henry VII to that of Elizabeth, could do more than rely on the support of a greater, or at least better-armed, military force, supplied by those of its people who chose to be loyal. It is at least arguable that one of the Tudor dynasty's greatest peace-keeping assets was its virtual lack of a standing, professional, army. In 1549, the great year of rebellions, only the fortuitous presence of foreign mercenary soldiers provided by Protector Somerset for Lord Russell's use against the rebels encamped around Exeter caused the almost unique and very considerable bloodshed with which this 'commotion' ended.

By the Statute of Westminster of 1285, confirmed in 1511, all able-bodied men aged between sixteen and sixty were required, according to their means and status, to be equipped with weapons, and skilled in their use. Firearms were prohibited until 1544 and again from 1546, except under licence, and the practice of archery was encouraged as an alternative recreation to the playing of tennis and bowls, cards and dice. Only if required to be absent from home, family and occupation for long periods, or to serve beyond the bounds of their own counties, could men expect to be paid a daily wage. From time to time, and until Elizabeth's reign usually only when foreign invasion or internal disorder actually threatened, they were required to muster for inspection and listing. Parishes were mustered by their constables under the supervision of commissions of local gentlemen, as far as possible simultaneously in order to prevent arms and even men being lent to make up numbers. Comparison of names of those listed for neighbouring parishes can be the despair of modern demographers. The Militia Act of 1558 prescribed for those with incomes of over £1,000 a year in land sixteen horses fully equipped for war, eighty suits of light armour, forty pikes, thirty longbows, each with a sheaf of arrows, twenty bills or halberds, twenty handguns and fifty steel helmets, and, more like a sumptuary law than a tax assessment, for men whose wives wore velvet kirtles or silk petticoats a light horse apiece. But the Tudor village green bore little resemblance to a field of battle, and not until 1573 were really determined efforts made to train as well as muster the militia. The later Elizabethan 'trained bands' were in fact smaller and more select, firmly excluding the poorer sort of men from whom Tudor politicians persisted in believing trouble was most likely to arise. In 1536 in Lincolnshire and Yorkshire muster rolls were in fact used to some effect by the rebel gentry to assemble a force of some 30,000 men at Pontefract, and when Henry Courtenay, marquis of Exeter, was sent to the south-west that same year to raise an army for the King there were those who said that it was his very success in attracting so many men to his side which led only two years later to his execution. For putting down trouble nearer home the militia were usually more obdurate. In 1525 the duke of Suffolk found it impossible to enlist the men of neighbouring villages to deal with those of Lavenham who were up in arms about taxation. Lord Russell was similarly discomfited in the south-west in 1549. In fact the only occasion on which the militia was actually used to quell a major rebellion was in 1569. By then some of the problems of leadership of

the militia had been solved by the appointment, beginning
under the duke of Northumberland's regime in the early 1550s,
of county or regional lords-lieutenants.

One of the limitations on the use of a national militia was
the traditional right claimed by most substantial landowners,
and indeed statutorily confirmed in 1558, to assume the leadership at least of their principal tenants. Far from declining with
the abandonment, not later than about 1300, of a national feudal
army, what may be called private armies had been recreated
in the later Middle Ages with the system of contracting with
the nobility and others to find contingents of men, equipped
and trained, to fight for the King under their command. The
nucleus, it was expected, would come from the captains' own
retainers. This worked well enough when kings went to war
on the continent of Europe and there was time to prepare. But
when internal disorder occurred there was no time for
formality. What usually happened, especially in the later 1530s,
was that men of power in their localities whom the government
thought could best be trusted received letters requiring them
to assemble such force as they could and repair immediately
to some rendezvous to join with other contingents. That law
and order was so often restored by such means was largely
due to the fact that the rebels were rarely large in number,
had fewer arms and less-experienced captains. A lot depended
on how many gentlemen were actively on their side. For very
minor affrays the nearest gentlemen to the scene, usually including one or more JPs, were expected to go with their own
household servants to talk the rioters into going home, always
with the hope of being able to isolate and arrest their leaders.
In fact, of course, it was the same men who comprised the
militia who formed the private armies of lords and gentlemen,
but it was on the informal rather than the formal method of
enlistment that the Crown relied.

What occasioned men in greater or lesser strength to leave
home and occupation to challenge the forces of law and order?
There was, no doubt, throughout the sixteenth century but
particularly towards the end, an element in society, not always

drawn entirely from the poor and the unoccupied, who would join any disturbance, either in the hope of opportunities for looting or even for the adventure and comradeship they missed in conventional society. Cities and towns in particular were for this reason alone always loath to make common cause with rebels, even if they sympathized with their aims. This was certainly the case in London in 1554 at the time of Wyatt's rebellion. There is ample evidence too that, especially in the early stages of rebellion, men were paid for assembling. This happened at Horncastle and Louth in Lincolnshire in 1536 and in Maidstone in 1554. On the other hand, many were drawn into rebel camps as hostages, though we need not believe that all the gentlemen who, after every major uprising, claimed that they were forced to go along for fear of their lives or the safety of their families, were thus involuntarily involved. There were, too, the families who hedged their bets, hoping thereby to save their property, by splitting up between the two sides. In 1569 Sir Ralph Sadler reflected ruefully on the loyalty of the northern gentry: 'If the father come to us with x men, his son goeth to the rebels with xx, and therefore guess you what trust is to be reposed in such men.' There were still, even in Elizabeth's reign, over-mighty subjects, and perhaps because of them there was no such thing as a purely peasant rising and virtually no class war. A rebel army was more likely to consist of a microcosm of contemporary society. Most rebels were, and certainly claimed to be, conservatives, defending their interests against what they regarded as innovation. Their intentions were in most cases to demonstrate their discontent, to bring their grievances to the notice of the king or queen. It was not only in order to save their skins in the event of failure that, even when armed in battle array, rebels invariably protested their loyalty.

Ironically, quite a few local commotions, especially in the reign of Henry VIII, were caused by the government's own licensed preachers. One of the worst offenders was Hugh Latimer, later bishop of Worcester, whose sermons at Bristol in 1533 against pilgrimages and the worship of saints both attracted sympathizers and also outraged conservatives, as did his performances in Exeter the same year. Only the fact that such preaching was always in the larger towns where mayors exercised very real authority prevented their ending in bloodshed. No serious riot was caused by Protestant militancy, and even at the height of Marian repression the 'professors of the gospel' denounced rebellion in the strongest possible terms. Nor did the public burning of heretical books, or even of heretics themselves, whether Protestant or Catholic, apparently engender any more public disapproval than that occasioned by the death of convicted criminals or political victims. Such spectacles always had their attractions as entertainment and were always staged in the larger and more law-abiding towns.

Trouble over religion, when it came, arose almost entirely from religious conservatives, feeling themselves to be assaulted by officially initiated reforms. Rumour invariably played a large part. The rebellions in 1536–7 in Lincolnshire and the north, in so far as they had a religious motivation, were concerned very little with doctrinal matters, which indeed had made little impact as yet, especially on ordinary laymen, but with churches, both secular and monastic, their furnishings and their clergy. Most rebellions are preceded by widespread popular 'murmuring' but are sparked off by some particular event, usually involving an assembly of some kind. In this case the initial assembly was one of parish clergy, called together in September 1536 to be put through their paces in accordance with the Ten Articles of religion and more particularly the first Injunctions to the Clergy just issued by Thomas Cromwell. There are thought to have been over seven hundred beneficed clergy at Louth in Lincolnshire and a further 160 at Caistor. They knew very well, of course, that they should not neglect their cures, should not haunt taverns, should make provision for the poor and send scholars to one of the universities, but it must have been more than they could stomach to be told so by the king's Vicar-General, a layman. They no doubt felt themselves not only to be on trial as pastors and as preachers, but to be valued in high places primarily as purveyors of government propaganda. They also knew of many former monks waiting to step into their shoes. However, the answer to the question why rebellion in 1536 occurred first in Lincolnshire may well lie simply in the fact that Bishop John Longland, though a conservative in matters of doctrine, was a strict disciplinarian and was the first – possibly the only – bishop to implement the Injunctions with vigour. That his clergy were not all ill-educated and underpaid was all the more reason for their being disturbed by rumours of confiscation of their glebe and tithes and their remuneration by fixed stipends like the unbeneficed clergy. There were also rumours circulating among local laymen that it was intended to confiscate the plate and other treasures of the parish churches, and when the clergy reached home, having agreed to call the people out by ringing the bells, they will hardly have needed to remind their parishioners that their church treasures had been given by their own ancestors. Further north in the Lake Counties, one of the rebels' main grievances was the demand for tithes, not so much by the clergy as by lay farmers and by monks. Even the dissolution of the monasteries was not a simple issue. By no means all members of the religious communities regretted their release, and the heads of houses had been well provided for. Only the very elderly monks and nuns will have resented being moved into larger communities, and for the younger men there was the possibility of being licensed to serve secular cures. It is true that many monks rode, fully armed, with the rebels, but not even Robert Aske, the most eloquent defender of the monasteries, dwelt overmuch on the religious implications of the Dissolution – that is, on the loss of prayers – but rather on the utilitarian value of monastic hospitality in out of the way places, hospitality more likely to be enjoyed by gentlemen like himself than by the poor. Although some attempts were made to restore those of the smaller monasteries which had already been dissolved, there were also instances of antagonism and even of intimidation of the religious by the rebels who were only too apt to assume that all who were not actively with them were against them.

Once banners had been raised there was no lack of reasons,

some highly personal, for joining in the demonstration. Most owners of land were strongly opposed to the Statute of Uses. Its repeal was one of the rebels' demands and Henry VIII showed how misinformed he was of their real identity when he upbraided 'the base commons' for bothering their heads about a matter which 'in no manner of thing' touched them. The powers that be always liked to believe that rebels were men of no account, but much of the pattern of the rebellion, especially in Yorkshire, can be explained by the attitude of the nobility, many of whom were with the rebels all the way, if only to embarrass the upstart Cromwell. Those parts of the West Riding dominated by the younger Percies, the disinherited heirs of the sixth earl of Northumberland, and by Lord Darcy, rebelled. Hallamshire stayed loyal under the earl of Shrewsbury and Lord Derby was able to keep Lancashire south of the Ribble unaffected. Beyond the Ribble there was much opposition to the Dissolution, the monks being very popular. Elsewhere the chief objection to the Dissolution was that it would drain money out of the region. There were many local grievances such as a shortage of land in Cumberland and Westmorland and there were many who took up arms in protest at what they regarded as the unreasonable rents and 'gressums' (fines) exacted by great northern landowners like the Cliffords and the Nevilles. The northern magnates for their part resented the fact that strangers had been appointed to northern offices, to the wardenship of the borders with Scotland, and to the Council of the North which had been re-established in 1525. Strangers had been given lands. In 1529, for instance, the duke of Suffolk, the King's own brother-in-law, had acquired the wardship of a Lincolnshire heiress, Katherine Willoughby, with the intention that she should marry his son who had been made earl of Lincoln. In 1534 Lincoln died and Suffolk had married Katherine himself, at the same time successfully resisting all claims by the male Willoughby heirs. In February 1536 Suffolk was also given estates in Lincolnshire ceded to the King by the earl of Northumberland and he acquired Tattershall Castle as a local residence. Naturally the Willoughbys joined the rebels, their anger intensified when Henry chose Suffolk to lead his army to quell the Lincolnshire rebellion. The northern counties rose in 1536 not only because a great many people at all social levels were at odds with the government and its policies but also because so many of them, including Aske, had faith that their grievances could be remedied if only they could make the King himself listen. Most of those grievances were secular, but there was more than a veneer of religious, if not spiritual, discontent, enough to give a righteous air to mundane matters. That, presumably, is why the men of Cumberland went into battle with processional banners flying, the five wounds of Christ having no particularly conservative religious significance.

By 1549 there had been a great deal more strictly religious change. The statutory compulsion to use the new English Prayer Book might have been, in parishes up and down the country, the last straw. The fact that it clearly was not should surely raise the question whether even in the south-west it was the root cause of a resort to arms. People assembled that Whit Sunday in thousands of other parish churches and, as in Sampford Courtenay, heard their priests use the new liturgy. We do not know why in that remote Devon parish they should have reassembled on Whit Monday and apparently persuaded their vicar to say the old words. Were they at that point really serious? Were the gentlemen who were quickly on the scene with a considerable retinue perhaps over-reacting? There had already been trouble in Cornwall but this had more to do with 'foreign' ecclesiastical administration than with the liturgy. It is easy to scoff, as they did at Westminster, about the demand for the liturgy in Cornish. As early as 1538 their bishop, John Veysey, had envisaged a Cornish Bible. Did the demand not simply represent rejection of English interference? The Cornish, after all, had lost more holy days than any other part of the kingdom. The processional banners under which they marched into England were, of course, symbols of the old ways, and in particular of the now outlawed local pilgrimages. The legendary leadership of the south-western rebellion by the

priests should surely be narrowed down to one in particular,
Robert Welsh, vicar of St Thomas's just outside Exeter, but
also a Cornishman, a wrestler and one skilled in the use of
firearms. He was clearly a born leader whose greatest achievement was to keep the rebel force from dispersing, especially
as harvest time drew near. The walled city of Exeter was probably never in any real danger, except of shortage of food.
The gentlemen of the south-west sustained a low profile, probably as much because of their desire to embarrass Protector
Somerset as from sympathy with the rebels. The leading gentleman activist, the forty-one-year-old Sir Thomas Pomeroy, had
his own good reasons for hating Somerset who had recently
obtained from him his ancestral lands near Totnes, no doubt
driving his usual hard bargain. It is at least arguable that the
gentlemen as well as their tenants were primarily incensed by
a levy on sheep and cloth imposed by Somerset and his parliament in the spring of 1549. Intended as a discouragement to
sheep-farming it was seen as a tax, and it is not without significance that way back in 1497 a large body of Cornishmen had
marched all the way to London to protest about being taxed
to pay for a war against those other foreigners, the Scots. It
was well known that Protector Somerset had the same end
in view. Moreover, it was provided in the statute that assessment was to be made by parish juries two weeks after Whitsun,
and that the rate would be higher in enclosed counties. It is
true that under Welsh's spell the rebel forces encamped around
Exeter lent their support to a long list of demands for a return
to the old religious ritual, but it is not difficult to imagine that
at Sampford Courtenay on Whit Monday the new Prayer Book
appeared to a lively community of farmers as just one more
imposition emanating from the King's uncle and his captive
Parliament.

The rising led this same year by Robert Kett and others
in East Anglia was also complex in its causes. It certainly had
little to do with religion although one of the assemblies out
of which it grew was the celebration at Wymondham of the
presumably quite illegal feast of St Thomas the Martyr. By

and large the region was by now thoroughly Protestant and had accepted the new Prayer Book. Nor was there much murmuring against enclosures, except in some of the wood–pasture areas, for, as we have seen, in sheep–corn Norfolk the farmers favoured enclosure as a means of denying to their landlords the latter's ancient right of folding their sheep on their tenants' arable. The rebels of East Anglia were for the most part tenant farmers and freeholders of considerable substance but no political power, that power lying, so they claimed, with a select group of magistrates who failed even to do justice. Indeed, the fecklessness of the gentry of East Anglia in dealing with the rebels was probably less calculated than that of their southwestern counterparts. Kett's was also a classic case of rebellion following rather than aiming at liberation from an oppressive landlord, in this case the Howard family. Thomas, third duke of Norfolk, was still alive in the Tower but his lands were in Crown possession.

Disturbances of a local nature were widespread in the late summer of 1549. In many counties, especially Somerset and Wiltshire, the trouble did arise from enclosure, either of common pasture alone or of erstwhile arable farms, not necessarily for sheep-walks but in some cases for conversion into deer-parks. Many of the unlawful acts were indeed popular attempts to enforce a royal proclamation of April 1549 ordering that the statutes against enclosure be observed. The rioters in such cases were more likely to be poor cottagers, victims not only of landlords but of mutual agreements by the larger farmers to exchange and enclose open fields. The fact that in Wiltshire, according to a contemporary report, there was 'neither gentleman nor yet a man of any substance' among the hedge-breakers is sufficient to explain why the disturbances petered out so quickly. If there was any one thread uniting the many disorders of 1549 it was distrust of Protector Somerset, both for what he was doing and also for what, in spite of promises, he was failing to do. It is possible too that many of the reports from magistrates exaggerated the problems with which they were dealing as their own form of protest against a regime which most of them thoroughly detested. But at no time was there any real liaison between rebels in different areas. In Devon the rebels hoped for support from the bishop of Winchester's men in Hampshire and indeed money was actually raised in Winchester for their succour, but that was all. As for an alternative to the Tudor dynasty, that was not for plebeian rebels to contemplate but only for a pillar of the established order such as the duke of Northumberland with his plans for a Queen Jane instead of a Queen Mary.

Mary Tudor was mistaken about many things, not least in her belief that all who tried to thwart her were doing so in the interests of Protestantism. There was only one serious rebellion against her regime and the main aim of its leader, Thomas Wyatt, if not of all his supporters, was to persuade her not to marry Philip of Spain. This was born not so much of patriotism as of a fear that with Spaniards entrenched at Court there would be less room there for English gentlemen. The attempts of Wyatt and his associates to arouse English xenophobia – he told the men of Devon that the Spaniards would ravish their women – misfired largely because as yet most Englishmen were far more suspicious of the French, with whom Wyatt was in communication, than of the Spaniards. Wyatt also played on the fears of landowners that Mary would restore all former Church lands, but such fears were not of course confined to Protestants. It is true that most of Wyatt's support came from his native Kent where by now over 75 per cent of wills were couched in positively Protestant terminology, and in particular from Maidstone, but the conspirators' plan to marry the Princess Elizabeth to young Edward Courtenay, whom they declared to be a Protestant, was unlikely to enable the radical and irresponsible Sir Peter Carew to rouse even those of his fellow-Devonians who shared his religion. In any case, the south-west had had enough of commotions. There had been a good deal of discontent in various clothing areas in Kent but some of the sporadic hedge-breaking had been directed against Wyatt's own new park at Boxley, and by no means all his own tenants responded to his call to arms. The Dudley conspiracy of 1556 was almost entirely the work of disgruntled gentlemen, one of whom, Henry Peckham, an otherwise loyal Buckinghamshire landowner, joined in because he thought he had not been sufficiently rewarded for his contribution to Wyatt's defeat. Except for Wyatt the leaders of Tudor rebellions did not look overseas for support. There had been some talk in the south-west in 1549 of an appeal to the Emperor, Charles V, but the whole rebellion would probably have collapsed overnight if the threatened invasion by the French had materialized. The English were infinitely easier to unite against external enemies than against any domestic regime, however unpopular. They were far more in sympathy with Sir John Cheke's *Hurt of Sedition*, written to convince Kett's supporters of the error of their ways, than with Christopher Goodman's *How Superior Powers Ought to be Obeyed*, published in 1558, which, for all its insistence on the duty of the nobility to resist what he called idolatry in high places, urged that if they failed then popular rebellion was a godly act. There were even Marian exiles who were sadly troubled by John Knox.

The rebellion of the earls of Northumberland and Westmorland in 1569 had no popular roots. That the former title once more belonged to a Percy who had recovered in Mary's reign a good deal of the family's land and some of its prestige was no coincidence. Religion played a part but one very personal to Northumberland who was a convert to Catholicism as the old faith could now be called. That the earls were virtually provoked into rebellion by the Queen and her ministers only underlines the disinclination of most Tudor people to rebel. The lack of support from their principal tenants demonstrated the growing anachronism of aristocratic territorial power in Elizabethan England. Even the Queen, as landed successor to the earls, found that tenants were no longer prepared to be, as such, her 'manrede', even on the Scottish borders. This, however, did not lead her to reverse her decision to limit the grant of licences to retain private armies. She never refused entirely to allow those she trusted to indulge their vanity by clothing their affinity in fine feathers but woe betide them if they appeared in her presence with retainers 'defencibly arrayed'.

The almost paranoiac fears of Tudor governments of the consequences for public order of food shortages and high prices might lead to the conclusion that these were indeed primary causes of rebellion. It is true, of course, that poor harvests, of which there were many in sixteenth-century England, or any cause of distress, including unemployment and plague, were unsettling. Unless local magistrates were vigilant, which they very often were not, there was always a danger of people taking the law into their own hands, and there must often have been occasions when, while the magistrates dithered and conducted inquiries, hungry people helped themselves. Proclamations, such as that of November 1527 advising hoarders of grain of the King's displeasure, must often have arrived when the worst of the crisis was over or, where authority was weak locally, have been regarded as invitations to break the law. In fact none of the major resorts to arms was directly occasioned by dearth of food. In Lincolnshire in October 1536 there was actually considerable jubilation on account of a rather better harvest than in previous years. Until the very end of the century there was very little real starvation outside the towns, except in very remote pastoral areas, and in the towns, even if relief was not very soon available, rebellious instincts were more easily curbed. London was a city with an almost continual food-shortage but never once did its governing body lose control. Also, not only do starving people make poor soldiers and attract no leaders of standing and ability, but when grain is short, farmers stay at home to protect their barns. Even in the 1590s when, partly owing to the great increase in population, poor harvests and high prices were causing distress in both towns and countryside such as had been unknown for the greater part of the century, organized rebellion or riots, as opposed to individual law-breaking, occurred very rarely. In the whole county of Kent between 1585 and 1603 only eleven food riots are known to have occurred, less than one a year, and most of these were little more than peaceful demonstrations, protestations about prices being accompanied by protestations of loyalty to the Queen. The protesters were largely poor craftsmen and un-employed labourers dwelling in forest areas and in the vicinity of towns. Their targets were the corn-dealers and farmers. The gentlemen, even if not actively involved, were not entirely un-sympathetic. No doubt far more resorts to arms were planned than were put into execution, and the nature of the protest becomes very clear when, for the first time, women were among the insurgents. On the river Severn south of Gloucester in April 1586 ships loaded with malt were boarded and unloaded by hundreds of hungry artisans and their wives, and at about the same time at Romsey in Hampshire a group of ordinary folk assembled with the intention of preventing a local farmer sow-ing woad instead of corn, the idea having clearly been put into their heads by a royal proclamation of October 1585. A plan to do likewise at Selborne was devised by five tailors, four weavers, a fencemaker, a mason, a tanner, a butcher, a black-smith, a carpenter, one gentleman and four husbandmen, which hardly supports William Cecil's firm belief that 'the people that depend upon making of cloth are in worse condition to be quietly governed than the husbandmen', or that other convic-tion in high places that trouble came largely from vagrants. In spite of the poor harvest of the following autumn there were few further reports of popular disturbances until 1594–5, by which time there was more real starvation and less purely industrial unrest. Even then real riots were few. At Hampton Gay near Oxford, Bartholomew Stere, a carpenter, and Richard Bradshaw, a miller, planned to seize food and arms and march on London from where, with the help of apprentices, they would 'overrun the realm', but on the appointed day less than a dozen supporters responded to their call and all were easily apprehended. These included, however, four men described as servants (resident employees) of the gentlemen whose heads Stere said he planned to cut off. Stere himself was not par-ticularly poor and was presumably a would-be demagogue. He admitted on examination by members of the Privy Council that he had first got the idea of a rising on hearing of a riot in London over the price of butter. His fate is unknown, but he told his examiners that he could die but once. Unlike poorer men he may have been worth fining. Such protests did have some effect. Although the leaders of the Hampshire rising of 1586 were arrested, so too were the woad-growers; and local magistrates were ordered by the Privy Council to see that both food and work were available. Men like Stere talked a great deal about destroying gentlemen and clearly, in these very late Tudor disturbances, great emphasis was laid on the distinction between the haves and the have-nots, but it was all very far from being class warfare. At the height of the crisis in 1549 when disorder seemed to have taken over large parts of the realm Sir Thomas Smith, certainly no lover of rebellion, wrote in his *Discourse of the Commonweal*, in response to a suggestion that England should, like France, establish a standing army: 'I would not have a small sore cured by a greater grief, nor for avoiding of sedition popular, which happens very seldom and soon quenched, to bring in a continual yoke and charge both to the king and his people.' He would almost certainly have been of the same mind in 1600.

Many Tudor threats to raise rebellion would have passed unnoticed and unrecorded but for the fact that by a statute of 1534 (withdrawn in 1547 and only re-enacted in 1571) words as well as acts were deemed to constitute treason. But although the law of treason was considerably extended in the sixteenth century, the power this gave to the courts to deal effectively with rebellion must not be exaggerated. The great treason statute of 1352 had been conceived in terms very personal to the monarch and members of the royal family. Early additions to the law, such as making it a treasonable offence to attempt to interfere with the royal succession or to counterfeit the currency, were in the same vein. Even after 1534 it was not easy to convict of treason those who caused disorder not directly aimed at the King, and the protestations of loyalty of so many rebels should perhaps be judged partly in this light. The medieval principle that all peace was the king's peace had worn a little thin. At any rate Henry VIII's judges found it necessary to decide that risings in support of increased wages constituted war against the King, and in the autumn of 1549 this was extended to cover any occasion on which twelve or more persons, having been ordered to disperse, continued in arms with the object of killing any member of the Council or of changing the laws of the realm. But even so, rioting for the purpose of doing damage, for example breaking up enclosures, or of reducing rents, was only treasonable if forty or more persons were assembled for two hours or more. Subsequently this was reduced to a felony, still, that is, punishable by death but not by the total rigour of hanging, drawing and quartering, loss of all goods, chattels and land, and corruption of blood. Not until 1597, following a serious anti-enclosure riot in Oxfordshire did the Queen's judges decide that risings against enclosure in general, as opposed to specific targets, were treasonable. But charges of treason in Tudor England were largely exemplary, aimed at removing ringleaders. Wholesale liquidation was not the Tudor way. In any case it was not always easy to obtain the essential indictment by a county grand jury. In 1541 Parliament provided that the trial of an alleged traitor could be held, by virtue of a commission of oyer and terminer, outside the shire in which the alleged offence had taken place, but it is unlikely that this improved the justice of the hearing. Allowed neither legal counsel nor defence, defendants, once put on trial, had little hope, for conviction for treason was possible on the evidence of only two witnesses. In cases of large-scale riot there was the possibility of a resort to martial law which involved no proper trial but the victims' heirs were not deprived of their inheritance. Wealthy rebels were usually dealt with by parliamentary acts of attainder. The Court of Star Chamber which had been specifically charged in 1487 with punishing crimes of violence quickly found other work to do. Contrary to traditional beliefs, the lawcourts of Tudor England were not kept especially busy dealing with rebels or even with armed protesters.

Was Tudor England's relative freedom from mass rioting

and rebellion more than made up for by an increase in criminal offences, either by individuals or small gangs? This question cannot be fully answered, for two reasons. Contemporary impressions that only a very small minority of offenders were ever brought to trial is clearly incapable of proof either way, and the records of the assizes, where most criminal charges were laid, survive for only a handful of counties, largely in southeast England, and only for the reign of Queen Elizabeth. Within these limits, and even allowing for increasing efficiency in the detection and charging of offenders, it would appear that felonies, that is, capital offences, largely murder, manslaughter and theft, were increasing. In Sussex indictments rose from an average of forty-three per annum in the 1560s, to fifty-eight in the 1580s, and sixty-nine in the 1590s. In Essex the annual rate trebled from thirty-eight to 116 over the same period. Corrected to allow for estimated increases in population the rise in Sussex was from fourteen to nineteen per 10,000, but in Essex it was from eight to twenty. Essex was, of course, very near London which was a honeypot for criminals. In Hertfordshire the proportions were much higher but more stable, from thirty-eight per 10,000 in the 1570s to forty-one by the end of the century, but the county's total population was only half that of Sussex and less than a quarter that of Essex. More than any other county it was plagued by highwaymen lying in wait for travellers on the road to and from the north. Berkshire, astride the Great West Road, if its records had survived, would probably show a similar pattern but Sussex was probably more typical of the country as a whole.

Analysis of the nature of the crimes dealt with at assizes indicate that homicide, that is, premeditated murder accompanied by gross brutality, was far outnumbered in all the counties investigated by killings resulting directly from personal quarrels between fellow-workers, fellow-drinkers, and even players at games. Perhaps most significant as a measure of the public disorder of the period is that about one fifth of the killings, if servants be included, occurred within the family circle. Husbands more often killed their wives than vice versa but wives, as might be expected, more often used poison. Of the few counties for which evidence has survived, Essex had the greatest incidence of the murder of children and servants. The statutes prohibiting the unauthorized possession of firearms would seem to have had some effect in that hardly one in twenty killings which we know about involved firearms, but even in 1600 these were probably still more lethal to the operator than to his target. The rapier, a weapon far more lethal than the older and heavier broadsword, only came to be used with any skill in England at about the time of the Spanish Armada.

Contrary to the literary evidence and to the lurid tales told in Star Chamber the slightly less serious crime of assault was by no means invariably the work of gangs, certainly not in Sussex where it characterized only about one third of the cases, although in Hertfordshire nearly three quarters of the cases of assault involved two or more persons. Highwaymen, like their victims, rarely rode alone. Predictably, nearly three quarters of all crimes indicted at assizes concerned theft, a situation which politicians and moralists alike attributed to a lack of disciplined upbringing. But the court records show that most thefts were committed by people in genuine need of food and clothing, and the number of theft cases rose considerably at times of famine and unemployment, especially in the years 1596–8. This suggests that, assuming the increase in convictions for theft arose to some extent from an actual increase in crime (and not merely from greater judicial efficiency), the criminals were acting on impulse rather than as professionals. There are grounds for believing that there was more lawlessness in forest than in fielden areas, but even the more manorialized villages had their quota of poachers and light-fingered people. At all times vagrants loomed large among those charged with theft, but they, of course, were marked men. But studies in depth of village communities reveal that the same men who served as constables, churchwardens, etc. – that is, the more settled element – also appeared not infrequently as defendants at the assizes. More often, however, their offences were not common theft but technical ones such as breaking the assizes of bread and ale,

working on Sundays, failing to pay the poor-rate, or polluting
the streets. Crime was not, in Tudor England, the prerogative
of the lower orders of society. Gentlemen, in proportion to
their numbers, figured equally, if not more prominently,
especially among highway robbers, and the criminal violence
perpetrated by many noble lords apparently exceeded what
could be condoned as youthful high spirits. Nothing less than
the Queen's personal disapproval could curb noble criminality,
but a good deal of aristocratic aggression, including the intimidation of juries, was directed at rivals and equals rather than
at those less able to defend themselves. Even in Elizabeth's reign,
examples of the worst excesses of bastard feudalism are not
hard to find, but this particular kind of civil disorder was no
longer endemic. The sixteenth century also saw a slow but sure
diminution in the offences for which men could be convicted
but avoid punishment by pleading benefit of clergy, and also
in places where criminals could find permanent sanctuary. There
is, however, some evidence that the very harshness of the law,
even petty theft being a felony, punishable with death, made
life easier for those who committed the more serious offences,
even those which local magistrates usually referred to the assize
judges. In Devon in the years 1598–1600, while nearly twice
as many people (550) were tried at assizes as at quarter sessions,
a greater proportion of them were either granted clergy, discharged, acquitted or pardoned. Moreover, the chances of those
punished being executed were almost as great if they were dealt
with by the JPs as they were if they faced the judges. The
former sent sixty to the gallows and sixty-eight to be whipped,
the latter seventy-seven and forty-four respectively. These,
however, are really not large numbers, spread over three years,
in a very large county. If this was only the tip of an enormous
iceberg of undetected crime and violence, would there have
been such widespread support for the appointing at Christmas
time, in cities, in institutions of higher education, and even at
Court and in noble households, of what has been called the
'institutionalized ridicule' of authority, that is, of Lords of

Misrule? The heavy hand of authority was surely a reality in Tudor England.

But the courts of law were not only concerned with the punishment of crime: they were also available for the settlement of disputes, and indeed civil litigation, 'between party and party', occupied by far the greater part of their time. Partly, this was due to the lack of adequate means of bringing lawbreakers into court. For example, most of those brought before the courts accused of the criminal offence of witchcraft were defendants in civil actions. While this could be more expensive for the victims than criminal proceedings initiated by indictment, the successful conclusion of a civil action had the advantage that it could bring compensation in the form of restitution or damages. In fact, much civil litigation was commenced either in the hope of inducing the defendant to settle out of court or in order to vex, that is, to put someone the plaintiff disliked or sought to annoy to trouble and expense. In Tudor England vexatious litigation was a very effective form of private warfare, provided, of course, that the lawyers could be persuaded to bring matters to an early conclusion.

A great deal of civil litigation was concerned with debt. For the recovery of small debts there were still available some at least of the old hundred courts and the equally ancient shire courts presided over by the sheriffs, as well as the far busier, and more businesslike, courts of the town mayors. Substantial debts, however, were pursued in the central Courts of King's Bench and Common Pleas, such cases increasing from rather over 40 per cent to rather over 60 per cent of their business between 1560 and 1600. But even more striking is the enormous increase in the overall number of cases being pursued in these two courts, from about 2,000 per annum in 1500 (after which business slackened somewhat), to 2,500 in 1560, and then to no less than 13,000 in 1580 and 22,000 in 1600, increases in the second half of the century out of all proportion to the increase in the country's population. About a quarter of the litigants were gentlemen and rather fewer were yeomen but as the volume of business increased so did the proportion of the litigants, both plaintiffs and defendants, who were merchants and craftsmen.

The increasing litigiousness of Tudor people was also reflected in the volume of business done in the conciliar Courts of Chancery, Requests, and Star Chamber where the common law could be implemented more flexibly. Early in the century these offered the advantage of speed in the determination of proceedings. The Court of Chancery in particular could deal very expeditiously and informally with civil disputes, but its very success inevitably led to delays, and by 1600 this court presided over by men with a multiplicity of other duties was dealing with some five hundred cases a year, with delays of up to three years. The number of cases in Star Chamber increased tenfold between the accession and death of Queen Elizabeth. Some of this was due to its spreading its wings over failures to observe royal proclamations, including those concerning the illegal printing of books, but very largely it was the result of its popularity for the resolution of civil cases, always of course providing the plaintiff alleged the use of armed force. Since 1495 poor men, even in Chancery, had been able to plead *in forma pauperis*, paying little or nothing in court fees and being served, free of charge, by some of the best barristers in Westminster. But by the end of the century the conciliar courts were failing in their purpose, the Court of Requests in particular, although set up especially for poor men, coming to be used more and more by those who only claimed in a purely technical sense to be poor. In Star Chamber, too, while during Wolsey's time as Chancellor nobles and gentlemen constituted only 29 and 35 per cent respectively of the plaintiffs and defendants, by the end of the century over half in both cases were gentry, including gentlewomen. The proportion of disputes concerning landed property seems not to have changed appreciably, but these had always accounted for about half the cases dealt with. One of the advantages of the Courts of Chancery, Star Chamber and Requests, especially to historians, was their use of written depositions, in English, in place of the largely oral proceedings and stereotyped Norman-French of the older common-law courts. Both plaintiffs and defendants were thus able, with the help of their counsel, but also with a certain amount of self-reliance on the part of gentlemen who had completed their education at the Inns of Court, to set down largely in their own words their version of the circumstances of their cases. For them, as they do to us, the records breathed an informality and an attention to the details of real life usually lacking in the common-law courts, preoccupied as they were with legal technicalities. Chancery in particular had far more efficient means of bringing defendants to court: instead of the cumbersome writs of the common-law courts it used the far more effective subpoena under the Privy or Great Seal, followed if necessary by the 'writ of rebellion' invoking the ancient but now territorially unbounded 'hue and cry'. Moreover, if less than satisfied with the evidence, these courts could direct lists of questions to be answered, also in writing and in English, by the most reliable (usually on account of age) local residents. Speed was not always the most important consideration. The assize judges must have worked infinitely faster but they asked few or no questions, the trial juries being presumed to know the facts. The Chancellor not only adjudicated with discretion, but he was able to concern himself with matters which the common law would not, or could not, touch, such as the interests of married women. In the case of Star Chamber, the court's punishments, as the century wore on, consisted, to be sure, less of fines and more of imprisonment, whipping, setting in the pillory (wearing a paper notice declaring the offence), public confession, and even physical mutilation such as the cutting off of ears. These pointed towards the court's eventual notoriety, at least among defendants, but to the majority of its plaintiffs the Tudor Court of Star Chamber offered better remedies for wrongs than were available in the common-law courts, central or local. Though it could not upset their verdicts the Tudor Star Chamber did deal very rigorously with JPs who failed to do justice in quarter sessions, and it taught them to offer greater protection to the poor and weak and to the victims of powerful neighbours. As far as practicable, copyhold tenants were referred back to their manorial courts, and if the defendant was the lord or his steward Star Chamber could commission a local gentleman to sit alongside him 'for knowledge of the truth'.

The example set and the influence wielded by the provincial conciliar courts, the Councils of the North, in the Marches of Wales, and (very briefly, 1539–40) of the West, must also be mentioned. By 1600 the second of these was hearing about 3,000 cases a year, very largely civil actions, and was some 2,000 in arrears. The Council of the North in particular achieved a great deal both by example and precept in bringing law and order to the region. Local magistrates were taught that their primary duty, as William Lambarde so well understood, was the 'compounding', that is, the pacifying, of controversy. The Church courts too, when not dealing with tithe causes, were occupied more and more as the century proceeded with charges of defamation, especially with allegations of sexual slander. In the consistory court of the bishop of Chester, between 1544 and 1594, the average annual number of defamation cases quadrupled. To the extent that this meant that English people were accepting litigation as an alternative to physical retaliation, the Church was helping to keep the peace. But the consequences of conviction in the Church courts were exemplary rather than brutal, the guilty party being made to walk around his or her parish church in front of the processional cross bearing a candle, or simply enjoined to contribute to the poor box.

Chief Justice Coke at the very end of the century attributed the enormous increase in litigation to the long period of peace and plenty early in Queen Elizabeth's reign. This was as if to say that litigation benefited the well-to-do. If this was so, then little had changed. In the later medieval period poor men feared the law as a weapon rich men used to trick them and there were still those in Tudor England who regarded the law not as a blessing but as a cause of social tension. The story of the efforts of Sir Anthony Cooke in the 1560s to frustrate the ambitions of his former bailiff, the now successful grazier Peter

Temple, to buy up the manor of Burton Dassett in Oxfordshire, of which he, Cooke, was part-owner, is interesting not so much on account of the prolonged litigation as for Cooke's tactics of physical harassment of Temple's controlled stock-breeding. By using his influence with members of the Privy Council – he was a well-known scholar and former tutor to Edward VI – Cooke contrived to have Temple imprisoned in the Fleet for over two years, a situation reminiscent of mid-fifteenth-century Norfolk. His former tenant, he complained, had 'from low estate grown to great wealth', which was true, and 'of late by subtle and crafty means crept in' to the property. Peter Temple, like John Paston, eventually triumphed but at what cost in lawyers' fees we can only guess. Whether or not the sixteenth century saw the law become for the first time a weapon in the hands of ordinary men it is certain that although justice in the courts of Tudor England was far from guaranteed, if pursued in the right place and with persistence it was able to provide an alternative to rebellion, riot and disturbance of the peace. In particular, the more knights and gentlemen who were absorbed in private litigation, the less inclination or means they had for leading rebellion. The hedge-breaking and food riots of lesser folk, without effective leadership, were little more than a nuisance.

10. New Horizons: 'By Little and Little'

It is part of the folklore of the English-speaking peoples that the Tudor period of their history, in particular the reign of Queen Elizabeth, was one in which their forebears showed considerable enterprise, long-dormant energies released by the renaissance of learning and the reformation of religion enabling them to discover a new native culture and to possess a material civilization with the aid of which they began that march of progress which ultimately led them to bestride the world. However, few people alive in the 1590s in an England racked by poverty, unemployment and commercial depression, would have said that theirs was a better world or that human inventiveness had restored a good and just society. As the great majority of English people were still, in 1600 as in 1500, engaged in agriculture, it is appropriate to begin and end with them, but also to survey, necessarily very briefly, those other spheres of activity, in particular industry and maritime affairs, where the sixteenth century saw, if not always great achievement, at least the opening up of new horizons. In particular, attention needs to be directed to the identity and social status of the promoters.

The publication in 1523 of Master John Fitzherbert's *Book of Husbandry*, the first practical handbook in its field to be published anywhere in Europe which was not only in the vernacular, but also was more than a mere repetition of classical texts, would suggest a readership able and willing to improve its techniques. Fitzherbert strongly advocated enclosure and such novelties as ley farming, that is, the conversion of arable land into temporary grass. But his book was expensive and only a few hundred copies were printed. In any case, very few of the country's preponderance of small family farmers could read, and even the slightly more literate yeomen or even gentlemen farmers had at this time little incentive to improve their corn-yields or the quality of their stock. A century and more of agricultural recession had also seen legislation prohibiting the export of wheat, except by licence, when it was more than 6s. 8d. a quarter and barley when it was more than 3s., levels unchanged since 1437 and certainly too low by the 1520s. There was no doubt a good deal of illegal trade, but the total recorded export of grain during the first three quarters of the sixteenth century was only about 6,000 quarters a year. Neither the requirements of the royal household nor victuals for armies, both of which farmers were obliged to supply at artificially low prices, added to the attractions of the market. The persistence of open-field farming was bound to have a stultify-ing effect on individual enterprise, but it did go a long way to outlaw really bad husbandry, and within its broad constraints it did not preclude the introduction of new crops and new rotations. For example, hops were being grown in many parts of south-east England in the early sixteenth century, though probably only for household use or for sale to local brewers and not for marketing on any scale, let alone for export. Ironically it was in those regions where there was still available a good deal of 'waste', that is, unoccupied land, for example in the hill-farming regions of the north and the south-west, where the soil was very thin, that the practice was followed of taking in patches for arable cultivation for a few years and then letting them revert to rough grazing. Here, rather than on the downland and the lowlands of the rest of the country, necessity was indeed the mother of invention. Manuring was vital everywhere, of course, and here early Tudor farmers had less to learn, the compulsory throwing open of fields after harvest to the villagers' total stock being one of the great virtues of the communal system. It was permanent change of use, especially if this upset the annual farming calendar, which placed strains on local society and its customary way of life which it could not easily bear.

By the mid-1540s population growth was no doubt beginning to press on food supplies and the immediate rise in grain
prices which followed poor harvests certainly testified to the
precariousness of the situation. On the other hand, the equally
precipitate fall in prices which accompanied a good harvest
would seem to show that, God willing, the farmers of England
could still supply the home market. Of the towns, only London
in the early sixteenth century provided an ever-increasing
demand for grain, vegetables and dairy products, and it was
largely for this reason that agricultural enterprise first began to
appear, slowly but surely, in those areas such as East Anglia,
Kent, and all the Home Counties from which London drew
most of its food.

The commercial wind in the early sixteenth century was still
blowing very strongly in favour of pastoral farming, particularly in the demand for wool for the manufacture of cloth, and
to their ability to sell, each year, more and more English cloth
abroad may be attributed the complacency of the early Tudor
merchant fraternity. Nowhere was this more evident than in
London whose cloth exporters, members of the Merchant
Adventurers' Company with its headquarters across the
Channel, were increasingly dominating the country's foreign
trade, except for that still in the hands of aliens. While London's
cloth exports rose from about fifty thousand a year in 1500 to
well over a hundred thousand by the late 1540s, the amount
of cloth exported through the outports, especially Bristol,
Exeter, Hull and Southampton, actually declined. None of the
outports, except possibly Southampton, faced the risk of total
shutdown, but at Exeter in the 1530s the outlook was so bleak,
particularly by comparison with the great expansion in their
trade from which the city's merchants had profited so much
in the late 1490s and until about 1505, that some thought was
given to obtaining the right to re-establish a merchant guild
with a strict monopoly of local overseas trade for its members.
In fact, Exeter's fairly stable trade with north-west France saw
her through.

A far more enterprising spirit was in evidence further west at

Plymouth. Already by the early 1530s, William Hawkins, of yeoman farming stock from nearby Tavistock, was sailing in his own ships to Upper Guinea on the coast of west Africa for malaguette pepper and ivory, and from there crossing the Atlantic to Brazil (only discovered as recently as 1500 by the Portuguese) for dyewood, a commodity 'in those days very rare, especially to our nation' (Hakluyt). What goods he took with him on these very early voyages we do not know, but in 1540 he loaded the *Paul* with 940 hatchets, 940 combs, 375 knives, copper and lead arm-rings and nineteen dozen nightcaps. Clearly many of these were re-exports, but at least they were a change from cloth. In 1531 he had brought home a Brazilian chief for the King's diversion. The man died on the return voyage but such was Hawkins's reputation that his own man whom he had left behind in Brazil as a hostage was released. The range of his voyaging was quite extraordinary, though he almost certainly employed a French pilot or possibly a renegade Portuguese. The failure of the early Tudor merchant community at Bristol to seek trade in the New World is quite extraordinary, especially in view of the enterprise shown by their fifteenth-century predecessors. This may have been due in part to the absence in Bristol, as in other large Tudor towns, of merchant dynasties to pass on the torch, as it were. Robert Thorne junior, whose father had sailed to North America and back in 1502, lived in Seville in the 1530s and was quite content trading, with Spanish permission, with the Canary Islands and the West Indies. Within a few years, however, English 'heretics' were to find life in Spain decidedly risky.

Henry VIII occasionally supplied one or more ships for an Atlantic crossing, once, in 1517 to the Coventry-born lawyer John Rastell, by then a London printer and poet, who blamed his failure to get further than Ireland on his mariners, 'Kaytyffes [who] wolde take no paine to saile further'. Rastell nevertheless felt qualified to print *A New Interlude* commending westward voyaging to his fellow countrymen. In 1527 a certain John Rut, who deserves to be better known, fitted in a return voyage to, and considerable exploration of, the east coast of America between his regular sailings to Bordeaux to fetch the King's wine. He took seventy men, twice the *Mary Guildford*'s normal crew, including skilled artisans, and carried a forge as well as other tools. Rather more idiosyncratic was a voyage to the Newfoundland coast made in 1536 by two of the King's ships carrying no less than 120 persons, a quarter of them gentlemen, including some London lawyers. The organizer was a wealthy London leather-dealer, Master Richard Hore, said by Hakluyt to have been 'given to the study of cosmography', but he clearly had little knowledge of navigation or of how to survive even in a country teeming with game and fish. His 'tourists' very nearly starved to death and were only saved by the seizure of a French vessel full of stores. It was perhaps little wonder that it was twenty-seven years before any other English explorers sailed that way. Fishing-boats from Bristol and the south-west ports made quick dashes every summer to the fishing grounds off Newfoundland but took no interest in the North American mainland. It is, then, perhaps unfair to say that there was no interest at all in early Tudor London in westward exploration: only that the cloth-merchants, those best able to finance such voyages, were not involved. Indeed, in 1521, when asked to support an expedition to Newfoundland which already had the King's support, the Drapers' Company took the lead in persuading the rest of the London merchant establishment that the voyage was too risky in waters where English seamen had no experience, and this at the very moment when Ferdinand Magellan was crossing the Pacific on the first circumnavigation of the world!

In so far as Englishmen were achieving anything on the ocean, the early sixteenth century was the period of individualism, of free enterprise by those who, owing very little to the Crown, were able, when opportunity offered, to move into the more lucrative privateering, a traditional sideline of English seamen, especially in the south-west, and one which the early Tudor kings tried hard to eradicate. No doubt the London merchants, secure in their trade with the Spanish Netherlands, were horrified at the activities of Robert Reneger, the Southampton merchant and shipowner, whose opportunities of legitimate trade through his own port they themselves had largely scuppered. In 1545 he was the first Englishman to capture a Spanish treasureship, the *San Salvador*, off Cape St Vincent, on her way home from the West Indies laden with gold, silver, pearls, and 124 chests of sugar. There is, however, some evidence that Reneger shared the proceeds with important persons at Court, and indeed in the same year Thomas Wyndham, the only son of a Norfolk knight and one of Henry VIII's naval officers, went out on a private venture in search of French shipping as captain of the *Mawdelyn Russell*, owned by the Lord Privy Seal, John Lord Russell.

The complacency of the London merchants was to be rudely shattered by the middle of Edward VI's reign. Due to a combination of factors, not least the government's attempt to halt inflation by calling down the value of the coinage which made English cloth more expensive abroad, London's trade with Europe declined sharply in 1551–2. Light now dawned and, although the situation had largely recovered by the middle of the decade, the Londoners now realized that it was, in the words of the Russia Company's charter of 1555, 'inconvenient that the utterance of the commodities of England, especially cloth, should so much depend upon the Low Countries and Spain'. But prudence dictated that the risks be shared. The considerable sum of £6,000 was raised from no less than 240 individuals, each originally subscribing £25, with subsequent calls raising each investment within twenty years to £450, the price of a fairly large manor. The ownership of the shares could be handed on by will and they could even be sold. The actual business, which as things turned out took the form of an extensive though not very lucrative trade with Russia, was conducted entirely by the paid employees of a company incorporated by royal charter. Clearly, those who drafted the charter simply followed the familiar form of town charters of incorporation, obtaining for the company the right to use a common seal, to exist in perpetuity, to plead and be impleaded, to hold property, and to have a governing body.

The initial subscribers included seven peers, twenty knights, of whom six were important Crown officials, thirteen esquires, eight gentlemen, 144 London merchants (including two widows), and a solitary merchant of Bristol. The London merchants, including many present and future members of the governing bodies of the city and its guilds, had long been used to making common cause in their affairs, but now for the first time they were trading for their common profit and not in competition. The joint-stock principle was followed a few years later, but with far fewer shareholders, by the promoters of the voyages to Guinea in search of slaves, a trade already pioneered by the Hawkinses of Plymouth, but in this case the capital and any profits were redistributed at the end of each voyage. The Russia Company itself, and also the Levant Company formed in 1581, was later to revert to private trading under regulation, like the older Merchant Adventurers' Company. Perhaps it was the open-field tradition, individual proprietorship under communal regulation, which best served Englishmen's talents for collaboration.

In at least one other respect the history of the Muscovy trade showed how old traditions died hard. In the three ships which set out in 1553, command was divided between Sir Hugh Willoughby, an experienced soldier, named as Captain-General and responsible for the engagement of ships' masters, mariners, shipwrights, and gunners, and the purchase of victuals, and Richard Chancellor, a skilled navigator, as Pilot-General. Willoughby and the entire crews of two of the ships perished during the first winter in Lapland 'for want of experience to have made caves and stoves' (Hakluyt), but Chancellor reached Moscow and delivered the King's letter to the Czar. The company's agents were made very welcome in Russia. One of them, George Killingworth, impressed the Czar with his beard, grown very long, London-fashion, and said to have been over five feet.

It was also during the early 1550s that the merchants of London made their first real drive to 'undo' the aliens, especially those who had taken up residence. Their first success came in 1546 with the ending of the aliens' privilege, granted as recently as 1539, of paying the same customs rates as natives. From 1551 Englishmen were even more determined to press their advantage, especially one of the ablest young men of the age, Thomas Gresham. The second son of a very successful London merchant (and landowner) he had studied at Cambridge before becoming a freeman of the Mercers' Company in 1544, having first married a mercer's widow. His fame rests on his establishment, early in Elizabeth's reign, of a money market in London, the Royal Exchange, but his fellow merchants had more reason to be grateful to him for the part he played in securing from Protector Northumberland in 1552 the withdrawal of the special privileges of the Hanseatic merchants, at least to the extent that the Hansards could only carry English cloth to their own towns and not to the Londoners' mart at Antwerp. Queen Mary temporarily restored the Hanse rights, but although they did not finally depart until 1598 the German merchants never really recovered their centuries-old position in London. Mary Tudor also frustrated to some extent the Londoners' efforts to be rid of the large Italian colony in their midst, and as late as 1573 there were attempts to vex the Italians by reviving an old regulation whereby aliens importing Mediterranean goods, especially wine, were required to import a quota of bowstaves. Informers had a field day and in the courts wealthy Venetians protested in vain that the yew forests were now in Turkish hands. However, in spite of traditional English hostility towards the 'Lombards', when Englishmen began trading directly with the Mediterranean by sea in the 1570s, fetching not bowstaves but silks, spices, oil and currants, they were aided by the more realistic of their erstwhile Italian rivals. In 1576 two ships belonging to Mr John Hawkins and Mr Francis Drake were actually chartered by a certain Mr 'Asharbo', alias Acerbo Velutelli, a native of Lucca but resident in London, who was himself importing currants from Zante. By the 1580s fourteen or so English ships were sailing regularly to the Mediterranean, employing some six hundred seaman and, inevitably, indulging in occasional piracy. Merchants of Hull and Newcastle were re-opening trade with the Baltic, though from 1579 they had to face stiff competition from the London-based Eastland Company. The merchants of Bristol were in like manner up against the London Spanish Company. The fight was now joined between London and the provincial ports rather than against aliens.

Without the assistance of alien craftsmen the diversification of English industry would have been even longer delayed. The same emissaries whom Henry VIII sent to secure for him a Protestant queen, Ann of Cleves, in 1539, were also buying arms, not only heavy guns but, so backward were the English, expert gunners to teach them how to use them. Henry liked neither but he dispensed with his queen more easily than with his alien gunners. In fact he had been employing at least a nucleus of alien gun-founders for some time. Peter Baude, a Frenchman, had been in the country since 1509 and since 1533 had been casting 'brass', that is, bronze, cannon for the King, and passing on his skill to two Englishmen, Robert and John Owen. The French had pioneered the making of cast iron which was more serviceable than wrought iron and cheaper than brass. Some iron had been cast in the Weald since the 1490s, but not until 1543 was the first cast-iron cannon made, at Buxted in Sussex, by a team comprising Peter Baude, Ralph Hogg, iron-smelter, and the rector of Buxted, William Levett, who seems to have been the manager. Levett lost his benefice for some reason in 1545, but he seems to have regained it at Mary's accession, so possibly he did not go along with Henry VIII's church. This did not prevent him continuing to function as the King's gun-founder. Two Sussex landowners, Ralph Hodson of Framfield and Arthur Mylton of Mayfield, were also casting iron cannon for the King in the 1540s, and another pioneer was the duke of Norfolk at Worth in the same county. At his fall in 1546 the whole of his outfit, furnaces and stock, were taken over by Thomas Lord Seymour. When he too fell in

1549 the Crown let the whole to a Clement Throckmorton for twenty-one years at the substantial rent of £60 which he could pay in kind. Although iron-smelting spread to many other forest areas, the making of cannon was still confined to Sussex in the 1570s, one of four gentlemen foundry owners there then being Sir Thomas Gresham on his estate at Mayfield. By now English cannon were in demand abroad, and in spite of strenuous efforts by the Crown to prohibit their export without licence, it was very easy to slip them out through the many havens along the Sussex coast. Gresham remained first and foremost a businessman to the end of his life, but it must be said in his defence that he received no salary for his considerable financial services to the Crown.

Blast-furnaces producing iron ore to supply to smiths for the making of tools and utensils, many of these previously imported, multiplied from a score in the 1540s in the Weald alone to over fifty by 1550 and over one hundred in 1574. The promoters here also were largely the nobility and more substantial gentlemen. At Robertsbridge in Sussex, on the former monastic land he had acquired in 1539, Sir William Sidney employed a small and largely seasonal work-force from the local farming population. The earliest accounts were kept by his steward, the parson of Salehurst, some of them being written on blank pages from the former abbey's service books. In the later 1560s, with the help of German expertise, some steel was made here, but the cost of labour made it difficult to compete with German imports. By the 1570s most of the Sussex ironworks were worked by local yeomen farmers as a secondary occupation or by lesser gentlemen, both of these tending to operate on a very small scale and to invest any profit in the purchase of land. It was essentially a rural industry and never big business, and it was claimed in 1548 that iron had doubled in price since so much had been made in England.

Barely a year later, however, Sir Thomas Smith, the former Cambridge professor of both classics and civil law, but now an experienced politician and man of the world, argued the cost-effectiveness of native industry. In his *Discourse of the Commonweal of this Realm of England*, besides setting down, through the mouth of his fictitious 'Doctor', his own explanation of the recent price rises, he provided a long list of imported consumer goods which he claimed had risen in price more than 30 per cent in the previous seven years. His approach was somewhat austere, reflecting the ideas of contemporary social reformers. Indeed, Clement Armstrong, as long ago as the 1520s, had deplored the excessive importing of 'strange merchandise and artificial fantasies', and he in turn was echoing the thoughts of the early-fifteenth-century author of the *Libelle of Englyshe Polycye*. Some of the less essential luxuries Smith thought people could well do without, and he showed the traditional English respect for the value of materials rather than labour. 'Artificialitie,' he argued, must be manufactured at home, preferably in the towns. Farmers should be growing food to keep prices down. He recognized that Englishmen were already skilled in the making of cloth, caps and pewter and in the tanning of hides but he looked also for 'the making of glasses, swords, daggers, knives and all tools of iron and steel, also making of pins, points, laces, thread and all manner of paper and parchments'. He criticized the towns for shutting their gates to non-freemen, especially 'cunning craftsmen', and compared the short-sightedness of most English towns with the good sense of the Venetians, but his concern was as much for a healthy balance of trade as for full employment, this being only 1549, and he only envisaged his new industries employing twenty thousand persons.

Smith was not to see many light industries established during his lifetime (he died in 1577) but he must have been gratified at what was achieved in the native manufacture of glass. A little had always been produced in England but not of a quality to satisfy those who could afford to pay for the superior imported product. Credit for the first move towards the establishment of a skilled native craft should probably go to a London merchant, Henry Smith (no relation), who in

1552 obtained both permission from the Crown to bring skilled men from Normandy and a monopoly of the making of window glass in England. But the real breakthrough came in 1567 when a similar patent was granted to Jean Carré, a native of Arras but trading in Antwerp. His alien craftsmen were highly skilled and productive and were paid as much as 18s. a day at a time when skilled English stonemasons earned about 1s. a day, but for this they were expected to produce three cases of glass with a selling price of about 90s. The Frenchmen's ability to produce large quantities not only of good but also of cheaper glass than had previously been available was a major factor in the widespread substitution of glass in place of wooden shutters in quite modest houses, at least in London and the south. North of Trent 'window cloths' persisted down to 1600, but for many Englishmen the outlook from the early 1570s was decidedly brighter. Carré gave no undertaking to train Englishmen but the demand he created encouraged native glassmakers. The Strudwick family of Kirdford in Sussex were yeomen farmers who both made and carried glass (to the glaziers) as a secondary occupation, and although their product was probably very inferior to the Frenchmen's it made them enough money to build up a modest freehold estate by 1600. Carré died in 1572 and by about 1580 the holders of the monopoly of window glass manufacture were no longer asserting their rights, demand by now far outstripping supply.

Whether the glass monopoly and the many others that were granted by Queen Elizabeth to promoters of allegedly new industries were defensible is arguable, to say the least. The principle of monopoly was, of course, centuries old, having been justified by medieval craft guilds as a safeguard to the consumer of high standards of workmanship. The argument used by those seeking Tudor industrial privileges was that they needed both protection as inventors of new techniques and compensation for the risks they took. What was new about so many of the Elizabethan patents of monopoly was that they were bestowed upon individuals, or small partnerships, and that the grantees, especially when they were

Englishmen, were not themselves necessarily actively involved in manufacturing processes but, by selling licences,
were enabled to profit from other men's skills. Those granted
to aliens in the early part of the Queen's reign were the least
objectionable and did introduce new industries, but later on
they became political currency, the recipients being mostly
members of the Court circle. The latter almost inevitably put
up the price of the commodities concerned, even to the point
where imports were cheaper. The most outrageous were
those permitting their grantees to license people to evade the
law and the great parliamentary debate (1597–1601) which
led eventually to their partial withdrawal was fought largely
over constitutional issues. By then very few aliens were
involved.

Most of the individual aliens who came to England as merchants or industrial entrepreneurs, including the German mining
engineers, men such as Daniel Hochstetter and Thomas Thur-
land, came to England simply to make a better living in an industrially backward country where there was little competition.
Certain individuals came from the Low Countries, too, for the
same reason, but most of the 'Dutch' who came in very considerable numbers in and after 1565 did so ostensibly as religious
refugees. It was quickly realized that they were highly skilled
craftsmen and although most of them arrived first in London,
Colchester, the Cinque Ports and Southampton, great efforts
were made by the government to settle them in towns further
inland. They arrived of course at a time when urban economies
were still pretty stagnant, and just ahead of the early Elizabethan
rise in population, but it was extraordinary how easily some
towns were persuaded to forget their old prejudices against
strangers in general and aliens in particular. The good work of
Sir Thomas Smith, now firmly entrenched at Westminster, is
surely much in evidence. The corporation of Maidstone asked
in 1567 for makers not only of says (serges), mockadoes (mock
velvet) and other woollen cloths, but also of frisadoes (linen,
sailcloth and canvas), paving-tiles and bricks, all kinds of
armour, and for those engaged in 'other arts and sciences which

are not [here] known, being both necessary and profitable for the commonwealth'. It asked for sixty families, none to exceed twelve persons, including servants, but was allowed only thirty. Houses were found for them to rent and they had to engage in the stipulated crafts, take only English apprentices, employ only English unskilled labour and sell only wholesale. By 1585 there were in Maidstone forty-three alien families comprising 115 adults. In fact, with the help of its alien settlers, Maidstone found that its vocation lay in the making of linen thread. This not only encouraged the growing of flax in the surrounding countryside but contributed to the conversion of English people from woollen to linen clothes for everyday wear. Blue linen became for ordinary men and women, in the summer, including many who later migrated to America, almost as popular as it already was in France. Other refugees settled in Canterbury and Sandwich and, in even greater numbers, in Norwich where a revival in the making of worsted cloths was already under way. By the mid-1580s there were over 4,600 aliens there, and 1,300 at Colchester. At Sandwich one third of the population was now of alien stock and the corporation began restricting entry to certain favoured occupations. York, by comparison, acquired nothing which could be called an alien community, not necessarily because of its antipathy to radical Protestants but largely because, like Bristol and Exeter, it lay too far from the ports of entry. In spite of Cecil's enthusiasm and his attempts to resuscitate his native town, an alien settlement in Stamford does not seem to have been a success. These early Elizabethan groups of aliens did not, on the whole, introduce much industrial diversification, for most of them were cloth-makers, but they did contribute substantially towards the firm establishment of the 'New Draperies', fabrics which required very skilled workmanship, something which the largely rural English cloth industry lacked, and, very important as population grew in the 1570s and 1580s, which were labour-intensive. Alien silk-weavers settled in London in the 1570s and among other industries brought to Elizabethan London by aliens was starch-making, which, of course, was associated with the growing use of linen, especially the fine fabrics such as lawn and cambric. All of these could be washed more easily than wool. It was a Dutchwoman, Mistress Boone, wife of the Queen's coachman, who starched Her Majesty's magnificent ruffs, and a Fleming, Mistress Dinghen van der Plasse, who in the 1560s taught London women how to make the starch from wheat. How incalculable the English were! By 1585 there was great public concern at the sacrificing to 'vanity and pride [that] which would staunch the hunger of many that starve in the streets for want of bread'. This was Cecil, more concerned about how to feed the poor than to provide them with employment. From 1588 to 1601 starch-making was controlled by a patent of monopoly.

While there had certainly been no industrial revolution in England by 1600 there had been a certain amount of diversification. A stocking-knitting industry had started in the 1570s and by 1600 was occupying, part-time, thousands of country people in no less than ten counties. Pin-making, a very labour-intensive industry, was developing, but as late as 1597 some £40,000's worth of pins were imported. That in this respect the law was being flouted enabled the Dutch, who employed their poor filing pins and attaching knobs to them, to afford the purchase of English cloth. England's real problem was that apart from her woollen cloth and a few cannon she had no manufactured goods to export. In particular, her people had not by 1600 discovered how to employ their now considerable labour-force in making saleable goods from cheap raw materials. Such new industries as had become established were under-capitalized and only in rare cases employed sufficient persons to make much impression on the employment situation. Even in the country's staple industry there were hardly any factories in the modern sense. William Stumpe may have gathered some of his workpeople together in the former monastic buildings at Malmesbury, but he probably had far more people working for him in their own scattered homes.

But if Tudor people rarely experienced the discomforts of working in close proximity on land, the latter part of the century saw many more of them doing so on the high seas, combining legitimate trade and privateering in such a fine balance that it is difficult to say which was the by-employment. Of the sea-captains who showed the way, one was outstanding. It was in the early or mid-1560s, that Francis Drake, whose yeoman family had moved in the later 1540s from Devon to Kent, returned to join up in Plymouth with his wealthy and influential cousins, the Hawkins brothers, William and John, sons of the man who had sailed to Guinea and from there to South America in the 1530s. His first Atlantic crossing was to the West Indies under Captain John Lovell in 1566. This was no longer a merely provincial enterprise. John Hawkins had actually moved to London in about 1559 and as the son-in-law of Benjamin Gonson, Treasurer of the Queen's Navy, he was well placed to attract Court and city financial backing. In 1567 he told the Queen that he would sell slaves 'in truck of [African in exchange for] gold, pearls and emeralds', and his objective was still legitimate trade. Drake was, of course, present at St Juan de Ulua in 1569 when John Hawkins's fleet of six ships, including two of the Queen's, was attacked by some Spaniards. He returned as 'temporary' Captain Drake (of the *Judith*) and made his first visit to Court as the Hawkinses' 'servant' to report what had happened, including the fact that only seventy out of an original complement of four hundred seamen had returned. It must have been as if plague had struck the younger male population of Plymouth. From now on the young mariner had no scruples about getting his own back on the Spaniards by privateering. To his material interests was added a radical religious conviction which antedated his experience at St Juan. In 1573, following the episode at Nombre de Dios and his own first sight of the Pacific, and frustrated by the Queen's anxiety to restore good relations with the Spaniards, he went off to serve the earl of Essex in Ireland. The timing is interesting for it was probably there that he first became acquainted with professional military men, including his future ship-mate, Thomas Doughty, gentleman, and also with the idea of English overseas colonization.

Since about 1520 Englishmen had been considering the possibility of settlement in Ireland, primarily for political reasons, but increasingly from the later 1550s with an eye to her landed resources which had obvious attractions for younger sons such as Humphrey Gilbert. Their greatest ally at court was Sir Thomas Smith who in 1565 wrote to Cecil concerning the conquest of Ireland:

In my mind [the project] needeth nothing more than to have colonies, to augment our tongue, our laws, and our religion in that isle, which three be the true bands of the commonwealth whereby the Romans conquered and kept long time a great part of the world.

Among Smith's many Irish projects was one of 1574 which promised that settlers bringing at least fifty footmen or thirty horsemen would enjoy the status of lords of manors, that those bringing one hundred men would be lords of 'hundreds' to be named after them, and that all would exercise private jurisdictions. All, however, were to live in towns which Smith would plan; urban life, he thought, 'engendereth civility, policy, acquaintance, consultation, and a firm and sure seat', but for the first two years there were to be no feasts or frivolities, for the settlers were to be there 'to lay the foundation of a good and, it is hoped, an eternal colony for posterity, not a May game or a stage play'. Smith obtained considerable support, Cecil contributing a large sum, John Thynne, esquire, of Longleat in Wiltshire both money and men, Sir John Berkeley of Gloucestershire £1,000, and many gentlemen sums of up to £500. Even the vicar of Smith's Essex village, Theydon Mount, subscribed. Two hundred men sailed but by 1575 it was all over, the Irish having mounted very stiff opposition; the planning, however, contributed quite a lot to the later attempts by Englishmen to settle in North America. One wonders what the Devon sea-captain made of it all. By comparison, Drake's preparations in 1577 for the voyage which was to take him around the world, if equally hazardous, had a more limited objective, this being merely to explore the possibility of establishing English trading posts, if not colonies of settlers, in those parts of South America which were thought to be beyond Spanish preserves. Being in a temperate latitude similar to England the area might offer a market for English cloth. Drake had been preferred by the Queen to lead this voyage over Sir Richard Grenville whose own dream was of a great Pacific continent which was thought to stretch from beyond South America to Cathay, Terra Australis, 'by God's Providence left for England'. Why Elizabeth decided to send a mariner rather than a soldier is not clear. Perhaps she had more immediate use for treasure, or at least for maritime rather than for territorial expansion. However, John Oxenham, a close friend of both Drake and Grenville, was later to tell his Spanish captors that in England there were many people and little land. Drake, of course, put paid to the idea of the existence of a great southern continent and found the Spaniards much further south than he and his backers had reckoned. Without doubt, he had always hoped for spoil, though he can hardly have dreamed how easy it would be. More important in the long run than his treasure was his penetration of the Pacific and the East Indies, the first Englishman to reach those parts of the world.

Drake's backers were the usual Court syndicate, one ship being the Queen's, but the *Pelican*, renamed the *Golden Hind*, in which he completed his circumnavigation, was his own. He had with him on board when he set sail a considerable number of younger sons of English gentlemen, though not perhaps as many nor as eminent a complement as the west-country men who had been prepared to finance and possibly accompany Grenville. While still in the southern Atlantic Drake faced and dealt with a near-mutiny by the gentlemen, or some of them, leading him to execute the alleged ringleader, Thomas Doughty. This established that for the rest of the voyage he, as Captain-General, was in sole command and that all on board, gentlemen or, like himself, mere mariners, would 'haul and draw' together. He thus achieved well-nigh perfect discipline, consulting with the gentlemen but so respected that none sat down or put on his hat in his presence without permission. Socially, as in so

many other respects, the voyage was an outstanding achievement. His eventual knighthood and royal grant of arms in
1581 seem almost superfluous. Nor indeed did he disdain the
mayoralty of his home port in 1581–2, though when his first
wife, Mary Newman, daughter of a former shipmate, died in
1583 his next choice was a Somerset heiress, Elizabeth
Sydenham.

Overseas colonization, whether in Ireland or across the
Atlantic, had achieved little success by 1600. Sir Humphrey
Gilbert even attempted, especially after the great increase in
recusancy fines in 1581, to organize a settlement of English
Roman Catholic families on the east coast of North America.
The Catholic gentry were not without resources with which
to provide initial support, and with their tenants and servants
they would have formed a complete microcosm of English
society. It was even agreed that one in ten of the emigrants
should be persons without a livelihood in England. The main
emphasis was not on religious freedom – participation was not
to imply exile – but on the availability of land on the north
American mainland. Gilbert's death at sea in 1583 spelled the end
of the scheme, but by then most of the potential settlers were
in fear of having their throats cut by the Spaniards. Between 1584
and 1587 Sir Walter Raleigh, yet another younger son, assisted
as commander of the fleet by Sir Richard Grenville, organized
three successive settlements on the island of Roanoke off the coast
of the land he christened Virginia, the third party including
women. Why the colonists eventually fell out with the native
population will probably never be known but hunger may have
led them to invite liquidation. There was some hope in England
not only that the Indians would buy woollen cloth but also that
the Virginia settlement would provide the homeland with sub-
tropical products. But whatever the market might have been for
cloth, Raleigh's colonists, most of whom were Londoners, had
no knowledge of how to cultivate new crops. Indeed, even the
promoters, as in Ireland, were obsessed with the idea of founding
great cities. What America needed was hard-working farmers
and artisans, and in the 1580s these were not yet desperate enough

in England to want to leave home for good. It was small consolation to his colonists that Raleigh was reputedly the first Englishman to grow American potatoes and to smoke tobacco, the former on his extensive Irish estates, nor that, largely under the influence of his Portuguese pilot, Simon Fernandes, the English ships contrived to fit in some privateering on both the outward and return journeys. In the short run Raleigh and his contemporaries achieved very little on the far side of the Atlantic. In Professor Quinn's words, 'Ireland was in a real sense the moving frontier of Tudor England', for in Munster, at least, the closing decades of the century did see Englishmen establishing, for better or for worse, a precarious settlement.

It is easy to attribute the failures of Elizabeth's later years, particularly the stagnation of the country's economy, to the shortcomings of the gentlemen, and to the fact that enterprise had become the plaything of politicians and the Court, and to argue that the effect of a benevolent despotism, a tightly reined economy, was inevitably the rise of unprecedented private privilege. But were the gentry really in command? An analysis of all those who were admitted to the membership of companies concerned to promote home or overseas enterprise between 1575 and 1600, whether as active traders, industrialists, explorers, privateers, or simply as investors, shows that gentlemen, defined as those whose main source of income was the land, comprised under 20 per cent, while merchants, those whose resources were mainly commercial, accounted for over 80 per cent. Moreover, of the two hundred and fifty or so gentlemen concerned, the great majority, over two hundred, invested between 1577 and 1587. The gentry's lack of investment in purely trading enterprises and the vastly greater participation in these by the merchants, very largely those of London, are not, perhaps, surprising; but how can we account for the amount of city money invested from the mid-1580s onwards in that alternative to legitimate trade, privateering? The answer seems to lie in the merchants' conversion to the idea that, particularly when the country was at war, the two could be engaged upon in the course of a single voyage, thus halving the overheads or doubling the profits. John Hawley of Dartmouth had had the same idea two centuries earlier. Now, however, Londoners dominated the game, and this is perhaps just one more example of the way in which the metropolis drew into itself, and indeed exemplified, the worst, as well as the best, features of Tudor enterprise.

Meanwhile in the country at large, out of sight and sound of London and the provincial seaports, the vast majority of gentlemen lived largely on their rents and the profits of a demesne farm or two, and their tenants farmed, as always, largely for subsistence. Concern in high places about the country's dependence on imports was not confined to manufactured goods, but also comprehended the raw materials of industry produced on the land. Great efforts were made to encourage the growing of flax and hemp, primarily for the making of linen, ropes and canvas but towards the end of the century for the oil which was in great demand for soap-making, cloth-manufacture, lighting and cooking. A succession of statutes from as early as 1532 ordered all occupiers of over sixty acres of land to devote a proportion to these crops, but to little avail except in those parts of Kent, Suffolk and Lincolnshire where the soil was particularly suitable. Official promotion of the growing of coleseed or rape, also for the production of oil, only really commenced in Elizabeth's reign and was inextricably entangled with grants of patents for the crushing of the seed. Farmers were not easily persuaded. After all, they could now usually sell all the corn they could produce, and even in government circles there was anxiety lest the qualified success achieved in stemming the conversion of land from arable to pasture might be undone if too much was devoted to industrial crops. The new crop (new at least to Tudor England) which made most headway was woad, needed in great quantity for dyeing woollen cloth. Although formerly grown here, by the fifteenth century it was all being imported raw from France and from the Azores. As early as 1542 Thomas Derby of Cranborne in Dorset obtained from the Privy Council (of which he was Clerk) permission to 'take up labourers to forward his intent touching the making of woad'. He was a pioneer, possibly sufficiently privy to govern-ment aims to judge that the London merchants might one day be forced to have their cloth dyed in England. In fact, Parlia-ment did not begin to encourage the growing of woad in England until 1559, and it was well into the 1580s before many farmers, and then very largely gentlemen, responded. In 1585 it was reported that nearly 5,000 acres, in twelve counties from Worcestershire to Hampshire and Suffolk, were devoted to woad, not perhaps a great many, but it has been calculated that even this scale of production will have employed 20,000 men, women and children for four months each year. Whether home-grown woad was any cheaper than that which had previously been imported, even allowing for inflation, we do not know. Nor do we know whether it was a more profitable crop than grain, though it is significant that Sir Francis Wil-loughby of Wollaton near Nottingham went in for woad-growing in 1585 at a time when he was short of money for the building of his great mansion there. Sir Francis's operations were directed by a certain Robert Payne of High Wycombe in Buckinghamshire, who called himself 'gentleman' but who was consistently referred to by his partner as 'yeoman'. In fact, the woad grown was unsold, or not paid for, and by 1588 the project had to be abandoned. Payne was at best a trier – he suggested all manner of other profitable investments to Sir Francis – but he was probably a practised confidence trickster. One wonders how many others of his kind bled the more impoverished and gullible gentlemen of Elizabethan England.

From the 1560s there are signs that not only gentlemen with land in their own occupation but also many of the more substantial tenant farmers were turning, not so much to new crops, as to improved farming techniques. Enclosure of arable ground by way of redistribution and consolidation of former open-field strips was a contributory factor but not an essential prerequisite. There was, too, a renewed coloniza-tion of waste ground in the 1570s and 1580s, especially in woodland areas where there was more scope. Land which had not been tilled since the fourteenth century, if then, was

taken under the plough, and a new beginning was made in
the 1590s on the drainage of fenland. Manorial rentals show
new 'intakes', and land which had previously only been
cropped occasionally was now regularly 'manured', that is,
added to the arable nucleus. By such means farming
horizons were quite literally changing. In the great midland
plain farmers were slowly but surely, from the 1560s,
abandoning the rigid distinction between arable and pasture
land and adopting the more flexible 'up-and-down' husbandry, 'up' for corn and 'down' for grass. This must have
led to radical changes, even total abandonment, of time-
honoured local customary rotations, with considerable consequences for community life. Corn-yields on some farms
crept up to as much as twice their former levels, and with the
better grass, though with as yet little selective breeding, the
quality of stock slowly improved. By 1600, too, many
lowland farmers were 'floating' their water-meadows by
diverting streams and constructing elaborate trenches from
which the land flooded in winter and gained invaluable
sediment. Slowly but surely, too, more farmers were realiz-
ing the value of lime-burning and the digging of marl (clay),
in both cases for spreading on their land to enhance its
fertility. Near the coasts, and indeed in some cases quite a
long way inland, the old practice of spreading sea-sand and
seaweed was considerably extended. Since 1555 the age-old
statutory ban on the export of grain had been replaced by
statutory encouragement, except in times of very real scarcity.
Internal long-distance trade in foodstuffs was growing too,
even, again with government support, to relieve local shortages.
But in spite of such official encouragement it is unlikely that
many Elizabethan farmers were exerting themselves more than
was normally necessary to produce sufficient food for their own
families and for nearby markets. From about 1577 there was
available in England a printed translation of Conrad Heresbach's
Foure Bookes of Husbandry which spelled out the benefits, aesthetic as well as economic, of growing vegetables. These, it was
argued, would both employ the poor and feed them, and also

save currency by obviating the need to import onions and cabbages from Holland. We should not assume, however, that many English farmers, except those in the immediate vicinity of London and the larger cities, read, let alone heeded, such advice before the end of the century. Far from offering a depressing picture this indicates a society not yet in a hurry for change.

Most of the sixteenth-century agrarian innovation of which there is evidence took place between 1560 and 1585, which might suggest a response to a growing number of mouths to feed. But who can be sure that the chain of cause and effect was not the other way round? Although by no means all the experiments and improvements were made by gentlemen or even yeomen, agricultural progress in Tudor England did not so much result in the making of fortunes as flow from them. Nor should the demoralizing effects of the bad harvests of the 1590s be underestimated as disincentives to change. It required quite unusual self-confidence to pit one's own wits and muscle against the will of God. There was much to encourage Englishmen in the decade following the defeat of the Spanish Armada to believe, even more firmly than had their medieval ancestors, that the golden age was in the past.

11. *The Poor in Very Deed*

In 'Utopia' those who were able worked and those disabled
by sickness, youth or old age were supplied from the common
stock. But early Tudor England was very different from Thomas
More's fantasy world, and those convicted of helping themselves were liable to suffer the full rigours of a law which made
theft a felony, an offence punishable by death. The medieval
state did not concern itself with the relief of poverty, regarding
that as the responsibility of the Church, one which the Church
welcomed, both as a means of salvation for its members, both
clerical and lay, and also as a justification for accepting and
soliciting material resources in excess of those needed for the
sustenance of the clergy, both secular and regular. The main
thrust of the Church's critics, from John Wyclif to Simon Fish,
was that she was not bestowing on the poor more than a very
small proportion of her surplus wealth. When, in the mid
sixteenth century, the Church was relieved of a substantial
part of that wealth, the poor were almost forgotten in the
scramble of the laity at large, including the Crown, to repossess
the resources bestowed on the clergy by their ancestors. However, from small beginnings even before the Reformation,
the state bestirred itself, slowly distinguishing not only between
the deserving poor and the merely idle, but also between the
genuinely unemployed and professional vagrants, and in part
took over from the Church, but through its agents in the
parishes, the task of extracting from men and women of some
substance a public purse from which the poor might be relieved.
Poor-rates were a long time coming, were very grudgingly
paid, and were probably always inadequate. Fortunately for
the poor, the layman's charitable impulse, though not especially

quickened by the Reformation, was very far from being extinguished by it. All in all, provision was probably not far short of demand, except for the needs of the sick, until the last decade of the century. In the 1590s, however, to the country's traditional quota of young, aged, and disabled poor were added large numbers of able-bodied poor, who through no wish of their own were chronically unemployed. But even then, as throughout the sixteenth century, poverty was very largely an urban problem.

Canon law, the law of the Church, required that at least one quarter of all ecclesiastical income be bestowed on the poor, and parish clergy were supposed to devote one third of their income to alms-giving and to 'hospitality', which could mean anything from offering lodging to wayfarers and keeping open house for neighbours, rich as well as poor, to employing servants. While failure to share their modest resources with their needy parishioners does not seem to have resulted in many appearances of parish clergy before the archdeacons, Thomas Cromwell in 1536 in his first Injunctions to the Clergy, equating the goods of the Church with the goods of the poor, added rather tartly that 'at these days nothing is less seen than the poor to be sustained with the same'. The bishops traditionally appointed special officials called almoners to dispense their direct charitable giving, but the sums they set aside for the purpose were usually quite small. Far more was spent on more indulgent forms of episcopal 'hospitality', both in the maintenance of very large households and in entertaining, but there was a spin-off for the poor in the distribution of left-over food at palace gates, sometimes in very large quantities. Nicholas West, bishop of Ely (1512–23), is reported to have fed two hundred men daily with 'warm meats' (hot meals), but with one hundred servants regularly employed he could presumably well afford to dispose in this way of the rents in kind from his many manors. The last pre-Reformation prelate to leave a substantial sum specifically for the poor in his will was John Morton, Archbishop of Canterbury, who bequeathed 1,000 marks in 1500.

When kings, wealthy churchmen, and laymen had founded religious houses, their primary requirement had been that the monks or nuns should pray for them, their kindred, and all Christian people. Good works were rarely stipulated, though towards the end of the medieval period certain augmentations of monastic revenue had been particularly designated for charitable disbursement, sometimes for very specific regular 'doles'. In the survey of ecclesiastical revenue, the *Valor Ecclesiasticus*, made in 1535, these obligatory outgoings, which were allowed for tax purposes against gross income, amounted in all to less than 2.5 per cent of monastic income. The monks, and nuns too, were expected to distribute 'broken meats' to the poor, and indeed to succour anyone coming to their gates, but, as in the case of the bishops, a good deal of their hospitality was bestowed on the more affluent of their friends and benefactors. Of their permanent lay residents those who on entry had paid a lump sum, often partly in kind, may well have outnumbered those nominated by lay patrons as 'corrodians' to be accommodated entirely at the cost of the monastery.

The Church, or rather its benefactors, also made provision for more institutionalized charity, in particular the establishment of hospitals for the care of the sick and of almshouses for those more able poor people who needed only shelter and a regular pension. Hospitals for lepers were, by 1500, a thing of the past in England, leprosy no longer being endemic. Some had been converted into refuges for the sick generally but most had just disappeared. Even some former hospitals had become just old people's homes, communities of 'bedesmen' (sayers of prayers), offering little by way of professional care to the infirm. Some no longer admitted the laity and had become simply chantry chapels. Most of those which still admitted sick people had no more than six to ten beds, but there were notable exceptions such as St Leonard's, York, which in the later 1530s still had over forty elderly and sick inmates. In the 1530s there still existed in England rather over four hundred hospitals, about twenty-seven of these being technically monasteries as their religious communities had adopted the Rule of St Augustine.

Very few had more than £100 a year to spend, most had less than £30 and quite a number under £10. All told there cannot have been residential provision for more than 5,000 sick people in all the English hospitals. The hospital of St Mary the Virgin at Newcastle upon Tyne, with a permanent household of a master, a chaplain, and six resident 'bedefolk' to bear the brunt of the intercessions, offered lodging to all destitute wayfarers, and there were houses catering especially for maimed soldiers and sailors at Dover, Hythe, Southampton and Hull. Gaunt's Hospital in Bristol had a paying guest, Lady Jane Guildford, who wrote to Cromwell begging that she not be disturbed. Some hospitals, as it happened to their eventual cost, or rather to that of potential inmates, had been at some time annexed to religious houses, as was the hospital of St Julian in 1505 to its near neighbour the abbey of St Albans. The hospital of St James and St John at Brackley, intended primarily for the relief of poor travellers, had been annexed to Magdalen College, Oxford, in 1484 and was still open in 1535 with an annual income of over £65. At Cambridge, however, the hospital of St John the Evangelist was in such a state of decay by 1509 that it had to be rescued and was eventually converted into St John's College.

In the later Middle Ages and early sixteenth century laymen were more likely to found almshouses, that is, buildings providing separate living accommodation either for unmarried or widowed men and women, usually living in pairs, or for married couples. The archetype was that founded in 1424 in accordance with the will of Richard Whittington, mercer, and former Lord Mayor of London. There was provision for thirteen poor freemen of the city, preference being given to freemen of the Mercers' Company who were not members of the livery. As long as possible those who fell sick were to be nursed by the other inmates but those who, having become chronic invalids or insane, had to be moved to other institutions, were allowed to continue to draw their food allowance of 1s. 2d. per person per week. In one respect in particular Whittington and his executors were ahead of their time: in spite of the emphasis on prayers for Richard and his wife Alice, the trust monies were left to the Fellowship of St Thomas of Acon, alias the Mercers' Company. By the end of the fifteenth century there were, in a scatter of ten counties in England, just over seventy almshouses, ranging from twenty-three in Yorkshire, through twelve and ten respectively in Kent and Norfolk, to none at all in Lancashire. Between 1500 and 1520 there were further foundations, most of them, as always, in towns, but, after that, for two decades the momentum was lost.

No one, least of all Henry VIII, pretended that the wholesale dissolution of monasteries or chantries would directly and substantially augment the country's provision for the relief of poverty. Even those who cried loudly for more schools had in mind not so much the education of the poor as the sons of gentlemen. But not even Cromwell was anxious to incur the odium of extinguishing charitable trusts and at worst the government followed a strictly legalistic line. In the case of monasteries some effort was made to safeguard the relatively minor portion of their resources which consisted of designated charitable trusts. A few were passed on as charges on their income to lay grantees of monastic property. Others became a charge on royal income. The statute of 1539 authorizing the establishment, out of former monastic property, of new bishoprics contained a preamble, thought to have been composed by the King himself, which actually promised that provision would now be made for 'old servants decayed to have livings, almshouses for poor folk to be sustained in, [and] daily alms to be administered...' Fourteen new secular cathedral churches were established, and a particular obligation was placed on their clergy to provide for those in need. The new dean and chapter of Worcester, for example, were instructed to set aside £40 a year, of which 48s. was to be given to prisoners in the city's gaols, 6d. per week to be given to twenty poor householders, and the rest to be distributed as occasion required. All in all, however, such provision was but a small proportion of the monastic resources unlocked by the Crown, and in 1546 Henry Brinklow, the former friar, was to remind the King of his promise and to warn him that he would surely 'stand before the judgement seat of God in no more reputation than one of those miserable creatures which do now daily die in the streets for lack of their due portion ... which they trusted to have received when they saw your Highness turn out the other sturdy beggars'. The preacher clearly knew his political jargon, but his was a voice crying in the wilderness.

Following the disappearance of the monasteries, the future of the hospitals and almshouses depended on a technicality. Those hospitals whose communities of priests had adopted a monastic rule were swept away between 1536 and 1540, their permanent residents provided with some compensation. In 1540 the forty inmates of St Leonard's Hospital at York were each awarded a pension of 26s. 8d., this having been their annual maintenance allowance, but of course they lost the roof over their heads, and the members of the community which had cared for them were rather better provided for. Many of those hospitals which remained were dissolved with the chantries in 1547, the only exceptions being those whose secular trustees, or in some cases friends, such as municipal corporations, fought hard enough for their survival, often with reduced endowments. Thus at York the two hospitals of Corpus Christi and St Thomas the Martyr, which had been taken over in 1478 by the Corpus Christi guild, survived, but all in all the city lost, between 1530 and 1560, thirteen of its former complement of twenty-two such institutions. All over the country, however, most of the almshouses survived, largely on account of their secular trusteeship, a substantial legacy from the later Middle Ages which was to serve as a model for the charitable inclinations of post-Reformation English society.

Only the really well-to-do laymen and clergy in late-medieval and early Tudor England could afford to found almshouses. For those of more modest means small cash sums had to suffice. Dependent as we are on the evidence of their wills, it is not easy to distinguish people's real concern for the needs of the poor from their own very deeply felt need for prayers after their death. It was believed – some might say very conveniently – that the prayers of poor people had particular efficacy in lessening the pains of purgatory. Most testators in fact simply left instructions that part of their estate be disposed of by their executors in a manner likely to be most beneficial to the 'health' of their souls. A sizeable minority specified that money was to be given to the poor, and many executors were no doubt only too happy to oblige all comers as far as the money would go. However, there were a few testators who wished their executors to be more discriminating: in 1528 Richard Clarke of Lincoln stated very firmly 'that there shall be no penny dole dolt for me at my burial, nor none assembly ... of poor folks, and I will that warning shall be given thereof'. Instead he wished each of one hundred poor residents of the town, in default of which those in neighbouring towns, to have one groat (4d.) apiece. Alice Spring, widow of the wealthy Suffolk clothier and landed gentleman who left £13 at her death in 1538 to be given to 'poor folks and indigent householders within the parish of Lavenham' also rejected the idea of a common dole 'where', as she declared, 'most commonly the unneedy taketh the relief of the needy'. This kindly old lady even went further and stipulated that the alms were to be delivered to people's homes so that they might be spared undue 'labour and travail', echoing parliamentary provision in 1531 that funeral doles should be 'sent home to the people'. What we shall never know, of course, is the extent to which householders in their lifetimes helped their needy neighbours in the same charitable but discriminating manner.

The real trouble was the almost complete lack of regular, sustained, communal provision, with funds in reserve for special emergencies. Some town corporations as well as guilds were trustees of one or more small endowments for the relief of poverty, and towns, to a far greater extent than rural communities, largely by virtue of their ownership of property and their ability to levy tolls on trade, did have corporate funds which could be tapped in dire emergencies and even augmented by appeals to or even levies on their wealthy establishment. There was, in fact, in the larger early Tudor towns a long-standing tradition of communal provision of free or subsidized grain in times of dearth. What could be done is well illustrated by what happened in Coventry in 1518–20. First of all, when John Haddon, a wealthy draper, made his will in March 1519, it was no doubt the poor harvest of the previous year which moved him to leave to the corporation the sum of £20, to be used, when necessary, to reduce the price of corn. Following an even worse harvest that year the city council took steps to control the market in the interests of the inhabitants, and finally, a year later, following a survey of the total population and of existing stocks, proceeded, just before Christmas, to buy from its own resources nearly a hundred quarters of grain. Three bad harvests coupled with unemployment in the cloth industry had suddenly and considerably increased the number of households in need. It was a situation faced far more regularly by London where even a slight rise in grain prices sent vast numbers below subsistence level, but less frequently in the countryside, except in those areas where little or no corn could be grown.

For most early Tudor towns, and London in particular, the most pressing problem was the growing number of beggars. There were, of course, existing laws forbidding people to give alms to the able-bodied and ordering both the able and the disabled to return to their place of birth, but that still left the complement of helpless, indigenous poor. Soon after 1500 some towns attempted to control numbers by issuing licences to beg. Gloucester is thought to have done so as early as 1504. At York in 1515 the sick and impotent were issued with badges to be worn on the shoulder of their outer garments, and here, as in many other towns, 'masters of beggars' were appointed. London too resorted to licensing in or before 1517, placing the responsibility on its aldermen, a limit being placed on the number of badges to be issued for each of the city's wards. At best this meant waiting for 'dead men's shoes' and at worst, no doubt, a trade in badges. The national statute of 1531 extended this duty to all JPs, adding to the existing municipal schemes only an insistence that beggars carry written descriptions of their territory.

It was in London in 1533 that the first real efforts were made to provide a continuing fund. The aldermen were instructed to appoint persons 'to gather the devotions of parishioners for the poor folk weekly and to distribute them ... at the church doors'. In 1538 the city's chronicler, Henry Wriothesley, thought it worthy of record that the Lord Mayor, Richard Gresham, arranged for various 'worshipful men' to collect money for the poor at the Lenten Sunday sermons at Paul's Cross, and to distribute it week by week to those 'which had most need thereof'. For a decade the collectors did their best with varying enthusiasm and success until 1547 when it was decided that there would have to be a compulsory levy, especially if the city was to make efficient use of the hospitals it was in process of acquiring from the Crown. London's example was quickly followed by the second largest city in the kingdom, Norwich, perhaps significantly in 1549, immediately after the putting down of Kett's rebellion. York followed suit in 1550. The towns were undoubtedly setting the pace, but only because, compared with the countryside, they had greater problems.

Meanwhile, at Westminster, the politicians were only gradually distinguishing the problem of genuine distress from 'idle vagabondage' and Parliament was, of course, concerned with country as well as town. There were suggestions being made, in or around 1534, that each parish should appoint two officials who would compile a register of 'old, sick, lame, feeble and impotent' persons and relieve them from a parish fund. All begging would thus be eliminated except that the disabled might be 'employed' soliciting contributions to the fund, part of which might be used to provide free medical attention for those of the sick capable of being rehabilitated. The Act which was actually passed in 1536, while often castigated for its failure to provide for work for the unemployed, did in fact follow up most of the suggestions for the disabled poor, except that for medical care. In the body of the Act the receipt of private alms-giving was limited to friars, shipwrecked mariners, the lame and the blind, though all poor people were permitted to continue to solicit 'broken meats' and 'refuse [waste] drink'. A proviso added by the Lords allowed noblemen and other householders, or their servants, to offer 'the fragments [of their] broken meats or drinks' to all comers, even strangers to the parish. Did not Thomas Cromwell himself give bread, meat and drink twice a day to two hundred persons at his gate, a manifestation of his status which no man of worship would lightly surrender? A further last-minute exemption somewhat inconsistently concerned persons who, 'riding, going, or passing by the way', gave alms to the deserving poor. The Act was in danger of losing its point. However, the establishment of parish funds was made obligatory, 'by gathering ... of such *charitable and voluntary* alms every Sunday, Holy Day, and other Festival Day', and parishes were threatened corporately with fines of 20s. a month for default. The Commons added, hopefully, that any parish having surplus funds should assist neighbouring parishes. Even so the Bill had a rough passage, no doubt because MPs regarded even a voluntary levy for the poor, quite rightly as it turned out, as the first step towards a new form of personal taxation. The duty placed upon the clergy to commend the Act in their sermons was the corollary to the reminder of their own obligations towards the poor given to them by Cromwell in his first Injunctions later in the same year, though all he required was that non-resident clergy with incomes of at least £20 should distribute a fortieth part in alms. Cromwell was nothing if not a realist. He also, incidentally, laid on church-wardens, or 'some other honest men of the parish', the task of seeing that the clergy complied. Indeed, the churchwardens now replaced JPs and parish constables (who had been made responsible in the Act of 1531) as administrators. The very reference to the officers of the ecclesiastical parish, coupled with a suggestion that any alms other than those permitted to be given directly might be placed in the church's common box, is a reminder that men were accustomed to regard the relief of the poor as an ecclesiastical preserve, or, to put it another way, that the relief of the poor was still regarded as part of a man's duty as a member of a Christian community.

Indeed, by avoiding the introduction of compulsory poor-rates, the members of the Reformation Parliament were, consciously or not, adhering to the traditional belief in the importance of good works. Unless entirely voluntary, the relief of the poor could not be an act of Christian charity. Being subject to confirmation by the next parliament, the statute was almost certainly never enforced.

Was the very failure to make the Act permanent due to a recognition that in the country at large the need was not urgent? An analysis of wills in ten of the most densely populated English counties, including Middlesex, shows that the amount of money left to the poor, having dropped slightly in the 1510s and 1520s, actually picked up considerably in the 1530s, and at over £21,000 in the 1550s, before inflation had really begun to bite, was four times what it had been half a century earlier. Most of this, in spite of the attempts at legislative prohibition, was being disposed of in the traditional manner. After all, belief in purgatory was not officially abandoned until 1563 and its holy terrors were no doubt still sufficient to induce those nearing death to make sure that they personally would be prayed for. So in 1545 Robert Gower of Terrington in Yorkshire, former professional soldier, left 20s. 'to be given in alms in the parish church ... to be prayed for', and Roger Tempest in the same county, when making his will in 1555, provided that 'every cottage house of Norton have one penny in money or else in bread'. Churchwardens and the parish poor box were not yet substitutes for the prayers of the children of Christ. However, those men of the world, the London mercers, certainly by 1560 and probably as early as 1552, released the inmates of Whittington's almshouses from their obligation to pray for the souls of their founders.

The Act of 1536 was, however, the thin end of the wedge, and even the otherwise entirely secular and vicious statute against vagabonds of 1547 had attached to it an invitation to parishes to erect houses for the accommodation of the disabled poor, no doubt an attempt to offset the disappearance of so many hospitals. It also contained a reiteration of the encouragement to parishes to collect for the poor each Sunday. An Act of 1552 not only called on the clergy and parish officers to compile registers of the poor, but offered them a little 'stick' in authorizing them to refer to the bishop for ecclesiastical censure parishioners who declined to contribute to the poor box. The next stage was reached in 1563 when the bishops, presumably having failed to find ways of disciplining their flocks, were authorized by Parliament to bind over recalcitrants in the sum of £10 to appear before the JPs, on whom was now placed the responsibility for assessing the culprits to pay weekly instalments under threat of imprisonment. The voluntary principle still held firm for those who chose to respond, the likelihood being, however, that little or nothing was yet happening at parish level either in the collecting of alms for the poor or in dealing with defaulters.

Meanwhile towns up and down the country were slowly but surely stepping up their efforts, mostly concentrating on controlling the number of beggars. Action was usually precipitated by an emergency, especially an outbreak of plague such as happened in Lincoln in 1550 when, to try to stop the spread of infection by confining even licensed beggars to their homes, a fund was opened for the relief of poor people, each alderman being assessed to pay 4d. a week, and other substantial citizens 2d. Following another epidemic in 1557 the cathedral clergy and all resident gentlemen and the better-off householders were invited to subscribe. Where London and Norwich had led the way, many other towns were following a decade later, perhaps driven to do something to relieve survivors of the flu of 1557 and 1558. Cambridge and Ipswich in 1557 and Exeter in 1560 were making the payment of money for the relief of poverty compulsory for all householders 'of ability', implying some sort of assessment, and with his council behind him a mayor did not need to rely on action by the bishop. By 1588 the city of York was able to afford to give 1½d. a day to all old and infirm people who had lived there for at least three years and did not beg. In 1591 it was laid down that all strangers caught begging would be treated as vagrants.

Towns in the middle of the Tudor period were also way ahead of the countryside in providing institutionalized relief. The founding of almshouses had fallen away immediately before the Reformation and not until the 1550s was as much money being left for this purpose as at the pre-Reformation peak of nearly £1,300 a year in the decade 1501–10. Needless to say it bought rather less. Hospitals for the care of the sick seemed almost a lost cause, especially as the Act of 1547 which gave some encouragement to their foundation was quickly repealed. Here again, however, London was the great exception. The city acquired as gifts from Henry VIII in 1546–7, and to all intents and purposes refounded, St Bartholomew's Hospital in Smithfield, with 100 beds, and the use, though not the ownership, of the much smaller Bethlehem (Bedlam) Hospital for the insane. Each had some endowments in the form of property, but that of Bedlam brought in by way of rents only just over £34 a year. For St Thomas's Hospital, also for the physically sick, together with the former Grey Friars, the city paid the Crown nearly £2,500. The benefit was twofold, for these hospitals were regularly remembered by the citizens in their wills and for the rest of the sixteenth century were not dependent on parochial poor-rates. This does not mean that their income was adequate or that there was never peculation by the paid officials, although they had on their new boards of governors most of the leading citizens, Catholics as well as Protestants, including one of the most eminent of the city's money men, Martin Bowes, goldsmith, who was also one of London's MPs. It was claimed in 1552 that during the previous five years over eight hundred persons per year had been healed and that only 172 had died, and in support of its request to the Crown in the same year for the former royal palace of Bridewell for use as a reformatory, the city corporation congratulated itself on having already provided for all those in need of care. The city was later to be affronted by Mary Tudor's refounding of the Savoy Hospital which it claimed would only serve to attract beggars. To add to its annoyance, Parliament was persuaded in 1553 to re-introduce licensed begging, and, statutorily confirmed, this was once again withdrawn in 1563. Meanwhile the corporation had adapted for use as an orphanage the former Grey Friary, which in 1552 was renamed Christ's Hospital. By 1553 this was said to be housing 280 children, and there were 100 more boarded out in the country, but that the city was unduly complacent is shown up by the fact that out of fifty-nine children aged between five and ten years admitted to the hospital proper in 1563 no less than sixteen had died before the end of the year. Mortality was even higher among those sent out into the country for wet-nursing. Even Bedlam must have been quite inadequate. It could only accommodate about twenty 'distracted' persons, and many of them were paid for by friends and relations. In 1598 the inmates included, besides Elizabeth Dicons of East Ham, one 'Hans' who was paid for by the governors of the Dutch Church, a fellow of Pembroke Hall, Cambridge, and a member of the Chapel Royal. The condition of the old building in Bishopsgate then was described as 'so loathesome and filthily kept [as not to be] fit for any man to come in'. Gifts of food, even from the Lord Mayor's table, were said to be appropriated by the Keeper and at best sold to those described very appropriately as 'the prisoners'. However, London's achievements shine by comparison with those of the city of Bristol which, although it purchased the former Gaunt's Hospital in 1541, made no provision for orphans until it founded Queen Elizabeth's Hospital in 1590. Of the other larger provincial towns the most remarkable and possibly unique success story was that of Norwich. According to an inquiry carried out in 1570, out of a total population of well over 10,000, 650 of the wealthier householders were contributing regularly to a fund which was relieving less than one third of that number who constituted the city's really poor population. The city council immediately prohibited begging entirely. The powers that be at Westminster were very impressed, especially Archbishop Matthew Parker, a native of Norwich, and when in 1572 Parliament appointed a committee to consider a new statute, one of its members was the city's MP, John Aldrich, who had been mayor in 1570–71.

By the beginning of Elizabeth's reign, and possibly even earlier, something was also happening in the rural parishes. The Act of Uniformity of 1559, in providing for the levying by churchwardens of fines of 1s. per Sunday on all persons failing to attend church, must in some parishes have offered a useful regular source of succour for the poor. The Act of 1563 involving the JPs may also have had some effect in the country at large. One swallow does not make a summer and it may be pure coincidence that the earliest evidence we have of a rural parish's efforts regularly to collect and distribute a poor rate comes from Northill in Bedfordshire and relates to the years 1563–5. John Nichols and Harry Clarke handled, it is true, very varying amounts of cash each quarter, usually only a few shillings and rarely over £1. This was distributed among about a dozen persons, each of whom rarely received more than 8d. a quarter, though some later accounts from the 1580s show 'old Mother Morris' costing the parish over £1 a year in board and lodging. Some of the cash even came from small private bequests. Scattered evidence tells of other kinds of rural parish effort. At Dry Drayton in Cambridgeshire, sometime after 1571, when barley was dear, the Puritan parson, Richard Greenham, 'by holy persuasions', got a score or so of local farmers to join with him in building up a common granary where the poor could obtain corn at under half the market price. In 1569, the year of the Northern Rising and one which inaugurated a very determined national effort to put down vagrancy, there was a government inquiry into the implementation of the most recent Act. Reports varied and although it is unlikely that either Cecil or the Queen were taken in by the many ambiguous replies that 'all things be well', it seems unlikely that either Northill or Dry Drayton was unique.

Norwich's success had demonstrated that the only really effective remedy was a compulsory poor-rate. The elaborate Act of 1572 which made this a universal obligation otherwise contained little that was new. The idea of compiling parochial censuses of the poor had appeared in the Act of 1552, the provision of housing in 1547, and the sending of vagrants

home to their native parishes and the prohibition of begging
were old ploys. Even the empowering of the civil authorities
to assess and levy weekly poor-rates by the appointment of
collectors, with imprisonment for defaulters, was little more
than a positive re-enactment of the fall-back provided in 1563
for operation when persuasion failed to extract voluntary alms.
One novelty was the provision for the appointment by the JPs
of local Overseers of the Poor, to be selected annually from
among the more substantial householders. Those appointed
were to be unpaid and unable to refuse to serve: no one could
escape, except by paying a fine. Service to the secular parish
community was becoming more compulsory than had ever
been the case with lay service to God and the Church.
There is no way of discovering, so meagre are the civil parish
records of the period, to what extent this particular Act was
implemented. In ten counties which have been searched only
four hundred assessments at most have been found for the years
between 1560 and 1600, which averages at only one per county
per year. An exhaustive search of the records of the county of
Kent led to the statement that 'it seems likely that a considerable
number of Kentish parishes were operating parochial relief'
before about 1590, and most by 1603. Perhaps they were, but
the few collectors' accounts which survive make no mention
of Overseers. Those who drafted the Act of 1572 clearly
envisaged that the number of deserving poor in any parish
would remain fixed and there was no provision for the accumulation of emergency reserves. Perhaps in 1572 this was still not
as unrealistic as it sounds. In that year licensed begging was
once more authorized in cases where parishes were quite unable
to provide adequate relief. But persons over the age of fourteen
discovered begging without a licence were not only to be
whipped but also 'burned through the gristle of the right ear
with a hot iron of the compass of an inch about, manifesting
his or her roguish kind of life', unless, for Members of Parliament were never averse to including a convenient escape-clause,
some substantial householder would offer employment. Young
persons under fourteen caught begging were merely to be

whipped, but the children of convicted beggars aged between five and fourteen were to be put to service with householders following honest occupations, to be bound thereto, if boys, until the age of twenty-four and if girls until eighteen. The formal apprenticeship of pauper children was not far away. In 1576 the licensing of begging was extended to cover able persons afflicted by loss of goods and to any poor persons having particular needs. A collection of licences issued in Norfolk in the early 1590s shows that the JP most involved was the bishop, Edmund Scambler. In July 1593 Thomas Jenkinson of Cromer in the same county, who had suffered an injury to his leg so severe that in the opinion of Mr Cropp of Norwich, surgeon, it should be amputated – and who on that account was unable to support his wife and three children – was licensed by the Justices to go the rounds of his kinsmen and friends in the county in order to raise the surgeon's fee of forty shillings.

By the later 1580s, and even more so by the later 1590s, the problem of poverty had escalated far beyond what anyone could have imagined in 1572. To the chronically disabled had been added wounded soldiers and, especially in the counties near the coasts, wounded sailors. There were also far more able people unable to support themselves. On the one hand the population had grown quite considerably, greatly increasing the number of able unemployed, and on the other, after the comparative freedom of the period from 1560 to 1585, plague had returned and left many families without breadwinners. To cap all this, there was the succession of disastrous harvests from 1594 to 1597 which more than doubled the price of wheat and carried that of barley, oats, peas and beans, the food of the poor, proportionately even higher. Probably for the first time in Tudor England large numbers of people in certain areas died of starvation. It was against this background of very widespread poverty and hunger that the switch of 1572 to the entirely civil authority was now once again to be reversed. In the statutes of 1597–1601 codifying the system of poor relief, the only real novelty was the restoration of parochial responsibility. Although still to be nominated by the JPs, the parish Overseers were now to include the churchwardens *ex officio*, and they were to assess as well as collect the poor-rate. They were required to meet at least once a month, in the parish church, 'upon the Sunday, in the afternoon, after divine service'. To this extent the moral authority of the Church was reinstated and the system which, for better or for worse, was to last until 1834 was established.

But while the Queen's officers, at Westminster and in the counties, had been pursuing their statutory experiments, the more affluent of her subjects at large had continued to play a role, as a matter of private conscience if no longer out of fear of eternal damnation, in the succour of the needy. The 1550s had seen a substantial increase in actual cash terms over the previous decade in the overall charitable bequests of laymen, but when some allowance is made for the mild inflation of the period the level was still below that of the very early decades of the century. The last forty years, 1560–1600, though they brought yet more income in cash terms, when corrected to take account of inflation show only a modest rise, especially in the 1570s and 1580s, and an actual decrease in real terms in the 1590s. There were regional variations, however, the value of bequests in the wills of Norfolk people rising even in real terms in the 1590s, probably largely due to the prosperity of the leading citizens of Norwich, while the real value of the Londoners' contributions (always much higher than that of any of the counties) showed a drop of one third between the 1560s and 1590s. The overall record may not be particularly impressive, especially bearing in mind an almost total lack of bequests for strictly religious purposes, but there does seem to have been some revival of interest in the founding of charitable institutions. Hospitals, especially new ones, required considerable initial capital and few of the provincial towns, and virtually no villages, could compare with London's achievement in caring for her sick. But almshouses could be very modest affairs, sometimes no more than a couple of cottages, needing no quarters for staff. The years 1570 to 1600 added very substantially to the provision of such homes for the aged, about one hundred being added to those which had survived the Reformation. One of the most enlightened – and well-documented – schemes was that at Ipswich. By the 1580s there was residential accommodation for forty poor persons. In addition there was a hospital for the sick and young orphans. Not all such institutions were as well endowed. At Sandwich it became necessary to sell places in the almshouses to those who could afford to pay, and there are reports of corruption by trustees. There was in the whole county of Kent probably accommodation for only about 270 sick and elderly poor, not nearly enough to provide for the proportion of the growing population which needed such help. At Warwick the earl of Leicester provided what would appear to have been the handsome annual income of over £200 to support the hospital set up in the town's former guildhall, but after his death in 1588 his widow withheld some of the endowment. But in any case the hospital accommodated only twelve poor men, of whom more than half usually came from outside the town, and, as censuses of the poor show very clearly, women in need outnumbered men by two to one. It was the Master of Leicester's hospital, the well-known Puritan Thomas Cartwright, who took the lead in collecting money and handing it out to the poor in their homes with discrimination. In one house he found Isabel Glover, aged sixty, her two sons, aged sixteen and eighteen, and a small child. Isabel was given 8d. per week for herself and the child but nothing for the older boys who presumably continued to beg. As far as possible Cartwright sent all children who were old enough into service. If he had had his way the parish church would have been run on Presbyterian lines with deacons appointed to look after such matters. He insisted on two of his own servants being publicly punished for bastardy, but his Puritan remedies for such disorders differed from traditional methods only in the zeal with which they were applied.

Again relying entirely on the evidence of wills it is possible to get some idea of where the money was coming from. It was not coming, any more than before the Reformation, from the clergy themselves. It was hardly to be expected that the bishops, living as most of them were on reduced incomes, would improve upon the record of their predecessors. Most of them continued the tradition of episcopal hospitality on a grand scale and there may still have been left-over food. A few Elizabethan bishops were generous to the poor, Archbishop Matthew Parker giving £160 a year to a hospital at Canterbury, Bishop Scory of Hereford leaving £600 for the poor, and the bachelor primate, John Whitgift, founding almshouses at Croydon, and although these were exceptions more than half left some money to the poor in their wills, twice as much altogether as they left for educational purposes. It is perhaps unfair to say of the Elizabethan parish clergy that we do not often hear of their hospitality or alms-giving and one would like to think that in years of bad harvests they and their families shared what little tithe grain they had with their most distressed parishioners. William Harrison, the Essex parson, thought that as their homes were run more efficiently married clergy could afford to be more open-handed. Turning to laymen, figures based entirely on their wills suggest that the Elizabethan nobility, in spite of considerable financial pressure, did more for the poor than their mid-century predecessors, over five times as much without allowing for inflation. This was not in compensation for any shortcomings during their lifetimes, for the later Tudor nobility not only lived well and entertained generously but also gave a good deal of left-over food to the poor. Gentlemen, both lesser fry and knights and esquires, maintained the level of their charitable bequests very well, especially the former, but then there were far more of them, probably enough to balance inflation. The same can be said for the yeomen, for they too were increasing in numbers towards the end of the century. Mere husbandmen, on the other hand, were, as a group, hardly keeping pace in their bequests to the poor with rising prices. Tradesmen too apparently did little better after 1560, hardly keeping up with inflation, but they, together with the merchants, had been generous in their bequests to the poor since the early decades of the century. The merchants, of all the groups analysed, probably made the greatest additional contribution after 1560, but even this was limited by the inroads of inflation. Not only, of course, were they mostly town-dwellers and as such very aware of the extent of the distress, but also they were the most likely to be in a position to leave ready money. The Ipswich almshouses and hospital were the outcome of one very large bequest in 1551 by a local merchant, Henry Tooley, and a gift such as his brought others in its train. The Elizabethan merchants' total contribution, under £2,000 a year in the ten counties investigated, was little enough, but their bequests do stand out in the shift of their interest from the simple bequest of money for a dole to the establishment of permanent trust-funds. From the income, and sometimes from the ongoing loaning of the capital, grants could be made to the poor at such times as the need was greatest, or young people could be helped to help themselves. The most generous were the entirely interest-free loans which were provided for in some provincial towns, but in London, even before the taking of interest was legalized in 1571, some return was usually expected. Humphrey Baskerfield in 1564 left £200 to the Mercers' Company, of which he had been Master, to be lent to four young men, each of whom was to provide two loads of charcoal each year for distribution to the poor. His money was thus doubly put to work. The revolving loan bequest was, except in London, very much a late Elizabethan trend, making its appearance in York, for example, only in the 1590s. By the founding of such charitable trusts the names of the civic establishment have achieved an earthly immortality to which even the donors can hardly have aspired. Old habits died hard, however, and at the funeral of a rich Elizabethan London merchant as many as one hundred poor persons might be provided with black gowns to add a sombre note to the occasion.

The supply of food and the control of its price were of course vital ingredients of any successful system of poor relief. Traditional methods of price control, the Assizes of Bread and Ale, aimed at the protection of all consumers from profiteering

bakers and brewers, merely related retail prices to the cost of
the raw materials, including fuel. It did not help a hungry
Londoner that whereas in 1558 1d. bought a loaf of wheaten
bread weighing 57 oz., in 1560 it weighed only 36 oz. and in
November 1597 only 8 oz., except that but for the Assize it
might have been smaller still. Proclamations concerning the
price of luxury foods, even if enforced, hardly helped the really
poor. For example, that of May 1544 reducing recent large
increases in the price of imported sugar could hardly pretend
to be for the benefit of the king's poorer subjects, nor that of
the same month laying down maximum retail prices for a great
range of meats, fowl and dairy products. 'The best crane, bustard
or stork not above the price of 4s. ... quails, of the best, the
dozen not above 4s.' or even 'the cony, the kidney half covered
with fat, 2½d.' were not of great interest to the poor. Attempts
to move food supplies from one area to another, even by the
authority of JPs backed by that of the Privy Council, were
only too likely to cause popular unrest, and even at Westminster
it was firmly believed that corn-dealers were largely responsible
for shortages. This had prompted a statute of 1552 providing
for their licensing by the county JPs. It was in the same year
that Parliament began to take steps, also by a system of licensing,
to stem the proliferation of alehouses, those modest places of
refreshment largely run by the poor for the poor. They were
not yet an offence to Puritan consciences but were thought to
consume too much barley. Both the number of corn-dealers
and that of alehouses nevertheless escalated in the second half
of the century as fast if not faster than inflation. Whenever
dearth of food occurred, or threatened, the authorities in both
town and countryside, with degrees of determination which
varied from time to time and from area to area, attempted to
force the producers to bring their stocks to the market-place.
In 1550 the JPs of Cornwall followed an old medieval ploy
in prohibiting, at a time of crisis, the 'forestalling' of the markets.
Fishermen were not to sell their catch at sea or anywhere but
on the 'strand', and for one hour 'all comers of the country'
might buy, after which the 'jowtars' (fish dealers) could have

their chance. Even before this time royal proclamations were occasionally concerned with the cost of the more basic and essential food supplies. One issued in November 1544 ordering that all stocks of grain be offered for sale claimed that grain prices had risen to such an extent 'that His Majesty's loving subjects cannot gain, with their great labours and pains, sufficient to pay for their convenient victuals'.

After the accession of Mary Tudor, the elaborate proclaiming from time to time of maximum prices came to an end. Queen Elizabeth proclaimed only the maximum price of French wine. Her attachment to Lenten and Friday fasts was perhaps not entirely unconnected with fears for the food supply, as were the still frequent prohibitions of the export of grain, but in fact the early decades of her reign also brought fewer efforts to 'furnish the markets', at least until after the disastrous harvest of 1586. What is especially interesting about her proclamation of January 1587, and the printed *Book of Orders* accompanying it, is their preoccupation with the needs of 'the poorer sort'. Those with stocks of corn were ordered to take them to market, except for any they sold 'to the poor artificers or day-labourers of the parish' in which they dwelt. Moreover, what they sold in the markets was to be available to the queen's subjects in small quantities of a bushel or less. The JPs were to see that the 'common bakers' baked rye, barley, peas and beans 'for the use of the poor' and 'where any notable offence shall be in the bakers, to cause the bread to be sold to the poorer sort under the ordinary prices in part of [their] punishment'. None should buy in the market for resale for the space of one hour from the opening of the market, 'that the poor may be first served', and the JPs were to use every means to see the poor provided with corn 'at convenient and charitable prices'. How far this typically Tudor mixture of threat and exhortation helped to lessen the rigours of starvation we have no means of discovering. Any diminution in prices helped, of course, to make the poor-rates go further, but as the bad harvest of 1586 was accompanied by a commercial depression which caused widespread rural under- and un-employment, the demands made on the poor-rates were almost certainly running much higher. In fact the harvest of 1587 was an abundant one and the crisis of the previous year, and the response to it, had been but a dress rehearsal for the much more prolonged one of 1594–8. Although the government, through the clergy, exhorted people both to accept the will of God and to pray for better weather, the iniquities of unlicensed corn-dealers and the sharp practices of the producers were still thought to be factors in causing a really menacing situation. In particular, the demands of London were seen as both effect and cause of the dearth, especially in Kent. In 1597 the people of Sandwich were reputed to be starving at the same time as a London baker was shipping 260 quarters of wheat from their port, but it was only too likely that many of the London poor were migrants from Kent. The Privy Council showed its awareness that the dearth was real and widespread when it decreed in August 1596 that no one should have meat for supper on Wednesdays, Fridays and fasting-days and that gentlemen and others should keep fewer dogs. The *Book of Orders* was re-issued, and many surveys of grain were carried out, but actually getting the corn to market was another matter. A letter to the Archbishop of Canterbury conveyed the Queen's request that sermons should be preached condemning 'engrossers' (hoarders) of corn. In Kent the situation was most satisfactory in those towns – for example, Canterbury, Faversham, Maidstone, and New Romney – where the wealthier inhabitants found the money to buy corn and sell it direct, at reduced prices, to the poor. In other words, in years of real crisis the only hope for the helpless poor in Elizabethan England lay in largely voluntary charity at town or parish level. Theft, particularly of food, increased considerably in these closing years of the century but, as we have seen, law and order were maintained until, in the fullness of time, the wet summers came to an end.

Tudor provision for the succour of the helpless really in the end proved inadequate largely because during the two closing decades of the century, and only then, the physically helpless were overwhelmed by the under- or un-employed. There were indeed those who argued, early in the next century, that the poor-rates were intended only for the 'lame, impotent, old, blind and such others as being poor are not able to work'. The traditional poor had comprised mostly children, widows, and the elderly, but the new poor were adult, usually married and with families to support. In 1598 the village of Grain in the isle of that name on the coast of Kent contained three 'impotent' poor, twenty-two 'respectable', that is, able, poor, composed of six married couples with children, over fifty households short of food, and only seven payers of the poor-rate. In New Romney in the same county families which had earlier paid poor-rates were by 1597 themselves in need of relief. A country whose social conscience was rooted in the religious necessities of pre-Reformation society, when most able-bodied idleness was voluntary, was not easily adaptable to a new situation in which poverty was not an absolute but a relative term. What, then, was the employment situation?

12. *The Banishment of Idleness*

To men and women of substance in Tudor England there were two kinds of poor, God's and the Devil's, the latter consisting of those who though physically able were, by their own choice, unemployed. Most reprehensible were the mobile labourers, little distinction being made between migrants genuinely seeking betterment and habitual vagrants. To be neither a master oneself nor in regular service was to be a social outcast, a potential if not an actual rebel, and this in spite of the obvious utility, especially in agriculture, of a seasonal work-force. However, the apparently unremitting effort of those in authority to force people to settle down and work for their living was matched only by the apparent determination with which a quite substantial minority contrived to avoid conventional employment. It must, however, be remembered that, although their number increased substantially during the course of the sixteenth century, full-time wage-earners, actual or potential, were never more than a minority of the population.

Underlying most official pronouncements and legislative provisions concerning employment was the assumption that all able-bodied people, if they had a mind to, could make an adequate living, and for at least the first three quarters of the sixteenth century that was probably broadly true. In most parts of the country until the late 1580s there were few settled bread-winners totally unemployed, though from about 1540 and certainly by the mid-1550s it was becoming more difficult for unskilled labourers to earn more than a bare subsistence. Until inflation, both of population and of prices, really began to bite, wage-earners were still enjoying the advantages of nearly two centuries of scarcity of labour. There were, of course, temporary and even very local unemployment crises. The effects of enclosure, especially for sheep-farming, though they must not be exaggerated, could be to deprive small tenant farmers not only of their land and common grazing but also of part-time and seasonal employment. Commercial crises, such as that of 1528, affecting the export of woollen cloth, were quickly felt over large tracts of countryside as merchants and clothiers stopped buying and employing. Those particularly affected were the small farmers and their families, part-time spinners and weavers, in the 'woodland' areas such as parts of Somerset, Gloucestershire and Wiltshire, mid-Kent and the Weald, the borders of Essex and Suffolk and the West Riding of Yorkshire. But such commercial crises were soon over and neither that of 1551 nor that of 1586, serious as they appeared at the time, had any long-term effect on the employment situation. Towards the clothiers, the only large-scale employers of labour, Tudor governments maintained an ambivalent attitude, becoming, as the century wore on, rather more susceptible to the blandishments of all who offered, usually in return for some concession, to provide employment, but also ever-fearful of the large employers' power to precipitate unemployment, distress, and hence the risk of commotions. But uppermost in the minds of the legislators ever since the late fourteenth century had been the supply of the labour-market. The more people there were on the road, they believed, the more difficult it was to hold down wages. Hence, in early Tudor England, all strangers, unless carrying a licence or testimonial of some kind, were liable to be apprehended, set in the stocks on a diet of bread and water, and sent back to their place of birth or most recent habitation. This was no novelty, Henry VII's Parliament in 1495 having merely allowed that the stocks were a more humane punishment for vagrants than the imprisonment provided for in a statute of Richard II. If indeed there was a really serious vagabond problem in early Tudor England the chief sufferers were the larger towns and cities, and they were not slow to take action. York in 1501, for example, ordered each of its six wards to provide stocks and fetters for beggars, vagabonds 'and other misdoers'. An Act of Parliament of 1531, however, ordered that idle vagabonds be tied naked to a cart and whipped until their bodies were bloody.

From the 1530s the insistence of the Protestant reformers on men's duty to work and to support their families, eschewing the receipt of alms, a theme continually recurring in the preaching of Cranmer, Ridley, Lever and other would-be reformers, helped to stiffen official attitudes, but in fact it was the very conservative *King's Book* of 1543 which equated begging for alms by those capable of work with the breaking of the eighth commandment. As in the matter of the relief of the impotent poor, so also in that of the employment of the able-bodied, ideas for practical measures from Catholic Europe were circulating in London parliamentary circles in or before 1536. Indeed, there were proposals which have been connected with the names of Christopher St German and John Rastell, both lawyers, as early as 1531. The proposal later favoured not only by Thomas Cromwell but by the King himself was that able unemployed persons should be rounded up and employed on public works such as harbours (that of Dover being specially mentioned), highways, fortresses and watercourses. Are we really to believe that this Henrician scheme was intended to relieve unemployment? Some draft proposals for legislation of the mid-1530s actually categorized the 'vagabonds' as brawlers and drunkards 'commonly called Ruffelers', unlicensed students, sailors pretending to be wounded, confidence tricksters, prostitutes and all who 'shall continue out of service by the space of forty days'. Was this not a ploy to obtain much-needed labour, at a price which the government could dictate, to put the country's defences in readiness for the invasion by foreign powers which the Crown's religious policy was already inviting? The fact that Henry himself was prepared to help finance the project seems to add weight to this argument. That Parliament also was asked to contribute by way of taxation put paid to the idea of public works and resulted in the passage of an Act in 1536 which merely provided, as far as sturdy vagabonds were concerned, that local authorities in towns and villages should finance, from voluntary alms, the provision of work, not, as is so often assumed, for those who could not find it, but 'that such as be lusty or having their limbs strong enough to labour may be daily *kept in continual labour*, whereby every one of them may get their own substance and living with their own hands'. Here was no charity, only opportunities for self-help. The draft proposal had provided for idlers to be branded on the hand at the second offence and to face death at the third, but in the Act as passed the only penalties were those to be exacted from negligent parishes. One of the Act's more practical provisions was that all vagrants, able as well as disabled, *en route* for home and carrying letters to that effect, were to be provided every ten miles by parishes on their route with 'competent meat, drink, and lodging for one night only'. Not surprisingly, not even the threat of a corporate fine galvanized parishes into activity. Most were probably unaware of any great need. Only contemporaries with a particular axe to grind believed that the Dissolution, now well in train, would add to the country's unemployed. There were, no doubt, especially in 1538 and 1539 when most of the larger monasteries were dissolved, some monastic servants surplus to local labour needs, but the provision in the Act of 1536 dissolving the smaller monasteries for the maintenance both of tillage and of 'an honest continual house and household' by the tenants or owners of the former monastic property, if implemented, should have ensured that most of the lay servants, indoor and outdoor, had not far to seek for work. Henry VIII's wars with France in 1544–5 underlined the country's continued manpower shortage, but we need not take too seriously John Lord Russell's report, when he was endeavouring to conscript seamen in the south-west in 1545, that all the fishing-boats were apparently manned by women. The following year the King, by proclamation, ordered all 'ruffians, vagabonds, masterless men, common players and evil-disposed persons' to the galleys, ending with a swipe at illegal retaining. Among those idlers whom the King saw 'daily with his noble eyes' he mentioned in particular the sturdy vagabonds of the city of London.

The proscribing of mobility was a harsh policy, harshest of all as laid down in the statute of 1547 closely associated with the

name of the soldier-statesman, Protector Somerset, whereby
those convicted of vagabondage were to be branded on the
breast and given into serfdom for two years. To abscond once
would incur branding on the forehead and permanent serfdom,
and a second time death as a felon. The Act was repealed soon
after it was passed, but in 1572, probably as a result of the panic
which resulted from the Northern Rising of 1569, the medieval
practice of imprisoning vagabonds was restored, and in 1597 it
was again enacted that all rogues, vagabonds and sturdy beggars
(and the Act contains a long list of categories including 'persons
able in body using loitering and refusing to work for such
reasonable wages as is taxed ...') were to be 'stripped naked
from the middle upwards' and whipped, before being sent back
to their places of birth, 'there to put him or her self to labour as
a true subject ought to do'. Incorrigible rogues were to be
banished from the realm or sent permanently to the galleys. No
one could guess, by reading this Act, that there was any lack of
employment in England as the century drew to its close. Tudor
governments knew better, of course, but could never get over
their traditional aversion to popular freedom of movement.

So much for the 'wanderers' as they were called in many
parish records. But what if they still avoided employment at
home? The Act of 1547 had depended for its implementation on
there being employers willing to take in convicted vagrants,
even if only for the 'bread and water or small drink, and such
refuse of meat as [they] shall think meet' stipulated in the Act.
Even allowing for the attractions to employers of cheap labour
this suggests that demand for labour still exceeded supply, and
as late as 1572, by which time, due to the increase in population,
the two must have been reaching at least equilibrium, the term
vagabond, as used in an Act of that year, clearly comprehended
any who refused to work except for what employers regarded
as unreasonable wages. It was, in fact, well before this, and,
predictably, in London and the larger towns, that the thoughts
of the powers that be turned to the provision of stocks of
material for the setting to work of the unemployed, as indeed
provided for in the now defunct Act of 1536. How far such

moves were motivated by a desire to help those unable to find
work rather than to discipline the work-shy is very difficult to
discover. It is even more difficult to gauge with any precision
the number in any town of men and women willing to work if
work were available. One thing is certain: there was no spare
cash in the poor-boxes for pump-priming. In 1549 John Hales
suggested that towns be discharged payment of their fee-farms
to the Crown on condition that 'the profits' thereof be used
for the purchase of stocks for employing the poor. His suggestion was not followed up, but in 1551 the decayed city of
Lincoln, on the initiative of four of its aldermen, provided a
range of accommodation at little or no rent where the city's old
cloth industry might be re-established. The aldermen undertook
to provide a stock of materials and payment in kind, but it is not
clear how far their concern was really charitable. Perhaps because the employees were clearly under pressure to occupy
themselves, the scheme failed and no further efforts were made
at Lincoln until the 1590s. It was in 1552 that the corporation of
London really made an effort to provide work for the able
unemployed, and it is perhaps significant that in a petition to the
young Edward VI for the use of his empty palace of Bridewell
as 'an house of occupations' the corporation did not state that
work was not available but rather that the beggars, that is, the
unemployed, whether willing or not, 'have so utterly lost their
credit . . . that few or none dare or will receive them to work'.
The city did, however, also refer very specifically to the need to
rehabilitate both those cured in the hospitals and also discharged
prisoners. As is always the problem in the public provision of
work there could be no question of competing with existing
businesses, and indeed the Court of Aldermen had no intention
of committing the city's own funds to the provision of a stock
of materials. This was to be the responsibility of already established entrepreneurs, who were to pay for the work done, no
doubt at rates which would be attractive to them. The success
of the scheme was bound to depend on there being a market for
the goods. The crafts proposed were cap-making, the making
of tick for feather beds and of wool-cards, wire-drawing, silk-

winding, and the making of nails. This was promising, in each case competing largely with imports. Bridewell was duly made over to the city and was in operation by 1557. During the remainder of the century it achieved a great deal in keeping the city's vagabond population under control. By and large those who came to London in search of work were able, in that rich and busy city, to find it. If, however, they came with criminal intent or to live as parasites they would have great difficulty in escaping the attentions of the powers that be and not ending up in prison, or in Bridewell, which was no less uncomfortable. Each of the city's wards had officials whose responsibility it was to keep an eye on lodgers and 'inmates', especially if they were not in regular employment. No wonder London was regarded with envy by most of the provincial towns.

London's example was not quickly followed. York, also a particular magnet for sturdy immigrants, established what amounted to civic weaving factories at St Anthony's Hall and St George's Chapel in the later 1560s, and this early effort may well have been intended as much for the benefit of those willing to work as for the incarceration of incorrigible tramps. It failed owing to difficulty in disposing of the cloth which was probably of very poor quality. Supervisors were appointed and some of those gathered in will already have learned and exercised industrial skills elsewhere, but it is difficult to see how the profitable industrial employment of unskilled persons could be reconciled with current official emphasis (in the Statute of Artificers of 1563) on many years of training. The town of Ipswich did rather better. It was as Christ's Hospital, for 'the aged, the orphans, the widows and the sick', that a new institution in the converted Black Friary received a royal charter in 1572, but the beadle was allowed 2d. as his reward for every 'unruly person' whom he brought in. Between July 1573 and September 1574 nearly one hundred persons were admitted and set to work to earn their keep by the 'Guider'. Refusal to work meant no food. A workshop was built and implements and materials provided for carding, spinning, and weaving wool, and for the making of candles 'for the better serving of the inhabitants [of Ipswich] . . .

and for the more benefit of the hospital'. The turnover was fairly rapid, indicating either that the inmates were quickly fitted for normal employment or that they fled the town for more comfortable pastures elsewhere. By the 1590s the majority of those in Ipswich's Christ's Hospital were children, girls as well as boys, most of whom were apprenticed when old enough. Indeed London too in 1552 had planned to accommodate in its Bridewell not only idle adults but also young people 'found unapt for learning' and for whom no other service could for the moment be found.

By the mid-1570s the growth in the population of England at large, coupled with the lack of new employment opportunities, was probably just beginning to create almost everywhere outside the capital a substantial class of involuntary unemployed. Still very frightened by the Northern Rising of 1569, Privy Council and Parliament aimed legislation principally at compelling people to work and to 'avoid' idleness. There was, however, some recognition in the Act of 1576 that not everyone could now find work. The preamble gave as its objectives not only that 'youth may be accustomed and brought up in labour', but also 'that such as be already grown up in idleness ... may not have any just excuse in saying that they cannot get any service or work'. Under the supervision of the JPs all cities, corporate and market towns, and other 'places' were ordered, with rather more precision than in 1536, to provide stocks of 'wool, hemp, flax, iron or other stuff' to be delivered to the unemployed in their own homes. The whole operation, including the collecting and sale of the finished product, was to be in the hands of local officials to be called 'Collectors and Governors of the Poor'. For those who offended, either by refusing to work, or by embezzling or spoiling the stock, there were to be provided what were called, significantly, 'Houses of Correction'. They were not in any sense factories for the employment of willing workers. For the law-abiding people the home or the small workshop was the proper place of work. Those received into the Houses of Correction were to be 'straightly kept, as well in diet as in work', that is, they were envisaged as penal not charitable institutions. The initial financing, both of stock and buildings, was to be met out of the new poor-rates, though one Member of Parliament suggested that the magistrates might also make available fines imposed on keepers of unlicensed alehouses. The Act also encouraged any 'well-disposed' landowner feeling confident of the 'good success which will grow by setting people on work and avoiding of idleness' to give or bequeath land in support of the venture. To administer such a scheme required the authority and administrative experience of the older towns, and indeed it is clear that the Act of 1576 was based very largely on local experiments. York for one was very quick off the mark, converting St George's Chapel in 1579 into a 'bridewell' for disciplining its idle poor and finding no less than £400 for a stock of wool. In 1584 further premises at Fishergate Bar were acquired but these were converted within a very short time into an ordinary prison. At Winchester, too, a bridewell established in 1578 was soon being used for the imprisonment of petty criminals. Exeter made a start in 1579 but not until about 1593 was its House of Correction supplied with a governor and finance, the latter in the form of a permanent loan partly supplied by money left by a Mr Lawrence Attwill in 1588 for employing the poor. Everywhere the old problem remained, how to find a market for products which, if the current demand was not already saturated, could be readily supplied by the expansion of the private sector. In 1571 the earl of Leicester suggested to the burgesses of Warwick, still very much a country town, that cloth or cap manufacture would employ large numbers of people and 'though they be children they may spin and card, though they be lame they may pick and fray wool'; but although he offered to lend capital he clearly expected a handsome return and his offer was turned down. His further suggestion that an even more specialized industry, such as the making of tapestry so successfully established by the Sheldon family at Beoley in Worcestershire, be set up would, if adopted, have required both industrial and entrepreneurial skills, as well as premises, which Warwick could not supply.

Only at Ipswich, where the poor-rate could be augmented from Henry Tooley's bequest, is there evidence of tools and materials being supplied for people to work in their own homes. Norwich, however, did arrange for certain 'select women' to take in up to a dozen poor children and to teach them a craft, mostly carding and spinning. It was their penal nature which prevented the Elizabethan bridewells from making any real contribution to the growing employment problem. Most of those who went there did so only after prolonged admonition by clergy, churchwardens, and local magistrates, and to be sent there was a fate hardly less disparaging to a person's reputation than conviction under the slavery Act of 1547. It is said that people would even risk death as a felon in order to avoid committal to a house of correction. Perhaps because unemployment was neither so widespread nor so immediately visible in the countryside – and that meant in by far the greater part of England – the county magistrates were in far less hurry to provide work opportunities, either in people's own homes or in Houses of Correction.

No account of the Tudor employment situation would be complete without a reference to efforts to achieve urban renewal, most Tudor politicians regarding prosperous and well-governed towns as one of the best guarantees of law and order. Legislative efforts in the later 1530s and early 1540s to compel owners of urban property to rebuild or relinquish derelict houses had done little more than indicate the government's interest and encourage towns to seek government support in dealing with their problems. Fears that the dissolution of the urban monasteries would reduce even further the prospect for urban employment were not realized to any extent, but the dispersal of the many urban communities and the conversion to lay uses of their buildings and extensive precincts did very little, in spite of extravagant promises by prospective grantees, to liberate urban enterprise. Most of the towns which, at the end of Henry VIII's reign, were still suffering from a sluggish economy could only think in traditional terms of even more restrictive monopolies. Sir Thomas Smith in his *Discourse* of

1549, concerned about the quality of English industrial products, argued that as far as possible all artificers should live in towns, and that those who could not, for technical reasons, be accommodated there should be subjected to urban supervision. He also urged the towns to be more liberal in admitting outsiders. It was, in fact, in the reign of Mary Tudor that the most determined government efforts were made to restore industry to the towns. In 1554 a statute sought to restrict the retailing of various goods, including woollen and linen cloth, haberdashery, and groceries, to corporate towns or to fairs, most of which were held in or very near towns. The Weavers' Act of 1555 was an attempt to entice cloth-makers back into the towns by restricting country clothiers to one and country weavers to two looms apiece. This was clearly aimed at the full-time working employers not the part-timers. Another Act concerning woollen cloth manufacture, that of 1556, actually referred to the drift of cloth-making into the countryside to escape urban regulation as though this was a very recent development. The penalty provided for starting up as a rural cloth-maker, a fine of £5 per cloth, was a stiff deterrent but the Act lost a good deal of its force due to the usual long list of exemptions.

Perhaps more important, Mary Tudor's reign also saw a considerable increase in the number of royal charters of incorporation granted to towns, twenty-six in all compared with Edward VI's ten and Henry VIII's eight between 1540 and 1547. Some of these only extended old privileges or legalized existing situations, naming leading townsmen as members of a self-perpetuating oligarchical council, and establishing autonomous judicial machinery, free of seignorial control. Many towns now for the first time obtained their own ex-officio JPs and parliamentary representation. Charters by themselves solved no problems, but they enabled mayors and town councils to exercise greater authority and, by enabling them to build up corporate funds, to promote local trading and industrial facilities and hence to increase employment prospects. As already indicated, powerful and respected urban corporations attracted legacies from wealthy townsmen, to be lent as initial capital to young men about to embark on industrial or commercial enterprise.

The towns of early Elizabethan England had by no means recovered entirely from the decline which so many of them had inherited from the later Middle Ages but their population was growing again and by no means all the newcomers were living by begging or theft. During the years 1568–71 some thirty English families, largely from the surrounding county, moved into the city of Norwich without any opposition and were rapidly absorbed into the working population. To some extent this was due to Norwich's insistence that her immigrant aliens employ natives. But what was particularly significant about Elizabethan Norwich was the change which was taking place in the occupational pattern. Admittedly the evidence concerns only the freemen, but they were also the town's employers. Comparing the years 1558–80 with 1530–58 there was in the later period, in spite of the New Draperies, a smaller percentage of cloth-makers and a considerable increase in that of makers of clothes, especially tailors and hatters. There were also more cordwainers (shoemakers) and glovers. The number of those processing and retailing food and drink hardly changed, but there was a considerable increase in those engaged in the building and allied trades, using brick and slate rather than timber and thatch, a sure sign of local prosperity. That prosperity was increasingly dependent on the city's progress as a provincial capital, the resort of gentlemen and their families from all over East Anglia. Norwich could support fifty grocers in 1569 compared with barely half that number in the mid-1520s, and they were able to dispose of enormous quantities of imported luxuries such as sugar and dried fruit. There were similar developments in Elizabethan York, Bristol, and Exeter, in each of which, as in Norwich, numbers of gentlemen acquired town houses in which they spent a good deal of the winter months. Exeter admitted forty-one tailors to its freedom in the first half of the sixteenth century and ninety-six in the second half. This suggests an expanding upper-class market. There were also new occupations appearing in the larger provincial towns, vintners, for example, taking their place along with brewers. Traditionally wine had been sold only at taverns. But the number of craftsmen making good quality articles for sale on the home market was still far from freeing the country from its dependence on the imports which Sir Thomas Smith so deplored. The mere market towns probably did rather better industrially during Elizabeth's reign than the larger county towns, and this in spite of legislative efforts in 1563 to frustrate their growth.

Most of these urban developments after 1560 were the results of economic and social changes owing very little to official policy and pressures. Indeed, by the beginning of Elizabeth's reign there was considerable concern at Westminster about the apparent 'avoidance' of employment in agriculture. Like a great deal of Tudor legislation the Statute of Artificers of 1563 is important more for what it tells us of the reaction of those in power to current circumstances than for what it actually achieved. Later to be regarded by skilled artisans engaged in the older crafts as their protection against unskilled competitors, at the time of its passage the main thrust of the Act, like that of the vagrancy laws, was to enforce the universal obligation to work. Comprehending in its vast bulk everything to do with employment – not just in the narrow sense of wage-earning – it can so easily be mistaken for an enlightened and forward-looking blueprint for a planned economy. It was in many respects, however, backward-looking, merely reiterating legislative provisions going back more than two centuries. It certainly ushered in no brave new world of justice for both master and man, nor indeed had it much relevance to the livelihood of the majority of the queen's subjects. Like so much Tudor legislation it derived a great deal from local experiments.

That the commercial crisis of the early 1550s, especially the decline in the export of woollen cloth, coupled with a fairly consistently rising population, did not create disastrous unemployment is partly to be explained by the continuance of a healthy home market for cloth, by the localized nature of the manufacture of most of the cloth formerly made for export, and by the cushioning effect of agricultural holdings for most cloth-

workers. Even so, the end of Mary Tudor's reign might have
brought a crescendo of unemployment but for the demographic
effect of the influenza epidemic of 1557–8. With corn un-
harvested and land untilled, hired men were demanding, and
employers being obliged to pay, wages which, compared with
the more or less fixed wages of the previous half century,
seemed, at least to the employers, to face the country with ruin.
The long-term upward trend in prices was upsetting the traditional wage structure, and all employers of labour felt to some
extent under pressure. Elizabeth's very first parliament in 1559
debated the problem but nothing was put on the statute book
until early in 1563. This in itself should warn us against assuming
that it was the fall in population caused by the influenza epidemic of 1557–8 which precipitated the legislation. It is perhaps
worth quoting the following passage from the proposals of
1559:

> So, by the heed of the masters, servants may be reduced to obedience,
> which shall reduce obedience to the prince and to God also; by the
> looseness of the time no other remedy is left but by awe of the law to
> acquaint men with virtue again, whereby the reformation of religion
> may be brought in credit, with the amendment of manners, the want
> whereof has been imputed as a thing grown by the liberty of the Gospel.

Elizabeth's ministers were wont to try to kill two birds with one
stone, and, on mundane matters, to enrol the Almighty on their
side.

William Cecil wrote on 27 February 1563, 'There is a very
good law agreed upon for indifferent [fair] allowances for
servants' wages in husbandry.' His use of the term 'servants
in husbandry' was correct: the promoters of the statute were
concerned primarily with the full-time, mostly resident and unmarried, man or woman, not with the casual, part-time, day-
labourer. In 1598 it was found necessary to confirm that the
statute applied to others besides agricultural workers. In fact its
preamble and no less than forty of its clauses were concerned
with occupations other than husbandry and with other matters
besides wages. Once started Members of Parliament found it

hard to stop. All able persons were required not only to seek work but to accept such regular employment as was offered to them. Young people were the Act's main target, all unmarried persons under the age of thirty being compelled to serve any employer who needed them. Agriculture was top priority. In time of harvest the JPs or other local officials might even require all artificers to lend a hand, on pain, for refusal, of two days and one night in the stocks. In fact everyone between the ages of twelve and sixty was required to work on the land unless (and the exemptions are interesting) a gentleman born, an heir to lands worth £10 a year or goods worth £40, already employed in a skilled craft or at sea, occupied in the supplying of London with grain, in mining, metal-working or glass-making, or attending a school or a university. Apart from these reserved occupations everyone was to be employed gaining his or her own living in supplying their own and the country's need for agricultural products, especially food. The universal obligation to work in fact only echoed principles first established in the labour legislation of 1349–50 and 1388, although the Act of 1563 applied to women only up to the age of forty. The Elizabethan Act also reinforced old regulations insisting on contracts of service, binding on both masters and servants, and requiring the giving and receiving of written testimonials to and by all employees moving out of a parish on completion of their terms.

The burning issue in 1563 was clearly wages and although the preamble to the Statute of Artificers recognized, somewhat disarmingly, that due to inflation the old wage regulations 'cannot conveniently without the greatest grief and burden of the poor labourer and hired man be put in due execution', the main purpose of the Act's authors was to set a limit to the inflation of wages. In principle this too was not new. Prior to 1500 practice had varied from the general wage-freeze at pre-plague levels in 1350 to a national maximum scale for all agricultural labourers in 1388, quickly followed in 1390 by local assessments by JPs, and a reversion in 1445 to revised national maxima. These left little room in theory for free bargaining, and a statute of 1514, the last before 1563 to deal with wages, merely corrected the levels to take some account of the very mild inflation which had occurred by then. London was permitted higher maxima in 1515, but there is very little evidence of any demand for, or the paying of, higher rates until the middle of the century. Pressure first became evident in the building trades, in London in 1551, in York in 1552 (where a corporation order that builders' wages be pegged at the level laid down in 1514 resulted in a local 'strike'), and in Coventry in 1553, that is, before the demographic crisis of 1557–8 which probably once again lessened the demand for building-workers. In London and Coventry small concessions were made but in York the authorities held firm. Most of the local experiments in the assessment of wage-rates which were made in the years 1560–62 were confined to agricultural labourers, but Worcester included the building crafts and King's Lynn confined itself to them. The Act of 1563 shows Parliament accepting the necessity for local assessments of all wages, industrial as well as agricultural, placing the duty on county and city JPs. In theory there were to be new schedules prepared annually, soon after Easter, but the Act connived at repetition. The rates were to be returned to Westminster for the Lord Chancellor to issue printed royal proclamations for display in all market towns by Michaelmas. This was the most common traditional time for hiring labourers, though some employers took on men at Martinmas and some on May Day. A statute of 1566 confirmed earlier prohibitions, in 1464 and 1512, of the payment of wages in kind. Always suspect by employees, 'truck' wages might in some cases have provided a useful hedge against inflation.

There were, then, few real novelties in the great Act of 1563 but in two respects it introduced national regulation in spheres previously left to local agencies. One of these concerned hours of work which were fixed in summer (mid-March to mid-September) from 5 a.m. to 7 or 8 p.m., with not more than $2\frac{1}{2}$ hours for meal breaks, and in winter from dawn to sunset. A penalty was laid down of 1d. for each hour of absence, a sum not lightly forfeited when the daily wage of a labourer was about 6d. It is unlikely that such a regime was adhered to unless it accorded with local custom. Far more intrusive though not necessarily more effective in its operation was the Elizabethan government's concern to extend apprenticeship. Widely adopted for over two centuries by urban fraternities, guilds, and companies of craftsmen, traders, and merchants as a ritualistic framework for the passing on of skills and experience, as well as a mechanism for controlling entry to skilled occupations, it had never been adopted in any formal sense in the countryside, and certainly not in farming households. The poor-law Act of 1536 had implied a degree of official formality in recommending that sturdy pauper children aged five to fourteen be put to service 'to masters of husbandry or other crafts to be taught' in order that they might be enabled later to earn their living. They were even to be provided with 'a raiment', but the word apprentice was not used, nor were guilds mentioned, and indeed the guild-registered apprentices of the towns were never either paupers or young children. In spite of the establishment of rural industry the very concept of a craft or mistery was urban, Thomas Starkey in the early 1530s putting into the mouth of Pole in his *Dialogue* the idea that 'if any man had no craft at all . . . he should be banished and driven out of the city, as a person unprofitable to all good civility'. To most people all rural skills were natural extensions of the subsistence economy of the traditional farming household. When those who passed the Act of 1563 made apprenticeship, for seven years at the least, compulsory for all exercising any 'craft, mistery or occupation', did they really intend this to include agriculture? This would appear to be so from the clauses laying down who might take apprentices, one of which reads, 'For the better advancement of husbandry and tillage, and to the intent that such as are fit to be made apprentices to husbandry may be bound thereunto . . .' any person, being a householder and occupying at least half a ploughland (about fifteen acres) might 'receive as apprentice' *anyone* aged between ten and eighteen, to serve until aged twenty-one or twenty-four. Such a provision must have seemed quite extraordinary both to farmers who would not expect any young adult to commit himself for more than a year at a time, and also to urban guilds who were very particular about those whom they accepted as apprentices. This freedom to receive anyone as an apprentice was also extended in the Act to a range of rural craftsmen – smiths, wheelwrights, ploughwrights, and millwrights – and to building and allied craftsmen, namely carpenters, rough masons, plasterers, sawyers, lime-burners, brickmakers, tilers, slaters, thatchers, shinglers and tile-makers. The list, presumably denoting rural crafts to be encouraged, was completed with the addition of turners, coopers, millers, earthenware potters, weavers of 'housewifes' or household cloth, fullers and, a late addition by some MP, burners of ore and of wood ashes. It is a splendid conspectus of what Members of Parliament saw as the elements of an ideal rural society.

As they had been since the early fourteenth century, towns continued to be restricted by statute as to the familial source of their immigrant apprentices, only London continuing to enjoy an ancient right of exemption, and Norwich one granted to it as recently as 1495. The citizens of Exeter in January 1563 instructed their MPs to get exemption for them too, and no doubt others did the same, but all without success. The Statute of Artificers in fact added some very detailed refinements whose effect was to narrow very considerably the recruitment of apprentices by masters dwelling in mere market, as opposed to the more privileged corporate towns. Certain occupations, namely merchants, mercers, drapers, goldsmiths, ironmongers, embroiderers (one wonders what lobby was at work here) and clothiers were presumably thought to be too popular and their masters were permitted to have as apprentices only their own sons or, depending whether they lived in a corporate or mere market town, the sons of parents worth, respectively, 40s. and £3 in freehold land. Urban renewal was clearly no longer top priority at Westminster. However, no restrictions were placed on the number of apprentices which any individual master might have, a disappointment no doubt to many of the guilds but in line with statutes passed earlier in the century limiting the entry-fines which craft guilds were permitted to levy on new entrants. Clearly Parliament had no intention of encouraging the restrictive practices of guilds, and indeed guilds as such were nowhere mentioned in the Act. Only one clause, apart from those concerning apprenticeship, echoed in a mild way a common guild ordinance. This, and it applied only to cloth-makers, tailors and shoemakers, required masters to employ at least one journeyman, that is, skilled employee, for every one of their apprentices in excess of two. The guilds, especially those outside London, had to some extent been weakened already by the confiscation of some of their property but while they adjusted themselves to their new role as entirely secular organizations they were prudently keeping a low profile in order to conserve such resources as they still owned. Their real enemies were the merchant-dominated city and town councils.

The Act's provisions regarding apprenticeship were probably among those least enforced during the rest of the sixteenth century. It was not to be expected that either husbandry or the country-based industries would adopt with any enthusiasm a system to which they were not accustomed. Not until the poor-law statutes of 1598 and 1601 was the principle of formal apprenticeship extended to pauper children, under the aegis of parish Overseers, a very different thing from the system run for so long by the guilds. By a quirk of the Act of 1563, probably not intended by its authors, industries not then established were exempt. It has been calculated that between 1563 and 1603 at least 75 per cent of all apprenticeship cases were brought before the magistrates either by professional informers or by persons seeking to vex the defendants. Informers, it is thought, also made considerable profits by persuading offenders to compound with them out of court. One result of this was that, by and large, only established masters were vulnerable, there being no point in prosecuting penniless illegal workmen. Nor was much effort wasted by magistrates on migrants, seasonal employees, or, in general, those following multiple occupations. If the apprenticeship clauses had been rigorously implemented then indeed the future development of rural industry might have been curbed, the supply of labour immobilized, and existing craft demarcations fossilized, all of which might have had very damaging effects on future industrial development and employment opportunities. It was perhaps as well that the power of Tudor governments was only as great as the determination of its local agents to put the law into effect.

Later generations were to concentrate their criticism on the Act's wage regulations, arguing that far from providing for employees what the preamble promised, namely a 'convenient proportion' – that is, wages related to current prices – it served only to hold down wages and to further degrade wage-earners by denying to them the right of free bargaining with their masters. Evidence that many employers paid more than the official rates does indeed suggest that the assessments were lower than the wages which most employers could afford to pay. There was no lack of published assessments but all too often the rates were repeated year after year – no doubt partly in the hope of holding wages down – regardless of price changes, short- or long-term. In Kent, for example, the assessment of 1563 was reissued each year, without change, until 1589. In general it was not until the 1590s that local magistrates were forced to recognize that wages could no longer be pegged at the old levels. At Chester the wages for master-carpenters, without food, were raised from £5 10s. per annum in 1593 to £5 13s. 4d. in 1596 and £6 6s. 8d. in 1597, the latter rise being 'with respect and consideration had of the great dearth and scarcity of things at this present'. The wages of those also provided with food remained unchanged. In fact, of course, annual reviews made, in accordance with the statute, in the early summer, could never realistically anticipate the quality of the forthcoming harvest. In spite of widespread evasion of the wage-assessments, their effect, helped very considerably by the late Tudor rise in population, must have been to bring about a progressive deterioration in the living standards of all who were wholly or largely dependent on wage-earning. Evidence is very difficult to find regarding contracts of service and the extent to which the Act's provisions in this respect were enforced. It had long been customary for those seeking employment to meet prospective employers at certain recognized locations and resident labourers and the more important non-residents, especially bailiffs and shepherds, had traditionally been employed for a year at a time. However, most agricultural labour continued to be performed on a very casual basis by part-time day-labourers for whom annual contracts, binding on both sides, were quite unrealistic.

What is very clear is that neither the Statute of Artificers, nor the various statutes against vagrancy, and least of all the increase in unemployment, especially in the 1590s, did anything to immobilize the population. Indeed, to the large number of those on the road seeking to better their fortunes were added, for the first time, men and women seeking, presumably because the poor-relief in their own parishes was inadequate, mere subsistence, if not regular employment. In spite of very energetic efforts by local magistrates both vagrancy and migrancy were on the increase, especially during the last decade of the century. Some of this was, of course, seasonal and traditional, and JPs had to recognize and condone very large-scale annual migrations, usually for harvest work and therefore mostly from forest to fielden country. As for the obligation for migrant persons to carry with them 'testimonials' – that is, licences under seal from their home town or parish – these, we may be sure, were more readily provided by the authorities for the disabled than for the able-bodied, except in times of very serious unemployment. Nor were prospective employers likely to refuse employment to anyone failing to produce a testimonial. It was, of course, the deserted employer whom the Act of 1563 was endeavouring to protect, but he would have had to be very hard-pressed – more particularly as the supply of employees increased – to pursue his departing servants in the lawcourts in the manner of a medieval lord of the manor hauling back his villeins. Nor were his chances of retrieval improved by the passage in 1572 of an Act which imposed the death penalty for a third attempt to escape from service. Tudor magistrates were not as savage as Parliament.

William Harrison, possibly writing in the mid-1560s, and certainly not later than the early 1570s, put the total number of vagrants at ten thousand, that is, at about 0.3 per cent of the

population, but he may just have meant that there were a great
many! A fairly comprehensive inquiry by the government in
1569 resulted in a figure of some thirteen thousand, so Harrison
may not have been merely guessing. Even searches carried out
at night on government instructions rarely discovered more
than half a dozen real vagrants in any one village or small town,
though they tended to appear in increased numbers on market-
days and at fairs. Magistrates varied considerably in their efficiency and severity in dealing with those apprehended, and their
records are few and difficult to interpret. Evidence drawn from
the judicial records of the town of Warwick and from a number
of counties for the middle years of Elizabeth's reign shows that
a substantial proportion of persons charged with vagrancy were
young, between fifteen and twenty-five years of age. Contrary
to the evidence of contemporary popular literature, few of them
were gypsies and few moved around in large bands or were
accompanied by their families. Most in fact were single men,
labourers, servants and time-expired apprentices. Of those who
admitted to an occupation the majority said they were cloth-
workers, and many, of course, were genuine pedlars and tinkers.
One effect of the Elizabethan laws against vagrancy was to make
life even harder for groups of touring entertainers, whether
these were the more old-fashioned and versatile minstrels or
more specialized actors and musicians. Noble patronage, however nominal, was becoming more difficult to obtain and full-
time employment in noble households even more so. For actors
in particular there was little hope of making a living except with
a troupe based in London; and even in the metropolis the scope
was very limited. Lord Leicester's company numbered only five
in 1574 and was probably not much larger when it emerged as
the Lord Chamberlain's twenty years later, by which time the
thirty-year-old glover's son and possibly former schoolmaster,
William Shakespeare from Stratford, was one of its actor–
playwrights.

There is some evidence that the general drift of migrants,
which earlier in the century had been largely from fielden to
woodland regions, was going into reverse towards the end of

the century. But this may be an illusion created by the records. Local magistrates were men of some experience in these matters and they would be more likely to deal firmly with those who turned up in fielden areas where there was still, as always, less scope for their settlement. It seems likely that most permanent movement was still from sheep–corn areas to woodland. This was certainly the case in the county of Sussex (especially in the eastern half where wealden woodland and downland mixed-farming areas lay in close proximity) and in the numbers still, towards the end of the century, moving into the forest village of Axholme in Lincolnshire. Some of those arrested as vagrants were hundreds of miles from home, but the majority wandered less than fifty miles from their place of birth or last permanent settlement. There is some evidence, however, that increasing unemployment in the 1590s led men and women vagrants to cover greater mileage, thus creating greater problems for magistrates anxious to send them home. This was particularly so in London and the south-east. It was, then, with understandable satisfaction that the constables of Hallingbury Morley in Essex reported in 1566 that they saw few vagabonds who could not be sent home the same day.

What led people, apparently in larger numbers than ever before, to seek fresh pastures? The evidence of the judicial records concerning the youthfulness of most migrant labourers points to the early Elizabethan increase in population as the main factor. The proportion of country people – for this is what most of them were – who could find part-time or secondary employment in industrial occupations was not increasing sufficiently to take account of the expansion of population. In fact it was probably decreasing, for the late Elizabethan English cloth industry, still the only really large-scale employer of skilled labour, was facing stiff competition overseas and, quite apart from serious commercial crises such as that of 1586, the demand was at most static and may even have been falling. Most at risk were the minority of full-time rural cloth-makers, mostly weavers, whose livelihood was dangerously dependent on the overseas market. The long period of peace until the 1580s had cushioned them to a considerable extent, but from 1585 the country was more or less continually at war and the resulting trade stoppages led to a good deal of sporadic and localized unemployment. It was perhaps the very localized nature of late Elizabethan unemployment that encouraged migration. Most important of all, on the land itself there were, by the last quarter of the century, rather fewer small farmers and more virtually full-time agricultural labourers. The supply of labour was thus sufficient to keep agricultural wages in what, in spite of statutory assessments, was still a free market, at bare subsistence level. If indeed there had been a real and universal shortage of agricultural labour in the early 1560s this was certainly not the case thirty years later.

The increase in the number of landless villagers can, of course, be traced right back to the late fifteenth century when, particularly in the midland counties, enclosure had resulted in many smallholdings being swallowed up in sheepfolds. How many of the victims of enclosure and their descendants had failed to find new farms we can only guess, though it is easy to exaggerate the number. Except for the division of farms in those parts of the country where partible inheritance customs prevailed, the trend towards the extinction of smallholdings and their absorption into larger units had never been reversed, though until after 1560 it had proceeded very slowly. What proved to be the downfall of so many smallholders was not so much enclosure, whether of arable fields or common pastures, even by agreement among the larger tenants, but engrossing, that is, the buying up or at least acquisition of smaller units to form larger farms. The property market at farm level shows continual aggregation, with virtually no compensatory fragmentation, except perhaps by the creation of sub-tenancies of which little record survives. Whether or not the engrossing of their tenancies added substantially to their rent-rolls, the pressure on Elizabethan landlords to respond to the argument that larger units made for higher production, greater scope for the adoption of improved techniques, and even economies in administration, was very considerable. The result was that many, especially younger sons, who in earlier times would have expected to find smallholdings were forced to become landless cottagers, earning a living, if they were lucky, working for the larger farmers. This by itself, however, need not have depressed agricultural wages, for the land still had to be worked. It is unlikely that larger units or even improved techniques had more than a marginal effect on the demand for labour, and very little Elizabethan engrossing was for the creation of new sheep farms. Some was for the grazing of cattle. So we come back to population growth. For even if there was only marginally less work there was no longer a penury of people, and this was reflected in the fact that, while during the course of the sixteenth century the cost of living more than quadrupled, the wages of agricultural labourers barely doubled.

But when all is said and done about Tudor employment – and much work remains – it still seems likely that overall, even including the towns, the number of people entirely dependent on wages was, even by 1600, far short of half the total working population. Some indication of this is to be seen in Gloucestershire just after 1600 when it appears that only one in ten of the county's vast number of husbandmen employed any labour. To this vast preponderance of family farmers the Statute of Artificers, with its provisions regarding hours of work, wages, contracts and so on, was a complete irrelevance.

13. *Family and Fortune*

Inflation, both of prices and of population, presented a challenge to every family in later Tudor England. One of its ironies was that in the particular economic circumstances of the time it often made a reality of what medieval people had tended to believe, that one person's good fortune was another's distress. Inflation of prices in a still relatively stagnant economy was bound to be socially divisive. The growth of population, itself the main cause of the increase in prices, ensured that those who suffered most were those most dependent on the earning of wages. But there were others, perhaps only a minority, at all social levels, whose income failed to keep pace with the rising cost of living, a situation not made easier for them to bear by the rise in the standard of material living which characterized the Elizabethan period. Sumptuary laws and statutes of apparel notwithstanding, and there were plenty of both during her reign, Elizabeth's subjects, and not only those in the upper ranks of society, discovered expectations of material comfort previously undreamed of. Perhaps it was as well, in the interests of social harmony, that although, as we have seen, new horizons were appearing, neither at home nor abroad were there really great fortunes to be made. By 1600, however, there were greater distinctions, in both town and countryside, between the rich and the poor, particularly between those of modest prosperity, the yeomen farmers and major urban tradesmen, and the poor husbandmen, small craftsmen and full-time labourers. The number of gentlemen had increased, but by comparison the number of really wealthy landed families, especially of those at the very top of the social scale, was remarkably static.

In William Harrison's categorization of English society one

looks in vain, apparently, for the ordinary husbandman or small family farmer, but, as we have seen, they are there all right, disguised by him as farm-labourers. While it ill behoved a parson thus to disparage hundreds of thousands of humble working farmers he was right, of course, in that by the 1570s, more than ever before, the ordinary husbandman's own farm provided neither a full-time occupation nor an adequate living. Manorial surveys show progressively fewer farms, especially in sheep–corn areas, of around thirty acres and more nearer ten or fifteen acres which in contemporary terms meant only bare subsistence. In the sheep–corn village of Chippenham in Cambridgeshire where, as we have seen, the concentration of the land into larger units had already gone some way by 1544, the process was proceeding even further when the manor was next surveyed in 1560. The smallest viable family unit, that of between fifteen and twenty-five acres of arable land, with appurtenances, was giving place to the cottage holding of a mere acre or so. Even so, the really precipitate decline of the Chippenham husbandmen came only from the later 1590s. Over at Willingham in fen country the process did not begin so early, but while in 1575 there were twenty-eight tenants holding between fifteen and twenty-five acres, by 1603 these were reduced to twenty. During the same period four holdings of twenty-five to thirty acres increased to seven. There were similar slow but significant developments in Wiltshire where, from about 1560 the sheep–corn country on the chalk saw a gradual reduction in the number of family farmers occupying forty to fifty acres. It was happening very slowly, however, only to the extent that while in the early sixteenth century the old type of self-sufficient husbandmen occupied rather over half of the land, their share declined to under one third by the middle of the seventeenth century. In the 'cheese' or woodland parts of Wiltshire where the average size of farms had always been smaller there was even less change, and in highland regions such as the far north-west, where there was greater concentration on stock rather than on arable farming, the old pattern persisted, as indeed it also did in areas such as the Weald or in Devon, in both of which the small farmer had always been a man of parts. Over the country as a whole, and especially in the lowlands, the 1580s may well have been the crucial decade, for by then to the absorption of more and more land by the larger farmers was added the new pressure of population, in other words, more sons to be provided for. Even in those parts of the country where partible inheritance had never been the rule – and that meant most of the sheep–corn areas – husbandmen were now to be found splitting their holdings into units of quite unviable size rather than cast out their younger sons as entirely landless labourers. Population pressure was by now such that there were rarely vacant holdings near at hand for them to move into, and in any case they stood little chance in competition with wealthier farmers who, at the very least, had similar familial responsibilities. By 1589 there was sufficient concern at Westminster for an Act to be passed prohibiting the building of cottages on the waste unless at least four acres of land was attached. Four acres was no living unless there were ample grazing rights.

There were a number of other factors besides population pressure contributing to the gradual disappearance of the more substantial husbandmen. In fielden areas, for example in parts of Wiltshire, the progress of enclosure by agreement may well have deprived some smallholders of both pastoral rights and also of access to meadow land. Not all exchanges of strips were fair, especially to those with least voice in the community. Whole villages no longer disappeared in Elizabethan England, only farms. The occupants of smaller farms were also likely to be harder hit by a run of bad harvests, and there is some evidence that there were more wet summers during Elizabeth's reign than before. The most obvious factor was an increase in rents, but this could usually only be achieved by the granting of entirely new and long tenancies, and once fixed the rents were soon overtaken, for those farming above subsistence level, by market prices for agricultural produce. Some farmers actually preferred to pay larger entry-fines than to see their rents increased, although this really amounted to the same thing. Richard Carew, writing of

Cornwall in the 1590s, can hardly have been thinking of farmers of substance, of which there were still very few in that county, when he referred to a general preference for a 'once smarting' to a 'continual aching'. But in the sheep–corn areas the majority of ordinary husbandmen were copyholders, more often than not 'of inheritance', and with nominal rents and fixed entry-fines, they had little to fear from their landlords. At Almondbury in the West Riding of Yorkshire as late as 1584 fines for copyholdings were stated to be one year's rent on inheritance or purchase, or half that amount for a tenancy in reversion. Indeed the tenurial situation of copyholders was improving as the common law moved slowly but surely to their defence, following the earlier lead given by Chancery and the conciliar courts. Insecurity really began when husbandmen were persuaded to exchange their copies for indentures of leases. Each manor and village had its own chronology but it was inevitable that sooner rather than later tenants-at-will would fall victims to landlords' realization of the advantages of fewer and larger tenancies. In some parts of the country, such as Leicestershire where they had been numerous, small freehold farms went the same way, sometimes bought up by lords of manors to lease out as part of larger units. In few places, however, did any of this happen in a hurry.

But while it is easy to exaggerate the decline of the later Tudor smallholding, it is difficult for us to appreciate how slight was the physical hold of many small farmers and their families on their land and livelihood. At Earls Colne in Essex a comparison of rentals compiled in 1549 and 1589 shows that out of 111 separate farms only thirty-one remained with the same family, even including descent through heiresses. In Suffolk only about one fifth of those families assessed for taxation in 1558 had descendants still on the same farms in the early seventeenth century. The really poor husbandmen, anyone with less than about fifteen acres, was always, of course, a potential pauper or vagrant, but why families should move into a neighbouring parish is often totally inexplicable. Some, of course, may have moved in order to avoid their creditors, for Elizabethan husbandmen were great borrowers of money from their more affluent neighbours, even on occasion from their parish priests. For many of them, however, money can have played so small a part in their normal lives that even the effort to go regularly to market can hardly have seemed necessary. Only on the death of a father or some other occasion when the payment of a substantial cash sum was required would panic set in. Indeed, many husbandmen might have fared better if their half-yearly rents had been increased rather than occasional entry-fines exacted. Many, too, must have invited a crisis by failing to look after such title deeds as their copies of the court roll. These must often have been lost or burnt in their fragile homesteads. Most farmers were hardly literate enough to know what they contained. Removal, whether voluntary or involuntary, was made easier, of course, by the very simplicity of the average husbandman's single-storey homestead, the one or two rooms, with an extension for animals, constructed in a matter of days from rough-hewn timbers, in-filled with wattle and earth, frequently rebuilt and deserted with scarcely a thought. Furnishings, including pots and pans, were minimal. John Tytmarche, husbandman, of Over Norton, Oxfordshire, lived at the time of his death in 1590 in a house consisting of a hall containing a small table, a form and a hen pen, some brass and pewter ware, a chamber containing one furnished bed, and a 'backside' in which were corn, hay, two 'beasts' and twelve sheep, the movables being valued all together at £7 13s. 8d. There were doubtless many who were poorer in worldly goods than this, too poor to need to make a will or have their possessions valued. These were the unsettled people, those whom William Harrison, without undue snobbery, described as having 'no voice nor authority in our commonwealth', and only for want of better, he went on, were churchwardens, ale-conners and constables chosen from 'such low and base persons'. He found their bawdy humour distasteful, though he admitted that when gathered together for weddings 'they are so merry without malice, and plain without inward Italian or French craft or subtlety, that it would do a man good to be in company among them'. It was indeed not yet time to write their epitaph.

Complementary to the gradual disappearance of the smaller farmers of Tudor England was the slow but steady advance in the number, and more especially the fortunes, of the larger farmers, those who occupied around sixty and even one hundred acres or more, depending on the area and the nature of their farming. Yeomen were not an Elizabethan novelty but by the later sixteenth century they were becoming much more clearly differentiated from their neighbours and their number was increasing so that instead of merely one or two there were usually half a dozen or more in villages of any size. It was these whom Thomas Wilson in his *State of England*, written at the very end of the century, referred to as 'the glory of the country and [providers of] good neighbourhood and hospitality'. Of those whom he called 'yeomen of the richer sort which are able to lend the Queen money', he reckoned there were in England at the time about ten thousand. Assuming that he was thinking only of the very rich yeomen, then an average of one per parish over the country as a whole may not be far wrong. Whereas many early Tudor yeomen had been descendants of old freeholding families who had added to their inheritance the newer yeomen of Elizabethan England were more likely to be the sons of customary tenants, men who had even leaned to good purpose on the protection of local manorial custom. When Sir Thomas Smith equated yeomen with the old 'forty shilling freeholders', he was using the term in its personal rather than its tenurial sense for he went on to say that most of them were farmers, that is, tenants, of gentlemen. Thomas Wilson, while allowing that there was 'yet good store of yeomen left', suggested that they were, as a group, already on the decline. But he wrote from the point of view of a gentleman on the defensive. He was thinking of those sons of yeomen who, 'not content with the state of their fathers', left the land and 'must step into velvet breeches and silk doublets and getting to be admitted into some Inn of Court or Chancery must ever after think scorn to be called other than gentleman'. His tract, written it is true not for his fellow-countrymen but for a foreign friend, deserves careful reading. In fact the least distinguishing mark of an Elizabethan yeoman was his tenure which could be freehold, leasehold or even copyhold, often a mixture of all three.

With their larger than average acreage, and hence surplus crops and animal products, yeomen were able to take full advantage of any increase in market prices. They were thus able to build up reserves of cash which enabled them not only to weather one or more bad harvests (and it had to be a very bad summer indeed to deprive them of any profit) but to buy either the freehold or a long lease of additional land when it became available. They could also tempt the lord of the manor with offers to buy reversions, a useful arrangement for providing for younger sons. Many yeomen, unlike the majority of husbandmen, occupied land in more than one parish, but above all, even within their native communities, they were the great engrossers of land. Thomas Dillamore, yeoman, of Chippenham in Cambridgeshire, held in 1600, still by customary tenure, almost two hundred acres, land which in 1544 had maintained no less than fifteen families. Men like Dillamore often set up as moneylenders, foreclosing on defaulting small copyholders and 'purchasing' their holdings in the manor courts. It was in this way that landlords connived at the ruin of their smaller tenants rather than actually exploiting them directly. Only their care to provide for their younger sons put a brake on the progressive enlargement of their farms with each successive generation. Once they had their foot on the ladder yeomen were probably the greatest beneficiaries from enclosure by agreement. Above all, they were the most stable element in the farming community, their names being those most likely to reappear in village records for generations. Their title deeds which, if they owned freeholdings, might include charters many centuries old, they kept in chests well away from the kitchen or 'firehouse', and indeed these latter were increasingly, in yeoman farmhouses, separated from the main hall or living-room. Few, however, built completely new houses, merely extending and improving them year by year, using more and more stone and inserting more substantial timbers. Extravagance was not their style. Chimneys to take away the smoke, window-shutters to keep out the wind, and the raising of roofs to enable them to insert upper floors seem to have been sufficient improvement for Elizabethan yeomen to refer to their houses as 'mansions', and so, compared with the cottages of their neighbours, they were. There is archaeological evidence that in the English lowlands some of the old 'long houses' containing accommodation for both men and beasts under one roof were disappearing, or to be more precise, were being deserted by their human inhabitants for new and separate farmhouses on higher ground a short distance away.

Yeomen were above all family farmers, working themselves and making full use of their wives and children. If they had resident farm-servants, male or female, these were expected to earn their keep, unlike those of gentlemen. The yeoman, wrote Thomas Westcote of Devon, 'speaketh to his servants ... in the plural number, we will do this ... intending to participate (in some easy sort) in their labours ... and so is well assured to have it done to his liking'. Moreover, they were usually to be found at home, on their land, not gadding about on public duties or visiting friends, like the gentlemen. Especially if there were no gentlemen resident locally, yeomen would both expect and be expected to be prominent in local affairs, to set a good example, for instance in turning up for the musters fully equipped in accordance with their rank. But at home, muck, carts, and harness lay all around them, and their upstairs chambers, when inventories came to be made, were as likely to contain stores of wool as feather beds. Thomas Taylor, yeoman, of Witney in Oxfordshire, who died in 1583, was clearly, on the evidence of his probate inventory, very much a working farmer. There was a good deal of money owing to him, most of it for such things as malt and leather and other products of his land, but some of it as small loans to friends and neighbours, in all no less than £246 out of his total assets of £408. His house contained ten rooms, apart from outbuildings, including a new parlour and even a guest chamber, each of these latter, as well as his hall or main living-room, hung with wainscot (wooden panelling) and even tapestry. His furniture and household goods were lavish in quantity but homely in quality and style. The Taylor family ate off a multiplicity of broad-rimmed pewter platters but they had no plate to speak of and, although they had pillows on their beds, most of their linen was coarse 'canvas'. It was no doubt of yeomen farmers that Harrison was thinking when he commented somewhat acidly on the increase, in his own lifetime, of domestic comforts such as pillows, previously only thought necessary for women in childbirth.

It was still, in Elizabethan England, rare for a family to progress into and out of the yeomanry in one generation and even for one born of a yeoman family it was easier for a younger son to be accepted as a gentleman if he had behind him a successful career, especially in the law. But a really substantial acquisition of freehold land would do just as well. Thomas Bradgate, already a wealthy yeoman, possibly of a second generation, in the village of Peatling Parva in Leicestershire, married in the 1520s the heiress of another yeoman of Carlton Curlieu. When his son Richard died in 1572 he owned, besides his inheritance, the two adjacent manors of Peatling Parva and Bruntingthorpe, both of which he had bought from Viscount Hereford. He was possessed of at least one thousand acres and he left chattels valued at over £700, much more than his father had done, but most of them consisted of stock and farm implements, his only luxuries being brass pots and pans and eighty pieces of pewter. But he did possess a rather better wardrobe than would probably have been deemed proper to one of his degree. Only at the very end of the century did his son assume the title of gentleman.

The husbandmen and yeomen of the countryside had their counterparts in the artisans and small traders of Elizabethan towns, but the equation must not be carried too far. For one thing there were much greater occupational differences in the towns, certain urban trades being intrinsically more profitable and conferring greater status. Another difference was that by and large the sons of the more affluent townsmen moved out and it was the poorer who stayed on. This was not incompatible with a continuing stream of migrants. At Oxford, for instance, entry to the freedom by patrimony, implying local birth, dropped from 20 per cent in the 1550s to only 7 per cent in the 1580s. But, in spite of increased competition, every town of any size had its complement of more successful artisans who lived, not uncomfortably by contemporary standards, much as did yeomen farmers. Anthony Osgarbie, tanner, of the parish of St Peter at Arches in Lincoln, occupied what was basically a two-roomed house of hall and parlour but with three chambers upstairs, one of these 'the maid's', and a separate buttery and kitchen at the rear. There were also in the towns far larger numbers of less independent craftsmen, the economic equivalent of husbandmen, though mostly slightly better housed. Many of these were employed as journeymen by the master-craftsmen or 'householders' as they were called in many towns. But the journeymen, having completed apprenticeships, were themselves an élite, head and shoulders above the very large numbers of semi-skilled casual labourers who possessed even less security, and far less chance of subsistence, than most rural labourers. On the whole, however, no doubt partly on account of the greater availability of poor-relief in the towns, they were less likely to move unless forced to do so by the town officers. Finally there were, in all towns, the hopelessly and abysmally poor people. The base of the urban social and economic 'pyramid' was becoming much broader. To what depths of temporary shanty dwellings it descended we can only guess, for it was the small master-craftsmen who inhabited the tenements into which so many of the older and more substantial urban buildings were now divided.

In the Elizabethan towns as well as in the countryside there was an ever-widening gap between the men of great wealth, who were almost invariably merchants, wholesalers if not actually engaged in overseas trade, and even the most successful of the master-craftsmen. Elizabethan merchants, not only in London but in the larger provincial towns, were very rich indeed and unlike the most successful yeomen farmers, whose material possessions they far surpassed, they usually made the bulk of their fortune in one generation. Their wealth was also

more conspicuous, especially in the large and very elaborate
houses which they built anew on the most prominent sites they
could find. It was no longer necessary for the civic authorities
to seek government help in rehabilitating building-plots. They
were now at a premium and so great was the competition that
even the town houses of the wealthy had to be built with very
narrow street frontages, and with overhanging jetties to enable
their occupants to live spaciously upstairs. Glazed windows and
interior walls hung with fabrics if not with elaborate 'seeling'
(carved wooden panelling) and ceilings in the modern sense
decorated with moulded plaster – all these proclaimed mercantile wealth, as too did the attics and 'cock-lofts' where they
accommodated their apprentices and domestic servants. The
number of their fireplaces, too, was coming to reflect merchant
wealth, as also were the elaborate 'cupboards' on which they
displayed their plate. In addition they had great need of large
'presses' in which to store their quite extraordinary collection of
gowns, some of them being their official robes as members of
the civic hierarchy. Velvet and fur abounded. Finally, ·to
comfort within they added even greater ostentation without,
utilizing their narrow street frontages for a profusion of
wooden, and in some areas plaster, decoration. It was undoubtedly the Elizabethan merchants who were setting the pace
in the great rebuilding of the age. To some extent their
knowledge of continental towns gave them the idea, but by
virtue of their occupation they usually had more ready cash at
their disposal than most countrymen. Compared with those in
the country, houses in towns at all social levels were more often
rebuilt from scratch rather than enlarged, if only because fire
was a perpetual hazard.

With the wealthiest of the provincial merchants and the quite
remarkable number of rich Londoners we are indeed moving
very near in status to the gentlemen and knights with whom so
many became related, if not united, by marriage. It is, however,
easy to exaggerate the anxiety of first-generation merchants,
even those who called themselves gentlemen and those many
Londoners who on or before attaining the Lord Mayoralty were

dubbed knights, to move very far from city streets. They bought land, often in many counties, not to bolster their status, which was already assured, but for investment or for the occasional retreat from their spiritual home which was London. Sir Thomas Gresham, the great Elizabethan financier, would occasionally escape from his large mansion in Bishopsgate to his house at Mayfield in Sussex, but this also enabled him to inspect his ironworks there. He was perhaps the extreme in Elizabethan absentee landlordship. After his death it was revealed in the course of a manpower inquiry in County Durham that he, or his agents, had evicted no less than thirteen of his fifteen tenants in the parish of Stranton, and three of the seven in Seaton Carew, presumably in order to let the land for grazing. In fact his lands were valued in 1579 at only £2,670 a year, most of his capital having gone into the building not only of Gresham House but of the great house at Osterley in Middlesex. Sir Roger Martin, a London mercer and a native of Long Melford in Suffolk, bought property in Nottinghamshire and Gloucestershire but continued to live until his death in 1573 no further from the city than Hoxton. It is true that he left £66 13s. 4d. to be given to 200 poor householders at Long Melford but he also took care to be remembered in London, leaving £40 for a dinner on the day of his funeral for his fellow members of the Mercers' Company and as many of their wives as could be accommodated.

One of the few wealthy city men with no previous roots in the countryside who did make the transition in his own lifetime in Elizabeth's reign was not an Englishman by birth but a native of Genoa. Horatio Palavicino, who was not of common stock, his family having been prominent in Italian public and mercantile life, came to England in about 1580 after first laying the foundations of his personal fortune in the Low Countries. During the ensuing decade he served the Queen as her principal financial agent in succession to Sir Thomas Gresham. He became a naturalized Englishman in 1585 and was knighted two years later. By then he was investing heavily in land, buying estates in Essex from the needy earl of Leicester and in Norfolk

from Lord Burghley's eldest son. In 1589 he bought a house and
land at Babraham in Cambridgeshire and by the time of his
death in 1600 he had spent in all some £20,000 and was lord of
over eight thousand acres of English soil. He became a not
inconsiderable sheepmaster and took an interest in agricultural
irrigation. His tenants found him a hard man to deal with. He
and his Dutch wife Anna whom he married in 1591, in so doing
acquiring a marriage portion of some £10,000's worth of land
in Holland, filled their Cambridgeshire house with Italian
servants and continental plate and furnishings. They did,
however, call their sons Henry and Toby, though their daughter
was christened Baptina. Palavicino's capacity for quarrelling
with his neighbours exceeded that of most English gentlemen
and even the friendship of the Cecils must have worn a little thin
when he sought their support for his protests about his
assessment for taxation and musters. Those who had most cause
to bless him were his English lawyers, for he left his affairs in a
hopeless tangle. But Sir Robert Cecil stood by Anna who, in
the manner of so many English widows, was allowed to
purchase her son's wardship. Within a year of her husband's
death, and contrary to his wishes, this eligible young widow
remarried, becoming the second wife of Oliver Cromwell,
esquire, of Hinchinbrook. The three children of each first
marriage were eventually neatly joined in matrimony and the
traditional business interests of this immigrant family were
pursued only by Horatio's bastard son Edward.

   In spite, however, of most of the successful merchants'
attachment to their counting-houses it was still very rare to find,
either in London or the provincial towns, more than two
generations of any family among the élite. Of the forty-eight
Lord Mayors of Elizabethan London no two had the same
surname, and in the names of aldermen and members of the
common council the repetition is minimal. Although at any one
time a large number of the city's governors were related by
marriage, there was, even in London, no civic caste. Likewise in
the Elizabethan city of Oxford, only one son followed his father
in the mayoralty and an analysis of the city council in 1600

shows that only one fifth had followed in their father's footsteps. At Worcester the situation was similar, and it seems that no more than two or three of her leading men or their descendants made any notable impact on local rural society. They simply returned, both here and elsewhere, very largely to the rural obscurity from which they had emerged. Presumably the existing county establishment was too entrenched for them to make any impression. By contrast the late Elizabethan coal-owners of Newcastle and the Tyne valley, whose business interests spanned both town and country, bought much land in the vicinity for what looks like purely social purposes. The defeat of the Northern Rebellion in 1569–70 gave them the opportunity, and their assimilation into local society was apparently eased by the fact that the survivors of the old landed establishment also owned both collieries and saltpans, and now sought to be admitted into the Newcastle trading oligarchy. By 1600 even local yeomen families in the north-east were producing pedigrees and seeking recognition for their arms. After centuries of domination by the great landed magnates this part of England became, towards the end of the century, one of quite unparalleled change.

The sector of Elizabethan society which continued to depend most on recruitment from families with other occupations was that of the clergy. At no time in Elizabeth's reign were there enough clergy to fill the parochial benefices, but even without pluralism they should not have suffered greatly from the effects of price rises. Their income derived mainly from tithe and from their glebe, and providing neither had been leased for long terms these should have provided a useful hedge against inflation. Small tithes, that is, of wool, lambs, fruit, etc., which most vicars enjoyed, actually trebled in value between 1530 and 1580, and though the price of corn and hay only doubled over the same period, after 1580 it provided the rectors, as owners of the great tithes, with an even larger proportional rise in income. It must not be forgotten, however, that the rectorial tithes appropriated by the monasteries had passed, via the Crown, into lay ownership, charged with fixed stipends for the unfortunate vicars. The glebe, which was more likely to be still in clerical hands, was, then, particularly valuable, especially if the priest farmed it himself and could adapt its produce to market-demand as well as to the needs of his own household which were not met by tithe. Some clergy were pioneers in growing such crops as hemp and flax and many will have been familiar figures in local markets, more so probably than before the Reformation and in spite of a good deal of lay disapproval.

But the great difference between the Elizabethan parish clergy and their early Tudor predecessors – and this too did not please all the laity – was, of course, their acquisition of wives and families. While this put some strain on their resources, there were savings by way of housekeepers and servants. But conjugal bliss did underline the fact that incumbents had only life tenancies of their houses and land and there arose problems not only of providing for possible widows but also for setting up sons and marrying daughters. If they were to accumulate the minimum capital out of income for the launching of their children, the parish clergy were in no position to improve their houses which were at best merely extended to accommodate growing families. Though on the whole better off materially than the ordinary husbandmen among their parishioners, especially towards the end of the century when their probate inventories show that many clergy owned chattels valued at over £50, this may only have meant that they were standing still while the situation of the poorer farmers deteriorated. Whether or not, like everyone else except the really poor, the Elizabethan parish clergy enjoyed increasing domestic comfort by the 1580s and 1590s, by which time an increasing number of the lesser clergy were university graduates, clerical probate inventories contained references to books, not only Bibles and service books but a range of theological and other literature. By then, too, parsonage houses almost invariably contained studies, even if they were only small chambers over the entry. But even by 1600 the lifestyle and social status of the parish clergy placed them with the more well-to-do yeomen, from whose families most of them had come, rather than with the gentlemen. In the matriculation registers of the university of Cambridge the sons of clergy were classified with those of tradesmen and farmers as *mediocris fortunae,* which indeed most of them were. They were in no real sense gentry, nor did their sons and daughters often marry into the families of gentlemen. As yet, though the possibility was already there, there were few clerical dynasties, the time not having yet come when family livings were bestowed, generation after generation, on patrons' younger sons. But the lesser Anglican clergy were becoming, by 1600, rather more of a professional group. An all-graduate clergy now seemed attainable, and although pluralism was still rampant, far fewer benefices were used to fund government posts. This provided more opportunities for promotion to the higher clerical ranks for priests with parochial experience. Moreover, they were still a privileged group. In spite of determined efforts by lords-lieutenants the clergy, led by the bishops, successfully resisted being required to muster with the shire militia. In Armada year they provided a separate levy of men, horses and armour. Even the drastic curtailment of benefit of clergy can only have served the interests of the priestly office proper.

There was, perhaps, among the Elizabethan parish clergy, less real envy of their superiors, especially the bishops, than had been customary, and indeed justified, in the medieval and early Tudor Church. The bishops certainly felt the full force of the re-establishment of the royal supremacy, and although they enjoyed rather greater personal security of tenure, their economic position was fraught with danger. There were plenty of laymen prepared to argue for the reduction of bishops to a merely supervisory function, and an Act of 1559 which forbade them to grant leases of their land for more than twenty-one years also enabled the Queen to effect unlimited 'exchanges' during vacancies. In fact it suited her not entirely to beggar her bishops, and although they lost a great many manors their income was maintained by grants of rectorial tithes still in Crown hands. They were allowed to keep their palaces and sufficient demesne to supply their still considerable households but, though often better pastors than their medieval predecessors, these post-Reformation diocesan managing directors had lost a great deal in local prestige. What the Queen did not welcome but was powerless to stop was the propensity of her bishops to marry, at least three quarters of them doing so, some of course before their elevation, and to beget, on average, four children. But only very gradually did Elizabethan gentlemen look with favour even on the higher clergy as prospective sons-in-law. In County Durham, for instance, it was not until the very end of the sixteenth century that the children of bishops, deans and prebendaries were marrying into gentry families, or that bishops were able to establish their heirs as landowners. Having for the most part come from humble backgrounds, once in possession of what, by contemporary standards, was great wealth, the higher clergy felt more obliged than their lesser brethren to find patrimonies and dowries sufficient to ensure all their children a standard of life such as they had enjoyed in the palace. Bishops could not, of course, actually pass to their children, except with royal permission, any part of their episcopal capital resources, but they could sell leases and, if able to accumulate the capital, purchase land for members of their family, including brothers. Most of Elizabeth's bishops managed to live very well, keeping plenty of servants and entertaining lavishly, but none of them built new, or even rebuilt their old, palaces, some of which were now very dilapidated. They continued to sit in the House of Lords but, except for their graces of Canterbury, they no longer had any place in the secular corridors of power, and most of them had to be content with the company of the leading country gentlemen rather than with their fellow peers.

Nor, in Elizabethan England, was there anywhere any lack of gentlemen to keep the bishops company. Contemporary commentators marvelled at, and historians rediscover, the burgeoning of gentility in England in the later sixteenth century. The mere self-styled gentry were becoming literally countless. The élite who were named in the county commissions of the peace multiplied two and even three times between the 1540s and 1580s. As Parliament found more and more for them to do perhaps all that was happening was that lesser men were being called upon. However, even more convincing evidence is available from the records of the heralds' visitations. In County Durham, for example, whereas in the 1530s only six gentlemen claimed the right to bear arms, by 1575 the number was fifty-six and by 1600 nearer one hundred. Even this could be evidence simply of a greater desire for outward and visible trappings. But there is also the evidence of the land market which indicates a growing demand for single manors or other medium-sized properties. It seems likely that by 1600 well over half the land in England was owned by gentlemen, and the disappearance of so many corporate landlords and sales by the nobility added considerably to the number of villages which had a resident 'squire'.

But when Sir Thomas Smith made his well-known comment that gentlemen were 'made good cheap', he was not so much remarking on how little landed wealth was necessary but making the point that the real test of gentility was occupation:

Whosoever studieth the laws of the realm, who studieth in the universities, who professeth liberal sciences, and to be short, who can live idly and without manual labour, and will bear the port [appearance], charge [cost] and countenance [assurance] of a gentleman, he shall be called master . . . and shall be taken for a gentleman.

William Harrison was even more explicit, preceding an almost identical passage by declaring that 'gentlemen whose ancestors are not known to have come in with William duke of Normandy . . . do take their beginning in England after this manner', implying that new gentlemen achieved occupational status first and land second. This was not entirely true, except in the case of lawyers, but it serves as a reminder that to acquire land, except by inheritance, a man had first to acquire capital, and even for marriage to an heiress a man had to have either lineage or prospects: the legend of the poor apprentice marrying his master's widow was wearing a little thin by the end of the sixteenth century. It remained true, of course, that landownership was the only sure way of passing on one's gentle status to one's descendants.

The inclusion in Smith's list of potential gentlemen of university men is a sign of the times, for not long since they would all have been called clerks. The matriculation registers of both Oxford and Cambridge continued to note the status of each student's father and if anything erred on the side of designating all who were not clearly gentlemen born or better as 'plebeians'. But by no means all those called plebeians were inferior and poor, many being sons of wealthy merchants. Especially was this true of St John's College, Oxford, founded in Mary's reign by Alderman Sir Thomas White of London, merchant-tailor, and required to reserve thirty-seven of its fifty scholarship places for boys from the Merchant Taylors' School of which White was also a benefactor. The other thirteen were to be drawn from the founder's kin and from the towns of Tonbridge, Reading, Coventry and Bristol. Even at St John's gentlemen made up over 40 per cent of its Elizabethan entrants, and although their sons were plebeians by Oxford regulations, the fathers of many of the town and city boys were themselves younger sons of country gentlemen. James Whitelocke who entered St John's in 1588 to read law, a *plebei filius* aged eighteen, was the youngest of the four sons of a London merchant, himself the youngest of the four sons of a Berkshire landowner. Sir James, as he later became, recalled that his mother, a country-woman (from Hertfordshire) and already a rich widow, 'did bring up all her children in as good sort as any gentleman in England would do [his father had died the year he was born], as in singing, dancing, playing on the lute ... Latin, Greek, Hebrew and French tongues, and to write fair'. Needless to say Mrs Whitelocke married a third London merchant, and her son James took as his wife a Bulstrode of Buckinghamshire, so the university played only a minor role in his return to his ancestral status. The fact is that there were in Elizabethan England far fewer really poor boys at Oxford.

If, as we have seen, gentility ran in the blood even of many of the new landowners of Elizabethan England, how far had their occupational diversions altered their attitude to land and its exploitation? How many of the Elizabethan gentry were, like so many of their ancestors, mere landlords, that is rentiers, and how many occupied enough of their land to enable them to augment their income by marketing surplus products? By no means all gentlemen were inclined to embark upon commercial operations and there were all kinds of other factors such as the nature of the terrain and the location of their property in relation to existing markets, especially those of London and the larger provincial towns. Equally important was the security of existing tenancies, and, for gentlemen of any substance, their pre-occupation with public duties. Indeed, it was possible for some landowners to make a virtue of necessity. Sir Thomas Cornwallis, forced into rural retreat on account of his recusancy, managed, by farming some of his lands in East Anglia himself, to increase his net income from under £700 a year in 1558 to over £1,000 by the end of the century. His wife kept his accounts and they lived in some style, rebuilding their house at Brome in Suffolk and another in Norwich. There were too, *pace* Harrison, many small backwoods gentlemen, mostly of very ancient lineage, who did accompany their labourers into the fields like any yeoman. Anthony Hall, gentleman, of South Newington, Oxfordshire, who died in 1588, had been living in a modest house consisting only of a hall and a few chambers, but he also had a barn and the stock and crops (valued together at about £30) of a modest husbandman. What distinguished him from his socially inferior neighbours was his possession of thirteen pairs of sheets, seven table-cloths, seventeen table napkins, some books and a sword, but it is unlikely that he never soiled his hands before sitting down to dine. Most gentlemen, old and new, if they farmed at all, were dependent on bailiffs. It cannot, however, be shown that there was any clear difference in attitude between the older-established families and the new ones, or even between those still actively engaged as lawyers etc. and those who had retired to live on their estates. To some extent the older gentry had a head start in the race against inflation if only because so much of the property on the market between 1540 and 1570, especially former monastic land, was encumbered with long leases. Many new landlords had to be

patient at least until the 1580s. One of the cleverest old-
fashioned tactics (a favourite of the monks) which could be
adopted by a modest landlord with estates conveniently located
was to insist on as much rent as possible in kind. The Acclom
family of Moreby Grange in Yorkshire, throughout Elizabeth's
reign, drew from their manor of Bonwick not only £11 in cash
but also ten quarters of seed barley and three of wheat and rye,
the value of the latter fluctuating from year to year but in both
the long and the short run at least part of the income was keeping
in line with prices. When the food rents were finally commuted
in 1600 the total rent was £60. It is doubtful whether many of
the legendary new and thrusting landlords did better than that.

It is impossible to distinguish clearly between the interest
of old and new gentlemen in the adoption of new techniques of
farming, though it is probably safe to say that more progress
was made in this direction by gentlemen than by yeomen
farmers. To some extent this was due to the same energy and
initiative which had got the new gentry where they were, and
it may also have owed something to their better education
which led them to read the growing number of printed books
on the subject. But most important of all, gentlemen travelled
further afield than most yeomen and had more time to observe
and to listen. Many will have learned when at the Inns of Court
of the benefit to be gained from having their land expertly
surveyed and its potential value assessed. Land also had its
industrial potential, of course, including the exploitation of
mineral resources, and here too gentlemen, especially as they
were more likely to own the freehold, were decidedly more
active than yeomen, but this is not to say very much. Most
mineral enterprises, especially ironworks, were not only owned
by substantial landowners but also managed on their direct
behalf. In Cornwall the majority of the more profitable tin-
workings, especially those where shaft-mining was in operation,
were owned and exploited by gentlemen. One of these was
William Carnsew of Bokelly, esquire. There may be some
connection between the fact that his mother was a Welsh woman
and that he was concerned in 1584 with the building at

Aberdulais near Neath in south Wales of a smelting works for processing Cornish copper ore, a project which has some claim to have been the first stage in the industrialization of the area. Carnsew's technical expert was a German. It is easy enough to cite examples but, as already indicated, there was no Tudor industrial revolution, and gentlemen who, either by themselves or in partnership with others, put capital into industrial enterprises were the exception and not the rule. Even Carnsew probably made more money from farming than from mining.

What is certain is that for every Elizabethan gentleman who invested in industry half a dozen or more at some time invested in some kind of maritime or overseas enterprise, which was more likely to be privateering than legitimate trade. Broadly speaking, as already indicated, their support and enthusiasm were more important in the earlier part of Elizabeth's reign. After 1590 few gentlemen invested and they apparently did not share, in 1599–1600, the merchants' enthusiasm for the East Indies, perhaps simply because there was less chance of privateering. There were many gentlemen who sold land, even land they had inherited, in order to chance their luck on the ocean. Edward Glenham esquire of Benhall in Suffolk even sold his family home to buy ships but few gentlemen were as reckless as that. On the whole those who did best were their younger sons, with rather less to lose, but the younger Gilberts and Raleighs and their like left to their descendants more glorious memories than landed or other wealth as a result of their maritime enterprise.

Elizabethan gentlemen were, however, not far behind the merchants in their desire for domestic comfort and ostentatious display, but, with outstanding exceptions, including those who were prepared to incur large debts to builders and craftsmen, they were more limited by their lack of ready cash. They also had rather different objectives, their domestic lifestyle being more public, more open to view. Living mostly in the country they also had more room, for instance, to erect elaborate gate-houses and to provide gardens beyond the dreams of most town-dwellers. They loved to set their houses against a back-drop of broad parkland where both sporting activities and table

delicacies could be nourished. Indeed, parks were as important
to gentlemen as pedigrees and not a great deal more costly.
Instead of narrow frontages, their houses faced the world
broadly, often with little depth, even the service quarters lying
alongside their spacious halls. They were rarely able to afford to
rebuild entirely and so their houses were more often than not
adapted and enlarged versions of traditional and much simpler
mansions, still with their central cross-passages. However, in
many parts of the country finely sculpted stone took the place,
both internally and externally, of timber-framing. Brick was
being increasingly used in the Home Counties but had not spread
far to the north or west by 1600. Above all, the wealth of the
more substantial gentry was to be seen in an excrescence of
chimneys. Rich wall-hangings, plaster-work and panelling
abounded inside, and the old simple wooden partitions gave
way to elaborately carved screens. Rooms, which were, in most
gentlemen's houses, not very large or lofty, were almost over-
powered by their fireplaces and huge chimney-pieces. The
furniture, at least of those who could afford to employ highly
skilled wood-carvers, also tended to be massive and heavily
ornate, in particular the great four-poster beds with their
elaborate hangings. Like his social inferiors, and perhaps even
more necessary in view of the still very public nature of life in
the gentleman's 'hall', he inserted a warren of upstairs chambers
for family privacy. Armorial bearings abounded, reminders of
the peregrinations of the heralds. The records of the College of
Arms show that the peak of grants of arms was reached in the
1580s, and that the last decade of the century, as in so many other
respects, was, even for the gentry, a period of anticlimax. While,
as a group, the Elizabethan gentry had increased in numbers, in
real wealth and in prestige many had outreached themselves by
the 1590s, and for most gentry families, sooner rather than later,
a period of quiescence arrived. This could be due to many
causes, including personal eccentricities. It was more likely to be
the result of an heir being under age. It could also be due to the
cost of being a religious extremist. In an age of inflation most
gentry families probably lived up to their income: this was

expected of them. More became rich, by contemporary standards, from the profits of office than from the exploitation, direct or indirect, of their lands, but even at Court a young man might hang about for years before he caught the Queen's eye and there were those who attached themselves to falling stars such as the earl of Essex. In fact, it is doubtful whether the Court of Queen Elizabeth was as open to real talent as that of her father or grandfather. Some gentlemen were never other than just solvent: some were occasionally or chronically in debt. For what the figures are worth, out of ninety persons with lands or goods in Wiltshire who, between 1551 and 1600, defaulted on their debts to the point where their creditors made use of the process of distraint available to those whose loans had been registered in the courts, over two thirds were gentlemen.

Even if an Elizabethan gentleman eschewed the perils of maritime, industrial or even agrarian adventures, farmed his demesnes, marketed his surplus crops and stock, steadily built up his rent-roll, and kept his expenditure within bounds, the future of his line was never assured. He had to find capital out of income to provide patrimonies for his younger sons and marriage portions for his daughters, and these might at the very worst lead him into mortgaging the very core of his estate. All was likely to be well, provided he lived long enough, and particularly if he lost one or more wives and married wealthy widows without too many children of their own. The great disaster was to have no sons but one daughter, or even worse, more than one, the effect of which would be to see the small estate split between sons-in-law. Many a disappointed gentleman must have almost welcomed the loss of an ageing wife, with the hope this brought of another chance with a younger woman. Remarriage among the Elizabethan gentry was very common indeed, often producing an embarrassingly large second family. Moreover, if it brought the first sons, it also increased the possibility of death while the heir was under age. The forfeiture of wards' estates to the Crown was not new, of course, but under Burghley's mastership of the Court of Wards central intelligence was vastly increased. The essence of gentility was to be known and there was no escape from the escheator.

In an age which saw such a growth in the number of gentlemen the order of knighthood was especially prized. It too had expanded during the middle years of the century but with scant regard for the views of Sir Thomas Elyot and his friends that those singled out for such distinction should be men educated in the arts of peace rather than of war. The increase was partly due to there being three coronations in fairly quick succession, and possibly even to something of a protest by those landed gentlemen returned by commissions of inquiry as being eligible, who resented being fobbed off with a fine for a technical 'refusal'. Queen Elizabeth refused, almost as a reassertion of her prerogative, to devalue the honour, and during the first decade and a half of her reign she created barely ten knights a year. The result was a fall in the total number from about five hundred and fifty at her accession to under two hundred and fifty by the mid-1570s. She then relented a little and although never particularly generous (the annual average from the mid-1570s until the end of the century was just over twenty) the total number had crept up to well over three hundred by the end of her reign. Many men of considerable distinction, especially soldiers such as Henry Killigrew, and naval administrators such as John Hawkins and William Winter, were only knighted at the end of long careers in her service. Unlike her father, the Queen disapproved of her generals knighting men on the field of battle, and it was during her reign that knighthood at last became overwhelmingly a civil rather than a military distinction. Above all, she was adamant that those knighted should already possess the means – usually land – to sustain their status. Even Francis Drake had been authorized to keep a substantial portion of the spoils of his circumnavigation of the world before being dubbed knight at Deptford in 1581. But there was no Elizabethan knightly class. In the three widely dispersed and very different counties of Lancashire, Norfolk and Sussex there were, altogether, only ninety families producing a knight, barely one third of these three or more, and over half only one. Knighthood ran in families far less than in the early sixteenth century, and even where son succeeded father there was often a long gap. Knights did not necessarily undertake more public responsibilities than the more substantial gentlemen, nor were they, by and large, any better fitted by their education. In Sussex by 1580, whereas over half the gentry had been to a university or an Inn of Court, only 23 per cent of the knights had done so, but all the latter were, as indeed were most knights, heads of families. It was then most important that, as an additional bonus to his accolade, a young knight, under twenty-one and fatherless, was allowed to escape the shackles of wardship.

After the profusion of titles of nobility which had characterized the Edwardian regime, the peerage settled down, as far as numbers were concerned, for the rest of the century. Mary created only half a dozen peers, though she did restore those titles previously forfeited by the Howard, Courtenay and Percy families. Whether, as in her parsimony in the dubbing of knights, Queen Elizabeth was determined to husband her prerogative, or, more particularly in the case of nobles, she had no wish to be prodigal in the granting of royal lands, or even had learned in the hard years of her young womanhood to be wary of over-mighty subjects, she never allowed the nobility to expand in size beyond that which she had inherited, many of them very recent creations. The total remained steady at just under sixty, of whom well over half were mere barons, and only a quarter were earls. There were never more than one or two dukes and marquises, this scarcity of men at the very top of the social scale being, of course, partly due to an almost complete lack of royal relatives. Even the Queen's first cousin, Henry Carey, became, in 1599, only Lord Hunsdon. Her most trusted ministers gained little by way of rank, William Cecil only becoming Lord Burghley in 1571, and stalwarts such as Francis Bacon, Walter Mildmay, Thomas Smith, Francis Walsingham, James Croft, Thomas Heneage, Francis Knollys and Christopher Hatton were never more than knights. The Queen's favourites, Robert Dudley and Robert Devereux, were earls of Leicester and Essex respectively, but the former was the son of a duke and the latter inherited his title at the age of ten in 1576.

In all, Elizabeth elevated only ten commoners to the nobility and restored or revived a further eight titles, all but three in the first few years of her reign. To balance this no less than fourteen titles became extinct during her reign through failure of male heirs, and six were extinguished by attainder.

What strikes one about the later Tudor nobles is how like they were, except in degree, to the generality of knights, esquires and even mere gentlemen. They still enjoyed certain unique privileges, of course – the personal summons to Parliament, trial by their equals, and special arrangements for taxation – but none of these availed them much in their primary role as very large landowners. Although most of them still regarded themselves as professional soldiers, the long peace of the 1560s and 1570s gave them very few opportunities for active service and they had to be content with the semi-military role of the county lords-lieutenancies, making them leaders of the county militia. When they went to war, especially in Ireland, it was largely at their own expense and neither there, nor on the continent of Europe, nor at sea, were there compensating spoils. Although some of the Elizabethan nobility were great builders, their ambitions were, except perhaps in London, to live not in castles or palaces but in large and magnificent country houses, built for lavish entertainment and hospitality. The scattered nature of their estates made some of Elizabeth's nobles go for quantity instead of quality in their residences, presumably so that they could spend a great part of each year moving, with their entourage, from one to the other. For example, the Cliffords, earls of Cumberland, had four houses in Westmorland, and two in the East Riding of Yorkshire. Others, of course, sank their all, and more, into one magnificent pile, but the great age of aristocratic building did not come until after 1600. In Elizabeth's reign many commoners' houses outdid, in magnificence if not in size, those of their social superiors. One thinks, for example, of Longleat, of Wollaton and also of Gresham's pile at Osterley. The chief concern of the Elizabethan peers, like that of all landowners, was the conservation and extension of their inheritance. Marriage, which in the great majority of cases had been crucial in the early accumulation of their estates, had to continue to be profitable, for only by continual augmentation could most inheritances be maintained in view of the very considerable 'portions' which had to be found for daughters. It sems to have been a particular hazard faced by the Elizabethan nobility to die prematurely, of natural causes, leaving their heirs saddled with jointures payable to one, and even two, long-lived dowagers. Between 1588 and 1595 the estates of the young earl of Rutland, Burghley's ward, were encumbered with no less than three widows' jointures. These were more likely to consume a young peer's substance than his gambling debts.

Inflation, the increasing cost of everything which contributed to the aristocratic lifestyle, was the real drain. The greater their estate the more time and energy were required to improve the cash income. The remedy, for some a never-ending tale and for most of Elizabeth's nobility a resort at some stage, was outright sale of land for cash which was immediately consumed. Between 1595 and 1600 the young earl of Southampton sold seven scattered manors to realize the sum of £20,500, as well as mortgaging others, to pay his creditors. This seriously depleted his immediate annual income. The third earl of Cumberland sold land to buy ships, initially as a means of getting himself out of debt. In 1600 he reckoned that he had spent on 'sea journeys' in the region of £100,000. He achieved neither wealth nor real fame for he was never other than an amateur pirate and only kept his head above water in the end by going into partnership with London merchants. But his sales at least had some purpose compared with the sale by Henry Hastings, third earl of Huntingdon, of no less than 170 separate parcels of land, including sixty-five manors, between 1561 and his death in 1595. Out of total proceeds of over £90,000 only about £13,500 was spent on purchases of land, the rest going on day-to-day expenses, including lawyers' fees. However, by 1600, as already indicated (as compared with 1561 and taking into account their purchases), the nobility as a group had sustained a net loss of only a little over four hundred manors, not a great deal over the country as a whole, though it varied considerably from county to county. Politics had little effect, for even the attainder of one of its members did not necessarily ruin a family. When Thomas Percy, seventh earl of Northumberland, was executed for treason in 1572, the estates, which were entailed, passed to his brother Henry and when he, in his turn, died in the Tower in 1585 they passed to his son and heir, Henry, the ninth earl. It was the same entail which precluded him from selling large parts of the estate during what remained of his profligate youth. The turning-point for him came some ten years later when he not only found what he had been looking for, a wife who could 'bring with her meat in her mouth to maintain her expense', but also buried his mother who had been enjoying land and an annuity together worth over £1,500 a year, a third of his total income. Even debt itself, at the rate of interest (10 per cent) legally permitted after 1571, was not by any means disastrous. Really wealthy men – and most peers had landed income running into several thousands of pounds a year – can afford to incur debts, and few owed at any time more than one year's income. It is perhaps worth stressing that the English aristocrats, unlike their European counterparts, did not live on feudal dues and labour services which could only be increased by oppressing their tenants. One of their great resources was woodland and, in a country getting very short of that resource, sales of standing timber saved many a menacing situation. Some peers, usually for short periods, augmented their income by exploiting their mineral rights, but few were as successful as the earls of Rutland with their ironworks at Rievaulx Abbey in Yorkshire. Many of the Elizabethan peers were remarkably successful in 'improving' their estates, that is, increasing their income by way of rents and fines without necessarily exploiting their tenants, most of whom were themselves profiting substantially from the inflation of prices. By 1600 the earl of Northumberland had doubled his annual income and was embarking on judicious purchases of land. Each family has its own peculiar history of estate management, often with long periods of neglect (or seignorial benevolence) followed by sudden onslaughts when, usually with the help of professional surveyors, yields were improved and tenants were made to face up to reality. When the earl of Rutland emerged from his wardship in 1597, farms which fortunately had been let on short terms during his minority realized in fines for renewal no less than £14,600, four times his total landed revenue. There was some exploitation, of course, and even enclosure, not so much for aristocratic sheep farming as to facilitate the engrossing of farms, but by and large the Elizabethan peerage was not particularly notorious for injustice towards its tenantry. Neither of the two leading Puritan earls, Huntingdon and Bedford, had bad reputations as landlords, and yet neither of them was especially thrifty.

Compared with what was expected of the gentry and even of yeomen in the service of their local communities the Elizabethan nobility was under-employed. Of those who were eligible, at least by age though not necessarily by capacity, it has been calculated that barely a third held high offices of state, most of which were held by those Elizabeth chose not to ennoble. As servants of the Crown, the sons of gentlemen had, of course, the edge over the sons of the aristocracy, being for the most part better educated. Few peers sent even their younger sons to the universities or to the Inns of Court, and Burghley's efforts to educate noble wards (of whom he had no less than nine in his own household) were largely in vain. As for the Queen's favours – cancellation of debts, grants of Crown lands, farms of the customs, patents of monopoly, and the profitable licences of all kinds which were the stock in trade of Elizabethan politics – the nobility almost certainly got less than their fair share, especially in the last two decades of the century. On the whole they had been loyal subjects, and it was with some justification that in 1601 no less than seven young earls joined with the earl of Essex, not, of course, in rebellion against the Queen but against the commoner, Robert Cecil, in an effort to make the Court a better place for the aristocracy.

14. *Community and Country*

As men stood ready, in June 1588, to light the beacons at the sighting of the Spanish Armada, and when they celebrated their deliverance, English people may have felt themselves to be one nation. The Queen, if only because none but the old could remember when she had not been there, was herself an institution, the centre of a highly artificial, but none the less national, cult. She it was who so often decided whose ideas were tried out, whose projects went forward and whose did not. There were still many men of great wealth and power, but it was during Elizabeth's reign that men's loyalties gradually became detached from the aristocracy, the great landowners *per se*, and that all but an eccentric minority looked up only to those men of influence, landed or not, who enjoyed the Queen's favour, and her ear. Noblemen still kept up large households and dressed their servants in their personal livery, but their magnetism was now much more local than in the past. They could, and on occasion did, muster their tenants and neighbours, but formal retaining, as understood and licensed by the Crown as late as the 1560s, was virtually a thing of the past by the 1590s. Patronage – and all men of ambition needed patrons – flowed downwards from the Court, all lesser centres of power existing only by royal licence, forming a ladder of vertical relationships and mutual aid from the most influential to the least privileged in the land. The new lord-lieutenancies of the counties were filled by royal commission, and were not hereditary. The earl of Huntingdon dominated Yorkshire by virtue of his presidency from 1572 to 1595 of the Council of the North, not as a local landed magnate. However, it required very hard work on the part of the Queen and her ministers to ensure that the knights and gentlemen who for the most part ran county affairs danced to her tune.

Most Tudor people lived, most of the time, in the context of their own local community, primarily that of their family and immediate neighbours in the fields and in the streets, or in local gatherings, secular and religious. At this distance of time it is not easy to identify the exact nature of those communities and even less to discover how men and women saw themselves away from their own firesides. This is particularly true of landlords and their tenants. The late medieval decline of the manor, seen in terms of the withdrawal of its lord from demesne farming and the commutation of tenants' labour services, is as well attested as the survival of the manor into the sixteenth century and beyond as a unit of landownership. Equally important, however, were the effects on the personal relationship between lord and tenant of the spread of leasehold tenure and also the persistence in hundreds of open-field villages of the making and implementation in manor courts of agrarian by-laws. Historical records, even when they survive in abundance, can in fact positively distort the realities of community life. The tenants who assembled in the court-rooms of manor houses, to pay their rents and to be recorded by name among the 'homage', will often have been strangers to most of those present, either because they were themselves newcomers, perhaps occupying enclosed farms, or because, as is rarely properly understood, manor and village did not in all cases coincide, especially in 'forest' areas. In many a region of hamlets and isolated farms there was neither a village nor in any sense an agricultural community, and certainly no need for agrarian by-laws. Even those Elizabethan by-laws which are to be found on court rolls often refer to decisions made by and applicable to the 'inhabitants' rather than just the tenants, and many villages, especially those with divided lordship, held 'town' meetings which in some cases had ancient roots. Contemporary pictorial maps, for example that of 1581 of Toddington in Bedfordshire, show that some villages even possessed 'town' or 'moot' houses quite distinct from either the ancient court-houses

or the newer 'church' houses. There is, moreover, evidence of
the creation in the later sixteenth century of new village
governors. It was, in fact, the manor court at the small village of
Burbage in Leicestershire which in 1584 appointed a committee
of nine 'wise men', including two gentlemen, to assess and tax
the inhabitants 'for the town's affairs', disburse the proceeds,
and render an annual account to the lord's steward. At Shrewton
in Wiltshire in 1596, following the dismemberment of the
manor and consequent loss of its court, such apparently was
the disorder, 'in breach of Christian charity and peace of the
neighbourhood', that the parson, Nicholas Barlow, and twenty-
two of his flock drew up seventeen by-laws, all concerned with
agricultural matters, and these were written down prior to
being submitted to a town meeting, Barlow and four others
adding their signatures and the rest their marks. Penalties were
to be placed in the parish poor box.

There was almost certainly a great deal more communal
activity of this kind than was ever placed on record and more
often than not the meetings were held in the churchyard, in
the nave, or in the adjacent church house where the remains
of the last 'ale' may well have put the assembly in good humour.
Much of the business had ecclesiastical connotations anyway.
Bulls, rams and boars kept for communal use often belonged
to the church and made their contribution to parish funds. Fines
imposed on those who contravened village by-laws were in
some cases made payable into church funds, and regulations
made at the manor court of North Walsham in Norfolk in
1598 actually specified that penalties were to be divided equally
between the lord, the poor, and the churchwardens for the use
of the church. Villages as such had no corporate identity.
Though not necessarily equivalent, the parish was more likely
to equate with the village community than was the manor. Territorially, it had a great advantage over the manor in that there
could be no argument about the identity of parishioners. The
inhabitants having long been required by canon law to pay a
tithe of their produce to the incumbent of its church, the limits
of the parish had been very exactly defined by the ecclesiastical

authorities. Its boundaries were marked by physical features in the landscape and these were regularly 'beaten' during the annual Rogationtide processions. On these occasions the boys of the community were 'bumped' to make sure they remembered, while the rest of the assembly sang Psalm 104: 'Thou hast set them their bounds which they shall not pass.' Since 1547 this had been the one exception to the general ban on traditional religious processions.

Laymen had long been encouraged to play an active part in the affairs of the parish church, in particular as churchwardens and as sidesmen ('synodsmen'), who were associated with the wardens in the presenting of offences to the church courts. To some extent lay involvement had been reduced by the removal of the shrines and images whose maintenance had so often been the main function of parish guilds. However, money still had to be found for repairs to the fabric, and the multiplicity of parish guilds was giving way to fewer but more select governing bodies of parishioners. It is perhaps significant that it is from some of the large parishes of the far north-west with their far-flung settlements that some of the earliest evidence has survived of the traditional two churchwardens being joined in the sixteenth century with representatives of the outlying settlements to form the first parochial church councils. The sixteen men appointed at Holm Cultram in Cumberland in 1568 to serve for three years represented the four quarters of the parish. Their 'election' was recorded on the roll of the manor court but they had their own 'foreman' and minute book. They even took it upon themselves to act as arbiters in disputes between parishioners. No doubt in many cases these were self-perpetuating oligarchies of the bigger farmers, but there is evidence, for example at Crosthwaite in Cumberland, of annual elections and of ineligibility for re-election. Such bodies, firmly rooted in the local rural scene, came in time to deal not only with parochial finances but with almost any 'laudable' local matter such as the repair of sea walls and the appointment of schoolmasters. The references to schoolmasters should probably serve as a reminder of the scatter of very small, privately endowed, village schools which had survived the Reformation, and whose number was probably still increasing. It was only natural for churchwardens to be appointed ex officio trustees. However, the foundation of a village school by public subscription at Willingham in Cambridgeshire in 1593 seems to have been unique. Although it may be construed as a community effort in that over one hundred people contributed, attendance was limited to the families of the subscribers and to the children of the poor. Most village schools in Elizabethan England were the result of private enterprise by unemployed university graduates and others even less well qualified, and they existed precariously and unsupervised.

In this growth of secular communal activity based on the parish, external forces also played their part. Even before the Reformation Cardinal Wolsey had used the parish in 1524–5 as the unit for the collection of his lay subsidy, and indeed for his military survey of 1522, the latter a useful precedent for all later musters of the militia. In Elizabeth's reign parish musters were the occasion of the biggest assemblies of the younger and middle-aged menfolk of the community, especially as fewer and fewer of them could claim exemption as the retainers of the nobility. One of the first statutory duties laid upon parishes was that of 1532 requiring them to provide nets for catching 'choughs, rooks and crows'. The registration of baptisms, marriages and burials inaugurated in 1538, although ostensibly an ecclesiastical matter, had civil uses well understood both by Thomas Cromwell and by many parishioners. Whether or not registration made for a more united and stable community it certainly contributed to order and decency, if not to oblivion. At Bramfield in Suffolk in 1539 the vicar recorded that he had during the past year performed fourteen baptisms, 'whereof men children 11, whereof bastards 2, women children 3'. The Act of 1555 concerning the upkeep of highways introduced no new principle in that this had since time immemorial been a local communal responsibility, but now all adult male inhabitants were required to work on the highways, unpaid, for four days of eight hours each year. This was increased to six days in

1563. Each parish was also required to appoint two surveyors to plan and supervise the work. Delinquent parishes could be presented and corporately fined, at quarter sessions, the precedent having been set at least as early as Cromwell's time. People continued, however, to bequeath money for the upkeep of highways which suggests that JPs were slack about enforcing the Highways Act. Even the ancient office of constable, formerly attached to the village, was by 1600 firmly tied to the parish. Finally there was the gradual identification of the parish as the unit of poor-law administration which, while it did little to call forth the charitable instincts of parishioners, certainly intensified traditional suspicions of the stranger.

The continuity in all this secular parish activity with the days before the Reformation must in its turn have helped to sustain the life of communities made poorer by the loss of feasts and holy days, especially those peculiar to individual parishes, and at a time when the spiritual life of most parishes was at a low ebb the increase in the secular activities linked with the church must have helped to sustain a sense of spiritual community which might otherwise have been lost. Manor courts in some places continued to support the church. At Burbage in Leicestershire in 1584 the manor court laid down that 'If any alehouse-keeper suffer any person to resort and room [*sic*] into their houses in time of service or sermons upon the Sabbath or holy day that then they shall forfeit for every such default 20s.' It was in 1563, while plague was raging, that the Lord Mayor of London (Thomas Lodge) not only ordered all churches to hold daily services at 8 a.m. but also all churchwardens to instruct each household to send at least two persons to church for at least one hour a day. Such links with the secular community may even have ensured that parish churches continued to be kept in a reasonable state of repair, that their towers continued to command the landscape and their bells to ring out over the countryside. In the year of the Armada each parish was ordered to silence all but one bell so that in the event of an invasion the pealing of all the bells could be used as a signal of alarm. On the other hand, while the Queen's insistence that all her subjects should attend church may not have made them more godly on weekdays it did ensure, with more and more permanent seating installed, that once a week each parish assembled as a tableau, the better sort in front and the poor at the rear, except that, especially in towns, servants and apprentices sat with their masters. In one parish in York in 1569 the sacrament was being administered in strict order of social precedence, and in some of the parishes, for example in County Durham in the 1580s, pews were already private property. In fewer churches was it now the custom for men and women to sit apart.

But the Elizabethan parish was far from being a structured and stable social entity. In spite of the dispersal among laymen of the lands of the Church, by no means all parishes had a resident landlord or even a gentle family in their midst. Freehold estates, including manors, changed hands with remarkable frequency. Even a gentleman technically resident and of a settled disposition might well be absent most of the time on the Queen's or his own business, and the lordship of several manors, while undoubtedly lending prestige, did not necessarily make a man an important local community leader. As for the village community at large, it could experience an almost complete turnover within little more than a generation. In Terling, Essex, between 1580 and 1619, of all the men and women who married and produced at least one child less than one fifth of the men, and barely one third of the women, had themselves been born in the parish. Here and elsewhere wills and other records show that people often found wives and husbands in neighbouring parishes and that bastardy too was frequently inter-parochial. What is surprising, and perhaps serves to underline the high degree of migration, is how few blood-relations people had in their own parishes. At their deaths they tended to remember only those of their kin whom they knew as neighbours, and indeed it was their neighbours, to judge by their bequests, with whom they felt the closest ties. The exceptions were the gentlemen and their wives who knew and often visited their relations much further afield, though rarely far beyond the county boundaries. The Elizabethan parish community was not, then, the unchanging, inbred, tightly knit, kin-centred or even highly structured community which people in the modern world imagine.

Nor were parishes havens of tranquillity. Riots and rebellions may have been few but strife was rarely absent for long. Witches typified the very worst aspects of local community life in that they exhibited not mere indifference but positive animosity towards their neighbours. Not being 'in love and charity' with their neighbours, they were presumably ineligible, according to the rubric of the Book of Common Prayer, to receive the holy sacrament. For the rest of the community, simple instincts of humanity towards both the witch and her victim were distorted and confused by fear of her apparently magical or supernatural powers. First offenders were liable to imprisonment but were much more likely to have to endure four appearances in the pillory, thus enabling the local community to play its part in inflicting punishment. Second offenders faced death. The Church courts, however, only required of those convicted of witchcraft public penance in their parish churches on a Sunday. But witchcraft, and all forms of anti-religious practice, were rare and localized, infinitely more so than the religious differences which, within a decade of Elizabeth's accession, were dividing many parish communities. In the long run, for all the hostages they have given to the Devil, both Protestant dissent and Roman Catholic survival have contributed a great deal to the spiritual life both of the national and the local community, but in the short run, as they tended to be minority interests, they did little to bind the inhabitants of ancient parishes together.

In few parishes at any time during Elizabeth's reign did either the Roman Catholics or the Puritans command total allegiance. To take the Catholic minorities first, it was of course only very gradually that they assumed an identity as recusants, and many who were Catholic in spirit continued to attend their parish churches, though contriving to refuse the sacrament. Analyses of those who, after about 1570, preferred to pay fines, show that they clustered very largely around certain of the gentry and the aristocracy, or more particularly their houses, the only places where missionary priests could officiate with any safety. This was accentuated by the fact that it was, on the whole, among the older landed families that the tradition of hospitality had survived, and in general the higher a man's social status the wider his circle of known blood-relations who were in the habit of paying visits. But even those Catholics who were prepared to take the risks of harbouring priests still felt a considerable attachment to their parish churches. They would, perhaps in a spirit of optimism, leave bequests for new bells and for repairs to the fabric, and in some cases even contrived, as did Roger Martin of Long Melford in Suffolk in 1615, to be buried in the family aisle, commemorated by a brass. In the parish of St Colomb Minor in Cornwall where most of the land belonged to the Catholic branch of the Arundell family, their many recusant tenants were made to contribute 3s. 4d. a year to the parish for 'refusing' to serve as churchwardens. Not all Catholic priests were fugitives: at least one Suffolk incumbent also said mass in Latin regularly in the private chapel of his patron, Sir Thomas Cornwallis. On the other hand there were also the real separatists such as Lord Vaux who in 1581 claimed that his own home was 'a parish by itself'. Few recusants, however, regarded themselves as socially separate from contemporary society. If they found it increasingly difficult to make marriage alliances with Protestant families it was largely because of their own financial straits.

While Catholics on the whole simply made their resources, including their houses, available to those of a like mind, the Puritan gentry and aristocracy were able to be more outward-looking. They made full use of whatever clerical patronage they possessed and used all possible means to further their cause. In many parishes Puritan laymen seized the opportunity, like latter-day Joshuas, to lead their fellow parishioners to a promised land of strict discipline and godly living. Church-wardens, in particular, found in Puritanism the zeal to enforce the rules about church attendance, though it was up to them to decide who among their neighbours were to be reported to the archdeacon, and by no means all Puritans disapproved of the traditional Church courts. Other Puritan laymen were enthusiastic 'gadders' to other parishes, ostensibly for the sermons many of them felt they lacked at home, but some no doubt with memories or at least folk traditions of the old pilgrimages. Indeed it was the Town Clerk of Barnstaple in north Devon who, with a touch of irony, wrote in his journal in the year 1586:

> On St Luke's day this year there was a trental of sermons at Pilton [a parish about a mile away] so that divers as well men as women rode and went thither. They called it an exercise or holy fast and there some offered [money] as they did when they went on pilgrimage. And the like was kept at Shirwell, to the admiration of all Protestants.

A minority of Puritans migrated permanently to other parishes. None of this can have made for peace in the parishes, and both radicals and conservatives (as well as those in the middle), depending who enjoyed the ascendancy, must have been subjected, both individually and with their families, to considerable harassment. But even in what are generally regarded as the most Puritan counties, such as Northamptonshire, probably less than one third of the parishes were seriously disrupted. Indeed, the many Puritan incumbents who were reported to their archdeacons for such offences as not wearing a surplice, for taking liberties with the Book of Common Prayer or even for ignoring the remaining holy days, were clearly not making much progress locally, and they may even have achieved a good deal in knitting their parish communities together, if only in opposition.

With the exception of the few English people who followed Robert Browne, the Cambridge separatist for whom 'the Kingdom of God was not to be begun by whole parishes but rather of the worthiest [people], were they never so few', the Elizabethan Puritan movement was wholly within the established Church. Even the conventicles and prophesyings were little more than occasional gatherings of clergy for mutual support and education of a kind which should have been regularly organized for them by the more or less inactive rural deans. What is interesting is the territorial grouping of these 'gatherings', often much more realistic than the old arch-deaconries and particularly the dioceses, neither of which formed convenient bases for regional Christian communities. But what really marked the Puritans, and in this they were not unlike the Catholics, was their household piety, the family prayers to which outsiders often came, conducted not in all cases by the head of the household but by 'friends' who, at least in the eyes of the more conservative bishops, were remarkably like unordained ministers. With hindsight we can see that there were greater pointers here to the future strength of English Dissent than in the well-known 'gatherings' of Londoners, for example those drawn from many parishes to Plumbers' Hall in 1567, to hear a good sermon and to receive the sacrament without the offensive 'idolatrous gear'. Over the country at large the Elizabethan Puritans never really became an 'alternative' society. By seeking, as was inevitable in a society so governed by rank and status, not Lazarus but Dives, they also missed the opportunity, especially in the 1590s, of enlisting the support of the increasingly numerous and suffering poor. Their very emphasis on Bible-reading meant that their main support had to come from the minority of better educated, or at least more literate, laymen, that is, the gentlemen, the merchants and the more substantial yeomen and urban crafts-men. At the time of the Bartholomew Day massacre of Protestants in France in 1585 there was, among the gentry, almost a crusading fervour. Sir Arthur Champernon, a Devonian, made an offer to the Queen to find sixty horsemen, all of them 'younger brothers to gentlemen, mean gentlemen being heirs, franklins [yeomen] and other lusty young fellows, the worst of them having in annuities and other yearly profits £20', as well as 500 foot soldiers who would require 8d. a day, all of whom would go to the relief of La Rochelle, fired, it may be assumed, with a desire to revenge the slaughter of their co-religionists. Nor were all Puritans bent on suppressing all pleasurable activities. Much of their bad name in this respect derives from municipal regulations which were inspired not necessarily by Puritanism but by an obsession, especially in the larger towns, for an orderly society. The city of York's ban in 1579 on the popular custom of blessing bridal beds was not necessarily inspired by Calvinist theology, and even in Parliament at Westminster the existence of specifically Puritan policies and pressure groups can be exaggerated. It has been noted that MPs more often quoted classical texts than the Scriptures and that some who opposed fish days were graziers. Nor did all Puritans draw attention to themselves by giving their children unusual biblical names, a practice we now know to have been followed only in a belt of parishes in the Kent and Sussex Weald, with echoes in Northamptonshire.

The regional spread of recusancy and Protestant dissent is hard to define and even harder to explain. For the most part the former was rural in location. According to a return made by the bishops in 1603, Catholics were numerically greatest in the diocese of Chester (nearly 2,500) which included a good deal of Lancashire, with the dioceses of York and of Coventry and Lichfield some way behind. They were fewest in the dioceses of Rochester, Canterbury and Ely (each under fifty), and otherwise the spread was fairly even. There were few, if any, in the towns, York and Winchester being notable exceptions. Rural Puritanism was undoubtedly strongest in the 'forest' areas, even in south-east Lancashire, Cheshire, the Yorkshire dales and almost everywhere where pastoral farming was the chief occupation and where people were by nature more mobile and less conformist. The latter point must not be pressed too far, however. Some of the pastoral areas of south-west Lancashire and the Fylde coast were predominantly Catholic, partly on account of their isolation behind the peat mosses but also because of close links with Ireland. A lot also depended on the degree of concentration of Puritan patronage of parochial livings. The counties of Essex and Leicestershire were largely won for Puritanism by the Rich and Hastings families although they contained both fielden or sheep–corn and also forest or dairy

country. In traditional agricultural villages even a godly landlord and parson found the going hard. The presence or absence
of resident gentlemen could affect the issue either way, but
genuinely popular Puritanism was to be found largely among
the cloth-workers of such old Lollard towns as Ashford and
Cranbrook in Kent. Towns and their neighbourhoods were
perhaps easier to win, one sermon on market day attracting
more hearers than a month spent by a preacher tramping from
village to village. There was also more money available in
towns for financing Puritan lectureships. By 1580 Ipswich was
finding nearly £100 a year to pay its two preachers and the
corporation of Yarmouth was paying one preacher £50 a year.
Having obtained the services of able men the town authorities
were wont to insist, on pain of fines, that at least one member
of each household attended the lectures, and this on one or
even two mornings a week. In particular those 'teachers' paid
for by public subscription underlined the continuing scandal
of deficient parish clergy and impropriated tithes. Town schoolmasters too could be more effective, having more pupils than
those in the county. It is not easy to explain why it was in old
cloth-towns such as Norwich and Colchester that merchant
oligarchies embraced Puritanism so completely and made it
virtually a civic religion, the parish church becoming almost
the corporation's chapel, complete with mayoral pew. Some
towns had actually acquired the patronage of one or more of
their parishes. In Ipswich, where the clergy of no less than five
of the twelve churches were actually chosen by the parishioners,
Parliament's approval was obtained in 1571 for the levy by
the churchwardens of a town rate for clerical stipends and
church maintenance. A year before this the leading householders
of Bury St Edmunds, not yet even an incorporated borough,
drew up by-laws not only concerning vagabonds and pauper
children but also providing for compulsory church attendance.
Ten years later, claiming by ancient usage the patronage of
the parish of St James, they appointed a young 'minister' for
a trial period. They found that he could do little more than
read the Book of Common Prayer and, as they told the bishop,

they might as well have appointed a boy of twelve. It was as well for diocesan discipline that more patronage did not fall into municipal hands.

Anabaptism now being no longer a serious threat, probably the greatest degree of real religious separatism in later Tudor England was to be found among the alien congregations, and this ran contrary to long traditions. For centuries English towns, especially seaports, had contained alien residents, both temporary and permanent, but apart from the German Hansards in London and King's Lynn they had had no buildings of their own, secular or religious. In spite of English xenophobia (mostly in London and in Mary's reign), their presence had not added perceptibly to the religious tensions of the immediate post-Reformation period. Even in Elizabeth's reign Italian merchants, presumably all good Catholics, were wisely left alone by the authorities, and some of them regularly attended Anglican parish churches, as did Benedict Spinola, accompanied by his nephew, his two Genoese clerks and his French cook. The change came with the organized settlements from predominantly Protestant continental regions. As early as 1549 Protector Somerset had organized the bringing of a whole congregation of Protestant Walloon cloth-makers to the Somerset town of Glastonbury which he had acquired after the dissolution of the abbey. Two hundred persons, with their pastor, were provided with both their own cloth hall and a church. The settlement failed but a precedent had been set. Although aliens were still officially encouraged wherever possible to attend English parish churches, in November 1551 the Privy Council decreed that they should be allowed to form their own congregations if they so wished. Indeed in 1548 part of the crypt of Canterbury Cathedral had been put at the disposal of Walloon refugees and in 1550 there was established in the former Augustinian Friary in London what became known as the Church of the Strangers, with Cranmer's friend, the liturgical reformer John à Lasco, as pastor. England at this time was becoming something of a haven for continental Protestants but they were not yet coming in large numbers.

Mary Tudor closed the Strangers' Church, but even so, remarkably few aliens found it necessary to leave the country in her
reign. After Elizabeth's accession London's alien population
continued to grow alarmingly, reaching by the 1570s nearly
one in ten of the whole. Hence, when strangers began to appear
in large groups in the 1560s every effort was made to disperse
them to the provinces.

Those of the Queen's ministers concerned undoubtedly did
their best to ensure the success of the new provincial alien settlements, including taking account of native prejudices, especially
in the matter of employment. The very restrictions imposed
by the municipal authorities were bound to set the strangers
apart, but to these were added promises of freedom of worship
to which by no means all the immigrants gave top priority.
Many came primarily to earn a living. However, churches were
provided and alien ministers welcomed, but it is significant
that when the English bishops proceeded to exercise a degree
of supervision, their greatest problem was church attendance.
There were in all ten Dutch (Fleming) and four Walloon
(French) churches in thirteen provincial towns, Norwich having
one of each. Bishop Parkhurst lent the chapel in his palace
grounds to the Walloons and the Dutch residents were given
the use of the former Black Friars church. The aliens tended
to be Presbyterian in organization with a strong body of lay
elders, and the latter, as well as the pastors, were permitted to
attend national colloquies, through which, incidentally, some
of the leading English Puritans were able to maintain links
with reformed churches on the Continent. It had been laid
down from the start that each alien church should organize its
own system of poor-relief, a harsh condition in a city such as
Norwich whose increasing prosperity was to a large extent
due to the aliens who, because of their economic disabilities,
remained poor. As if to ensure their separation from the local
community, the Norwich strangers were assigned two aldermen, one a JP, 'to hear their causes and appease them'. This
was no doubt very well meant but it is surely no coincidence
that the first English Brownist church was established in

Norwich and that when its congregation went into exile it made for Middelburg in Zealand with whom the Dutch Church had contacts. The old tradition of intermarriage with English families largely disappeared, partly, of course, because these skilled artisan cloth-makers, unlike many earlier alien settlers, brought their families and even their servants with them. By contrast the aliens who came as iron-smelters, iron-founders and glass-makers came largely as temporary residents, without families.

The cities and larger towns of Elizabethan England, including London, exhibited interesting developments as communities, largely the result of a growing self-confidence on the part of their civic leaders. If little Bury St Edmunds could take on the bishop, how much more arrogant could be those towns with communal liberties centuries old, and even those granted charters shortly before the Queen's accession! Their conduct of their own affairs took on a new thrust, even though their form of government remained largely unchanged. They began seriously to organize their internal defences against the infections from which no one, rich or poor, was totally immune. York, for example, embarked on an energetic programme of street cleansing. Much more local charitable effort was now possible, for by and large urban economies were expanding, partly due to a national increase in internal trade, and this put more money into civic chests. Roads were improving, the printed road tables listing by 1570 as many as seventeen routes into London and by 1588 there were more than a dozen recognized cross-country roads, for example those linking Bristol with Oxford, Cambridge, Southampton, Shrewsbury and Chester. Another factor in urban renewal was increasing local specialization, both in agricultural production and in markets. The traditional country markets too were attracting larger weekly gatherings of people within a five to ten mile radius, bringing not only their farm produce but, especially in forest areas, their weekly production of woollen yarn or woven cloth. Many market crosses (covered places where goods could be displayed) date from the later sixteenth century.

In the larger urban centres there were no longer complaints about empty houses. Indeed, especially in London, the real problem was overcrowding, for, although still dependent on migration, the population of towns was growing internally. By 1600 nearly one in ten of the population were town-dwellers, London accounting for most of the increase. This alone called for more of the surplus produce of the countryside. Towns such as Plymouth in the south-west and York in the north were, on account of the resort there, respectively, of seamen and administrators, providing the same kind of boost to the local agricultural economy as London had long done on a larger scale. All of this tended to raise the status of Elizabethan towns not only in the estimation of their own residents but in the eyes of their rural neighbours. Most of the trading was still based on traditional markets and fairs but there was also a great increase in private trading, much of it, in spite of official disapproval, in urban inns whose number was increasing steadily. According to a census of 1577 there were at least 1,600 in the one half of the English counties for which the record has survived. Many provided not only sleeping accommodation but also storage for goods, and even, contrary to urban tradition, private rooms for business. Those who forgathered there were members of a growing fraternity of regional if not countrywide corn dealers who were now winning their way against age-old prejudices; their obligation, by a statute of 1552, to be licensed by the JPs almost made them respectable. An Act of 1563, however, laid down that dealers in foodstuffs might not be licensed unless they were married householders, were at least thirty years of age, and had been resident in the county for at least three years. Licences were only valid for one year. But even now the traditional open market was probably the safest place for the countryman to dispose of his produce. Although not needing to be licensed, full-time carriers were still preferred by the powers that be to husbandmen using their oxen and wagons to ply as part-time carriers.

Government efforts to expand urban industry had had only limited success, partly due to the opposition, at least in the larger towns, of existing craft guilds. While merchants were still the wealthiest people in the towns, industry there remained the preserve of small master-craftsmen. Governing bodies, dominated by the merchants, while anxious to preserve guild monopolies in the interests of an ordered society, were in favour of encouraging an increase in the number of craftsmen, especially of those who supplied their own export trade. To do this they needed to reduce the level of admission-fines. Guilds, arguing that standards would fall, resorted to working to rule, that is, to admitting at the statutory rate only those who had served a full apprenticeship with one of their own members. That craft guilds were not even mentioned in the Statute of Artificers of 1563 suggests that at Westminster their elaborate ritual was not even regarded as essential to the institution of apprenticeship. Indeed, the minutes of Elizabethan guild meetings suggest that there was still little corporate interest in industrial regulations, unless one or more members were thought to be indulging in practices which gave them an unfair advantage. The monthly meetings of the Guild of Weavers, Fullers and Shearmen at Exeter, in its now completely secularized hall, dealt very largely with the guild's property and its charities, and of course with what to do about interlopers. The guild had no desire whatever to embrace the much larger body of rural cloth-workers, one of its strictest conditions of entry being residence within the city boundaries. They, or their governors, were becoming, far more so than the civic oligarchies, inward-looking and obstructive. Even the level of admission-fines was, one suspects, connected with the current state of guild finances. The old tension between the craft guilds and the town and city governing bodies increased still further when trade depression set in towards the end of the century. The tendency for urban guilds, both those of craftsmen and those of traders, to become largely 'social' organizations, never more impressively demonstrated than by attendance at members' funerals, was especially marked in London. There, besides the guilds of master-craftsmen, there were the companies of merchant wholesalers, all of these latter now outshone by the Company of Merchant Adventurers, which still had its headquarters on the other side of the Channel. Although by ancient custom in London freedom of any of the trading companies entitled a man to trade in any commodity, the Merchant Adventurers' virtual monopoly of the export of undyed cloth made membership of their organization essential for all cloth-exporters, and its admission-fine was prohibitive for all but men of substance. The cloth-merchants also strove to exclude from their company all retailers, laying down minimum quantities in which its London members might deal: for example, a whole cloth, a hundredweight of currants, or a gross of haberdashery. One effect was that for many of the most active London merchants the domestic affairs of their original companies were of little interest. Members of the Merchant Adventurers' Company meanwhile virtually monopolized both London's Lord Mayoralty and seats on its Court of Aldermen. In 1565–6 those members of the Clothworkers' Company who were still craftsmen, virtually the 'yeomanry' as compared with the 'livery' of merchants, challenged the Adventurers' ability to preclude all dressing of cloths at home. They emerged from a complicated fight with the statutory provision that all Suffolk and Kentish cloths and one in ten of all other cloths exported should be finished in England. It was only a minor victory but it was a dent in the metropolitan mercantile armour. It had no parallel elsewhere. In all the larger provincial towns the merchants still ruled the roost.

In all the guilds and companies, and in the government of towns and cities, the trend was almost invariably towards rule by a tighter and tighter oligarchy, by a circle made even smaller by the continuing habit of contracting out, at a price. Of necessity, certain individuals served as mayor many times. Although all guild freemen were expected to attend meetings, and could be fined for absence, the clerk usually only bothered to list by name the present master and other officers and the past masters. These clearly constituted the governing body and to them all others were expected to show proper respect. At Warwick in 1586 when Richard Brookes was dismissed from the town council as a 'breeder of troubles and procurer of great outrages' it was more specifically laid against him that he was wont to appear in 'unseemly' dress 'of a light or whitish colour, betokening him rather to be a miller [which he was] than a magistrate'. If they were men of integrity the rulers earned the dignity they assumed. Their material rewards, largely in the form of feasting and a certain number of perquisites such as first refusal of loans of the city or guild's capital, were really very limited. Prestige in the community, not forgetting that enjoyed by their wives, was presumably worth the expenditure of time and indeed on occasion of money. Civic ceremonial, every bit as elaborate, especially in London, as that which, it is claimed, had sustained the ailing early Tudor urban communities, added to the satisfactions of those who had made it to the top. But the ruling élite usually had the sense to make sure that some of the entertainment was extended, within bounds, to the whole body of inhabitants. At York and Chester the traditional miracle plays were kept up as long as possible and after 1570 were replaced by new 'midsummer' plays. In London the Lord Mayor's Show had become as spectacular as the early Henrician royal pageants.

In all this apparently communal activity, and even allowing for the essential part played in it by the enthusiasm of the inner ring, some consideration must be given to the contribution of the civic officials, not so much the town clerks, who usually had a busy private practice, as those called by some such title as 'chamberlain'. They kept the civic engine running. Such a one was John Hooker, City Chamberlain of Exeter from 1555 until his death in 1601. He salvaged and put in order the city's archives, wrote its history, administered its property, master-minded projects such as the obtaining of new charters and the construction of the new ship canal, and even served as one of the city's MPs. One of his achievements was the establishment of Exeter's Court of Orphans. This was a field in which the Crown's effort to profit from wardship was not lost on the more enterprising municipalities, with London, as always, setting the pace. Courts of Orphans have a spurious air of charity, of paternalism, and indeed there were those members of civic oligarchies who genuinely believed that they had a duty to assume the guardianship of the estates of those freemen who died leaving sons and daughters under age. Whether the widows and mothers always welcomed such civic attention is open to doubt, for the fact is that the property was temporarily appropriated by the courts with considerable advantages for the corporations' cash flow. Marriages too were arranged. At their best, the Courts of Orphans, which existed in at least seven other cities, though not in Elizabethan Coventry or Norwich, protected the interests of fatherless children against their inevitable, though not necessarily wicked, stepfathers. By 1585 the city of London was holding nearly £6,000 in capital belonging to its orphans, and here as elsewhere the impetus was not so much an increase in charitable concern as a great renewal in civic competence and efficiency. Orphans with estates worth under £10 in goods were usually ignored. Those towns which insisted that expenditure on the funerals of those leaving orphans be limited (usually in accordance with the economic status of the deceased) were motivated not so much by Puritanism as by the desire to conserve what was temporarily their own. Civic solvency was paramount. Hooker wrote and, by his own admission, also preached a good deal about civic loyalty, a loyalty which he would have regarded as running much deeper than loyalty to the Queen. But as long as he and his kind believed so firmly in the need for an ordered society, a need which even in the 'godly' Hooker's eyes transcended all religious differences, then this loyalty contributed to the network of loyalty centring on the Queen.

The competence, administrative, judicial and financial, of Elizabethan town oligarchies was not yet equalled in the countryside. There were, even in the later sixteenth century, manor courts which still went through the formality of dividing the tenants into groups of ten, a kind of judicial muster known as the 'view of frankpledge', the theory being that the members of each group were collectively responsible for each other's good behaviour. This, however, had been largely superseded by the growth of the jury system, another extension of communal responsibility, but with the greatly extended competence in the sixteenth century of the Justices of the Peace, the initiative in keeping the peace had become rather less of a communal task and one to be shouldered personally by royal nominees. In theory JPs were supplied with the names, and sometimes with the persons, of alleged offenders by the parish or village constables, but these, like the juries, only did their duty when made to do so. However, some of the old communal involvement remained, not least the resort to the 'hue and cry' for catching offenders. Many a Puritan gentleman found more scope for preaching the virtues of honesty and hard work as a JP than as a mere local squire, and it is easy to see how to the really radical Puritan, the godly lay magistrate made bishops and the whole apparatus of ecclesiastical courts dispensable.

The number of JPs continued to rise, and Burghley for one thought there were too many of them and that a smaller bench would be more effective. In fact here too there tended to be an active élite, officially designated a quorum, containing the most substantial resident knights and gentlemen in each county. Individually, and more and more as time went on in the small groups who held fairly frequent 'petty' sessions, the JPs had their own local stamping ground, but their authority extended over the whole county. Four times each year they forgathered in the county town, or elsewhere, for quarter sessions, and twice for the assizes. They and their families brought custom to local traders and hostellers, and employment for a whole range of urban occupations, skilled and unskilled. More important, these occasions brought together for several days a fairly representative selection of the inhabitants of the whole county, a cross-section of its community, poor as well as rich, and not all in answer to a criminal charge. Corn-badgers, for instance, had to attend once a year for the renewal of their licences. For many, even for substantial yeomen, this was the limit of their travels and provided a rich opportunity for exchange of news and gossip, and, especially for the gentry, opportunities for marriage-making. Indeed, it was often

remarked upon by contemporary observers and has been confirmed by historians that a large proportion of the sons and
daughters of the gentry married within the county or at the
furthest just over the border.

In fact, as in the case of the parish, it would be unrealistic
to draw the boundaries of county society too tightly. It was
not unknown for gentlemen who lived near the boundary
between two counties, and who owned land in both, to be
named in both commissions of the peace. Within certain limits
gentlemen were very mobile, spending a good deal of time
away from home, usually visiting near relations, and it was
within a radius of a day's ride from home that they usually
found their future daughters-in-law. William Carnsew, JP, the
Cornish landowner and tinner, married a lady from over the
border at Tavistock, and although he seems usually to have
travelled alone, this connection offered a greatly increased range
of hospitality. During the course of the year 1576 he covered
over 1,000 miles, mostly in Cornwall where most of his cousins
lived, but occasionally in west Devon. His diary suggests that
he was always welcome, for he was a great gatherer, and no
doubt dispenser, of news. There were, of course, a minority
of the gentry who made the occasional longer journey to represent their shires or local boroughs in Parliament, but Elizabeth
did not summon her subjects to, or keep them at, Westminster
often or long enough for them to develop more than a very
superficial *esprit de corps*. This suited the Queen, not because
she really feared a united Commons but because in her eyes the
only justification for gentility was service, and for most gentlemen that meant in their own 'country'. Even her own very
lengthy progresses into the provinces were at least an indication
that London was not, as Giovanni Botero would have had his
readers believe, the only place worth living in.

Underlying almost everything that can be said about community in Elizabethan England, counterbalancing almost all
we know about migration and about the wanderlust, sometimes
enforced, of the poor, was the sense that everyone belonged
to his own particular 'country', meaning that part of the

kingdom where he or she had spent his or her youth or had settled down. Loyalty to 'country' was reflected in a growing intellectual interest among the gentry in their own localities, an interest not unconnected with the surveying of their own estates. Elizabeth's reign saw the writing, and in a few cases the publication, of the first county 'histories' or, more correctly, topographical surveys with an antiquarian bias. For many gentlemen there was the particular satisfaction of establishing, wherever possible, the antiquity and therefore the respectable status of their own lineage, and this very serious hobby occupied much of their time when they met on the Queen's business, swapping and comparing notes and seeking every opportunity to search other men's records as well as their own. Only a handful, and in no case more than one in any shire before 1600, succeeded in converting their notes and jottings into literary form. Those who did so found it easiest to conduct their readers on a tour or 'perambulation'. They had the military man's eye for terrain but were less interested in buildings, except newly built mansion houses. Most were Protestants and hence their attitude to such monuments of antiquity as monastic ruins was, to say the least, ambivalent. An exception was Sampson Erdeswicke of Staffordshire, a recusant, who described with unalloyed nostalgia the stone imagery of Lichfield Cathedral. Most of these county topographers had been at one of the universities, and although they had moved away from an environment given over largely to moral philosophy and theology they never lost an opportunity, even in their local writing, of parading their knowledge of classical authors, switching easily for the purpose in their manuscripts from 'secretary' to 'italic' hand. The work of such men reflects a good deal of local pride and even a jingoism verging on the absurd. John Hooker in his *Chorographical Description of Devonshire*, still today largely unpublished, claimed that his native county was so well furnished with all manner of animals, vegetables and minerals that it could do without the rest of the kingdom better than the rest of the kingdom could do without Devon. Could pride in locality go further? If the remark does no more than remind us of the deep vertical as well as horizontal divisions in Tudor society it will have been at least worth making.

But we must be wary of seeing in the antiquarian pre-occupations of Elizabethan gentlemen a local literary culture. As composers of anything more than rough jottings these county historians worked alone, the best of them communicating their efforts not so much to a local circle as to an antiquarian fraternity which had its existence only in London. What was later to become the Society of Antiquaries began meeting in about 1586, its members supping together before listening to and discussing a paper, their deliberations encompassing all secular knowledge. Their chief link was with the Inns of Court with a notable absence of clergy or university dons. Their philosophy was well expressed by one of their number, William Lambarde, who declared in his *Perambulation* (1576) of his adopted county of Kent that 'The inwards of each place may best be known by such as reside there ... whereby good particularities will come to discovery everywhere ... to amplify and enlarge the whole.' The last phrase is significant. Indeed, a good deal of the impetus behind local topographical surveys came from individuals such as the great Ralph Holinshed who encouraged local scholars to contribute to his *Chronicles*, first published in 1578, and William Camden, Westminster schoolmaster and later herald, who drew extensively on the labours of local antiquaries for his *Britannia*, the first edition of which appeared in 1586. Camden also had links with European scholars and his methods closely resembled those of men like John Dee and the Hakluyts in their compiling of the literature of overseas exploration. All writers, whether or not their work was published, sought patrons, no longer the nobility as such but persons at Court, especially those nearest to the Queen. It is true that Richard Carew, esquire, in dedicating his *Survey of Cornwall* in 1602 to Raleigh, made much of Sir Walter's services to the county, but it was no doubt Raleigh the courtier, now back in favour, whose 'favourable countenance' Carew valued.

And so it was too with the writers of fiction, especially poetry and drama, for here too we look in vain for evidence of local cultures. This was not the result of London's virtual monopoly, from 1556, of the country's printing presses, for there was no bar to the printing of provincial literature in London. In any case only a small proportion of imaginative literature was ever printed. Elizabethan literature, especially poetry, survives in manuscript in great quantity but most of it is written by and for the Court circle. It was in a very real sense the work of amateurs in that writing was still not a full-time occupation and there was no livelihood in it. All that authors sought or expected was recognition in the form of a favour, protection, employment or even recommendation to an office of profit. There was in Elizabethan England still no literary profession, and even the writers of plays were only just beginning to support themselves by the end of the century. There were, no doubt, many provincial oral cultures, represented by folk-tales, rhymes, ballads and songs, most of them passed on from generation to generation, but even those which are on record are, by their very nature, difficult to date with confidence. As for the printed ballads which were appearing on the shelves of London booksellers in large numbers by 1600, few of them represent truly provincial writing, the lurid tales they tell of strange happenings bearing all the signs of pandering to the Londoners' love of the sensational. And when Court musicians incorporated into their musical fantasies the cries of street vendors, did they ever go further than the streets of London for their tunes? The great flowering of Elizabethan literary and musical culture was almost exclusively London-based. Only in London were there concentrated the support and protection of the Queen, her Court, the nobility and, particularly where the theatre was concerned, audiences of sufficient size prepared to pay for their entertainment. Touring companies were no doubt welcome visitors to provincial towns, but unless some 'reward' was forthcoming from public funds it is unlikely that they earned more than bare expenses.

But although for men and women of talent and ambition

London's attractions were irresistible, for the great majority of the queen's subjects provincial community life, in all its variety, was the only world they would ever know. Lacking, as it may have, the capital's sophistication, it had a stability and, as the Queen grew old, a potential magnetism which the people of London might well have envied.

15. *Marriage and the Household*

With such developments as the dispersal of the larger monastic communities and the retrenchment, both financial and political, of the higher nobility, the really large household had become by the later sixteenth century a rarity in England. Indeed, in most parts of the country and among ordinary farming and artisan families, and especially among the poor, the 'extended family' comprising several generations and various blood-relations had probably never existed. Certainly by Elizabeth's reign, except at Court and in the houses of the older and less prudent nobility and of a handful of the Queen's chief ministers, the number of persons sharing table, kitchen and hearth was confined to 'nuclear families' consisting only of parents and their younger children, plus in many cases non-related servants. The total number of people living even for part of the year in such institutions as college halls, boarding-schools, hospitals, houses of correction or even prisons was infinitesimal, as too was the number of men who as members of ships' companies spent more than a few weeks at a time cooped up together at sea. Censuses of the population by household are virtually unavailable for the period before 1600, but the evidence of parish registers, augmented by that of such other sources as wills, is sufficient to indicate how small was the domestic unit in which most Tudor people lived. If, as has been confidently calculated, the average size of households, including servants but excluding children who had left home, remained at about 4.75 throughout the sixteenth century, then the increase in the population of nearly 50 per cent between 1540 and 1600 must mean that there was an equivalent increase over the same period in the number of households. What is more, the great majority

of these were themselves self-contained units of production, as
well as of consumption and procreation, for in Tudor England
very few people went out daily to work.

When in our attempts to 'reconstitute' Elizabethan families
we take as our starting-point the parochial registration of church
weddings we are following the natural contours of Tudor
society, for, to an extent not always appreciated by those whose
interest lies in genealogy, every marriage was a new beginning.
It signified, particularly in rural communities, the point in the
lives of both men and women when they emerged from a
position of economic and social inferiority. This was particularly the case with eldest sons, few of whom could enter
into either the state of matrimony or the status of householder
until their fathers had at least retired, if not actually died. The
insistence, from 1538, on the registration of weddings, added
to their traditional solemnization at the church door, can only
have underlined the public nature of this creation of a new
social unit, and one, moreover, not easily undone.

In fact Tudor England had inherited a widespread belief in
the importance, if not the absolute primacy, of espousal, the
making of a contract in advance, or occasionally even in lieu,
of a church wedding. Protestant England, unlike post-
Tridentine Catholic Europe, continued to recognize that mutual
verbal acceptance by a man and a woman, if made in the
present tense, created an indissoluble bond. Hence what
amounted to bigamy could occur before marriage if there were
conflicting contracts. Promises made in the future tense,
especially if conditional on parental consent or on settlement
of land or goods, were not so binding, unless followed by
intercourse. The more notorious child-marriages arranged by
parents, usually the more well-to-do, were even less binding,
and indeed of no effect if either party dissented on reaching
the age of consent, fourteen years for boys and twelve for girls.
Most of the disputed spousals upon which the Church courts
were called upon to adjudicate were found to have been made
without witnesses in fields and backyards, there being, on
balance, slightly more aggrieved men than women. On balance,

too, there seem to have been more cases alleging undue influence by parents in breaking contracts than pleas by parents seeking to prevent what they regarded as unsuitable marriages. However, interesting as such cases are, they were not numerous, the bishops of Ely, Norwich and Winchester each dealing with barely a dozen cases a year towards the end of the century. The Church, following long tradition, was not in favour of interfering in young people's freedom of choice, but the Elizabethan bishops, like those in the Catholic Church, were anxious to establish marriage in church, preceded by banns or episcopal licence, as the only really valid union. At the same time the common-law courts were just beginning to entertain suits alleging breach of promise to marry. They could award damages against the guilty party, a sanction denied to the Church courts.

The lingering belief in the validity of spousal may have had a bearing on the high incidence in Elizabethan England, and probably earlier but not so easily discernible in the parish registers, of bridal pregnancy. Migration and incomplete registration mean that all statistics must err on the low side. In two parishes in the city of York in the half century from 1550 to 1599 one in five of the brides gave birth to a child within seven months of their weddings, and to this figure must be added at least some of those who gave birth within eight or nine months. Comparable rates have been discovered in many parts of the country. At Colyton in east Devon the proportion giving birth within nine months of marriage was as high as 40 per cent, thirty-one out of seventy-nine first live births, during the second half of the century, and at Terling in Essex and Gainsborough in Lincolnshire over the same period, although the numbers were much smaller than at Colyton, the proportion in each case was 33 per cent. The fact that most premarital conceptions seem to have occurred less than three months before marriage would seem to argue against the myth of the trial pregnancy, though the rate for young widows who had already borne children was significantly lower. For first marriages it occurred at all age levels. Although discouraged by the Church it seems to have carried no stigma and even a child born to a couple before their marriage not only became legitimized by the ceremony but was customarily given a place of honour at the wedding. It was not unknown for the child to be baptized on the same day. It is not difficult to imagine causes for the delay of weddings: the need to accumulate sufficient dowries, the cost of the traditional wedding feast, and even the finding of the entry-fine for a cottage or small farm. At Terling in Essex, for instance, the rate rose during the years of economic depression at the very end of the century. For whatever cause premarital pregnancy was very much more common in Elizabethan England than the bearing of what would be permanently illegitimate children.

Bastardy, while it had never been officially condoned, became doubly reprehensible in an age of population growth and the possibility of additional charges on the poor-rate. Its incidence is not so easily charted in the registers. Pregnant women with no hope of marriage were often sent away and their children lost sight of. Following their confinement, they could be refused churching, the ancient rite of purification, and their children denied baptism, at least until they themselves had confessed. Midwives, who partly for this reason were required to be licensed by the bishops, were expected to elicit, if necessary during labour, the identity of the father and it was on the basis of such evidence that the Church courts endeavoured to insist on putative fathers providing maintenance. Traditionally all this was the Church's business but the secular authorities could hardly fail to regard bastardy as a symptom of disorder and an Act of Parliament of 1576, significantly concerned largely with idle vagabonds, gave JPs the power to require both mothers and such fathers who could be identified to support their illegitimate children. Those who failed to respond were liable to be imprisoned. From then on the Church courts concentrated their attentions on those regarded as accessories to 'bawdry', that is, on parents, masters and mistresses, and those favourite targets of later Tudor moralists, the keepers of inns and alehouses. Indeed, most of the more human particulars concerning 'incontinence', as the lawyers called it, in the later sixteenth century come from the records of quarter sessions. But these survive for very few parts of the country. Such statistics as can be derived from parish registers indicate that the bastardy rate was actually dropping from about 3 per cent of live births in the second quarter of the century to about 2 per cent between 1560 and 1590, to rise again to over 3 per cent in the last decade, an effect, it would seem, rather than necessarily a cause, of increased population. But such averages mask great variety, in the 1590s, for example, from only 0.7 per cent in Gedling, Nottinghamshire, where, as it happened, bridal pregnancy was above average, to 4.7 per cent in Alcester, Warwickshire. In Hartland in Devon it had reached nearly 5 per cent by the 1590s (sixteen out of 343 live births), and here, at least, if not in the country at large, it was clearly contributing to the inflation of population, and probably to the problems of the Overseers of the Poor. There was some connection with age at marriage but not in the way one would expect, for in general bastardy increased as age at marriage fell. It was not confined to the poor. Indeed, a high proportion of bastardy cases brought before the courts involved servants and they were not, of course, the real poor. Rarely, it seems, were individual women repeatedly in trouble, although there are instances of this in Alcester. Nor, contrary to contemporary belief, do the registers suggest that vagrant or migrant women were especially prone. Although it has been calculated that bastards were more likely than other young persons to move away from their place of birth, they were quite frequently mentioned in their fathers' wills, almost like 'tithes forgot', and it may well be that the registers do not tell the complete story. However, the high proportion of cases of defamation, in both the secular and ecclesiastical courts, in which the epithet 'whore' is alleged to have been used, suggests that Elizabethan society did not take sexual misconduct lightly even though it was indulged in at all social levels. The presence at Elizabeth's Court of so many young and lusty men and women, usually with a lot of time on their hands, created a situation which

might have got completely out of hand had not the consequences of the Queen's displeasure been less easy to avoid and
more chilling to contemplate than the penalties of any court
of law, Christian or secular.

The practice of abortion seems to have left little record but
medical books spoke of certain supposedly effective 'medicines'. Infanticide, however, was a capital offence, though
when alleged in the common-law courts it was always difficult
to prove against the defence that the child had been stillborn.
Perhaps for this reason the total number of persons recorded
as having been indicted for this offence in the three counties
of Essex, Hertfordshire and Sussex in the later sixteenth century
was less than 1.5 per annum. Over the whole spectrum of what
might be called sexual offences only in the case of rape did the
common-law courts enjoy a monopoly. Rape was a wide term
covering not only forcible intercourse (though it was popularly
believed that pregnancy could not result unless a woman was
willing), but also that particular hazard of the woman of
property, abduction. Outraged parents and disappointed
suitors, especially in cases where the 'victims' were not entirely
innocent, required stronger arms than the Church courts could
provide. But if the three counties mentioned above were
typical, indictments alleging rape were even fewer than those
alleging the murder of unwanted children. This does not, of
course, prove in either case that such crimes were not committed. Finally, prostitution seems to have attracted little
attention in Tudor England, unless practised by vagrants. The
corporation of London endeavoured to confine it to the 'stews'
of the suburb of Southwark on the further bank of the Thames.
Indeed, it was not in itself a criminal offence and only came
to the notice of the JPs if it was thought, or alleged, to prejudice
public order. There is no evidence that it played more than a
marginal part in reconciling young men to the long period
which, as we shall see, separated puberty from marriage. Philip
Stubbes, who could be relied upon to see the worst in his
contemporaries, complained, in his *Anatomie of Abuses* (1593),
only of the imprudent young man who cared not whether he

could afford to marry 'so he have his pretty pussy to huggle withall'. It seems to have been over-hasty marriage that bothered Tudor moralists rather than illicit sex.

Before the Reformation the parish clergy had made considerable use of the confessional rather than of the pulpit to impress upon married women the moral dangers of enjoying the sexual act. By the time auricular confession had been discarded, even chastity had lost its primacy as a vocation. The clergy could now preach, more positively and with personal experience, of the marital virtues. But the changes wrought by the Reformation must not be exaggerated. There had long been available, albeit largely through the teaching of the clergy, advice in plenty for the wife and mother. With the invention of printing and the hope of an increase in the number of literate women, conduct books multiplied, all of them still written by men, and in particular by Puritans. These continued, however, to reflect largely traditional teaching, for example never giving the slightest encouragement to women to avoid conception, all efforts to obstruct the will of God being sinful. Even pre-Reformation priests had habitually urged wives afflicted with straying husbands to try showing them a little more affection. Both before and after the Reformation the Church taught that the primary purposes of marriage were the procreation of children and the regulation of sexual relations. Even the ideal of companionship was not a Protestant invention, Cranmer's 'mutual society, help and comfort that the one ought to have of the other, both in prosperity and adversity' not only echoing Tyndale but also many medieval clerical authors. Some Elizabethan Puritans, such as Thomas Cartwright, actually put partnership first, but otherwise had very little new to say. In fact, it is difficult to show that Puritanism had any really revolutionary effect on either public or private attitudes to matrimony or the household. The reformers did, it is true, place considerable emphasis on patriarchal authority, but whereas medieval women had been advised to beat their children, the Puritans merely advised them to see that their husbands did so.

Elizabethan men did not have to be Puritans to be persuaded that women, for all their legal disabilities, could, in the domestic context, be wilful, calculating and remarkably self-reliant, perhaps never more so than when they became widows or were deserted, temporarily or permanently. Except for those who were heiresses to property, or whose marriages could be used to effect useful political alliances, most Tudor women had always enjoyed considerable freedom in their choice of husbands. Many, especially those in service, in London and the larger towns, were far from home when the time came. For them, and for many other migrants, parental consent would have been quite inappropriate: they had moved into another family. Had the Anglican Church taken on board the new canons denied to it by the accession of Mary Tudor, parental consent might have become a necessity, with considerable consequences for English society, but there was no great anxiety to revive this and other novelties in Elizabeth's reign. As it was, then, even women still at or near home remained free from undue constraint. There were no doubt many battles of wills, with no holds barred, even from beyond the grave. In 1590 Thomas Wylede of Temple Normanton near Chesterfield, husbandman, left 'one cow [and] a coverlet or some part towards a bed' to his daughter Ann, 'if she will forsake Robert Huit and be ruled by her mother'. But whatever the consequences Ann would clearly make her own decision.

In this connection it cannot be too clearly stressed that, as in most of the countries of western Europe, men and women in sixteenth-century England married late, that is, in relation both to their attainment of the legal age of consent and also to their physical maturity. Men, on average, married for the first time in their middle to late twenties and women some four or five years younger. This pattern was not new, and indeed there are reasons for thinking that the average age, both for men and women, may have been falling after 1540. Averages, of course, can hide wide ranges, but just as there were few first marriages in which either bride or groom was over thirty so, except for those in the upper ranks of society, there were few teenage weddings. William Shakespeare, though a fairly ordinary town boy, was an exception in that he married at eighteen in 1582, but this was no doubt due to the fact that his twenty-six-year-old bride, Ann Hathaway, was already pregnant. It is by no means clear whether the custom of sending teenage children into other households was a cause or an effect of late marriage. What is certain is that official opinion was against any lowering of the age of marriage. In 1556 the city authorities of London prohibited the granting of the city's freedom to anyone under twenty-four, their reason being the need to inhibit 'over-hasty marriages and oversoon setting up of households'. Romantic love-affairs were probably only for a minority: if commonplace they would presumably not have been of such exquisite interest to courtier poets. If we are to judge by their portraits, Elizabethan women, at least of the upper classes, did not display their physical attractions, their natural contours being camouflaged by their clothes. Even Elizabethan men were far less manly than their Henrician forbears, the more fashionable being almost effeminate in their dress. No doubt there were many at all social levels who were carried away by mutual physical attraction but if so, if we are to believe foreign observers, they behaved most discreetly in public, both before and after marriage. Even genuine affection was perhaps more often bestowed upon, rather than the foundation of, Elizabethan marriages. On the whole, most brides and grooms were suitably matched as regards age and social status, with their combined economic prospects a prime consideration. Mere mutual acceptance was perhaps made easier by the lack of any escape. Divorce, that is, the legal dissolution of a marriage, even in cases where adultery had been proven, was virtually impossible. Even annulment was obtainable only if some impediment such as consanguinity could be discovered. Again the Reformation had made little difference except that, to suit Henry VIII, the law against marrying within the Levitical degrees had been tightened up. An Act of 1540 swept away the 'spiritual affinities' created by baptismal sponsorship. This may have widened the range of possibilities of marriage but it lessened the chances of retreat. For those sufficiently unhappy to seek a remedy it was permissible for couples to live apart, the wife separated 'from bed and board', but for most women this was not economically feasible as it precluded remarriage. Only in London, however, was the bishop's court kept busy with such problems.

Pauper women seeking charity often claimed to have been deserted by their husbands, and indeed in the census of poor families of Norwich compiled in 1570 there were many such as Margery, 'wife of Thomas Collins, hatter, now dwelling at London, by whom she have no help'. She was twenty-eight and had two daughters, one aged nine being a spinner of white warp, and the other an even younger child. Another Margery, aged forty, in the same parish of St Martin at Bale, was described as the wife, though never married, of John Hill, lime-burner, who had 'departed from her a four year past and she know not where he is'. These particular women may well have been the victims of economic circumstances, even of their husbands' genuine departure in search of employment, but there were also many women in reasonably comfortable circumstances who had to endure long periods alone, or with only their children for company, while their husbands were away buying and selling goods or engaged on seasonal work such as mining. It was on their good management that their families' survival depended should misfortune descend on their husbands' more adventurous enterprises. William Fells, yeoman, of Arrow in Cheshire regularly ran men and goods in his own ship across to Ireland. He did some fishing for herrings and he also owned two farms stocked with over a hundred head of cattle, besides crops. His wife spun flax, possibly for the sails of her husband's ship, and, although she had a comfortable house containing quantities of silver plate, pewter and linen she probably did far more than keep William's house, Puritan notions of patriarchy according ill with her responsibilities. However, there is some evidence, especially from the towns, that Elizabethan women were not increasing their standing in the local community. In Oxford, for example, no woman was named with her husband in an indenture of apprenticeship after 1583. This may have meant nothing but it could have been symptomatic. In general, it is quite clear, women had failed to grasp the opportunities which had seemed to be presenting themselves earlier in the century of becoming, if not highly educated, at least able to read and write. Literacy is difficult to quantify but it has been calculated that even in London during the last two decades of the sixteenth century barely more than 10 per cent of women could write their names, and that in the country-side not more than two or three in a hundred could do other than make their marks. Paradoxically, they were appearing more often than before as witnesses, especially in the ecclesiastical courts.

In spite of their late marriage, Tudor women were still left with about twenty years of childbearing. They bore, on average in the later sixteenth century, only six children, including those spread over more than one marriage. On the whole, children did not follow one another very quickly and it seems clear that the intervals between births were largely due to what was, and probably still is, the most effective form of contraception, prolonged breast-feeding, children being suckled for as long as three years. This period could even be extended, especially if their own infants died, by their acting as wet nurses for other women's children. Between 1578 and 1601 no less than thirty-seven of the babies buried in Chesham in Buckinghamshire were 'nurse children', out of an unrecorded number who survived this hazardous assault course. But these wives of wood-turners must have had some success or the London gentlewomen and charitable institutions would have taken their custom elsewhere. The results are evident in the parish registers. Ann, wife of Richard Smythe, having during the years 1567–72 successfully reared two girls and a boy of her own, then avoided further pregnancies until 1579, although she buried during these seven years no less than three nurse children. She then became pregnant but lost that child in 1581, and immediately became pregnant once again. Altogether she lost two of her own six babies, no more than she and her husband would expect to die young. Calculations based on a very small sample of parishes for the period 1550–99 indicate that about 13 per cent of infants died before they were twelve months old, about half as many between one year and four, and only 3 per cent between five and nine, a total of 24 per cent of the boys and 21 of the girls born alive. Boys were apparently particularly vulnerable during their first year. Although English families were, on average, smaller than those on the continent of Europe in the later sixteenth century, individual children had a far greater chance of survival into their teens and beyond, possibly due to the absence in England of real crises of subsistence.

From these figures it should be clear that by no means all Elizabethan men and women married. It has been calculated that this was the case for at least 8 per cent of those born in 1556. For those born ten years later the percentage was about half, but of those born in 1576, who would have been marrying in the later 1590s, the proportion who never married rose to over 13 per cent, possibly due to poverty and unemployment, though the connection is difficult to establish. But few bachelors and spinsters lived alone and most of them, along with widows and widowers, will have accounted for the minority of older indoor and outdoor servants. Elderly people, of whom those who were over sixty formed only about one tenth of the population, rarely comprised married couples, even in almshouses, most of them being 'relicts', men on the whole predeceasing their wives. Few children will have known more than two of their four grandparents and those elders who lived on in the family house did not do so for long. A very high proportion of the population, perhaps as many as 40 per cent, consisted of married adults aged between about twenty-five and sixty. Their children aged up to about fifteen constituted about one third, most of them still living at home. Their older, unmarried children aged between about fifteen and twenty-four, making up about one fifth of the total population, lived for the most part in other people's houses, in service, even including some eldest sons. In Coventry in 1523, as appears from the unique census of that year, 41 per cent of the population consisted of married couples, children and servants accounting for nearly a quarter each. Assuming, then, that all teenagers, if not contributing to the income of their own families were at least earning their keep elsewhere, it is clear that the Elizabethan domestic unit contained few dependants. The census of the poor carried out in Norwich in 1570, containing an above-average number of one-parent households, gives an average number of children per family of 2.10, and fewer than one family in five contained more than four persons. Here, of course, there were no servants, resident grandparents or other relations. To return to the rural population of tenant farmers the ubiquity of the two-generation family is amply borne out by the widespread use of the lease of land for *three* lives, these, however, being almost invariably husband, wife and one, usually the oldest, surviving child.

The employment of young people, almost all of them un-married, as resident servants – the girls largely for domestic work though they also worked along with their masters' wives in the fields and with the stock, and the boys in all branches of husbandry – was carried to an extreme in England which amazed foreign visitors. Domestic servants were especially numerous in London and the larger towns to which many girls moved in their late teens, sometimes forced by their eldest brothers to fend for themselves when their parents died or retired. However, they often found husbands among their masters' apprentices, for, like them, they usually came of good settled families. Such women tended to marry later rather than earlier, their future husbands having to complete their apprenticeships and find employment for a year or so as journeymen before setting up as householders. Dowries, too, had to be saved for, although in the larger towns there were often small sums available from charitable trusts for 'poor maids' marriages'. The donors were often rich widows. Many women servants married their widowed employers and pro-vided them with second families. Although, being far from home, they were free from parental influence, while in service all these young people were to all intents and purposes members of their employers' families, and as such endured a discipline which was an extension of that of their own homes. Such a situation met with the hearty approval of all those in authority concerned with the maintenance of public order. Moreover, particularly on the farms, the availability of this particular form of migrant labour enabled everyone, from the lesser gentry down to quite modest husbandmen, to be far more flexible in the size of their work-force than their European counterparts, burdened as the latter were with more or less permanent extended families, including impoverished relations whose claims on their hospitality were far more tenacious than those of non-related servants. There were, indeed, parts of England, notably the upland areas of the far north, where kinship, in this and in other respects, was a far more important element in family life, but these were exceptions to the general rule, and probably always had been. These were areas where farming was on the whole less labour-intensive, so fewer servants of husbandry were needed. It is possible to argue, though difficult to prove, that the availability of resident servants of husbandry was one factor in relieving Tudor wives from the pressure to bear large families as essential and cheap labour. Of course, all children on farms, and in the houses of craftsmen, were put to work as soon as they could make themselves useful, but they were not as essential to their families' economy as they would have been in most of the rest of Europe. Was this why, though most Tudor women no doubt wanted children, barrenness was not a cause of shame? Inability to bear children was not a legal ground for the annulment of marriage. It was not even a term of abuse inviting a charge of defamation, nor were witches often accused of procuring sterility in their victims. Of all the afflictions Tudor women suffered at the hands of God this was one of the most readily accepted, except by gentlewomen and the wives of the nobility. Was not a substantial dowry to many a Tudor husband worth more than a dozen sickly children?

A remarkable confirmation of English family and household structure, albeit for the south-east, is contained in the almost unique census compiled in 1599 of the inhabitants of the village – that is, the rural area – of Ealing in Middlesex. Here eighty-five separate households contained between them 426 persons. These included eighty-eight resident children under fourteen and thirty-seven older sons and daughters of whom only one appears to have been married, he being the twenty-six-year-old son of the parson, described as a weaver. Grandparents were few, but there was a fair sprinkling of stepchildren, indicating second marriages. Thirteen of the householders were women, some, but not all, described as widows, and all but three having with them one or more young children. The compilers quite naturally headed the list with the household of Edward Vaughan, JP, an official of the Exchequer, after which came that of Dr Thomas Lancktonn, a physician. There were two other gentlemen, two merchants, eight yeomen, a handful of craftsmen, including the Queen's mole-catcher, and a large number of husbandmen. Over a quarter of the households contained servants, most of them farm-workers, except in the gentry houses, and these accounted for over a quarter of the total population. Robert Tayler, yeoman, and Alice his wife, aged fifty and thirty-six respectively, had no children, or at least none still at home, but they employed two women domestic servants aged twenty-two and eighteen, and four servants of husbandry aged thirty-one, eighteen, eighteen and thirteen. There were no married men in Ealing under the age of twenty-five nor married women under twenty. Not surprisingly, so near London, there were six nurse children. There was, however, one very unusual household of over twenty persons, of which Master Peter Hayward, formerly a merchant of Salisbury and now a widower aged eighty, was the nominal head. It is clear that he had moved in with his thirty-eight-year-old bachelor son Thomas who kept a boarding-school. The eighteen boys, ranging in age from six to seventeen, were the sons of gentlemen, merchants and yeomen and included several pairs of brothers. Except for two women domestic servants, this was an all-male household, one which in every respect is the exception which proves the rule. But in general the community of rural Ealing was a microcosm of the country as a whole, only one in four of its households containing more than six persons, including servants, and the average number of persons per household was exactly 4.75.

Even when facing death, most heads of households, rich and poor, concerned themselves only with their immediate families. People only made wills if they still had goods and chattels to bequeath. Even quite poor men would provide for the disposal of their few possessions, but by no means all really elderly people did so, many of them having already passed on what they had to their children. Most of the tens of thousands of surviving wills were in fact made by men in middle age, 'sick in body but sound in mind', which is why so many of them mention quite young children, and even some as yet unborn. Late age at marriage meant that one or both parents often died before their eldest children were out of their teens. Some men left all the goods they possessed to their wives but most remembered each of their children, even poor husbandmen leaving, for instance, to each daughter a cow. Godchildren, employees and also neighbours were left something but, except in the more kin-orientated families of areas such as Teesdale and Weardale, brothers or more distant relatives rarely figured, but the older the testator the more likely he was already to have provided for his own children and to find small legacies for his nephews and nieces. Family historians need to be reminded that wills do not in fact tell the whole family story, older children sometimes being omitted altogether if they had already been provided with marriage portions or set up with apprenticeships. Younger children were frequently left most of the animals, leaving the oldest son to restock the farm. By a widespread and ancient custom widows were supposed to receive one third of their husbands' goods, the children one third between them and the remaining third disposed of for pious and charitable uses, including funeral expenses. In the detailed provisions which many of the more elderly male testators made for their widows' accommodation, implying that they did not feel able to rely on their children's sense of filial duty, there is confirmation of what foreign observers regarded as a certain heartlessness among Tudor people. All but very elderly widows were, of course, expected to remarry, and parish registers indicate that as many as a quarter did so. This too amazed foreigners: the Flemish painter, Joris Hoefnagel, was surely poking gentle fun at English eccentricities when in his 'Wedding Feast at Bermondsey', painted about 1570, he depicted the bride as a well-to-do lady in mourning and the bridegroom surrounded by a motherless family, the youngest in the arms of a nurse. Manor courts usually left widows in possession of farms until their eldest sons reached the age of twenty-one. But the largely urban custom of 'free bench' which, where it operated, assured to a widow occupation of her husband's house for her life or until she remarried seems to have been dying out in later-sixteenth-century England. Even those grandparents who were provided by their married sons with separate quarters, with access to the kitchen and the fire, tended to be regarded merely as 'sojourners', that is, temporary residents with no continuing claim on their families' resources. Their plight may have been exacerbated by the economic problems of the 1590s, and in 1601 Parliament thought it necessary to require the children of elderly poor people to contribute to the latter's maintenance to the extent to which they were able, on pain of 20s. a month for failure to do so.

Wills on the whole were concerned with goods and chattels, the former including cash and the latter leases for years, supervision of the disposal of which, in accordance with the wishes of the deceased, being the Church's preserve. But annuities charged on land and payable, for instance, to younger brothers and even mothers, were forms of real property, as also were leases for lives, and as such were enforceable only in the courts of common law. The descent of leases for lives was, of course, implicit in existing contracts and the land concerned passed to the remaining life-tenants, but freehold land and also copy-holdings normally descended from one generation to the next in accordance with local custom. By and large, England adhered (like her immediate continental neighbours, northern France and the Low Countries, but unlike much of the rest of Europe) to the custom of primogeniture, the preferment of the eldest son. This was the system favoured by all owners of lordship, from the Crown to lords of manors, and it had a long history. Hence it tended to be most firmly entrenched in the more manorialized and fielden regions. But primogeniture did not preclude previous disposal of portions of an estate, provided that it was not entailed (a legal limitation on sale or disposal), to younger sons, *inter vivos*. Even entails could be broken, given sufficient determination, and in theory there was nothing to stop a freeholder disinheriting all his sons. Even copyholdings, unless they were 'of inheritance', could be sold out of the family by recourse to the manor court. Landowners were, however, bound by common law to leave one third of their freehold land to their wives for their lives as their portion or jointure. Thus the custom of primogeniture did not necessarily lead to the progressive accumulation of land generation after generation. Even the most determined of engrossers usually looked after their younger sons. In some parts of England, more especially the woodland areas, local custom decreed that land should be divided at death between all the children ('gavelkind') or even left to the youngest son ('borough English'). The consequences of the latter could be modified in advance like those of primogeniture, but especially among small landowners and tenant farmers the effect of partible inheritance could be disastrous for the continuing viability of the agricultural unit, leading in many places, as we have seen, to the necessity for by-employment. By the end of the sixteenth century, excessive fragmentation among sons, and not only in areas where partible-inheritance customs applied, was causing real poverty, which in its turn played into the hands of the would-be engrosser. In fact, the smaller the holding, it would appear, the more likely it was to be divided at its occupier's death. In some cases, however, the consequences were avoided by one son buying out his brothers. In fact, the difference in practical terms in the consequences of different inheritance customs can be exaggerated, as can the difference between the descent of freehold and tenanted land. This latter was perhaps just as well for the many, especially yeomen, farmers whose holdings formed far from homogeneous estates. Most fathers in fact contrived to leave the core of their estates or farms to their eldest sons. The most serious situation, at all social and economic levels, was death leaving no male heirs and a multiplicity of daughters, for primogeniture did not apply to heiresses.

There were a number of ways in which the households and familial concerns of the gentry and the aristocracy differed from those of lesser folk. To begin with, their households were usually larger. They not only employed more domestic servants, but these traditionally stayed rather longer, and even when aristocratic resources were strained staffing arrangements were less flexible than those in lesser households. The upper classes also had, on average, more children. The mothers, in spite of the hazards – of which they had ample warning – normally employed wet nurses, with the consequential shortening of birth intervals. Perhaps more important, upper class people on the whole married rather younger, often in their teens, though rarely under fifteen. Even in the towns, the more affluent the family, the larger the number of children. In Elizabethan York, for example, while aldermen had on average four children at home, common labourers usually had only one. However, towards the end of the sixteenth century when over the population at large age at marriage had fallen somewhat, the aristocracy were just perceptibly moving against the trend. Even so, considering that one in five of the Elizabethan peers married before they were seventeen and over three quarters before they were twenty-five, almost invariably to younger women, it is surprising how many of them seemed to lack direct male heirs. But the chief reason for the larger establishments was that the children tended to remain at home for longer, especially if they had resident tutors. Eldest sons in particular would remain at home even after marriage, provided with their own hierarchy of servants, even although their ageing parents, supported by an army of officials, were less likely to retire into the background.

Marriage for the children of the gentry and the aristocracy was arranged with a great deal of parental deliberation and pressure on those concerned. Casual spousals, without witnesses, were almost unthinkable. Weddings were very elaborate and expensive. Whether as a result the marriages were less happy and companionable than those of lesser folk is very difficult to judge. What is certain is that it was far less easy for either partner to disappear without trace. The fact that highly placed public men such as Sir Ralph Sadler in 1545 and William Parr, marquis of Northampton, a few years later, were driven to secure private Acts of Parliament, with all the attendant publicity, to legalize second and technically bigamous marriages, far from indicating that life at the top was more libertarian, attests to the very considerable difficulty with which gentlemen and peers could make a fresh start.

The higher and older the family, with a few exceptions, the greater was the determination to avoid undue fragmentation of the estate, the effect of partition being not only economic but social and political. Lineage and dynasty became more and more important the higher a family climbed, for, as Gervase Markham, gentleman, wrote in 1598, 'If I shall leave my land and living equally divided among my children ... then shall the dignity of my degree, the hope of my house ... be quite buried in the bottomless pit of oblivion.' Nevertheless, the younger sons of the gentry and aristocracy were provided with small patrimonies, though these often took the form of grants for life, or grants in tale male so that in the event of their death without male heirs the land would return to the senior line. Hence, whereas nearly all the daughters of the gentry and nobility married (that is, were found husbands), many of their younger brothers, possibly as many as one fifth, remained bachelors. Almost to a man the younger sons of the English upper class felt themselves to be proportionately less well done by than their counterparts lower down the social scale and their social equals on the continent of Europe. For those without too much natural ability (and indeed everyone needed a patron of some sort), younger sons of gentlemen and peers were hot on the trail of anyone they could call cousin, even by marriage, who could assist them to an office, or better still an heiress. In this and in other ways the gentry in particular were more kin-orientated than farmers and artisans. But this did not lead them to encourage their relations to form an extension to their household. The gentry were great visitors but for short stays only. Was it not in order to avoid the expense of entertaining all and sundry in the manner of their ancestors that the aristocracy gradually learned from the gentry and the wealthier merchants the virtues of family privacy?

Throughout Europe, we are told, towards the end of the sixteenth century, though the trend is very difficult to chart chronologically, there was developing in families of the better sort a new attitude towards children. This took the form of a recognition that even when past infancy and absolute dependence children were not just undersized adults but interesting and even companionable people in their own right. There was, of course, in England far more than in the rest of Europe, a growing determination among the gentry and some of the aristocracy that their children should be educated, not only being efficiently tutored but even sent to school and university. But the great pre-Reformation campaign of the humanists to make classical learning popular with young gentlemen had only been marginally successful. The rod was increasingly used on young scholars and not until the very end of the century were there available in print expurgated editions of the classics suitable for children to read. In the case of upper class children the trend towards personal identity was perhaps more obvious to the eye, for they were beginning to be dressed differently from adults, though their long and rather old-fashioned garments did nothing to give them greater freedom of movement, and this at a time when their more fashion-conscious older brothers were wearing much shorter gowns and cloaks. But if little gentlemen had to suffer the indignity of wearing clothes very like those of their sisters, their reward was to be cherished, even pampered, and to be a centre of attraction, and even of concern, in their family circle. Thomas Phayre's *The*

Regiment of Life, first published in 1545, although derived largely
from classical writings, devoted particular attention to childhood ailments such as colic, his declared intention being 'to
do them good that have most need'. But people generally still
accepted infant and child mortality with resignation. However,
one senses that the Elizabethan laity were becoming at least as
anxious as the clergy to have their sickly infants hastily
christened, not so much for what might be called religious
reasons, to ensure them of immortality, but to establish their
identity, with a name, though the custom of giving a subsequent
child the same name as that of one deceased, or even in some
cases, of one still alive, had not yet completely died out. One
of England's few unique contributions to sixteenth-century
European art was the carving in stone of memorials showing
effigies not only of husbands and wives but of all their children,
including those who had died young, the whole composition,
although placed in a church, being not only secular but almost
homely in tone. Children were also being encouraged to follow
their own pastimes and to play their own games, though for
the great majority of children, once able to be useful, there
can have been little leisure.

Does this mean that English people, by 1600, were giving
vent to expressions of sentiment, even in public? If parental
affection is to be judged by their anxiety to keep their older
children at home, then for the great majority of parents nothing
had changed since 1500 when the author of the *Italian Relation*
had expressed such shock at the English habit of sending their
young people into other households, as they said, to be
disciplined. The Italian thought it mere self-indulgence, but it
could be interpreted as a recognition of a natural instinct to
over-indulge their children. How is the historian to judge? Real
affection is difficult to measure. We cannot recover, let alone
quantify, conversations, and least of all unspoken thoughts.
Bearing in mind how few Tudor people could write, or at
any rate write fluently, it is not surprising that so little private
correspondence has survived. Contemporary literature and

comment are unsatisfactory substitutes. What are we to make of the fact that while both the Italian observer in about 1500 and also Thomas Platter, the German tourist who visited London and a few other towns a century later, remarked on the freedom with which English women visited and drank in taverns and alehouses, Platter adding what was to him the surprising information that English husbands apparently accepted not only with equanimity but even with gratitude any attention paid to their wives by strangers? Here we have, perhaps, not so much indifference as that self-confidence – some called it arrogance – which all foreigners saw in Englishmen. It was surely more than an empty phrase which lawyers used when they recognized 'natural love and affection' between kin as 'adequate consideration' in deeds of bargain and sale. Who can doubt the tenderness with which so many dying widowers asked to be buried near their wives? It was no lawyer, or parish priest, who devised the instruction of Richard Watson, husbandman, in 1570 that he be buried in Chesterfield church, 'at the end of the form there where my wife [is] accustomed to kneel or some place nigh thereabouts'. Few Tudor marriages may have been made in heaven but when the Church enjoined upon the newly wed that they should cherish each other until death separated them it was not, this never having been its way, holding up an unattainable ideal. No Elizabethan Puritan was more insistent than Thomas Cranmer had been in all his injunctions, both to clergy and laity, on the duty of parents to maintain a caring as well as a godly and disciplined household. That most Tudor parents were able to do so was, of course, due in no small measure to the country's continued and providential escape from the worst horrors of foreign invasion, civil wars and above all crises of subsistence. Even the troubles of the later 1590s were on their way to being dispelled when the harvests of 1598 and 1599 were middling and good respectively. A people which had taken in its stride very profound changes in its religion, in its economy and in its external orientation and yet in its essentials had retained its dominant late-medieval characteristics was better placed than any other in western Europe to face the political conflicts which lay ahead, conflicts of which few Elizabethans can have had the slightest premonition and which might well have destroyed a more rigid and less resilient society.

Further Reading

Bibliographies are best kept as short as possible, selective guides to enable readers to build up their own. Almost any historical work concerned with the people of sixteenth-century England will throw some light on contemporary society and there is no end to the books and articles which could be included, especially those which communicate the rich diversity of English local life and institutions. There is also the point that the author of a book of this kind must attempt to acknowledge the debt she owes to those scholars upon whose researches she has so freely drawn. However, what follows will be confined very largely to the more accessible books and to the more important articles, especially, in the case of the latter, those which have opened up new lines of research. For more extensive bibliographies the reader is referred to the books which follow and to the following works of reference: Conyers Read, *Bibliography of British History: the Tudor period* (2nd edn 1959); M. Levine, *Tudor England* (1968), and W. H. Chaloner and R. C. Richardson, *British Economic and Social History: A Bibliographical Guide* (1976). Also useful are the *Annual Bulletin of Historical Literature* published by the Historical Association, the *Annual Bibliography of British and Irish History* edited by G. R. Elton for the Royal Historical Society and, especially valuable for periodical literature, the lists of books and articles on social and economic history published each year in the *Economic History Review*.

In what follows, to save space few items are mentioned more than once, and if so in a shortened form. Straight reprints are not mentioned but new editions are noted as far as possible. The following abbreviations are used:

AgHR   *Agricultural History Review*
BIHR   *Bulletin of the Institute of Historical Research*
EcHR   *Economic History Review*
EHR   *English Historical Review*
HJ   *Historical Journal*
JBS   *Journal of British Studies*
PP   *Past and Present*
TRHS   *Transactions of the Royal Historical Society*
VCH   *Victoria History of the Counties of England*

General

There is no single work embodying the results of recent research
on English society in the sixteenth century. L. F. Salzman's
England in Tudor Times (1926) is still useful but has been
superseded by *Life in Tudor England* by P. Williams (1964). It
is, however, the latter's far more substantial *Tudor Regime* (1979)
which, though concerned primarily with government in its
broadest aspects, in its chapters on social administration comes
nearest in recent years to dealing with Tudor society as a whole.
W. G. Hoskins, *The Age of Plunder* (1976) is confined to the
first half of the century and is followed in the same series by
D. M. Palliser's excellent book, *The Age of Elizabeth* (1983).
There is as yet no precursor to K. Wrightson, *English Society
1580–1680* (1982). One of the few general books on late-
medieval English society to include the sixteenth century is C.
Platt, *Medieval England: A Social History and Archaeology, from
the Conquest to 1600* (1978). The main social and economic
problems of mid-Tudor England are dealt with in W. R. D.
Jones's *Tudor Commonwealth, 1529–1559* (1970), but the author's
assumption that there was a coherent body of reformers is open
to question. Of the many descriptions of Elizabethan England,
most of them heavily dependent on literary sources, one of
the best is M. St Clare Byrne, *Elizabethan Life in Town and
Country* (revised edn 1961). The four books by A. L. Rowse,
The England of Elizabeth (1950); *The Expansion of Elizabethan
England* (1955); *The Elizabethan Renaissance*, I: *The Life of the*

Society (1970) and II: *The Cultural Achievement* (1972) are lively and scholarly but are not about society at large. One of the main influences in redressing the balance in recent years has been P. Laslett, *The World We Have Lost* (1965, revised edn 1971). The lack of general works on early modern English social history has been made up for in part since the mid-1970s by the publication of collections of essays on particular themes such as crime, bastardy, etc. (see below), usually with useful general introductions by the editors.

It is difficult to draw a clear line between social and economic history and although the two disciplines are becoming separated they can never be completely divorced. Economic historians have of late tended to encompass longer periods, especially in outline books. One of the best short summaries is D. C. Coleman, *The Economy of England, 1450–1750* (1977). Also useful are L. A. Clarkson, *The Pre-industrial Economy in England, 1500–1750* (1971) and R. O'Day, *Economy and Community: Economic and Social History of Pre-industrial England 1500–1700* (1975). Older but more specialized and still very useful is P. Ramsey, *Tudor Economic Problems* (1963).

The flourishing of local studies since the Second World War, and the recent emphasis on 'total' history, have not produced many books dealing exclusively with the sixteenth century. A. L. Rowse's *Tudor Cornwall* (1941), although a pioneer in the field of county history, does not comprehend the whole of Cornish society. From the north of England have come C. M. L. Bouch and G. P. Jones, *Short Economic and Social History of the Lake Counties, 1500–1830* (1961) and R. B. Smith's far more specialized *Land and Politics in the England of Henry VIII: The West Riding of Yorkshire, 1530–46* (1970), but the most penetrating work to come from that part of England is M. E. James, *Family, Lineage and Civil Society: A Study of Society, Politics and Mentality in the Durham Region, 1500–1640* (1974). *Tudor Cheshire* by J. Beck (1968) and G. A. J. Hodgett, *Tudor Lincolnshire* (1975) follow in Rowse's footsteps and A. Hassall Smith's masterly *County and Court: Government and Politics in Norfolk, 1558–1603* (1974) is also concerned largely

with those who ruled. Local studies of the Reformation (see
below, p. 401) cast their nets over a wider social spectrum and
the most substantial contribution to Tudor county history of
recent years has been P. Clark's *English Provincial Society from
the Reformation to the Revolution: Religion, Politics and Society
in Kent, 1500–1640* (1977). There have been some outstanding
recreations of early modern village communities: M. Spufford,
*Contrasting Communities: English Villagers in the Sixteenth and
Seventeenth Centuries* [Cambridgeshire] (1974), D. G. Hey, *An
English Rural Community: Myddle* [Shropshire] *under the Tudors
and Stuarts* (1974) and K. Wrightson and D. Levine, *Poverty
and Piety in an English Village: Terling* (Essex) *1525–1700* (1979).
The Victoria County History of England is a mine of information,
but the coverage of the sixteenth century in the parish histories
varies, depending to some extent on the availability of source
material.

Last but by no means least the reader is urged to contemplate
sixteenth-century English society with the help of the following
contemporary surveys, using the best modern editions: *A
Relation of England about the Year 1500*, translated by C. A. Sneyd,
Camden Society (1847); *The Itinerary of John Leland, c. 1535–43,*
ed. L. Toulmin Smith, 5 vols. (1907–10); *A Discourse of the
Commonweal of this Realm of England*, ed. M. Dewar (1969)
[written *c.* 1549, probably by Sir Thomas Smith]; *De Republica
Anglorum*, by Sir Thomas Smith, ed. M. Dewar (1982); *The
Description of England* by William Harrison, ed. G. Edelen
(1968); *The State of England A.D. 1600*, by Thomas Wilson, ed.
F. J. Fisher, Camden Miscellany 1936. Extracts from all of these
and a wealth of other source material are to be found in the
still invaluable *Tudor Economic Documents*, 3 vols., ed. R. H.
Tawney and E. Power (1924).

1. Occupations

The most important work on the occupational structure of a
predominantly rural society must be J. Thirsk (ed.), *The
Agrarian History of England and Wales*, IV: *1500–1640* (1967),

especially the chapters by the editor herself and by A. Everitt on 'Farm Labourers'. To this must be added J. Thirsk, *Fenland Farming in the Sixteenth Century* (1953) and *English Peasant Farming* [Lincolnshire] (1957). For the communal implications of common fields see W. O. Ault, *Open-field Farming in Mediaeval England* (1972), especially the appendix of documents. On industrial occupations in general there is D. C. Coleman, *Industry in Tudor and Stuart England* (1975) which has a useful bibliography. The best local study of the woollen cloth industry is G. D. Ramsay, *Wiltshire Woollen Industry in the Sixteenth and Seventeenth Centuries* (1943, new edn 1965), supplemented by E. M. Carus-Wilson's chapter in *Wiltshire VCH*, v l. IV (1959). There are also H. Heaton, *Yorkshire Woollen and Worsted Industries* (1920, new edn 1965) and N. Lowe, *Lancashire Textile Industry in the Sixteenth Century* (1972).

J. Thirsk, 'Industries in the Countryside' in F. J. Fisher (ed.), *Essays in the Economic and Social History of Tudor England* (1961) is essential reading for by-employment. Mining is best pursued in G. R. Lewis, *The Stannaries: A Study of the English Tin Miner* (1908), J. W. Gough, *The Mines of Mendip* (1967 edn), A. Raistrick and B. Jennings, *History of Lead Mining in the Pennines* (1965) and I. Blanchard, 'The Miner and the Agricultural Community in Late Medieval England', *AgHR* 1972. The standard work on building-craftsmen is D. Knoop and G. P. Jones, *The Medieval Mason* (1933). For wool-dealers see P. Bowden, *The Wool Trade in Tudor and Stuart England* (1962) and for dealers in foodstuffs A. Everitt, 'The Marketing of Agricultural Produce' in J. Thirsk (ed.), *Ag. Hist.* IV (1967). The history of the early Tudor mariner and fisherman is largely unwritten except for F. W. Brooks, 'A Wage Scale for Seamen, 1546', *EHR* 1945, D. Burwash, *English Merchant Shipping, 1460–1540* (1947), G. V. Scammell, 'English Merchant Shipping at the End of the Middle Ages', *EcHR* 1961 and 'Manning the English Merchant Service in the Sixteenth Century', *Mariner's Mirror* 1970. A useful local study is R. Tittler, 'The English Fishing Industry in the Sixteenth Century: The Case of Great Yarmouth', *Albion* 1977. Shipowning is investigated in G.

Scammell, 'Shipowning in England, 1450–1550', *TRHS* 1962 and seamanship in D. W. Waters, *The Art of Navigation in England in Elizabethan and Early Stuart Times* (1958). For the coastal pilots see G. G. Harris, *The Trinity House of Deptford* (1969).

The pre-Reformation clergy have received considerable attention, the regulars in D. Knowles, *The Religious Orders in England* III (1959) and D. Knowles and R. N. Hadcock, *Medieval Religious Houses: England and Wales* (1971 edn). The secular, and in particular the parish, clergy are the subjects of M. Bowker, *The Secular Clergy in the Diocese of Lincoln* (1968), P. Heath, *English Parish Clergy on the Eve of the Reformation* (1969) and M. L. Zell, 'Economic problems of the Parochial Clergy in the Sixteenth Century' in R. O'Day and F. Heal (eds.), *Princes and Paupers in the English Church, 1500–1800* (1981). Still very useful are F. W. Brooks, 'The Social Position of the Parson in the Sixteenth Century', *Brit. Arch. Assoc. Journal* 1945–1947 and W. G. Hoskins, 'The Leicestershire Country Parson in the Sixteenth Century' in his *Essays in Leicestershire History* (1950). Chantry priests are admirably dealt with in A. Kreider, *English Chantries: The Road to Dissolution* (1979), and school-masters, both clergy and laymen, in N. I. Orme, *English Schools in the Middle Ages* (1973) and *Education in the West of England, 1066–1548* (1976). For authors and musicians see J. W. Saunders, *The Profession of English Letters* (1964), P. Sheavyn, *The Literary Profession in the Elizabethan Age* (revised by J. W. Saunders, 1967) and W. L. Woodfill, *Musicians in English Society from Elizabeth to Charles I* (1953).

On early Tudor lawyers the pioneering work of E. W. Ives in such articles as 'The Common Lawyers in Pre-Reformation England', *TRHS* 1968 has been subsumed in W. Prest (ed.), *Lawyers in Early Modern Europe and America* (1981), especially the paper by J. H. Baker entitled 'The English Legal Profession 1450–1550'. Informers have perhaps become over-notorious through G. R. Elton, 'Informing for Profit', *Cambridge HJ* 1954 and M. W. Beresford, 'The Common Informer, the Penal Statutes and Economic Regulation', *EcHR* 1957. Employment in government service is dealt with by R. C. Braddock, 'The Rewards of Office-holding in Tudor England', *JBS* 1975 and by P. Lock, 'Officeholders and Officeholding in Early Tudor England *c.* 1520–1540', Ph.D. thesis, Exeter, 1974, which has a very full bibliography. G. N. Clark's *History of the Royal College of Physicians* (2 vols., 1964/6) perhaps exaggerates the importance of these doctors in contemporary society and should be supplemented by M. Pelling and C. Webster, 'Medical Practitioners' in C. Webster (ed.), *Health, Medicine and Mortality in the Sixteenth Century* (1979). There is food for thought in K. Charlton, 'The Professions in Sixteenth-century England', in *Univ. Birmingham Hist. Journal* 1969. For the heralds see below, p. 396.

2. *Landlords and Tenants*

J. Thirsk (ed.), *Ag. Hist.* IV (1967) again provides the basic reading, especially the editor's own chapter on 'Enclosing and Engrossing', and 'Landlords in England' by G. Batho and J. Youings. R. H. Tawney, *The Agrarian Problem in the Sixteenth Century* (1912) still has much to teach us, including how to write social history lucidly and without jargon. It has by no means been superseded by the smaller E. Kerridge, *Agrarian Problems in the Sixteenth Century and After* (1969) which is, however, a useful corrective. General works include M. W. Beresford and J. G. Hurst, *Deserted Medieval Villages* (1971), K. B. Macfarlane, *The Nobility of Later Medieval England* (1973) and B. P. Wolffe, *The Crown Lands, 1461–1536* (1970), each of which is not only based on meticulous research but links the early sixteenth century with what went before. A useful article is J. J. Scarisbrick, 'Cardinal Wolsey and the Commonweal', in E. Ives *et al.* (eds.), *Wealth and Power in Tudor England* (1978), which testifies to the pressure put on enclosers.

Most of the local studies which contribute to this topic, other than those already mentioned, cover more than the sixteenth century. They include F. G. Davenport, *The Economic Development of a Norfolk Manor* [Forncett], *1086–1565* (1906), G. H.

Tupling, *Economic History of Rossendale* [Lancs.] (1927), W. G. Hoskins, *The Midland Peasant* [Wigston, Leics.] (1957). H. P. R. Finberg, *Tavistock Abbey* (1951) and C. Dyer, *Landlords and Peasants in a Changing Society: The Estates of the Bishopric of Worcester 680–1540* (1980) testify to the continuing interest in the Church as a landowner. Family history is well represented by J. Wake, *The Brudenells of Deene* (1953), J. M. W. Bean, *The Estates of the Percy Family* (1958), A. G. Dickens, *The Clifford Letters of the Sixteenth Century*, Surtees Society, 1962 and C. Rawcliffe, *The Staffords, Earls of Stafford and Dukes of Buckingham, 1394–1521* (1978). The analysis of Devon landownership comes from J. Kew, 'The Land Market in Devon, 1536–1558', Ph.D. thesis, Exeter, 1967 and that of Norfolk from T. H. Swales, 'The Redistribution of the Monastic Lands in Norfolk at the Dissolution', *Norfolk Archaeology* 1962–6. J. Hatcher, *Rural Economy and Society in the Duchy of Cornwall, 1300–1500* (1970) and I. S. W. Blanchard, *The Duchy of Lancaster's Estates in Derbyshire*, Derbys. Arch. Soc. Rec. Ser. 1971 throw a good deal of light on the Crown's relations with its tenants. L. A. Parker, 'The Agrarian Revolution at Cotesbach, 1501–1612', in W. G. Hoskins (ed.), *Studies in Leicestershire Agrarian History* (1949), K. J. Allison, 'Flock Management in the Sixteenth and Seventeenth Centuries', *EcHR* 1958 and H. Thorpe, 'The Lord and the Landscape' [Wormleighton, Warwicks.], *Birmingham Arch. Soc. Trans.* 1962 all concern early Tudor graziers, as also do the unique financial records printed by N. Alcock in *Warwickshire Grazier and London Skinner, 1532–55* (1981). For the dispute at Combe Martin, see N. Gregory, 'The Freedom of Hangman Hill', *Devon Historian* 1979. The exercise of wardship is lucidly explained in J. Hurstfield, 'The Revival of Feudalism in Early Tudor England', *History* 1952.

3. People in Towns

J. H. Thomas, *Town Government in the Sixteenth Century* (1933) is still the only book devoted exclusively to Tudor towns but, especially for the social historian, it has been completely overtaken by the spate of recent work on the early modern English town. Attempts to uncover the anatomy of provincial urban communities began with W. G. Hoskins, 'English Provincial Towns in the Early Sixteenth Century', *TRHS* 1956. J. Cornwall, 'English Country Towns in the 1520s', *EcHR* 1962, is concerned largely with population but P. Clark and P. Slack (eds.), *Crisis and Order in English Towns, 1500–1700* (1972), followed by their *English Towns in Transition, 1500–1700* (1976), precipitated a great debate, which is still going on, concerning what some scholars see as a catastrophic decline in the economy and quality of life of late-medieval and early-modern towns. The extreme view is that propounded by C. Phythian-Adams in 'Urban Decay in Late-medieval England' in P. Abrams and E. A. Wrigley (eds.), *Towns in Societies* (1978) and in his *Desolation of a City* [Coventry] (1979). For a useful summary, with a very comprehensive bibliography, see the editor's Introduction to P. Clark (ed.) *Country Towns in Pre-industrial England* (1981). Work so far published on the major cities includes D. Charman, 'Wealth and Trade in Leicester in the Early Sixteenth Century', *Trans. Leic. Arch. Soc.* 1949, J. W. F. Hill, *Tudor and Stuart Lincoln* (1956), J. F. Pound, 'The Social and Trade Structure of Norwich, 1525–75', *PP* 1966, A. D. Dyer, *The City of Worcester in the Sixteenth Century* (1973), J. A. Youings, *Early Tudor Exeter* (1974), C. Platt, *Medieval Southampton: The Port and Trading Community 1000–1600* (1973). A. Rosen, 'Economic and Social Aspects of Winchester, 1520–1670', D.Phil. thesis, Oxford, 1975, A. D. Dyer, 'Northampton in 1524', *Northamptonshire Past and Present* 1979, D. Palliser, *Tudor York* (1979) and R. S. Gottfried, *Bury St Edmunds and the Urban Crisis, 1290–1539* (1982). The debate takes a new turn with J. Kermode, 'Urban Decline? The Flight from Office in Late Medieval York', *EcHR* 1982. At a more sober level many of the larger cities have whole volumes devoted to them in the *Victoria County History* and all urban communities have large sections in the topographical volumes. Many of the larger towns also figure in M. Lobel (ed.), *Historic Towns*, I (1969) and II (1975).

Early-sixteenth-century London is best approached through S. Thrupp, *The Merchant Class of Medieval London* (1948) and the all too few publications of the late T. F. Reddaway, such as 'The London Goldsmiths, *c.* 1500', *TRHS* 1962 and 'The Livery Companies of Tudor London', *History* 1966. G. D. Ramsay, *The City of London in International Politics* (1975) contains some very useful background information and the same author's 'The Recruitment and Fortunes of Some London Freemen in the Mid Sixteenth Century', *EcHR* 1978 is invaluable. For east London see K. McDonnell, *Medieval London Suburbs* (1978). The introduction by Dr L. M. Cronne to her as yet unpublished edition of the Minute Book of the Mercers' Company, 1527–58 is a mine of information on that august body and its members, and much can be learned about the London scene from W. Hamilton (ed.), *A Chronicle of England* (by Charles Wriothesley), 2 vols., Camden Society 1875–7, but the people in the streets of Henry VIII's London still await their historian.

4. Belonging and Not Belonging

The tax assessments of 1524–5 have been subjected to extensive analysis, notably by R. Schofield in an unpublished Ph.D. thesis (Cambridge, 1963) and by J. Sheail in 'The Distribution of Taxable Population and Wealth in England during the Early Sixteenth Century', *Trans. Inst. British Geographers* 1972. Those in print include A. C. Chibnall and A. V. Woodman (eds.), *Subsidy Roll for the County of Buckingham, 1524*, Bucks. Rec. Soc. 1950 and J. Cornwall (ed.), *Lay Subsidy Rolls for the County of Sussex, 1524–5*, Sussex Rec. Soc. 1956. Most of the town histories already mentioned include some information on migration, and to these should be added A. Butcher, 'The Origins of Romney Freemen, 1433–1523', *EcHR* 1974, C. I. Hammer, 'The Mobility of Skilled Labour in Late-medieval England' [actually largely early-sixteenth-century Oxford], *Vierteljahrschift für Sozial- und Wirtschaftsgeschichte*, 1976, and there is a good general discussion in J. Patten, *Rural–Urban*

Migration in Pre-industrial England (1973). For one early Tudor city's catchment area see *Calendar of the Bristol Apprentice Book*, I, 1532–42, ed. D. Hollis, and II, 1542–52, ed. E. Ralph, Bristol Rec. Soc. 1949 and 1980.

Internal communications and trade-routes in particular are dealt with in J. Crofts, *Packhorse, Waggon and Post: Land Carriage and Communications under the Tudors and Stuarts* (1967), T. S. Willan, *The Inland Trade* (1976), and J. A. Chartres, *Internal Trade in England, 1500–1700* (1977). Also useful in this connection are T. C. Mendenhall, *The Shrewsbury Drapers and the Welsh Wool Trade in the Sixteenth and Seventeenth Centuries* (1953), and B. C. Jones, 'Westmorland Packhorse Men in Southampton', *Trans. Cumb. West. Antiq. Arch. Soc.* 1960. Tudor fairs are dealt with in L. F. Salzman, *English Trade in the Middle Ages* (1931) and by A. Everitt in J. Thirsk (ed.), *Ag. Hist.* IV (1967), pp. 532–43. For the lawcourts see below, pp. 404–5, and for minstrels and travelling players, J. Wasson, 'Visiting Entertainers at the Cluniac Priory of Thetford, 1497–1540', *Albion* 1977.

Details of the Percy household and administration are contained in T. Percy (ed.), *The Northumberland Household Book* (1905) and in M. E. James, *Change and Continuity in the Tudor North: The Rise of Thomas, First Lord Wharton* (1965). Retaining and private armies are the subject of W. H. Dunham, *Lord Hastings' Indentured Retainers, 1461–83* (1955), M. E. James, *A Tudor Magnate and the Tudor State: Henry Fifth Earl of Northumberland* (1966), A. Cameron, 'The Giving of Livery and Retaining in Henry VII's Reign', *Renaissance and Modern Studies* 1974, J. Goring, 'Social Change and Military Decline in Mid-Tudor England', *History* 1975 and R. Virgoe, 'The Recovery of the Howards in East Anglia, 1485–1529', in Ives *et al.* (eds.), *Wealth and Power* (1978). *The Lisle Letters*, edited by M. St Clare Byrne (6 vols., 1981) provides a rare insight into the domestic affairs of an aristocratic family between 1533 and 1540.

5. *Rank and Status*

W. S. Holdsworth, *History of English Law* (1923), especially vols.
I (revised 1956) and IV, contains much of interest to the social
historian. For the sumptuary laws see W. Hooper, 'Tudor
Sumptuary Laws', *EHR* 1915 and also N. B. Harte, 'State
Control of Dress and Social Change in Pre-industrial England',
in N. B. Harte, *et al.* (eds.), *Trade, Government and Economy
in Pre-industrial England* (1976).

For the nobility K. B. Macfarlane (above, p. 391) is quite
outstanding in its range and scholarship, and invaluable are H.
Miller, 'Subsidy Assessments of the Peerage in the Sixteenth
Century', *BIHR* 1955 and two articles by J. R. Lander, 'Attainder and Forfeiture, 1453–1509', *HJ* 1961 and 'Bonds,
Coercion and Fear: Henry VII and the Peerage', in J. G. Rowe
and W. H. Stockdale (eds.), *Florilegium Historiale* (1971).

G. E. Mingay, *The Gentry: The Rise and Fall of a Ruling Class*
(1976) ranges over many centuries, but more useful for the early
sixteenth century is J. Cornwall, 'The Early Tudor Gentry',
EcHR 1965. There are not too many studies of early Tudor
families but the following are very sound: B. McClenaghan,
The Springs of Lavenham (1924) and J. Wake, *The Brudenells
of Deene* (1953). M. E. Finch, *The Wealth of Five Northamptonshire Families, 1540–1640*, Northants. Rec. Soc. 1956, A. Simpson, *The Wealth of the Gentry, 1540–1660* (1963) and J. T. Cliffe,
The Yorkshire Gentry (1969) all contain some early-sixteenth-
century material. H. Leonard, 'Knights and Knighthood in
Tudor England', Ph.D. thesis, London, 1970, deserves to be
better known. J. H. Round, *Family Origins* (1930) and three
books by A. Wagner, *English Genealogy* (1960), *Heralds and
Heraldry in the Middle Ages* (1956) and *Heralds and Ancestors*
(1978) are very relevant.

One of the first (and still few) local historians to take note
of the smaller gentry and large freeholders is W. G. Hoskins
in his *Essays in Leicestershire History* (1950), *The Midland Peasant*
(1957) and *Devon* (new edn 1972). For information on the Leigh
family of Churchstow I am indebted to Mr Beric Morley of

the Department of the Environment. M. Campbell, *The English Yeoman under Elizabeth and the Early Stuarts* (1942) was a pioneering work in its time and is still good reading.

J. Simon, *Education and Society in Tudor England* (1967) provides not only a good general background but also an excellent bibliography of the works of such contemporary writers as Sir Thomas Elyot, Thomas Starkey, Richard Morison and John Cheke, and D. Cressy, *Literacy and the Social Order: Reading and Writing in Tudor and Stuart England* (1980) displays great ingenuity in exploring this difficult subject.

Early Tudor women find little mention as a group in any of the more specialized works but their particular problems are highlighted in E. Ives, '"Agaynst taking awaye of Women": The Inception and Operation of the Abduction Act of 1487', in Ives *et al.* (eds.), *Wealth and Power* (1978). Bondmen, by comparison, have been very fully dealt with by historians as far apart as F. Davenport and M. Spufford (see above, p. 391, 388) and in R. H. Hilton, *The Decline of Serfdom* (1969). Aliens, too, have been very thoroughly covered by W. Cunningham, *Alien Immigrants to England* (1897), A. Ruddock, *Italian Merchants and Shipping in Southampton, 1270–1600* (1951) and T. Wyatt, 'Aliens in England before the Huguenots', *Huguenot Soc. Proc.* 1953. See also below, p. 406.

6. *Inflation of Population and Prices*

Before tackling E. A. Wrigley and R. S. Schofield's *Population History of England, 1541 to 1871* (1981), a truly massive work based on the resources of the Cambridge Group for the History of Population which is unlikely to be superseded for a very long time, readers would be well advised to read J. D. Chambers, *Population, Economy and Society in Pre-industrial England* (1972). They should also not ignore the less sophisticated local studies based on simple 'aggregative analysis' (counting annual totals of births and deaths) such as M. Drake, 'An Elementary Exercise in Parish Register Demography' [Yorkshire], *EcHR* 1962, D. Palliser, 'Dearth and Disease in

Staffordshire, 1540–1670', in C. W. Chalklin and M. Havinden (eds.), *Rural Change and Urban Growth* (1974), N. Annett, 'North Molton: The Pre-Census Population', *Trans. Devonshire Assoc.* 1976 or those based on tax assessments and other 'census' data such as W. G. Hoskins, 'The Population of an English Village, 1086–1801' [Wigston, Leicestershire], *Trans. Leics. Arch. Hist. Soc.* 1957.

For the medieval demographic background readers are referred to J. Hatcher, *Plague, Population and the English Economy, 1348–1530* (1977) and to the works cited there. Also relevant is H. H. Lamb, *The Changing Climate* (1966). J. Sheail (see above, p. 394) has made good use of the muster rolls and tax assessments of the 1520s but the most ambitious analysis is that of J. Cornwall, 'English Population in the Early Sixteenth Century', *EcHR* 1970. The early part of the century is also the subject of a stimulating paper by I. S. W. Blanchard, 'Population Change, Enclosure and the Early Tudor Economy', *EcHR* 1970. A pioneering effort to relate demographic developments with the economy which is still of value is F. J. Fisher, 'Influenza and Inflation in Tudor England', *EcHR* 1965, and finally there is M. W. Flinn, *The European Demographic System, 1500–1820* (1981).

C. Creighton, *History of Epidemics in Britain*, 2 vols. (1891 and 1894) is still useful but is being superseded by the local researches of P. Slack, so far only available in his D.Phil. thesis, Oxford, 1972 and in articles such as 'The Case of Bristol, 1540–1650' in P. Slack (ed.), *The Plague Reconsidered* (1977) and his two very substantial contributions to C. Webster (ed.), *Health, Medicine and Mortality* (1979). Other notable contributions are D. Palliser, 'Epidemics in Tudor York', *Northern History*, 1973 and J. A. H. Wylie and I. J. Linn, 'Observations upon the Distribution and Spread of the English Sweating Sickness in Devon in 1551', *Trans. Devonshire Assoc.* 1980. L. A. Clarkson, *Death, Disease and Famine in Pre-industrial England* (1975) is a useful general survey, but A. B. Appleby, *Famine in Tudor and Stuart England* (1978), though valuable, is largely concerned with the north-east in the 1590s.

The best short introduction to the subject of prices is R. B. Outhwaite, *Inflation in Tudor and Early Stuart England* (1969), based partly on E. H. Phelps Brown and S. V. Hopkins, 'Seven Centuries of the Price of Consumables Compared with Builders' Wage Rates', *Economica* 1956. J. Thorold Rogers, *History of Agriculture and Prices in England*, 7 vols. (1866–1902) is a mine of information but the most usable data is that provided by P. Bowden in J. Thirsk (ed.), *Ag. Hist.* IV (1967), with the appendices of tables. On food supply and prices there is W. G. Hoskins's invaluable and very readable 'Harvest Fluctuations and English Economic History, 1480–1619', *AgHR* 1964, with which should be read C. J. Harrison's note in *AgHR* 1971. For rents see E. Kerridge, 'The Movement of Rent, 1540–1640', *EcHR* 1953–4, and a useful article by B. J. Harris, 'Landlords and Tenants in England in the Later Middle Ages: The Buckingham Estates', *PP* 1969. For valuable information on wages see D. Crossley on the Sidney ironworks (below, p. 406).

7. *The Land Market*

No one should assume that R. H. Tawney had the worst of the argument which he so happily (for us) triggered off unless he or she has read carefully his 'Rise of the Gentry', *EcHR* 1941 and his postscript in *EcHR* 1954. The rejoinders he attracted, references to which will be found in J. H. Hexter, *Reappraisals in History* (1961), are now past history, and local studies of the land market are still too few to allow of a national picture. J. Kew's work on Devon (see above, p. 392 and 'The Disposal of Crown Lands and the Devon Land Market, 1536–58', *AgHR* 1970) is a model of what can be done, given adequate documents, but otherwise so far we have only the more limited studies of the West Riding of Yorkshire and of Norfolk (see above, pp. 387, 392), K. Wyndham, 'In Pursuit of Crown Land: The Initial Recipients of Somerset Property in the Mid-Tudor Period', *Somerset Arch. Natural History Soc.* 1979 and 'The Royal Estate in Mid-sixteenth-century Somerset', *BIHR* 1979, and M. Zell, 'The Mid-Tudor Market in Crown Land in Kent',

Archaeologia Cantiana 1981. But there have been intensive studies of individual landed families spanning county boundaries, besides J. Wake on the Brudenells (see above, p. 396), H. P. R. Finberg, 'The Gostwicks of Willington' and A. G. Dickens, 'Estate and Household Management in Bedfordshire, *c.* 1540', both in *Beds. Hist. Rec. Soc.* 1956. Among the many biographies of rising individuals the following are especially relevant: F. G. Emmison, *Tudor Secretary: Sir William Petre* (1961), A. J. Slavin, *Politics and Profit: Sir Ralph Sadler* (1966), R. Tittler, *Nicholas Bacon: The Making of a Tudor Statesman* (1976) and D. Willen, *John Russell, First Earl of Bedford* (1981). For the acquisitions and disposals of land by the peers see L. Stone, *The Crisis of the Aristocracy* (1965, abridged edn 1967) and by the bishops, P. M. Hembry, *The Bishops of Bath and Wells, 1540–1640* (1967) and F. Heal, *Of Prelates and Princes* (1980). Very useful on the closing decades of the century are R. B. Outhwaite, 'The Price of Crown Land at the Turn of the 16th Century', *EcHR* 1967 and 'Who Bought Crown Lands? The Pattern of Purchases, 1589–1603', *BIHR* 1971 and D. Thomas, 'Leases in Reversion on Crown lands, 1558–1603', *EcHR* 1977.

On the dispersal of monastic property there is J. A. Youings, 'The Terms of Disposal of Devon Monastic Lands', *EHR* 1954, 'The City of Exeter and the Property of the Dissolved Monasteries', *Trans. Devonshire Assoc.* 1952 and *The Dissolution of the Monasteries*, 1971, H. J. Habakkuk, 'The Market for Monastic Property, 1539–1603', *EcHR* 1958 and G. W. O. Woodward, 'A Speculation in Monastic Lands', *EHR* 1964.

For those, besides lawyers, for whom the land market brought employment see E. G. R. Taylor, 'The Surveyor', *EcHR* 1947 and *Mathematical Practitioners of Tudor and Stuart England* (1954) and also D. Coleman, 'London Scriveners and the Estate Market in the Later Seventeenth Century', *EcHR* 1951. V. Morgan, 'The Cartographic Image of "The Country" in Early Modern England', *TRHS* 1979 also has much to contribute on this and other topics.

8. Clergy, People, and Schools

A. G. Dickens, *The English Reformation* (1964) will long remain the most balanced and illuminating study of this central theme in Tudor history, but local studies are now throwing more and more light on its social implications. One of the first was Dickens's own *Lollards and Protestants in the Diocese of York, 1509–58* (1959) and more recently there have appeared D. Palliser, *The Reformation in York, 1534–53* (1971), C. Haigh, *Reformation and Resistance in Tudor Lancashire* (1975), P. Clark on Kent (see above, p. 388) and R. Whiting, 'The Reformation in the South West of England', Ph.D. thesis, Exeter, 1977. Rather slighter is J. E. Oxley, *The Reformation in Essex to the Death of Mary* (1965). Some of the best recent work has been published in two collections of essays edited by F. Heal and R. O'Day, *Church and Society in England: Henry VIII to James I* (1977) and (by O'Day and Heal) *Princes and Paupers* (1981). Among a great many other articles scattered in various journals mention may be made of the following: A. G. Dickens, 'Robert Parkyn's Narrative of the Reformation', *EHR* 1947, R. M. Fisher, 'Reform, Repression and Unrest at the Inns of Court', *HJ* 1977, N. L. Jones, 'Profiting from Religious Reform: The Land Rush of 1559', *HJ* 1979, S. Brigden, 'Youth and the English Reformation', *PP* 1982 and R. Whiting, 'Abominable Idols: Images and Image-breaking under Henry VIII', *Journal of Ecclesiastical History* 1982.

In addition to works already mentioned on the pre-Reformation secular clergy (see above, p. 390) two major contributions are M. Bowker, 'The Henrician Reformation and the Parish Clergy' [Lincoln diocese], *BIHR* 1977 and R. O'Day, *The English Clergy, 1558–1642* (1979). Of the utmost relevance to the laity's response to the Reformation is R. Houlbrooke, *Church Courts and the People during the English Reformation, 1520–70* (1979), a very readable treatment of what has usually been regarded as an obscure subject.

C. Cross, *Church and People, 1450–1660: The Triumph of the*

Laity in the English Church (1976) places great emphasis on native
Lollardy. In her paper, together with those of D. Loades and
B. Hall, in D. Baker (ed.), *Reform and Reformation: England and
the Continent c. 1500–c. 1750* (1979) the contributions of the continental reformers to the English Reformation come under
scrutiny. I. Luxton has some useful local material on Lollardy
in 'The Lichfield Court Book: A Postscript', *BIHR* 1971, and
J. Fines, *Biographical Register of English Protestants, 1525–58*,
part 1, A–C (1981) promises to be a very useful work of
reference.

The effect of the Reformation on education is dealt with
in books by J. Simon and N. I. Orme (see above, pp. 390, 397)
and a strong case for less change and more continuity is con-
tained in R. O'Day, *Education and Society 1500–1800* (1982).
E. L. Eisenstein, *The Printing Press as an Agent of Change:
Communications and Cultural Transformation in Early Modern
Europe* (2 vols., 1979), though obviously very important for
Europe as a whole does not supersede H. S. Bennett, *English
Books and Readers*, I: *1475–1557* (1969 edn) and II: *1558–1603*
(1965). Both need to be read in conjunction with D. Cressy,
Literacy and the Social Order (1980). D. M. Loades, 'The Theory
and Practice of Censorship in Sixteenth-century England',
TRHS 1974, is also very relevant.

For the suppression of the monasteries and chantries readers
are referred to D. Knowles's classic work (see above, p. 390),
to G. W. O. Woodward, *The Dissolution of the Monasteries*
(1966) and to the books by Youings and Kreider mentioned
above, pp. 390, 400. Treatment of the subject at a local level has
been uneven in quality but among the best contributions are
G. A. J. Hodgett (ed.), *The State of the Ex-Religious in the Diocese
of Lincoln*, Lincs. Rec. Soc. 1959 and C. Haigh, *The Last Days
of the Lancashire Monasteries and the Pilgrimage of Grace* (1969).

Witches have attracted more attention than their number
probably warrants, particularly in England. A. Macfarlane,
Witchcraft in Tudor and Stuart England, 1560–1680 (1970) and the
same author's 'Witchcraft in Tudor and Stuart Essex' in J. S.
Cockburn (ed.), *Crime in England, 1550–1800* (1977) testify only

to localized appearances, but witches also loom quite large in K. Thomas, *Religion and the Decline of Magic* (1971), a brilliant book which also encompasses a great deal of popular religion of a more orthodox kind.

Finally readers will find A. G. Dickens and D. Carr (eds.), *The Reformation in England to the Accession of Elizabeth I* (1967) a very useful source for the essential official pronouncements, to which should be added P. L. Hughes and J. F. Larkin, *Tudor Royal Proclamations* (3 vols., 1964, 1969) and S. E. Lehmberg, *The Reformation Parliament* (1970). The most important statutes are in G. R. Elton, *The Tudor Constitution* (1982 edn).

9. *Armed Rebellion, Popular Commotions, Mere Lawbreaking, and Litigation*

A. Fletcher, *Tudor Rebellions* (1973 edn) provides a good short survey both of the causes and the course of events. P. Williams, 'Rebellion and Revolution in Early Modern England', in M. D. R. Foot (ed.), *War and Society* (1973) provides an illuminating analysis which anticipates the chapter in his *Tudor Regime* (1979). C. S. L. Davies, 'Peasant Revolt in France and England: A Comparison', *AgHR* 1973 and N. Z. Davies, 'The Rites of Violence: Religious Riot in Sixteenth-century France', *PP* 1973 are helpful. A number of very substantial and penetrating articles on the risings in 1536 serve to illustrate the multiplicity of causes and differ only in their emphases, C. S. L. Davies, 'The Pilgrimage of Grace Reconsidered', *PP* 1968 and M. Bowker, 'Lincolnshire 1536: Heresy, Schism or Religious Discontent?', in D. Baker (ed.), *Studies in Church History* 9 (1972) contrasting with M. E. James, 'Obedience and Dissent in Henrician England: The Lincolnshire Rebellion, 1536', *PP* 1970. Each of the local studies on the far north of England already mentioned make their contribution, to which must be added S. M. Harrison, *The Pilgrimage of Grace in the Lake Counties, 1536–7* (1981).

The disturbances of 1549 are well summarized by M. L. Bush, *The Government Policy of Protector Somerset* (1975) and J. Corn-

wall, *The Revolt of the Peasantry* (1977). Two exploratory articles
are D. MacCulloch, 'Kett's Rebellion in Context', *PP* 1979
and J. A. Youings, 'The South-Western Rebellion of 1549',
Southern History 1979. The Marian rebellions are dealt with by
D. Loades, *Two Tudor Conspiracies* (1965) and *The Reign of Mary
Tudor* (1979). M. E. James, 'The Concept of Order and the
Northern Rising, 1569', *PP* 1973 is a characteristically pene-
trating paper. The incidence of food riots is investigated by
J. Walter and K. Wrightson, 'Dearth and the Social Order in
Early Modern England', *PP* 1976 and B. Sharp, *In Contempt
of All Authority: Rural Artisans and Riot in the West of England,
1586–1660* (1980). A useful local study is P. Clark, 'Popular
Protest and Disturbance in Kent, 1558–1640', *EcHR* 1976.

The resources of the powers that be are the particular concern
of G. Scott Thomson, *Lords Lieutenants in the Sixteenth Century*
(1923) and L. Boynton, *The Elizabethan Militia, 1558–1638*
(1967). For retaining see above, p. 395. Also very relevant are
G. R. Elton, *Policy and Police* (1972), J. Hurstfield, 'Was There
a Tudor Despotism After All?', *THRS* 1967, and K. Thomas,
Rule and Misrule in the Schools of Early Modern England (1976).
The value in this connection of P. Williams, *The Tudor Regime*
(1979), especially chapter 10, can hardly be exaggerated.

J. Bellamy, *The Tudor Law of Treason* (1979) is important
but rather more relevant to social history are the analyses of
lesser crimes in J. Samaha, *Law and Order in Historical Perspective:
The Case of Elizabethan Essex* (1974), and the contributions,
especially that by the editors, to J. S. Cockburn (ed.), *Crime
in England* (1977) and J. H. Baker (ed.), *Legal Records and the
Historian* (1978). Also useful are J. A. Guy, *The Cardinal's
Court: The Impact of Thomas Wolsey in Star Chamber* (1977),
T. G. Barnes, 'Due Process and Slow Process in the Late-
Elizabethan/Early-Stuart Star Chamber', *American Journal of
Legal History* 1962 and W. J. Jones, *The Elizabethan Court of
Chancery* (1967). For litigation in local church courts see, besides
Houlbrooke (above, p. 401), R. A. Marchant, *The Church under
the Law in the Diocese of York, 1560–1640* (1969), C. A. Haigh,
'Slander and the Church Courts in the Sixteenth Century',

Trans. Lancs. and Cheshire Antiq. Soc. 1975 and J. A. Sharpe, *Defamation and Sexual Slander: The Church Courts at York* (1980).

10. New Horizons: 'By Little and Little'

For the wide range of subjects touched on in this chapter it is only possible to indicate introductory works and publications which throw light on social dimensions. For new techniques in agriculture the editor's own chapter in J. Thirsk (ed.), *Ag. Hist.* IV (1967) is more readable than E. Kerridge's monumental *Agricultural Revolution* also published in the same year, but see also A. R. Bridbury, 'Sixteenth-century Farming', *EcHR* 1974. The overall pattern of change, including its chronology, is still far from clear, but there has been a great deal of research at a local level, from W. G. Hoskins, 'The Reclamation of the Waste in Devon', *EcHR* 1943, to more recent studies such as those of C. E. Brent published in *Sussex Arch. Collections* 1976 and 1978. Also useful is R. S. Smith, 'A Woad-growing Project at Wollaton in the 1580s', *Trans. Thoroton Soc.* 1961. For the grain trade see N. S. B. Gras, *The Evolution of the English Corn Market* (1926), and for metropolitan demand in the later sixteenth century F. J. Fisher, 'The Development of the London Food Market, 1540–1640', *EcHR* 1935. The pattern of wool and cloth exports is graphically illustrated in E. M. Carus-Wilson and O. Coleman, *England's Export Trade 1275–1547* (1963).

For the history of English adventuring overseas see J. A. Williamson's *Maritime Enterprise, 1485–1558* (1913), *The Age of Drake* (1938) and *Hawkins of Plymouth* (1951); D. B. Quinn, *England and the Discovery of America* (1973) and 'Renaissance Influences in English Colonization', *THRS* 1976; G. Connell-Smith, *Forerunners of Drake* (1954), T. S. Willan, *The Early History of the Russia Company, 1553–1603* (1956) and *The Muscovy Merchants of 1555* (1953), and K. R. Andrews, *Elizabethan Privateering* (1964). Among the many publications about Drake the reader is particularly referred to K. R. Andrews, 'Beyond the Equinoctial: England and South America in the Sixteenth

Century', *Journal of Imperial and Commonwealth History* 1981,
D. B. Quinn, *Drake's Circumnavigation: A Review of the Evidence*
(1981) and P. Williams, 'The Ownership of the *Golden Hind*',
Mariner's Mirror 1981. There are useful statistics in T. K. Rabb,
Enterprise and Empire 1575–1630 (1967). F. J. Fisher, 'Commerical
Trends and Policy in Sixteenth-century England', *EcHR* 1940
is still very relevant, but R. Davis, *English Overseas Trade, 1500–*
1700 (1973) provides a convenient short review. Among many
local studies some of the best are R. Davis, *The Trade and*
Shipping of Hull (1964), D. Woodward, 'Ships, Masters and
Shipowners of the Wirral 1550–1650', *Mariner's Mirror* 1977
and J. Vanes, *The Port of Bristol in the Sixteenth Century* (1977).

Aliens are dealt with by G. D. Ramsay, 'The Undoing of
the Italian Mercantile Colony in Sixteenth-century London',
in N. B. Harte and K. Ponting (eds.), *Textile History and*
Economic History (1973) and by L. Williams, 'Alien Immigrants
in Relation to Industry and Society in Tudor England',
Huguenot Soc. Proc. 1956 and 'The Crown and the Provincial
Immigrant Communities in Elizabethan England', in H. Hear-
der and H. Loyn (eds.), *British Government and Administration*
(1975). Very closely related is D. C. Coleman, 'An Innovation
and its Diffusion: The "New Draperies"', *EcHR* 1969 and short
but immensely valuable is G. D. Ramsay, *The English Woollen*
Industry 1500–1700 (1982).

Of the newer industries there is D. W. Crossley, 'The
Management of a Sixteenth-century Ironworks' *EcHR* 1966
and (ed.) *The Sidney Ironworks Accounts, 1541–73*, Camden
Society 1975, together with J. J. Goring, 'Wealden Ironmasters
in the age of Elizabeth' in E. Ives etc. (eds.), *Wealth and Power*
(1978) and B. G. Awty, 'The Continental Origins of Wealden
Ironworkers, 1451–1544', *EcHR* 1981. G. H. Kenyon, *The Glass*
Industry of the Weald (1967) and E. S. Godfrey, *The Development*
of English Glassmaking (1975) should be read in conjunction with
D. W. Crossley, 'The Performance of the Glass Industry',
EcHR 1972. Mining and the metallurgical industries loom large
in J. W. Gough, *The Rise of the Entrepreneur* (1969), but for
the smaller and more independent operators see I. S. W. Blan-

chard, 'Labour Productivity and Work Psychology in the English Mining Industry, 1400–1600', *EcHR* 1978.

The versatility of Sir Thomas Smith is fully explored in M. Dewar, *Sir Thomas Smith: A Tudor Intellectual in Office* (1964), including his interests in native light industry. J. Thirsk, 'The Fantastical Folly of Fashion: The English Stocking Knitting Industry, 1500–1700' in N. B. Harte *et al.* (eds.), *Textile History* (1973) is a worthy successor to her earlier paper on the growth of rural industry (see above, p. 389), and she has pursued her study of the early modern consumer society even further in *Economic Policy and Projects* (1978). There is, however, still much food for thought in F. J. Fisher's 'Tawney's Century' in the volume he edited in 1961 (see above, p. 389). On monopolies the standard work is still W. Hyde Price, *The English Patents of Monopoly* (1906). Finally, for Ireland, the best concise account, and one which draws out the New World connection, is D. B. Quinn, *The Elizabethans and the Irish* (1966).

11. *The Poor in Very Deed*

J. Pound's *Poverty and Vagrancy in Tudor England* (1971) and A. L. Beier, *The Problem of the Poor in Tudor and Early Stuart England* (1983) are short but succinct surveys of the causes of poverty and of the measures for its relief, but both show how remarkably little progress at a local level has been made since E. M. Leonard, *The Early History of English Poor Relief* (1900) which is still, for all its discursiveness, indispensable. Recent intensive research into the records of some of the larger towns (see above, p. 393) has added marginally to our knowledge, though rarely produced any hard evidence of the magnitude of the problems. Norwich is outstanding, both in what the city achieved and in the survival of its records which have been exhaustively investigated and published in J. Pound, 'An Elizabethan Census of the Poor', *Univ. Birmingham Hist. Journal* 1962 and (ed.) *The Norwich Census of the Poor, 1570*, Norfolk Rec. Soc. 1971. Ipswich has come a close second with J. Webb (ed.), *Poor Relief in Elizabethan Ipswich*, Suffolk Rec. Soc. 1966, and A. L. Beier's 'The Social Problems of an Elizabethan Country Town: Warwick 1580–90', in P. Clark (ed.), *Country Towns in Pre-industrial England* (1981), is a penetrating study of more than local importance. Relevant rural records for the sixteenth century are very rare but have been used in F. G. Emmison, 'Poor Relief in Bedfordshire, 1563–98', *EcHR* 1931, B. Clarke, 'Norfolk Licences to Beg', *Norfolk Archaeology* 1972 and in M. Spufford (1974), P. Clark (1977), and K. Wrightson and D. Levine (1979) as above, p. 388.

E. M. Leonard's account of the Tudor poor-laws can be augmented with the help of G. R. Elton, *Reform and Renewal: Thomas Cromwell and the Common Weal* (1973), P. Slack, 'Social Policy and the Constraints of Government, 1547–58' in J. Loach and R. Tittler (eds.), *The Mid-Tudor Polity, c. 1540–1560* (1980) and in the same author's 'Books of Orders: The Making of English Social Policy, 1577–1631', *TRHS* 1980. Also very relevant is R. M. Benbow, 'The Court of Aldermen and the Assizes: The Policy of Price Control in Elizabethan London', *Guildhall Studies* 1980. It is also still worth reading the full text of the statutes and proclamations. For continental parallels and comparisons see B. Pullan, *Rich and Poor in Renaissance Venice* (1971) and 'Catholics and the Poor in Early Modern Europe', *TRHS* 1976.

For pre-Reformation religious institutions and their confiscation and dispersal see the books listed above, p. 390, especially D. Knowles (1969) and D. Knowles and R. N. Hadcock (1971). London's administration of its newly acquired hospitals is investigated in C. Cunningham, 'Christ's Hospital: Infant and Child Mortality in the Sixteenth Century', *Local Population Studies* 1977, and P. Allderidge, 'Management and Mismanagement at Bedlam, 1547–1633', in C. Webster (ed.), *Health, Medicine and Mortality* (1979). For the Mercers' record see J. Imray, *The Charity of Richard Whittington* (1968). Finally there are the many books by W. K. Jordan, beginning with what is perhaps the most useful, *Philanthropy in England, 1480–1660* (1959) and followed by volumes on London and the west of England (both in 1960), Kent and rural England (both in 1961) and Lancashire (1962). The results of enormous industry these books have been widely criticized for their author's failure to take account of inflation (see the attempt to revise Jordan's figures by W. G. Bittle and R. T. Lane in *EcHR* 1976), but they still have much to say about the nature and source of Tudor philanthropy.

12. *The Banishment of Idleness*

Employment, or the lack or avoidance of it, is usually dealt with in the books along with poverty and its relief as listed in the previous section. To these may be added E. Lipson, *Economic History of England*, vol. III (1956 edn). Again, resort to the text of the statutes is recommended. For government interest in urban renewal see R. Tittler, 'The Emergence of Urban Policy, 1536–58', in J. Loach and R. Tittler (eds.), *The Mid-Tudor Polity* (1980), and for urban occupations and local experiments in providing work the various town histories listed above, p. 393. For wages see E. H. Phelps Brown and S. V. Hopkins, 'Seven Centuries of Building Wages', *Economica* 1955 and also W. E. Minchinton (ed.), *Wage Regulation in Pre-industrial England* (1972) which contains, besides a useful introduction by the editor, reprints of papers by R. H. Tawney and R. K. Kelsall first published in 1914 and 1938 respectively. Also very relevant is D. Woodward, 'Wage Rates and Living Standards in Pre-industrial England', *PP* 1981. On the legislation of 1563 see S. T. Bindoff, 'The Making of the Statute of Artificers', in Bindoff *et al.* (eds.), *English Government and Society* (1961) and D. Woodward, 'The Background to the Statute of Artificers: The Genesis of Labour Policy, 1558–63', *EcHR* 1980 and for the sequel, M. G. Davies, *The Enforcement of English Apprenticeship, 1563–1642* (1956). Also useful are A. Kussmaul, *Servants in Husbandry in Early Modern England* (1981) and K. R. Andrews, 'The Elizabethan Seaman', *Mariner's Mirror* 1982.

On vagrancy by the able-bodied see C. S. L. Davies, 'Slavery and the Protector Somerset: The Vagrancy Act of 1547', *EcHR*

1966, A. L. Beier, 'Vagrants and the Social Order in Elizabethan England', *PP* 1974, and the rejoinders which followed the latter. Also relevant are various local studies, especially J. Thirsk, 'The Isle of Axholme before Vermuyden', *AgHR* 1953, W. G. Howson, 'Plague, Poverty and Population in Parts of North-west England, 1580–1720', *Trans. Hist. Soc. Lancs and Cheshire* 1960, P. Clark, 'The Migrant in Kentish towns, 1580–1640', in Clark and Slack, *Crisis and Order* (1972), P. Slack, 'Vagrants and Vagrancy in England, 1598–1664', *EcHR* 1974 and A. L. Beier's work on Warwick (above, p. 408).

13. Family and Fortune

Most of the relevant books have already been mentioned. Especially important are the local studies of Finch (p. 396), Simpson (p. 396), Cliffe (p. 396), James (p. 395) and Spufford (p. 388), together with J. E. Mousley, 'The Fortunes of Some Gentry Families of Elizabethan Sussex', *EcHR* 1959. A. B. Appleby, 'Agrarian Capitalism or Seigneurial Reaction? The Northwest of England, 1500–1700', *American Historical Review* 1975 on the whole supports Kerridge rather than Tawney (see above, p. 391). R. C. Braddock, 'The Rewards of Office-holding in Tudor England', *JBS* 1975 is especially useful for the lower echelons and H. R. Trevor-Roper, *The Gentry, 1540–1640* (1953) skilfully rebuts one of Tawney's main arguments but proves nothing. To L. Stone's large study of the Elizabethan aristocracy (1965) must be added the same author's *Family and Fortune* (1973), C. Cross, *The Puritan Earl: Henry Hastings, Third Earl of Huntingdon, 1536–95* (1966), an excellent study in depth, and B. Coward, 'Disputed Inheritances: Some Difficulties of the Nobility in the Late Sixteenth and Early Seventeenth Centuries', *BIHR* 1971. All the town histories already listed are relevant, as also are F. F. Foster, *The Politics of Stability: A Portrait of the Rulers of Elizabethan London* (1977) and C. I. Hammer, 'Anatomy of an Oligarchy: The Oxford Town Council in the Fifteenth and Sixteenth Centuries', *JBS* 1978. The clergy, both lesser and higher, are very thoroughly covered by R. O'Day (1979) and F. Heal (1980), to which may be added J. Berlatsky, 'The Elizabethan Episcopate: Patterns of Life and Expenditure', in O'Day and Heal (eds.), *Princes and Paupers* (1981). There is as yet no detailed study of the profits and lifestyle of professional lawyers but a beginning has been made in W. Prest (ed.), (1981), see above, p. 390.

For the resort to the universities see L. Stone (ed.), *The University in Society* I (1974), especially the chapter by J. McConica, and also E. Russell, 'The Influx of Commoners into Oxford before 1581: An Optical Illusion', *EHR* 1977.

On houses there is W. G. Hoskins, 'The Rebuilding of Rural England, 1570–1640', *PP* 1953, together with R. Machin, 'The Great Rebuilding: A Reassessment', ibid. 1977, N. Pevsner, *The Planning of the Elizabethan Country House* (1961), M. W. Barley, *The English Farmhouse and Cottage* (1961), D. Portman, *Exeter Houses, 1400–1700* (1966) and 'Vernacular Building in the Oxford Region in the Sixteenth and Seventeenth Centuries', in Chalklin and Havinden (eds.), *Rural Change* (1974), M. Girouard, *Robert Smythson and the Architecture of the Elizabethan Era* (1966), E. Mercer (ed.), *English Vernacular Houses* (1975), C. Platt, *The English Medieval Town* (1976) and P. Hembry, 'Episcopal Palaces, 1535–1660', in Ives *et al.* (eds.), *Wealth and Power* (1978). Of the various collections of probate inventories now in print two of the best are M. Havinden (ed.), *Household and Farm Inventories in Oxfordshire, 1550–90*, Oxfords. Rec. Soc. 1965, and J. M. Bestall and D. V. Fowkes (eds.), *Chesterfield Wills and Inventories, 1521–1603*, Derbys. Rec. Soc. 1977.

For moneylending R. H. Tawney (ed.), *Thomas Wilson's Discourse on Usury* (1925) is still useful, there being little else except H. R. Trevor-Roper, 'The Elizabethan Aristocracy: An Anatomy Anatomized', *EcHR* 1951 and B. A. Holderness, 'The Clergy as Money-lenders in England', in O'Day and Heal (eds.), *Princes and Paupers* (1981). A. Conyers (ed.), *Wiltshire Extents for Debt*, Wiltshire Record Society, 1973, explores a new and fruitful source. J. Hurstfield, *The Queen's Wards* (1958), is masterly.

14. Community and Country

Again, most of the books relevant to this topic are contained in the regional studies of Bouch and Jones (p. 387), Smith (p. 387), Clark (p. 388), Hey (p. 388), and Wrightson and Levine (p. 388). A vivid picture of the physical dimensions of local communities is provided by M. W. Beresford, *History on the Ground* (1971 edn), and excellent documentation in W. O. Ault, 'Village By-laws by Common Consent', *Speculum* 1954 and 'Open-field Husbandry and the Village Community', *Trans. American Philosophical Society* 1965. A. Macfarlane, with S. Harrison and C. Jardine, *Reconstructing Historical Communities* (1977) offers excellent guidelines. Still very useful is J. C. Cox, *Churchwardens' Accounts* (1913), and there is some discussion of the role of the ecclesiastical parish in C. Hill, *Economic Problems of the Church* (1956). A good starting point for the pursuit of popular ritual and pastimes is C. Phythian-Adams, *Local History and Folklore: A New Framework* (1975). On the decreasing magnetism of the aristocracy see M. E. James, 'The Concept of Order and the Northern Rising of 1569', *PP* 1973 and chapter 13 in P. Williams, *The Tudor Regime* (1979).

Of the very extensive literature on Elizabethan Catholic recusancy the following are most relevant: P. McGrath, *Papists and Puritans under Elizabeth I* (1967), J. Bossy, 'The Character of Elizabethan Catholicism', *PP* 1962 and *The English Catholic Community* (1975), and C. Haigh, 'From Monopoly to Minority: Catholicism in Early Modern England', *TRHS* 1981. For Puritanism see C. Hill, 'Puritans and the "Dark Corners of the Land"', *TRHS* 1963, P. Collinson, *The Elizabethan Puritan Movement* (1967) and N. Tyacke, 'Popular Puritan Mentality in Late-Elizabethan England', in P. Clark *et al.* (eds.), *The English Commonwealth* (1979). In addition to the local studies mentioned above (pp. 387–8) readers are referred to the following: R. B. Manning, *Religion and Society in Elizabethan Sussex* (1969), R. C. Richardson, *Puritanism in North-West England* (1972), P. S. Seaver, 'Community Control and Puritan Politics in Elizabethan Suffolk', *Albion* 1977, W. J. Sheils,

Puritans in the Diocese of Peterborough, 1558–1610, Northampton-shire Rec. Soc. 1979, J. C. H. Aveling, 'Catholic House-holds in Yorkshire, 1580–1603', *Northern History*, 1980 and D. MacCulloch, 'Catholic and Puritan in Elizabethan Suffolk: A County Community Polarises', in *Archiv für Reformations-geschichte* 1975. For aliens see L. Williams (1975), as above, p. 406, and L. Stone, *An Elizabethan: Sir Horatio Palavicino* (1956).

For Elizabethan London there is F. J. Fisher, 'The Development of London as a Centre of Conspicuous Consumption in the Sixteenth and Seventeenth Centuries', *TRHS* 1948, G. D. Ramsay, 'Industrial Discontent in Early Elizabethan London: Clothworkers and Merchant Adventurers in Conflict', *London Journal* 1975 and *The City of London in International Politics* (1975). Also largely concerned with London is D. Bergeron, *English Civic Pageantry, 1558–1642* (1971). A useful addition to the extensive literature on later Tudor towns is P. Clark, '"The Ramoth-Gilead of the Good": Urban Change and Political Radicalism at Gloucester, 1540–1640', in Clark *et al.* (eds.), *The English Commonwealth* (1979). For a well-documented Elizabethan guild see J. A. Youings, *Tuckers Hall Exeter* (1968) and for the urban trading network the works of Everitt (1967), Willan (1976) and Chartres (1977) already mentioned above, pp. 389, 395. C. Carlton, *The Court of Orphans* (1974) is very illuminating, as also is A. Everitt, 'The English Urban Inn, 1560–1760', in A. Everitt (ed.), *Perspectives in English Urban History* (1973), on a subject not to be confused with that dealt with in P. Clark, 'The Alehouse and the Alternative Society', in D. Pennington and K. Thomas (eds.), *Puritans and Revolutionaries* (1978) and by the same author in *The English Alehouse 1200–1830* (1983).

An invaluable and pioneering study of the county community will be found in A. Everitt, *Change in the Provinces: the Seventeenth Century* (1969), to which should be added his 'Country, County and Town', *TRHS* 1979. J. H. Gleason, *The Justices of the Peace in England, 1558–1640* (1969) is informative but far more illuminating is N. J. G. Pounds (ed.), 'William Carnsew of Bokelly and his Diary, 1576–7', *Jour. Royal Inst.*

Cornwall 1978. For antiquarianism, both local and metropolitan, see F. J. Levy, *Tudor Historical Thought* (1967), M. McKisack, *Medieval History in the Tudor Age* (1971) and R. M. Warnicke, *William Lambarde, Elizabethan Antiquary, 1536–1601* (1973). On the communal world of the later Tudor university see V. Morgan, 'Cambridge University and the Country, 1560–1640' in L. Stone (ed.), *The University in Society*, I (1974). Attempts to discover local literary cultures have not been very successful, but for a brave attempt see A. G. Dickens, 'The Writers of Tudor Yorkshire', *TRHS* 1963. For music in the provinces see Woodfill (above, p. 390).

15. *Marriage and the Household*

Most of the demographic evidence has been published in the following books which, however, are largely concerned with the period after 1600 and with Europe and a wider world: P. Laslett and R. Wall (eds.), *Household and Family in Past Time* (1972), P. Laslett, *Family Life and Illicit Love in Earlier Generations* (1977), J. Goody, J. Thirsk and E. P. Thompson (eds.), *Family and Inheritance: Rural Society in Western Europe 1200–1800* (1976), P. Laslett, K. Oosterveen and R. S. Smith (eds.), *Bastardy and its Comparative History* (1980), M. Mitterauer and R. Sieder, *The European Family: Patriarchy to Partnership from the Middle Ages to the Present* (1982) and by far the most readable, R. B. Outhwaite (ed.), *Marriage and Society: Studies in the Social History of Marriage* (1981). M. Anderson, *Approaches to the History of the Western Family* (1980) provides a short but valuable introduction. A. Macfarlane, *Origins of English Individualism* (1978), although it overstates the obvious, is well worth reading, as also is the same author's 'Modes of Reproduction', *Journal of Development Studies* 1978, especially pp. 109–20. L. Stone's *Family, Sex and Marriage in England 1500–1800* (1977, abridged edn 1979) is largely confined to the élite whom the author deals with much more convincingly in his *Crisis of the Aristocracy* (1965). M. Spufford's *Contrasting Communities* (1974) and K. Wrightson and D. Levine, *Poverty and Piety* (1979), especially the former, deal with real families in real rural communities but, with the notable exception of C. Phythian-Adams, *Desolation of a City* (1979), urban families have received little attention. P. Ariès, *Centuries of Childhood* (1960, English edn 1962) was a brilliant book in its day but has been overtaken by more precise analysis. Much more relevant is I. Pinchbeck and M. Hewitt, *Children in English Society* (1969), but their subjects only really come alive in such records as F. J. Furnivall's *Child Marriages* [diocese of Chester, 1561–6], Early English Text Society 1897, and in D. Maclaren, 'Nature's Contraceptive, Wet-nursing and Prolonged Lactation: The Case of Chesham, Bucks., 1578–1601', *Medical History* 1979. K. J. Allison's 'An Elizabethan Village Census', *BIHR* 1963 is almost beyond price, but J. F. Pound, *Norwich Census of the Poor* (1971) is also unique in its details of poor households.

Index

Acclom family, 324
actors, *see* plays
Adwick-le-Street (Yorks.), 196
agriculture, 25–30; by-laws of, 27, 335–6; improvements in, 148, 230–31, 251–3, 302–3, 316, 324; profits of, 28–9; regional pattern of, 16, 26–7, 349; *see also* cattle; crops; 'fielden' areas; fields; 'forest' areas; land
Akes, Richard, 126
Alcester (Warwicks.), 365
Aldrich, John, MP, 260
alehouses, 383; licensing of, 275, 287
aliens, 13, 127–8, 181, 187, 347–9; churches for, 127, 267, 347–8; as craftsmen, clothmakers, 242–3, 347, 349, glassmakers, 241, 349, metal-workers, 238, 325, 349, mining engineers, 242, shipwrights, 35; denization of, 127–8, 315; families of, 128, 141, 243, 349; hostility towards, 127–8, 216; in London, 13–14, 127–8, 141, 237, 242–4, 347–8; as merchants, 232, 236–7, 242, *see also* Hanseatic merchants; numbers of, 128, 141, 243, 347;

as religious dissenters, 181; as religious refugees, 242, 347–8; their ships, 72; taxation of, 127; in towns, 128, 242–3, 347–8
aliens (by nationality): Dutch people, 127–8, 181, 183, 195, 242, 244, 267, 316, 348; French people, 90, 127–8, 238, 241, 347–8; Germans, 181, 242, 325; Italians, 128, 237, 315–16; Spaniards, 127, 187, 216
Almondbury (Yorks.), 307
almsgiving, 262–4, 271; by abbots, etc., 191, 256; by bishops, 255, 273; casual, 191, 260, prohibition of, 261–2; by cathedrals, 258; by gentry, 273; by husbandmen, 273; by merchants, 273–4; by nobility, 263, 273; by parish clergy, 255, 273; by yeomen, 273
almshouses, 256–9, 264, 266, 271–4, 372
Althorp (Northants.), manor of, 60
Amadas, Robert, 43
America, 223–4, 246–7, 248–9
Antiquaries, Society of, 358
Antwerp, 96, 237, 241; fairs at, 71
Appletreewick (Yorks.), manor of, 166